Virgil, 'the classic of all Europe' in T. S. El
: in his own lifetime and was the centre ᴏɪ ᴛʜᴇ ᴡᴇꜱᴛᴇʀɴ ᴄᴀɴᴏɴ ᴏᴏᴏ ᴏᴏᴏ
,800 years, exerting a major influence on European literature, art, and
:s. This *Companion* is designed as an indispensable guide for anyone,
er a classicist or not, who is seeking a fuller understanding of an author
l to so many disciplines. It consists of specially commissioned essays by
een scholars from Britain, the USA, Ireland and Italy which offer a
of different perspectives both traditional and innovative on Virgil's
;, and a renewed sense of why Virgil matters today. The *Companion*
ded into four main sections, focusing on reception, genre, context, and
This ground-breaking book not only provides a wealth of material for
ormed reading but also offers fresh and sophisticated insights which
to the shape of Virgilian scholarship and criticism to come.

A

The Unive

CAMBRIDGE COMPANIONS TO LITERATURE

THE CAMBRIDGE
COMPANION TO
VIRGIL

Simone Martini: frontispiece to Petrarch's Virgil manuscript, 1340. (Biblioteca Ambrosiana (Codex A.49.inf), Milan.) (A description of this picture can be found on p. x.)

THE CAMBRIDGE
COMPANION TO
VIRGIL

EDITED BY
CHARLES MARTINDALE
Professor of Latin, University of Bristol

CAMBRIDGE
UNIVERSITY PRESS

CAMBRIDGE UNIVERSITY PRESS

Cambridge, New York, Melbourne, Madrid, Cape Town, Singapore, São Paulo,
Delhi, Tokyo, Mexico City

Cambridge University Press
The Edinburgh Building, Cambridge CB2 8RU, UK

Published in the United States of America by Cambridge University Press, New York

www.cambridge.org
Information on this title: www.cambridge.org/9780521498852

First published 1997
7th printing 2011

Printed in the United Kingdom at the University Press, Cambridge

A catalogue record for this publication is available from the British Library

Library of Congress Cataloguing in Publication data

ISBN 978-0-521-49539-4 hardback
ISBN 978-0-521-49885-2 paperback

CONTENTS

ILLUSTRATIONS

FRONTISPIECE

Simone Martini, Frontispiece to Petrarch's Virgil manuscript, 1340. Biblioteca Ambrosiana (Codex A.49.inf), Milan. Photo by courtesy of the Veneranda Biblioteca Ambrosiana. (This photograph is the property of the Biblioteca Ambrosiana. All rights reserved. No reproductions allowed.)

The picture is an allegory showing Virgil seated beneath a tree composing one of his books. The figure drawing aside the muslin curtain is the fourth-century grammarian Servius, whose commentary on Virgil was an influential source for later writers and readers: he symbolically 'reveals' Virgil to posterity. The other figures personify Virgil's books: Aeneas stands beside Servius, while below them a farmer pruning a vine represents the *Georgics* and a shepherd symbolises the *Eclogues*. The two Latin inscriptions make the meaning of the image clear: 'Italy, benevolent country, nourishes famous poets. Thus this one [Virgil] enables you to achieve Grecian genius', and 'This is Servius, who recovers the mysteries of eloquent Virgil so they are revealed to leaders, shepherds and farmers.' The miniature was painted for Petrarch when he recovered his prized manuscript copy of Virgil's work in 1340 after losing it twelve years earlier.

PLATES

(Between pages 110 and 111)

1a Mosaic from Hadrumetum in Africa, *Virgil seated between the Muses of History and Tragedy*. Bardo Museum, Tunis.

1b Roman relief, *Aeneas sacrificing*: fragment of the frieze from the Ara Pacis, 13–9 BC. Ara Pacis Museum, Rome. Photo: Mansell Collection.

2a *Dido and Aeneas*. Mosaic pavement from Low Ham Villa, Somerset, fourth century. Somerset County Museum, Taunton. Photo: Somerset County Council Museums Service.

2b *Portrait of Virgil*. Miniature from the Roman Virgil, early fifth century. Vatican Library, Rome (Cod. Vat. Lat. 3867, fol. 3v). Photo: Biblioteca Vaticana.

CONTRIBUTORS

ALESSANDRO BARCHIESI is Professor of Latin Literature at the University of Verona. He is the author of a work on Virgil and Homer, *La traccia del modello* (1984), and other publications on Augustan poetry, including *Il poeta e il principe: Ovidio e il discorso Augusteo* (1994).

WILLIAM BATSTONE is Chair of Classics at the Ohio State University. He has recently published work on Catullus, Cicero and Virgil, and has an article forthcoming on 'Bakhtin, Catullus, and the possibility of a dialogic lyric'. His current work includes projects on the *Georgics*, on 'Sulpicia and the language of men', and on the construction of self in Republican literature.

COLIN BURROW is University Lecturer and Fellow in English at Gonville and Caius College, Cambridge. He has written extensively on the reception of Classical literature in the English Renaissance, with publications including *Epic Romance: Homer to Milton* (1993) and *Edmund Spenser* (1996).

FIONA COX is a lecturer in French at University College, Cork. She wrote her PhD thesis, 'Virgil's presence in twentieth-century French literature' at Bristol University.

JOSEPH FARRELL is Associate Professor of Classical Studies at the University of Pennsylvania. He is the author of *Virgil's Georgics and the Traditions of Ancient Epic* (1991) and of the forthcoming *Latin Language and Latin Culture*.

DON FOWLER is Fellow and Tutor of Classics at Jesus College, Oxford, and University Lecturer in Greek and Latin Literature. His articles on Virgil include treatments of focalisation, ecphrasis, and god.

PHILIP HARDIE is Fellow of New Hall, Cambridge, and University Lecturer in Latin. He is the author of *Virgil's Aeneid: Cosmos and Imperium* (1986) and of a commentary on *Aeneid* Book IX (1994).

DUNCAN KENNEDY, Senior Lecturer in Classics at the University of Bristol, is the author of *The Arts of Love: Five Studies in the Discourse of Roman Love Elegy* (1993). He is a leading expert in the application of modern literary theory to the study of ancient texts.

ANDREW LAIRD teaches Classics at the University of Warwick and has written a number of articles on narrative in Latin literature, including a study of ecphrasis in Catullus.

MICHAEL LIVERSIDGE teaches History of Art at the University of Bristol and is Dean of the Faculty of Arts. His specialist interests are in British art and the classical tradition. He co-edited *Imagining Rome. British Artists in the Nineteenth Century* (1996).

CHARLES MARTINDALE, Professor of Latin at the University of Bristol, is author of *John Milton and the Transformation of Ancient Epic* (1986), *Redeeming the Text: Latin Poetry and the Hermeneutics of Reception* (1993), and co-author of *Shakespeare and the Uses of Antiquity* (1990). He is editor of *Virgil and his Influence* (1984), *Ovid Renewed* (1988), and (with David Hopkins) *Horace Made New* (1993).

SUSANNA MORTON BRAUND is Professor of Latin at Royal Holloway, University of London. She has published extensively on Juvenal and Roman satire, has translated Lucan's epic poem *Civil War*, and (with Christopher Gill) has co-edited *The Passions in Roman Thought and Literature* (1997).

JAMES O'HARA, Associate Professor at Wesleyan University, has taught Classical Studies there since 1986. He is author of *Death and the Optimistic Prophecy in Vergil's Aeneid* (1990) and *True Names: Vergil and the Alexandrian Tradition of Etymological Wordplay* (1996). He is currently working on a study of inconsistencies in Roman epic.

ELLEN OLIENSIS is an Assistant Professor of Classics at Yale University. She is the author of a number of articles on Augustan poetry, including a study of Horace's *Epodes* (1991). Her current work includes a forthcoming publication on Horace's self-construction as a poet.

RICHARD TARRANT has taught at the University of Toronto and at Harvard University, where he is currently Pope Professor of the Latin Language and Literature. He has published commentaries on Seneca's *Agamemnon* (1976) and *Thyestes* (1985), and is one of the co-authors of *Texts and Transmission. A Guide to the Latin Classics*. He is now completing a critical edition of Ovid's *Metamorphoses*. His Virgilian work includes *Aeneas and the Gates of Sleep* (1982), and his next project is a commentary on *Aeneid* XII.

ELENA THEODORAKOPOULOS is a lecturer in Classics at Birmingham University. She wrote her PhD on 'Closure in Roman epic' at Bristol.

JAMES ZETZEL, Professor of Classics at Columbia University, was educated at Harvard and previously taught at Brown and Princeton Universities. His main areas of research are the literature of the first century BC and the transmission of Latin texts. He is the author of a number of articles on Latin literature, and of a commentary on Cicero's *De republica* (1994).

PREFACE

cui fidus Achates
it comes et paribus curis vestigia figit.

The Concise Oxford English Dictionary defines a *fidus Achates* as 'devoted follower, henchman'; and one of the aims of this *Companion* is to be as helpful as possible to its readers. It is devised for anyone, whether a classicist or not, who is seeking guidance and orientation for a fuller understanding of Virgil. We have assumed that most of those who consult this volume will have read parts of Virgil's poetry if only in translation – for those with Latin the best introduction is to read some of the texts with a good commentary, of which there are many. We certainly cannot attempt to replicate the work of the commentators here; rather we offer a series of essays on topics which can constitute useful entry-points for the devoted student of Virgil. And though we aim to help and to provide what is sometimes called 'basic information', we do not seek to simplify or to offer any sort of bland orthodoxy. We assume that our readers (even if not expert on the subject) are seeking intelligent and sophisticated comment, and we hope that the book will prove exciting as well as useful, and will point to the shape of Virgilian scholarship and criticism to come.

This book is very much a collaborative endeavour; and I am grateful to all the contributors for responding so positively to the various demands made upon them. Genevieve Liveley took time off from her PhD to assist me most efficiently in the editorial work; she is also responsible for the 'List of works cited' and for the 'Dateline'. I would particularly like to thank Pauline Hire of Cambridge University Press who gave patient help and advice throughout to a sometimes recalcitrant editor. Finally I would like to express my general pleasure in the task; all those who have helped to produce this book, whatever their differences of view about particulars, would surely be happy to be described as devoted followers of the poet whom Dante hailed with the words *tu se' lo mio maestro e 'l mio autore*.

Charles Martindale
Bristol, October 1996

I

CHARLES MARTINDALE

Introduction:
'The classic of all Europe'

The Irish poet Seamus Heaney's *Seeing Things* was first published in 1991, to immediate acclaim. The collection is framed by translations of two passages of canonical poetry, Virgil's account of Aeneas' consultation of the Sibyl and the instructions he receives from her about finding the golden bough, often read as a symbol of wisdom and initiation, prior to his descent into the Underworld, and Dante's meeting in *Inferno* 3 with Charon the ferryman of Hell, itself inspired by another episode in *Aeneid* 6. The first original poem in the book, 'The journey back', describes an encounter with a more immediate poetic predecessor, Philip Larkin, whose shade quotes from Dante and describes himself as 'A nine-to-five man who had seen poetry'; the piece resonates with earlier poetic meetings, T. S. Eliot's with the 'familiar compound ghost' in part two of 'Little Gidding' and – one of Eliot's intertexts here – Dante's with the shade of Virgil at the outset of the *Divine Comedy*. In his new pursuit of the visionary Heaney was also coming home to some of the most influential traditions of Western poetry. Five years later Heaney is a Nobel Laureate, and *Seeing Things* is already in Britain an A-level set text. Successful canonisation can be achieved with surprising rapidity – the *Aeneid* itself, greeted (according to some with a degree of irony) by the elegist Propertius in advance of its publication as 'something greater than the *Iliad*', almost instantly became a school text, and part of the furniture of the minds of educated Romans. And for Heaney, and therefore potentially for some of his readers, even at this late hour when Latin is no longer the object of widespread study, there is seemingly still power in the canonical name. We could say, following the argument of Colin Burrow's essay on translation in this volume, that Heaney, coming from what some might see as the 'margins' of Europe, seems to be laying claim to a share of the dominant cultural authority of the 'centre'.

There has recently been vigorous and often acrimonious debate about the status and significance of the canon, regarded at one extreme as a conspiracy of the ruling elite and at the other as a collection of masterpieces that transcend history and constitute, in Matthew Arnold's terms, 'the best that is known and thought in the world'.[1] In this connection Heaney's success, which hardly suggests a world in headlong flight from the canonical (whatever the fears and hopes of contestants, conservative or radical, in the contemporary culture wars over the future of the curriculum) can be used to make two observations. First, it illustrates how writers frequently themselves take the lead in canon-making. In *Inferno* 4 Dante, a great lover of lists of the famous dead, recounts how in Limbo he mingles with the *bella scuola*, the excellent school, of five great classical poets, 'masters of exalted song', Homer (whom in fact he had never read), Virgil hailed as '*l'altissimo poeta*', Horace, Ovid, Lucan, and by implication claims equality with them: 'They made me one of their company so that I was sixth among those great intellects' (101–2). Authors elect their own precursors, by allusion, quotation, imitation, translation, homage, at once creating a canon and making a claim for their own inclusion in it. So Virgil himself in the *Georgics* gathers into a single work features of the various strands of non-narrative *epos* (Hesiodic, technical, philosophical), thereby in effect making his own work the climax of a Graeco-Roman 'didactic' tradition. Secondly, the case of Heaney reminds us that canonical flourishing is always and necessarily sustained by and within institutions which enable dissemination (which include in this case publishing houses, the media, schools and universities), with the consequence that such flourishing is never simply a matter of intrinsic aesthetic merit (whatever quite that is taken to mean) but is necessarily also implicated in a range of socio-economic and (in the broad sense) political factors; we cannot wholly separate great books from the wider culture in which they have been, and are, embedded. The great medievalist E. R. Curtius begins his discussion of the canon thus: 'The formation of a canon serves to safeguard a tradition ... the literary tradition of the school, the juristic tradition of the state, and the religious tradition of the Church: these are the three medieval world powers, *studium*, *imperium*, *sacerdotium*.'[2] A canon established which texts were to be accorded authority and also ensured an authorised interpretation of them. Quintilian, who, in Book 10 of his *Institutio oratoria*, listed the 'best' authors both Greek and Latin in all the major genres for the practical benefit of the rising orator (with Virgil providing 'the most auspicious opening', *auspicatissimum exordium*, for the Latin writers), uses the phrase *ordo a grammaticis datus*, 'the corpus of accepted writers given by the scholars of literature' (10.1.54); significantly *ordo* is the word for a social grouping within a hierarchy (thus the senatorial 'order'), just as 'classic' was first used by Aulus Gellius to

---

[1] Arnold (1964) 33.　　[2] Curtius (1953) ch. 14 'Classicism', 256.

denote 'a first-class and tax-paying author, not a proletarian'.[3] The connections between the literary and the social and the political are thus inscribed within the very vocabulary of canon-making.

It is highly appropriate that Virgil should be the first classical poet to obtain an entire volume in the Cambridge Companions series, since, if we look at the whole of the last 2,000 years, it is hard not to agree with T. S. Eliot's description of him as 'the classic of all Europe'.[4] This is not to say that he is the greatest European poet (many would argue for the rival claims of, say, Homer or Ovid or Dante or Shakespeare), rather that he occupied the central place in the literary canon for the whole of Europe for longer than any other writer (Shakespeare today holds a similar position but mainly within the Anglophone world). As a result Virgil's significance extends far beyond his influence (massive as it is) on other writers and artists, itself something that can only be gestured towards in this book. For example as the poet of empire – given the importance, for worse or better, of the European imperial project – he speaks, at least on the most influential readings of his works, for many of the values and attitudes that have shaped the West. When Charlemagne was crowned Holy Roman Emperor in 800, the *translatio imperii*, the transfer of the Roman empire to the Franks, was accompanied by an analogous *translatio studii*, the scholarly appropriation of the Roman past, with Virgil at its core; the two acts of succession are indeed profoundly implicated in each other. Similarly Camoens turned to Virgil for the *Lusiads*, his poem justifying Portuguese global expansion. In that sense poems like the *Aeneid* have effects beyond the literary, can even, in Mandelstam's memorable words, 'get people killed'. Analogously a piece of landscaping like Henry Hoare's garden at Stourhead (discussed here by Michael Liversidge) is not Virgilian merely in the sense that it alludes to events and persons in the *Aeneid*; rather this whole way of seeing and shaping the 'natural' world is profoundly informed by a particular response to Virgil's texts. The traces of Virgil are everywhere in European culture whether recognised or not; and in that sense Virgil should be of interest both to traditionalists who espouse the timeless value of great poetry and to radicals alert to the ideological work performed by 'literature' within history. Not without reason the Austrian Catholic writer Theodore Haecker, socialist and staunch anti-fascist, called his popular and influential book on the poet first published in 1931 *Virgil, Vater des Abendlandes*, *Virgil, Father of the West*.

Eliot – like Curtius – saw the link between Dante and Virgil as central to European civilisation, a link which thus became, in Frank Kermode's

---

[3] Curtius (1953) 249.   [4] Eliot (1957) 70 ('What is a Classic?').

words, 'a sort of key to his historical imagination',[5] with Roman culture as a prefigurement, a *figura*, of Christian culture. This view of Virgil as *anima naturaliter Christiana* and a bridge between pagan and Christian Europe has of course a venerable ancestry; the Fourth Eclogue was early read as a prophecy of the Incarnation, while Aeneas became 'the prototype of a Christian hero'.[6] Eliot did not suppose, any more than Dante himself, that Virgil was in any way conscious of these things. Virgil's works can be read under the aspect of time, but also under the aspect of the timeless; neither reading excludes the other, and neither reading is adequate without the other. One can argue that what Eliot does here overtly is what any interpreter of past texts does – and must do. The Christianising interpretation of Virgil is thus not less historical than any other, it is simply *differently* historical; all historical narratives, it can be claimed, depend on teleological structures, however occluded, as a very condition of their possibility, and all historical narratives involve a simultaneous double reading of the past, backwards and forwards at the same time. If the Eliotic narrative seems different from other, 'secular' narratives, that is only because the ideological entailments of that teleology and that double reading are made explicit and because, in this explicit form, they are no longer acceptable to the majority of Eliot's readers. Frank Kermode argues that there are two ways of interpreting the revered texts of the past, the one philological and historiographical, the other accommodatory, accommodation being effected by various forms of allegory (even if not recognised as such).[7] However the distinction may all too easily be dissolved, since even the most austere philological scholarship can be represented as involving accommodation (for example, in the translation of terms), while even the most unconcealed allegorisation usually contains, at some level, an appeal to inherent or originary meaning.

In this respect there is an important connection between Virgil's status as a classic and his imperial vision (visible even as early as the *Eclogues*): as Kermode observes (quoting from the final section of Eliot's 'Burnt Norton'), 'The classic, like the Empire, must be thought of as "timeless . . . except in the aspect of time".'[8] Both classic and empire exist within history, but also transcend history, evincing both permanence and change and enabling us to grasp, or at least to experience in practice, the relationship between them. This shuttle between the aspect of time and the aspect of the timeless is operative at some level within any act of interpretation, and constitutes, we might say, an organising principle of the *Aeneid* itself.

---

[5] Cited Reeves (1989) 1.   [6] Eliot (1957) 128.
[7] Kermode (1983) 40.   [8] Kermode (1983) 60.

One could take an episode analysed by a number of contributors to this volume, the account of Aeneas at the site of Rome (8.306–61), where Aeneas walks over spots hallowed in later Roman history, and Virgil superimposes on Evander's rustic settlement the stately buildings of his own day, contrasting the pastoral simplicity of Pallanteum with the contemporary grandeur of Rome. The narrator draws our attention to both difference (*then* a wooded spot, *now* the golden Capitol, 347–8) and continuity (*even then* the Capitol was instinct with divinity). Finally Virgil shades a third layer on to the other two, when Aeneas sees the remains of ancient cities, their walls collapsed, monuments of the men of old, citadels built by Saturn and Janus. A reading which foregrounds the aspect of time produces a narrative either of progress or decline. An optimistic version would give us the rise of Rome from primitive settlement to mistress of the world with an empire without end. A pessimistic version would give us a reversed trajectory, as pastoral idyll gives way to imported luxury and modern vulgar display; or such might be the implication of lines 360–1 where cattle low in what will be a fashionable district of the city, the 'chic' Carinae (*lautis Carinis*). The *nunc/olim* figure in 348 is itself ambiguous since *olim* can refer to past or future: either 'golden now, once densely wooded' or 'golden now, one day to be densely wooded'.[9] So it is not only a matter of whether we prefer woods or gold; the trajectory of history is itself unclear, either from gold to woods or vice versa, and the lines might allow us to see beyond Augustan grandeur to a return to the wild. *Nunc* may introduce a further wavering, since it could mean 'now in Virgil's day' or 'now in Aeneas' day', and 'golden' could be literal or metaphorical, 'belonging to a golden time' or 'made of gold / gilded'. In this way a more complex narrativisation would give us *cycles* of growth and decay; so too ancient cities powerful long ago are ruined already in the time of Aeneas, perhaps thereby portending the eventual fall of Rome itself. On the other hand we might prefer to read the whole passage under the aspect of the timeless; then all the elements in Virgil's description can be held together synchronically. Rome the eternal city is always both the world capital, *caput rerum*, the metropolis which Augustus found brick and left marble, and sweet especial rural scene, both the *res publica* restored by political and military might and the locus of a renewed Age of Gold. Such a Rome, itself a new Troy, could be simultaneously always both standing proud and yet in embryo or in ruins. Bruno Snell famously argued that Virgil discovered a spiritual landscape which he called Arcadia; analogously Aeneas' visit to Pallanteum discloses a spiritual city which Europeans have always called Rome. So too

---

[9] I owe this point to a lecture by J. E. G. Zetzel: compare his chapter in this volume.

a literary classic, like the Virgilian *imperium*, is both here-and-now and eternal. But of course such a timeless synchrony can in turn be challenged by appeals to the aspect of time.

All readings of past texts, even those claiming 'historical accuracy', are representable as acts of appropriation. But an unusual and unusually evident openness to appropriation, so that the meaning of the text is configured within the value system and personal life-history of the individual reader, seems throughout the centuries to have been a particular feature of the response to Virgil, reaching its extreme point in the practice of the *sortes Virgilianae*, a practice whose efficacy has been amply confirmed by the historical record: a passage, arbitrarily chosen and torn from its context, could possess readers to the extent of revealing, and shaping, their futures. The most familiar examples concern famous men (for example Charles I during the Civil War, who consulted a copy of Virgil in the Bodleian Library in Oxford) but in 1783 Dr Johnson's friend Hester Thrale, agonising over whether to marry the Italian musician Gabriel Piozzi and go with him to Italy, against the opposition of family and friends, 'seeing a very fine Virgil was tempted to open it with something of a superstitious intention by way of trying the *sortes Virgilianae*: the book spontaneously opened where Turnus welcomes Camilla, and fixing his fine eyes upon her cries out with a mixture of admiration and gratitude *O decus Italiae* etc. I thought it a good omen.' Perhaps we have here a back-door way (not without irony) of appropriating in a 'female' amatory context the authority of a venerated writer much less accessible to women readers than to men, or at any rate less accessed by them.[10] We can represent this prophetic conception, constantly lurking within Virgil's reception history, in rather more orthodox terms using the words of Ronald Knox in *Let Dons Delight* (1939): 'Virgil – he has the gift, has he not, of summing up in a phrase used at random the aspiration and the tragedy of minds he could never have understood; that is the real poetic genius.'[11] So Helen Waddell found comfort in Virgil in the face of the Nazi threat:

> It was expedient that Rome should die. For one must die to become a legend:
> and the Roman legend was the inspiration of Europe. It is a strange thing to

[10] Thrale (1942) vol. 1, 560–1. For an example in fiction see Maria Edgeworth, *Belinda* (1801) ch. 13. I am indebted to Jackie Pearson for these references. In a review of *Oxford Readings in Vergil's Aeneid* George Steiner observes that of the 26 papers none are by women (Steiner 1990). The male dominance of twentieth-century Virgilian scholarly discourse could be said to replicate the marginalisation of women within Virgil's own texts (even the unforgettable Dido must die). This *Companion* represents a slight, but only a slight, advance in this respect. See also Ellen Oliensis' chapter.

[11] Cited by Stephen Medcalf, 'Virgil at the turn of time', in Martindale (1984) 222.

remember that in the meridian of her power, she herself looked back to her beginnings in a conquered city and a burning town: and the man who gave her immortality was the hollow-cheeked sad-eyed Virgil of the Hadrumetum mosaic. If all else goes from the schools, let us at least keep the second book of Virgil. I speak of it with passion, for something sent me to it on that September afternoon when the Luftwaffe first broke through the defences of London, and that night it seemed as though London and her river burned. You remember the cry of Aeneas waking in the night, the rush, arming as he went, the hurried question – 'Where's the fighting now?' – and the answer:

> Come is the ending day, Troy's hour is come,
> The ineluctable hour.
> Once were we Trojan men,
> And Troy was once, and once a mighty glory
> Of the Trojan race.[12]

For reasons such as these this volume devotes an unusual degree of emphasis to Virgil's reception within European culture (hence the choice of the traditional spelling Virgil rather than the more 'correct' Vergil). Virgil, or 'Virgil' (the very name can be regarded as a trope), even if he should not be wholly collapsed into what his readers have made of him, can never be the originary, reified text-in-itself that so many classical scholars fantasise about uncovering. In his presidential address to the Classical Association in 1995 Professor David West, translator of the Penguin *Aeneid*, opined:

> Reception theory . . . is concerned with the theory of reading, a theory which leads nowhere, or with the history of the reception of texts in later periods. As distinct from general interest, which may be intense, the classical scholar's only duty towards, say, the medieval reception of Virgil's *Aeneid*, is to peruse it for surviving evidence and for medieval insights which help our understanding of the ancient text in its own historical context. Medieval history is for medievalists.[13]

West, who has a triumphalist Whig conception of the progress of scholarship, takes the view, common among classicists, that the meaning of a text is its original meaning which the modern scholar tries to restore (usually identified with the hypothetical intentions of the author and responses of the first readers) – by contrast the history of its reception becomes largely a history of the errors that we have outgrown. Part of the objection to this is that it rests on a singularly crude epistemology, and part of the value of a theory of reading is that it may lead us to reflect not only on *what*

---

[12] Waddell (1976) 40 and 43. [13] West (1995) 16.

texts mean but on *how* they mean. A reception-theorist would argue that readerly responses, including our own, can be seen as strategies for mediating cultural change and for negotiating relationships with the past which are deemed significant for the present; moreover our own views of classical works have been affected by later responses and constructed as a further link in the chain of receptions. In the historicised version of reception-theory associated with the Constance school in Germany the meaning and interpretation of texts is thus inseparable from what readers and reading communities, employing particular reading practices, have made of them, and in this way reception-history becomes hermeneutically vital. Antiquity cannot be studied merely *in itself*, because there is always a 'fusion of horizons' (in Gadamer's somewhat awkward metaphor) between text and interpreter. It is not merely that in practice we cannot read Virgil like a Roman (which Roman?); it would not be desirable if we could, since it would no longer be 'we' who were doing the reading.[14] Interpretation is situated, contingent upon time and place and ideological preconception, is always made from within history. The point seems so obvious as to be not worth labouring were it not that scholars so often ignore it when it comes to their own interpretations. Stephen Harrison in his survey of twentieth-century Virgilian scholarship writes of the so-called Harvard Pessimists, who stressed the darker aspects of the *Aeneid* and the poem's sense of the cost of imperialism, that 'for an outside observer it is difficult to separate such an interpretation from the characteristic concerns of US (and other) intellectuals in these years: the doubt of the traditional view of the *Aeneid* has at least some connection with the 1960s questioning of all institutions, political, religious, and intellectual, and in particular with attitudes towards America's own imperialism'.[15] But something similar could be said of *all* readings – any reading can be historicised in similar fashion. Moreover it is not clear that the history of interpretation is best figured as a history of progress; a comparison of David West's Penguin translation of the *Aeneid* with the version of Dryden does not suggest that West is in any simple sense a 'better' reader of Virgil, even if he is possession of certain scholarly data that Dryden did not have. The mistake of scholars is to suppose that the discourses within which they work are the only ones that can deliver valid 'findings'. For example the view that the *Aeneid* must be understood in relation to its sources is taken as the only 'natural' or 'appropriate' one. Yet

[14] For this view of reading see especially Gadamer (1975). A more productive metaphor might be interpretation as dialogue. For a fuller exploration of these arguments see Martindale (1993a).

[15] Harrison (1990) 5.

did not the Greekless Dante effect one of the two or three most powerful and exciting readings of Virgil – what Harold Bloom, who argues that all readings can be construed as 'misreadings' (either strong or weak), would call a 'strong misreading'[16] – in the *Divine Comedy*, his own narrative revision of the *Aeneid*? The scholarly concern with source criticism – however illuminating within its own discourse – is bound up with the whole ideology and power-structure of Classics as an institution. It is perhaps no coincidence that some of the most innovative work on Virgil is now being done by scholars outside the discipline.[17]

This is not to say that reception-theorists, any more than other interpreters, can escape the shuttle between temporality and timelessness that I described earlier. Kermode describes Eliot's theory of tradition as 'Cubist historiography, unlearning the trick of perspective and ordering history as a system of perpetually varying spatial alignments',[18] in which apparent opposites, tradition and novelty, classicism and modernism, change and stasis, can co-exist. A canon is precisely a site where the diachronic is organised into a synchrony, or, to put the point in the more Eliotic terms I have been employing, where the aspect of time is reconciled with the aspect of the timeless. Thus a secular canon, as much as a religious canon, has metaphysical entailments – with some reason Bloom doubts whether, in high literature, secularisation has ever taken place.[19] And indeed Virgil operates for the committed Virgilian like a sacred book, endlessly repaying meditation, and part of a system of belief and cognition; it is not so much that Virgil imitates, effectively, an extra-literary world as that, for the lover of Virgil, the experience of the world, including the experience of other people, is significantly informed by his works. A canon is an assertion of what is valuable *for us*, and we need canons both because we cannot read everything and because we have no choice but to make value judgements about what we read. We organise the synchrony as a way of showing that our experience of the texts (which, to be sure, originated historically) is *our* experience. And as Kermode rightly insists 'there is no magic by which immanent value ensures survival; that belongs to our ability so to construct history that the valued object stands out from the unvalued and belongs to a totality of literature rather than to an archive of hopelessly diverse documents'.[20] One obvious sense in which a classic like the *Aeneid* could be described as 'timeless' is its capacity (itself a function of its reception) for constant reinscription within new temporal contexts. In this process the

---

[16] Bloom (1973). [17] E.g. Burrow (1993), Quint (1993), Ziolkowski (1993).
[18] Kermode (1968) 229. [19] Bloom (1995) 247. [20] Kermode (1988) 145–6.

'same' text means differently, and in that sense is not the same; or rather it is precisely this sameness-in-difference and difference-in-sameness that is the mark of such a classic.

Some of these points can be illustrated by further consideration of the political significance of the poems, an issue which remains at the centre of much current discussion. Are the poems firmly pro-Augustan, or are they in some sense a critique of empire and emperor? And if Virgil indeed wrote in support of an autocratic regime, does this compromise the value of those writings? A history of the British reception of the *Aeneid* from 1600 shows how the politics of the poem are always interconnected with the politics of talking about it. A necessarily simplified narrative might go something like this.[21] In the early seventeenth century the *Aeneid* was widely regarded as the greatest of epic poems. Virgil's comprehensive grasp of human knowledge, including ethics, politics and metaphysics, had created a work of unique profundity and profound unity, celebrating the Roman Empire and its values and the merits of royalism and one-man rule. Aeneas, the hero, was exemplary, or virtually so, for the Christian prince and leader, and reflected the qualities of Augustus. Virgil's mastery embraced all the arts of rhetoric (with its tropes and figures) including pathos. This reading, however, came under pressure as a result of the English Revolution and the subsequent rise of Whiggism, with its commitment to British liberty and its enthusiasm for the old Roman Republic. Those who wished to dispraise the *Aeneid* argued that Virgil had prostituted himself to the service of a tyrant and autocrat. The poem was also 'borrowed, unconnected, broken and ill-placed', or so thought a critic in 1763, and had no clear or single subject – it had only the virtues of good style. Those who wished rather to continue to praise the *Aeneid* countered in various ways; Virgil could be represented as, covertly or in reality, a friend to liberty, or as trying to charm Augustus into clement behaviour. The poem could be seen, not as a unity, but as disunified in a productive way, or as unified in sensibility if not in structure and theme. Pathos was privileged over patriotism (and indeed narrative), along with sublimity, sensibility, the picturesque and tenderness. Joseph Warton, in the Postscript to his edition (1763), wrote: 'the art of Virgil is never so powerfully felt as when he attempts to move the passions, especially the more tender ones. The *pathetic* was the grand distinguishing characteristic of his genius and temper.' One of the clearest cases of this revisionism was the treatment of the line *sunt lacrimae rerum*

---

[21] See in particular Harrison (1967); for the quotations see pp. 11 and 85. For an account of the importance of reception to the political interpretation of the *Aeneid* see White (1993) 95–109.

et mentem mortalia tangunt, 'there are tears for things, and mortality touches the heart' (1.462). In seventeenth-century editions and translations the line was treated as wholly intrinsic to its local context, but by the end of the nineteenth century it is widely seen as a general comment on the tears of the world (so, for example, the commentator James Henry in 1845) or as both general and specific at the same time.

As always 'findings' only make sense within the terms of the enquiry that produces them, which is one reason why different readings are possible in the first place. In an extraordinarily influential essay Adam Parry argued for a division, within the *Aeneid*, between a public voice celebrating Roman achievement and a private voice of mourning.[22] The passage from which he started in order to illustrate this competing elegiac strain was the lament of the Italian landscape for the dead Umbro (7.759–60), an example of what Ruskin named the 'pathetic fallacy' (*te nemus Angitiae, vitrea te Fucinus unda, | te liquidi flevere lacus*, 'For you the grove of Angitia mourned, and Fucinus' glassy waters, and the clear lakes'). In opposition to this liberal, New Critical, reading, S. L. Wofford, working within a neo-Marxist framework, sees the figure as reinforcing rather than undermining the workings of Augustan ideology.[23] For such a passage aestheticises death and distances grief, thereby partly occluding the violence in 'political and poetic claims to the land'. Violence is rendered natural or beautiful by 'the compulsion exercised by the text's figures'. The sense of history's (retrospective) inevitability survives all such gestures of protest. In other words there is a paradoxical element of 'congruence' between a poetics of loss and absence and an ideology of conquest and war. The process of naturalising *imperium* is as much at work in the lines on the dead Umbro as in more obviously patriotic passages. The structure of temporality (past as future) and the grand figural frame establish the Augustan settlement as history's *telos*, and render invisible, or inevitable, the sacrifices involved in its achievement; and in that sense history and causality become among the poem's principal figures. It would be pointless to say that the text simply 'means' one or the other interpretation (or neither), but this does not absolve us from the freedom, or burden, of choice – for that too is what it means to live in history. If for a moment we accept an account like Wofford's, does it undermine the value of the *Aeneid* today? On such a view the poem tracks the achievement of civilization through the exercise of *imperium*, which includes a claim of the right to rule others. And one recalls Walter Benjamin's resonant saying 'There is no document of

---

[22] 'The two voices of Virgil's *Aeneid*', reprinted in Commager (1966) 107–23.
[23] Wofford (1992); quotations 196–7, 199.

civilisation which is not at the same time a document of barbarism.'[24] On the other hand an observer of current events in the Balkans might conclude that perhaps the choice on occasion is between a version of *imperium* (a UN-sponsored peace or whatever) and a collapse into tribal violence. Some models of *imperium* may favour diversity-within-unity more readily than the modern homogenised nation-state. In general Don Fowler well describes the twentieth-century response to Virgil thus: 'If there is a common element ... it lies in the sense of crisis that has been so central to the century's rhetoric – whether it is that Virgil's poems are figured as a refuge from cultural disintegration, an answer to it, or merely the fellow-feeling of someone who has been through the same.'[25]

No single book on Virgil could be comprehensive, if only because history continues (we might say that interpretation is itself figured within the *Aeneid* in respect of its desire for finality, a desire which is a feature both of imperialist projects and of interpretative texts). Partly for reasons of space 'Virgil' here means the author of the three canonical 'authentic' works accepted as such by modern scholarship, though the poems collected by J. C. Scaliger in 1572 as the *Appendix Virgiliana* and particularly the *Culex* (which Lucan, for example, apparently thought genuine and which Spenser in his Virgilian progress Englished as 'Virgil's Gnat') have their significance from the perspective of reception and for the construction of 'Virgil'. This *Companion* can obviously be consulted piecemeal (the area covered by each chapter is clearly indicated in its title), but its structure has been planned for continuous sequential reading. Histories of reception tend to come as final chapters or postscripts; however, since this volume is based on the premise that reception and interpretation are closely intertwined, we have reversed the conventional order. Interpretation of a foreign classic obviously and necessarily begins with translation, so we begin here too with a substantial essay on Virgil in English translation, in which Colin Burrow argues that Virgil has been most alive when his translators have had a constructive sense of distance from him. No translation, not even the humblest crib, is a neutral transcription, but always an exercise in interpretation, a reading. George Steiner's starting-point in *After Babel* is that translation constitutes the primary hermeneutic act, that all acts of understanding and communication are configurable as exercises in translation. As he puts it:

> *After Babel* postulates that translation is formally and pragmatically implicit in *every* act of communication, in the emission and reception of each and every mode of meaning, be it in the widest semiotic sense or in more

---

[24] Benjamin (1970) 258, from 'Theses on the philosophy of history'.   [25] Fowler (1994).

specifically verbal exchanges. To understand is to decipher. To hear significance is to translate. Thus the essential structural and executive means and problems of the act of translation are fully present in acts of speech, of writing, of pictorial encoding inside any given language. Translation between different languages is a particular application of a configuration and model fundamental to human speech even where it is monoglot.[26]

The next chapter continues to explore the nature of the reading process as it affects our response to Virgil. Duncan Kennedy shows how modern readings of Virgil rest on strategies of appropriation, ideological assumptions, and changing notions of historical understanding; he illustrates this general thesis by a close reading of Eliot's influential critical essays on Virgil. The rest of this first part comprises fragments of a reception-history from antiquity onwards, including a short chapter on Servius as the oldest and most influential scholarly reader who engages with all the poems; necessarily we operate here under the sign of the figure synecdoche and with a particular emphasis on the Anglophone tradition – anything less selective would in the space available be little more than a list which would not teach the reader a great deal.[27] And indeed all historical narratives or views of the past are, and must be, synecdochal.

Part 2 focuses on genre, for most classicists – trained as they are within a strong tradition of literary formalism – a key defining concept for ancient texts. However, genres can be differently theorised: Virgil's career is usually seen as a determined ascent through the genres from lower to higher, from pastoral to didactic to epic, a model for the developing careers of future laureates, but for Quintilian Virgil wrote in only one genre, hexameter *epos*. And, like the Bible, Virgil's works have often been seen as constituting a higher unity, a notion explored in the final chapter in this group by Elena Theodorakopoulos. The idea of Virgil as a continuous text links with the way that Virgil has been constructed – partly as a result of his own self-constructions – as an *auctor*, at once author and authority. Post-modern theorists have frequently sought to contest such authority, proclaiming the death of the author:

We can easily imagine a culture where discourse would circulate without any need for an author. Discourses, whatever their status, form, or value,

---

[26] Steiner (1992), preface to the second edition, xii.

[27] Sadly one major omission is music (reception history is less practised in music studies than in the literary sphere). Among major works inspired by Virgil are the massive *Les Troyens* of Berlioz, whose literary deities were Virgil and Shakespeare, and Purcell's *Dido and Aeneas* with its eloquent concluding lament over a ground, 'When I am laid in earth' – the latter, so familiar today, whether originally written as a court masque or for a girls' school (the issue is currently debated), had no great immediate impact on the history of opera.

and regardless of our manner of handling them, would unfold in a pervasive anonymity. No longer the tiresome repetitions: 'Who is the real author?' 'Have we proof of his authenticity and originality?' 'What has he revealed of his most profound self in his language?' New questions will be heard: 'What are the modes of existence of this discourse?' 'Where does it come from; how is it circulated; who controls it?' 'What placements are determined for possible subjects? Who can fulfil these diverse functions of the subject?' Behind all these questions we would hear little more than the murmur of indifference: 'What matter who's speaking?'[28]

However, even the most perfervid believer in the Death of the Author needs to pay attention to the modes in which the author, of which Virgil has been so canonical an example, was born.

How Virgil's works are interpreted varies in accordance with the way they are contextualised. And contexts are not self-evident or unproblematic but are themselves constructions composed by juxtaposing texts which in turn have to be interpreted. The third part explores a number of contexts within which meanings – often conflicting meanings – might be determined or generated. And it concludes with a substantial essay on intertextuality. The question of originality has been central to discussion of Virgil's poems since antiquity because of the abnormal extent to which they are saturated in previous Greek and Roman literature; Joseph Farrell takes the view that modern discussions of intertextuality provide a framework for a more positive assessment of Virgil's relationship with his predecessors than a belated romantic embarrassment that Latin poets were not more 'original'. Moreover intertexts – like contexts – do not simply resolve problems of interpretation, they complicate them still more, multiplying possibilities. Steiner makes the point thus in relation to Shakespeare:

> And where are the confines of relevance? No text earlier than or contemporaneous with Shakespeare can, *a priori*, be ruled out as having no conceivable bearing. No aspect of Elizabethan and European culture is formally irrelevant to the complete context of a Shakespearean passage. Explorations of semantic structure very soon raise the problem of infinite series. Wittgenstein asked where, when, and by what rationally established criterion the process of free yet potentially linked and significant association in psychoanalysis could be said to have a stop. An exercise in 'total reading' is also potentially unending.[29]

The final part assembles a more loosely connected collection of topics which deal with matters of form and content which traditionally have been

---

[28] Foucault (1977) 138.

[29] Steiner (1992) 7–8. One might add that no later text can be excluded either, if one accepts the importance of reception.

felt to be an important part of the appeal of great literature: the aesthetic appeal of the writing, narrative power, skill in characterisation. The whole *Companion* is designedly pluralist; a variety of approaches are demonstrated, the contributors disagree among themselves on numerous issues, and some of them would not accept the major propositions advanced in this introduction. This very diversity we hope adds to the volume's usefulness, reflecting the diversity of responses to Virgil today as in the past. Contributors were asked to include material that, in their opinion, would be useful to the reader, give a state-of-the-art treatment of their topic as currently conceived, and point to possible future developments; they were free to reconceptualise the topic if they felt it appropriate (for example Philip Hardie shares the now traditional view of the *Aeneid* as in some sense a 'tragic' text, but shifts our sense of what that tragic element might comprise, while Andrew Laird's discussion of characterisation in terms of narratological strategies is very different from older Bradleyan accounts of 'the character of Dido or Turnus'). None the less some common presuppositions can be observed. Discussion of Virgil (somewhat becalmed of late in comparison with some other authors) is still largely dominated on the one hand by a philological tradition descending from Richard Heinze, whose seminal study *Virgil's Epic Technique* first published in 1903 is still regarded by many as the best book on the poem,[30] and on the other by the New Criticism, with its emphasis on poise, ambivalence, patterns of language and imagery and how they signify.[31] The well-wrought urn is still clearly on view in this volume; it is remarkable how many of the contributors stress the rich complexities and ambiguities of the poems (rather than seeing them, say, as containing faultlines that point to internal contradictions within Augustan ideology, as might a New Historicist for example). The various binary tensions seem to constitute an eternal return of those two voices.

The title of the envoi, 'The death of Virgil', carries various resonances. It recalls modern debates about the Death of the Author. It alludes to the story that the dying Virgil sought to burn his unpublished and unfinished *Aeneid* (similar stories are told of a number of subsequent writers including

---

[30] The book has recently been translated into English. For its significance see Hardie (1995).

[31] A copy-book example is Bernard Knox's essay 'The serpent and the flame', reprinted in Commager (1966) 124–42. The employment of imagery as a key to meaning is especially prevalent among 'pessimists'. But the New Criticism has to a remarkable degree colonized the study of Latin poetry in general. There is also continuity between the New Criticism and poststructuralist notions of textualism and fractured signification. The slide can be illustrated in the chapter on the *Aeneid* in Feeney (1991); Feeney never abandons the notion of Virgil's overall writerly control, but increasingly edges the text's discontinuities in the direction of an achieved undecidability.

Kafka). Most obviously it recalls Hermann Broch's novel constructed around this event, a novel which is regarded by George Steiner as one of the supreme masterpieces of literary Modernism and which Fiona Cox here relates to some major strands in twentieth-century accounts of Virgil. And it also raises the question of whether Virgil is still living for us today, or whether he is a species of dead classic, still a potent name perhaps but not widely influential. Theodore Ziolkowski in his *Virgil and the Moderns* goes so far as to present the period between the Two World Wars as a renewed *aetas Virgiliana*, with Virgil as 'a prophet of modernity'[32] able to provide succour for the contemporary *mal de siècle*, the widespread sense of disintegration and fracture; but he sees us as no longer, since 1945, living in so obviously Virgilian a world. Against such a view Steiner convincingly argues that Virgil can be seen as speaking to many of our current preoccupations and discontents:

> Our landscapes at evening, our manifold intimation of 'town and country', the ambivalent stance we take towards warfare, towards the exactions which public, civic life places on privacy, are at many points consequent on the *Bucolics* and *Aeneid* ... Above all, Virgil is European, or so we take him to be ... The Virgilian Mediterranean, the *Aeneid*'s vision of Carthage, the cardinal themes of the instauration of civic institutions, of a state cult, of a politically-animate historicity, are ours, or, more precisely, they lie at the roots of our European conditions. Neither Homer nor Shakespeare has very much to say of the illusions or potentialities which now engage European self-consciousness. Virgil and Dante are talismanic and exemplary of just that consciousness and of its singular contamination of Classical and modern, of pagan and Christian, of private and public modes. We follow on disaster as does Aeneas. The dead swarm at us with dire demands both of due remembrance and future resolve as they do in Book VI of the *Aeneid*. We are twilit, uneasy imperialists or exploiters of less privileged peoples in ways for which Virgil found the most searching expression. Being survivors in Europe, we grow wary of vengeance as Odysseus did not.[33]

Appropriated like this, Virgil remains as much 'ours' as for Seneca he was *Vergilius noster*. And for the diminishing number who can read Virgil's Latin there are also countless lines to haunt the memory and crowd the imagination. Sophisticated critics no longer cite with approval Housman's test in 'The name and nature of poetry' for the greatness of poetry that it made his skin bristle along with a shiver down the spine, or share Arnold's commitment to poetic touchstones 'for detecting the presence or absence of high poetic quality';[34] these seem too much like mere mystifications of

---

[32] Ziolkowski (1993) 6.   [33] Steiner (1990) 10.   [34] Arnold (1964) 242.

the aesthetic. Yet we read poetry as embodied beings, and poststructuralists have said too little about the rhythms of writing, of the danced and gestural elements in *poesis*, and the response of the body to sound and metre. C. S. Lewis records one of his teachers saying that a particular line in Milton had made him happy for a week.[35] We can document how for 2,000 years quotations of Virgil have provided solace or inspiration or material for reflection for thousands of readers in a fashion which cannot be confined to their paraphrasable meaning. We may end in Arnoldian fashion by citing a few famous instances of such possible 'touchstones':[36] take Silenus' picture of the new-created world in Eclogue 6:

> iamque novum terrae stupeant lucescere solem ...

Take the picture in the *Georgics* of hilltop towns and rivers flowing under ancient walls:

> tot congesta manu praeruptis oppida saxis
> fluminaque antiquos subter labentia muros.

take the lament of Orpheus' severed head for his twice lost Eurydice:

> Eurydicen vox ipsa et frigida lingua,
> a miseram Eurydicen! anima fugiente vocabat:
> Eurydicen toto referebant flumine ripae.

take Aeneas' dream address in Book 2 to the ghost of Hector:

> o lux Dardaniae, spes o fidissima Teucrum,
> quae tantae tenuere morae?

take his realisation that Troy's doom has finally come (already cited in Helen Waddell's version):

> venit summa dies et ineluctabile tempus
> Dardaniae. fuimus Troes, fuit Ilium et ingens
> gloria Teucrorum ...

take the words to him of the Sibyl of Cumae about descending into Hell:

> sate sanguine divum,
> Tros Anchisiade, facilis descensus Averno:
> noctes atque dies patet atri ianua Ditis;
> sed revocare gradum superasque evadere ad auras,
> hoc opus, hic labor est.

---

[35] Lewis (1995) 109.
[36] The references are *Ecl.* 6.37; *G* 2.156–7, 4.525–7; *Aen.* 2.281–2, 2.324–6, 6.125–9, 6.314–15. In this instance I deliberately refrain from offering translations.

and finish with the gesture of the dead seeking to cross the river of death into oblivion:

> stabant orantes primi transmittere cursum
> tendebantque manus ripae ulterioris amore.

even if we no longer have the confidence to conclude as Arnold concluded: 'these few lines, if we have tact and can use them, are enough even of themselves to keep clear and sound our judgements about poetry, to save us from fallacious estimates of it, to conduct us to a real estimate'.[37]

---

[37] Arnold (1964) 243. I have reworked material from two previous essays for this introduction; see Martindale (1993a) and (1996).

I

TRANSLATION AND RECEPTION

2

COLIN BURROW

Virgil in English translation

'Virgil' does not just denote the 13,000 or so lines of verse which are now usually attributed to the poet who is believed to have lived between 70 and 19 BC: the word also connotes all the interpretations which have accreted around those lines over the past two thousand years. A study of English translations – over a more modest period of five hundred years – can help us to understand what kind of Virgil has become embedded in English culture. Someone who has taught us, or someone who has taught someone who has taught us, will have read and absorbed, say, Dryden's Virgil – and Dryden had read widely in earlier translations, and was read by almost all later translators. When we interpret we usually think that it is simply we alone who are doing the interpretation. But our language contains buried fragments of the past, and to know the origins of at least some of these fragments can enable us to realise that some of what we think of as being our own views come from dark corners of history. This chapter aims to show the genesis of two more or less irreconcilable tendencies in recent responses to Virgil. The first is the belief that Virgil is a poet of divided loyalties, whose poems cannot completely align themselves with the empire of Rome. The second is the very widespread view that a perfect translation of Virgil would be so accurate that its translator would be invisible. Both of these beliefs emerge, as we shall see, at very specific and surprisingly early periods. What also comes out of this survey, albeit partial, of Virgil in English translation is that Virgil has only rarely appealed to poets who enjoy the patronage of English monarchs. Most English translators of Virgil are anxious about their own standing, and usually they support losing political causes. Virgil tends to be adopted into English by poets who need the consolation of his authority or the sustaining dream of his imperial vision.

The earliest rendering of Virgil in English occurs in Chaucer's *House of Fame* (*c.* 1380) as part of a dream vision. 'Geffrey', the dreamer, is a comically anxious figure, who doubts that his poetic labours will be rewarded. He encounters a version of the *Aeneid* in Venus' temple, engraved in brass in a form which is, like many medieval manuscripts of Virgil, part text and part picture. His first response to the image is tentatively to translate its words:

> 'I wol now synge, *yif I kan*,
> The armes also the man . . .' $(143-4)^1$

Geffrey, though, is not quite as modest as he sounds, and manages to associate himself with the power of Virgil's verse. In witnessing Aeneas' story engraved on the walls of a temple he makes himself a double of Aeneas, who sees a picture of the sack of Troy in Dido's Temple of Juno. Chaucer then summarises the action of the *Aeneid* in chronological order, and, like many a medieval reader of the *Aeneid*, is overwhelmed by the pathetic tale of Dido, which comes to dominate his paraphrase. The strength of his pity for Dido enables him to forget that his poem has a source in Virgil ('Non other auctour alegge I' (314)), and to present himself as the author of the poem. In a poem about Fame this is a significant thing to do: Chaucer introduces the idea that Virgil is the poet to be imitated by those who are eager to press their own claims for a place in the House of Fame, but who fear they might belong on its threshold.

Gavin Douglas's translation of the *Aeneid* into Middle Scots (1513) is often seen as marking a new age in the reception of Virgil, in which the 'Medieval' free paraphrase of Chaucer is superseded by a 'Renaissance' concern with the accurate understanding of ancient literatures and *mores*. Douglas is traditionally praised as a rugged Scot, whose surging descriptions of storms exploit the magnificent sibilance of Middle Scots (winds which 'quhissil' do sound so much more vivid than those which just whistle). Douglas, however, makes full use of the recent painstaking philological commentary of Jacobus Badius Ascensius, and promises 'Virgillis verse to folwe and no thing fain' $(1.\text{Pr}.266).^2$ He attacks the free prose paraphrase of the *Aeneid* which Caxton had printed in 1490, and his outrage at Caxton is designed partly to tell his readers that he, Gavin Douglas, is closer to the 'real' Virgil than his English predecessor. Douglas's professed literalism serves to unite Virgil's authority with his own. His prologues to each book counterpoint his own experiences with those of Aeneas, and, like Chaucer, his strongest responses to the *Aeneid* are to its pathos. He describes the poem as 'feilabill in all degre' ('affecting to the highest degree', 1.Pr.13), and his 'pius Aeneas' is, like Chaucer's narrator, a man of pity more than piety,

---

[1] References to Chaucer (1987). On medieval English Virgils, see Baswell (1995).
[2] References to Douglas (1957–64), book, chapter and line.

who introduces himself as 'Rewthfull Ene'. Douglas, though, struggles to erase the dominant medieval reading of his original as a chivalric tale of pity, adding a long philological note on the meaning of *pietas*, which he claims to interpret 'quhylys [sometimes] for "rewth", quhils for "devotion" and quhilis for "pyete" and "compasson"' (note on 1.vi.125).

Douglas also is very responsive to the dynastic plot of the *Aeneid*. He repeatedly strengthens words in the Latin which concern kinship, such as *gens* (family) and *proles* (offspring), by introducing a touch of blood ('Troian blude', or, his favourite, 'kynrent [kindred] and blude', lace his version), or by seeing the family of Aeneas as having all the closeness of a Scottish 'clan' (3.iii.61). Douglas creates in his *Eneydos* a world where families feel almost magically drawn together by blood: Ascanius is a 'tendir get' (tender offspring) of Aeneas, as is Lausus of Mezentius. Euryalus' bereaved mother cries out 'O my maist tendir hart, quhar art thou gane?' (9.viii.56). Families, and the pain to which they can give rise, are of course a central preoccupation of the *Aeneid*, since the *pietas* of its hero encompasses the emotions felt towards parents as well as duty to the gods; but in exaggerating this element of Virgil's poem Douglas may well have had one eye on his own search for fame. His translation is dedicated to his kinsman Lord Henry Sinclair, with whom he claims to be 'neir coniunct ... in blude' (1.Pr.90). Douglas owed all his subsequent advances to his ties of blood with the Earls of Angus: he became Bishop of Dunkeld two years after completing his Virgil, and died in 1522 having been exiled to France after the fall of his kin from favour. He produces a distinctively Scottish *Aeneid* ('Kepand na sudron [southern English] bot our awyn langage' (1.Pr.110)) not just in its dialect, but also in its insistence that blood is what makes a dynasty grow, and what makes people 'tendir' to each other.

It has been claimed that cultures which are uneasy about their own status are more likely to produce translations than those which are confident about the strength of their native literature.[3] In the case of English translations of Virgil, however, this thesis applies more to the individuals who translated Virgil than to the nation. The act of translating Virgil gives English writers the sense of writing an empire even if they could not themselves participate in one. A case in point is the Earl of Surrey's translation of *Aeneid* 2 and 4. The first blank verse in English, Surrey's is also the first English translation which sought to replicate the impacted rhetoric of the *Aeneid*: *timeo Danaos et dona ferentis* (2.49) is crisply rendered as 'I dred the Grekes, yea, when they offer gyftes' (2.66).[4] It is also the first to make the poem voice not the tender effects of pity, but the experience

---

[3] Basnett (1991) xii.   [4] References to Surrey (1964).

of isolation. Surrey's Dido is above all a solitary, shut off from human companionship by the imperial ambition of Aeneas. Surrey artfully opposes the solitary 'I' of Dido to the collective 'they' of the Trojans in a way that carries over into his own verse, which frequently dwells on the experiences of those who are compelled into solitude as a result of political events. Surrey's public life was isolating: unsuccessful military missions in France were interspersed with repeated imprisonments at home. As a powerful magnate who unwisely boasted of his Plantagenet blood, he never enjoyed the favour of Henry VIII, and in 1547 was executed on a charge of treason. How far these experiences influence his *Aeneid* is impossible to say, since scholars are unsure of its date; but the poem is for him less about the collective power of a nation, than about wounded isolation and imperial aloneness.

Surprisingly, no complete translation of Virgil was dedicated to a reigning monarch until 1849. In 1558 Thomas Phaer dedicated his translation of *The Seven First Bookes of the Eneidos* to the Catholic Mary I, only months before her death. Later editions sought more modest patrons, as Mary was succeeded by her Protestant sister Elizabeth. Even in its later editions Phaer's version contains hints that its author remained loyal to the old faith – images and icons leap out of the heavy matter of his fourteeners, and marginal notes make catholicising remarks such as 'no grace without prayer' (Sig. o3b).[5] By 1584, when his translation was completed by Thomas Twyne, it read like a remnant of an earlier epoch, harking back to an age when Virgil's Rome could be used to evoke the universal authority of the Church. The translation remained in print until 1620, however, and played a part in associating the *Aeneid* with the archaic. In *Hamlet* the Player King recites a Virgilian pastiche of the death of Hecuba in insistently archaic language, and Shakespeare may well have been thinking of Phaer's version, which is jolted into a thickly alliterative manner when Pyrrhus, that cultural throwback to the world of the *Iliad*, enters to kill Priam. Phaer was both out of time and out of place: no successful courtier, he was an obscure solicitor in the Welsh marches. He is an example of how writers on the margins of England have turned to Virgil in order to persuade themselves that they are at the nation's centre.

The *Aeneid* claims great strength and influence for Rome, and this can generate an uneasy relationship between English translators and their Latin original. Many Virgilians insist that 'native' words, by which they usually mean words with Anglo-Saxon roots, be used in translating Rome's chief epic: Dryden in 1697 cries up the value of good native monosyllables, and

---

[5] References to Phaer (1596).

24

in 1859 Singleton boasts of his 'choice of Anglo-Saxon words' (p. xvii). By employing native English words translators strive to make Virgil truly English, rather than succumbing to the weight of his, and Rome's, linguistic authority. The first English writer to attempt what is as much a linguistic conquest as a translation of Virgil was Richard Stanyhurst, whose translation of four Books of the *Aeneid* first appeared in 1583. Stanyhurst's version is in English quantitative metre, which attempts to naturalise in English the effects of Virgil's hexameters. The quantitative verse movement had distinctive national ambitions in the late sixteenth century. For its advocates it was a means of effecting not just a translation, but a full *translatio imperii* from Greece, to Rome, to England by grafting Roman versification onto the native tongue.[6] In Stanyhurst's version Germanic words, words redolent of English folklore such as 'pouke [Puck] bugs', strange coinages, such as 'to ferret' for 'to follow', are compelled to march in Latinate measures. His version attempts to make English triumph over Latin, but it succeeds only in hobbling on vernacular monosyllables, limping, like his Ascanius, after its cultural father:

> My father on shoulders I set, my yong lad Iülus
> I lead with right hand, tripping with pit pat unequal.   (p. 40)

Stanyhurst was Irish, and by the time his translation appeared he was in exile at Leiden, having in 1579 converted to Catholicism. Against this background the eccentricity of his language becomes significant: Stanyhurst does not wish so much to English Virgil, as to impose, through Virgil, a new vision of Englishness on a language to which he did not wish to render himself fully subject.

This short phase of Catholic Virgils was followed by royal, or would-be royal Virgils. George Sandys' translation of Ovid's *Metamorphoses*, dedicated to Charles I, contained in editions after 1632 a translation of Book 1 of the *Aeneid*, which its author presents as having been composed 'divers yeares' (p. 532) before. In the later seventeenth century followers of Sandys develop a self-conscious tradition of royalist versions of Virgil. The ramshackle translation by the Presbyterian John Vicars (1632), and the free rendering by the republican theorist James Harrington (1659), were both laughed into oblivion by royalists such as Samuel Butler, for whom the only true Virgil was one who spoke to princes in an austerely classical English which had roots in earlier English heroic poems. Richard Fanshawe, who became secretary of war to Prince Charles in 1644, rendered Book 4 into Spenserian stanzas and dedicated it to his prince. Printed as

---

[6] Helgerson (1992) 25–40.

it was by a royalist in 1648, during Charles I's imprisonment by Parliament, Fanshawe's work suggests a new role for the Virgilian translator, as one who uses the protection afforded by his prestigious Latin original to stand against the tendencies of the age. The volume concludes with a summary of Rome's civil wars, which connects the lives of Virgil and Horace to Roman political history, as well as making explicit links between Rome's civil wars and England's. Fanshawe then concludes by transforming Anchises' advice to Aeneas (to spare the subject and subdue the proud) into words fit for a future King of a war-torn Britain:

> Breton remember thou to governe men
> (Be this thy trade) And to establish Peace,
> To spare the humble, and the proud depresse.

The Prince of Peace protect your Highnesse most excellent life. (p. 312)

Anchises' maxim had often been quoted in sixteenth-century manuals of advice to Princes, and Sir John Harington, dedicating his manuscript version of Book 6 to Henry Prince of Wales in 1604, had emphasised the value of Virgil's precepts to future Kings. But where Fanshawe marks a new development in the English reception of Virgil is in his suggestion that the *Aeneid* offers consoling prophecies to losing causes.

Sir John Denham (another Irish-born English Virgilian) printed his *Destruction of Troy: An Essay Upon the Second Book of Virgil's Æneis* anonymously in 1656, at the height of Cromwell's supremacy. Like Fanshawe and Sandys he presents his version as having been written earlier, in 1636, well before the outbreak of the civil war. He does this both in order to disarm any efforts to apply his version to contemporary events by hostile readers, and, presumably, to alert his sympathisers to the possibility that a poem which ends with the headless body of a King has more than a little to say about the desperate position of Royalist exiles after the execution of Charles I in 1649. Denham's influential preface on the theory of translation might alert the wary to think that his Virgil speaks of the present: 'if *Virgil* must needs speak English, it were fit he should speak not onely as a man of this Nation, but as a man of this age' (Sig. A3a) – which he does, in the description of the death of Priam with which Denham's version abruptly ends:

> On the cold earth lyes this neglected King,
> A headless Carcass, and a nameless Thing. (p. 28)

The circumstances of these civil war translators sensitise them to the complexities of the *Aeneid*. There is no simple triumphalism: fragments of the poem are produced by disparate translators, each commenting on their own life and their flagging state, and looking forward to an age which might allow for the whole imperial fabric of Virgil to be replicated. John Ogilby's Virgil of 1649, radically revised in 1654, is the last of this camp. The 1654 edition contains elaborate engraved plates, protected from piracy by royal warrant at the Restoration, which mark the volume as one which, had there then been a King in England, would have sought royal patronage. Ogilby lost everything in the civil war, and was shipwrecked on his return from Ireland in the 1640s. He rarely takes a royalist peek over the parapet in his translation, since that might have led to the suppression of his expensive volume; but his Virgil showed just enough of its allegiances to win for its author the enviable job of composing the poetry for the coronation of Charles II. The version is a royalist work printed in a notionally republican country, and this compels it to equivocate. Brutus, the republican hero, is jeered at in the text as a man who would 'o'er his Sons the cruel Axes shake, | For *Specious Liberty*, and to judgement bring, | Because they rais'd new War for their old King.' Ogilby's notes, though, are more cautious, and suggest that he was aware that Cromwell, frequently praised as a new Brutus and no friend of kings, might cast an eye over the work. They circumspectly describe Brutus as 'The avenger of Lucretia's injur'd Chastity . . . and of the opprest Commonwealth groaning under the Tyrannie of *T. Superbus*' (p. 362). The civil war compelled Virgilians to present a Virgil who had divided political loyalties, and alerted them to the ways in which the aftershocks of Rome's civil wars are registered in Virgil's poem.

Virgil is not quite a Vicar of Bray: his text changes with the times, but always resists the simplicities of an imposed ideology. With the Restoration he is marched into Toryism, and a number of the resistant voices which might oppose this transformation are forcibly repressed, or surface in parodies such as John Phillips's scurrilous *Maronides* (1678). Gone are the voices of despair and unease which had been heard by Denham. In the copiously annotated translations of Books 3 and 6 by John Boys, printed a year after the Restoration in 1661, Virgil becomes an imperial triumphalist. *Æneas his Errours* is remarkable only for the extraordinary predictability with which Boys relates Aeneas' wanderings to the exile and Restoration of Charles II 'by the undeniable conduct of the divine Providence' (p. 60). Boys' prolix annotations to *Æneas His Descent into Hell* remove Ogilby's unease with the figure of Brutus, claiming, with a clear slash at the Cromwellian era, that 'under that specious and plausible pretence of asserting the people's liberty, those popular Magistrates did drive on their own sinister and ambitious designes' (p. 185). We are entering a world of party political Virgils, in which the Fourth Eclogue could be read, not as a prophecy of the birth of Christ, but of how, in William Walsh's parody, 'The Vile,

Degenerate, Whiggish Offspring ends, | A High-Church Progeny from Heaven descends.'[7]

John Dryden tried his hand at imitating Virgil after the Restoration. His *Astraea Redux* draws on the Fourth Eclogue for its rejoicings at the return of Charles II, and the anti-Dutch mini-epic *Annus Mirabilis* is nourished by allusions to the *Aeneid*. When Dryden came to translate Virgil in 1697, however, times had changed around him. He had become a Catholic in 1685, and had lost his post as poet laureate after the Glorious Revolution of 1688, when the Dutch Protestant William of Orange was installed on the throne and the Catholic James II was deemed to have abdicated. Virgil's translators need adversity to alert them to the painful worth of a Virgilian prophetic future, and to the complexities of the *Aeneid*'s embedded politics; and Dryden's Virgil is the greatest offspring of the line of resistant Virgils composed by displaced writers. It appeared in a rich folio ornamented with the plates from Ogilby's version, and was ostentatiously *not* dedicated to William III. Dryden's heroic couplets are elastic, sometimes jocular, sometimes as strictly disciplining as the moral environment of Virgil's poems. In his critical writings Dryden frequently associated Virgil with 'retrenchment', a word which he uses to mean that Virgil, unlike Ovid, curbs his style (he speaks of 'the sober retrenchments of his Sense' (p. 326)),[8] and sometimes too to mean that Virgil's chief ethic is that of cutting back the potential excesses of individual emotion. Dryden, however, rarely retrenches his own wish to elaborate the original. Often his version brings to the surface currents of metaphorical suggestion at which Virgil only hints. In the *Georgics* this habitual working-up of Virgil's metaphors enables Dryden to reproduce the continual interweavings of politics and agriculture which run through his original. When, for example, Virgil writes that ploughing is necessary to prevent sterile reeds from overrunning (*dominantur*) the carefully nurtured corn, Dryden turns this into an outright battle:

> So that unless the Land with daily Care
> Is exercis'd, and with an Iron War,
> Of Rakes and Harrows, the proud Foes expell'd,
> And Birds with clamours frighted from the Field ... (1.231–4)

'Exercis'd', 'Iron War' and 'proud Foes' are all Dryden's importations to Virgil, which together make the innocent 'field' of the original into a field of battle, in which the cultivator tries vigorously to expel the interloping weeds.

Dryden was himself embattled in 1697. In his 'Postscript to the Reader' he noted 'What *Virgil* wrote in the vigour of his Age, in Plenty and at Ease,

---

[7] Wells (1970) 491.   [8] References to Dryden (1987).

I have undertaken to Translate in my Declining Years: strugling with Wants, oppress'd with Sickness, curb'd in my Genius, lyable to be misconstrued in all I write' (p. 807). Dryden's age and sickness everywhere lend a feverish energy to his version. His *Aeneid* displays a fitful zeal for the fresh energies of younger characters, which draws from the poem a sympathy for the youthful Turnus, and a fascination with the death of youth which parallels Virgil's own. When young men such as Pallas die Dryden's language becomes tenderly ambiguous:

> One vest array'd the Corps, and one they spread
> O'er his clos'd Eyes, and wrap'd around his Head:
> That when the yellow Hair in Flame shou'd fall,
> The catching Fire might Burn the Golden Caul.   (11.107–10)

'The catching Fire' seems almost protective, arresting Pallas as he falls into it, at the same time as igniting him. The pun brings out the tenderness of those who burn him in order to release his spirit. The translation is not at its subtlest when it renders the ethical framework of the poem (*pius* Aeneas is usually just 'good', and far too often Dryden baldly states that actions are 'ordain'd by Fate', rather than struggling to render Virgil's delicate elisions of human and divine agency); but Dryden's fascination with age and youth can enable him to provide living equivalents for the pains of Virgilian family feeling.

When Dryden spoke of himself as 'lyable to be misconstrued in all I write' he was referring to his position as a Catholic Tory within the literary and political world of the 1690s. His Virgil has been seen as a 'Jacobite' work – that is, as a poem which shows his support of the exiled James II. Dryden quite often introduces the language of legitimate kingship and succession to his version. His Aeneas, at 1.8, 'setl'd sure Succession in his Line', and that added word 'Succession' may have been designed to remind sympathetic readers that William III's hereditary claims to the throne were tenuous. In Dryden's *Georgics* the bee-keeper must 'to the lawful King restore his Right' (4.134), whereas in Virgil's poem he must simply ensure that the more healthy of two would-be King bees goes on to rule the hive. Luke Milbourne in his censorious *Notes on Dryden's Virgil* of 1698 accused Dryden, with some justice, of 'Still girding at the Publick Management' (p. 173). Dryden's loathing of William often makes him read into Virgil a hostility to foreigners, and especially towards foreign kings. In hell, always a place where translators vent their animosities, he inserts those who 'To Tyrants ... have their Country sold, | Imposing Foreign Lords, for Foreign Gold' (6.845–6). Dryden's friend the Earl of Roscommon said that translators should 'chuse an *Author* as you chuse a

Friend' (p. 7), because of some affinity they feel for the original. Dryden himself advocated a form of translation which was very close to that of Denham: 'I have endeavour'd to make *Virgil* speak such *English* as he wou'd himself have spoken, if he had been born in *England*, and in this present Age' (pp. 330–1). His translation of Virgil draws on his own experience as a resistant member of a persecuted minority, compelled to bite his lip in a political milieu which was an abhorrence to him. In his 'Life of Virgil' the Roman poet is presented as a man like Dryden himself, at odds with the political order of his day, who resisted Augustus' imperial revolution as quietly and firmly as Dryden resisted the Revolution of 1688: 'Yet I may safely affirm for our great Author . . . that he was still of Republican principles in his Heart' (p. 280). Dryden's Virgil is no simple imperial poet, but a closet republican, prudently muting his admiration for Brutus and Cato in an age when support of Augustus was the only politic course.

Dryden's own political position is not simply imposed on his original, however. His hostility to foreign invasions is qualified by his own awareness that he, as a translator, is bringing a foreign text into England (and in the *Georgics* this can lead him to stress the benefits of hybridising native stock: a grafted apple tree 'admires the Leaves unknown, | Of Alien Trees, and Apples not her own' (2.116–17)), and by the inescapable fact that Aeneas is a foreigner who is seeking to settle in a new land. His translator's wish to absorb the foreign, rather than being overwhelmed by it, leads Dryden to have a strong, almost anti-imperial, bias in favour of the native people who resist Aeneas. Parry and Lyne have drawn attention to the 'other voices' of private lament which qualify the imperial triumphalism of the *Aeneid*. Dryden's Virgil is not quite the reluctant imperialist of later twentieth-century criticism; but he is, like his civil war predecessors, a Virgil of divided loyalties. Dryden is sure that Lavinia prefers the indigenous Turnus to Aeneas, and his Jove is far more explicit than Virgil's that the invading nation will have to assimilate its customs to those of the natives:

> The *Trojans* to their Customs shall be ty'd,
> I will, my self, their Common Rites provide,
> The Natives shall command, the Foreigners subside.
>
> (12.1209–13)

For Dryden, Aeneas' victory in Italy is not complete: foreign rulers must yield to the customs of native peoples just as foreign texts must be absorbed by the language and customs of their translators.

Later translators of Virgil shrink anxiously away from Dryden's example, and many claim to produce 'literal' translations, far removed from what they often term the 'indulgences' of Dryden. Theories of translation have always adopted a terminology which connects the translator's activity with larger questions of national identity, politics and morality: Horace spoke of a *fidus interpres* (a *faithful* interpreter), and Dryden himself had in his Anglican days presented his preferred form of translation as a *via media*, like his own Church, which afforded a 'latitude' to translators between the extremes of 'metaphrase' (word-for-word translation) and imitation. After 1700 the translator's task is often described in terms which represent his obligation to Virgil as a moral one. Joseph Trapp, in his blank verse Virgil of 1718–31 accuses Dryden of being 'extremely licentious' (p. xlix), and that moralised term of criticism marks an epoch in the history of translating Virgil: for Trapp rendering the very word of Virgil is akin to being virtuous, and Dryden's fertile overlap between his own concerns and those of Virgil is a culpable indulgence. Trapp, comfortably ensconced as Professor of Poetry at Oxford, begins the process of disentangling Virgil from the political and spiritual battles of the translator's own times. The Virgil who could voice the dislocation of an embattled royalist, or who could speak like a friend to an expropriated Catholic, died, and in his place came the Virgil of dons, parsons, and schoolmasters. Christopher Pitt (Rector of Pimperne in Dorset) and Joseph Warton (a headmaster of Winchester) produced the most influential eighteenth-century Englishing of *The Works of Virgil* (1740), which prompted Samuel Johnson (justly) to remark that 'Dryden's faults are forgotten in the hurry of delight, and Pitt's beauties are neglected in the languor of a cold and listless perusal.' Pitt's version, over-burdened with adjectives, is set in amber by the surrounding antiquarianism of the annotations by Warton and his friends. Book 6 in the Pitt–Warton Virgil is not a mirror for Princes, or a fable for poets such as Dante who wish to explore their debts to earlier writing: in Warburton's lengthy disquisition it is turned into an allegory of the mysteries of Eleusis. With that long note begins the shower of dusty antiquarianism which was to dull the surface of Virgil in English for generations.

By the later eighteenth century translators of Virgil were presenting themselves as accurate copyists. The preface to James Beresford's *Aeneid* in 1794 quotes with approval Pierre-Daniel Huet's assertion in *De interpretatione* (1661) that translators should, like painters, copy from the life, and states his ambition to be 'a faithful Representer' of Virgil (p. vii). This leads Beresford to write with a tortured Latinity ('Relume the altars' (p. 95)) which is the lineal ancestor of Housman's parody of translationese ('O suitably attired in leather boots'). Many translators in this period, however, and even those who claim to replicate the true shape of their original, render Virgil into an English which bears the unmistakable imprint of Milton. The preface to Alexander Strahan's version in blank verse of 1767 insists on its fidelity, and, like Beresford, quotes approvingly from Huet. But Strahan's professed admiration for Milton leads him to paint a Virgil in Miltonic dress: 'High on a royal throne' sits not Milton's Satan, but Strahan's Aeolus (1.75; cf. *Paradise Lost* 2.1).

Milton's dominance as a model for translators can influence the politics as well as the vocabulary of the English Virgil. In the eighteenth century, nourished by an odd alliance between Milton's austere anti-royalism and Dryden the Catholic Tory's insistence that Virgil was a closet republican, Virgil first becomes a Whig.[9] Robert Andrews, a Presbyterian minister, wrote in the preface to his *The Works of Virgil* (1766) that Virgil 'never inspires in his intelligent and unaffected Admirers any other than the spirit of liberty'. As befits an enemy of untrammelled royal authority Andrews presents Juno as a would-be absolute monarch rankling over an infringement of her royal prerogative ('Say Muse! the Cause; what touch'd Praerogative | Or what Affront mov'd heaven's Queen . . .' (1.8)). The Whig Virgil lived on in the version of Charles Symmons in 1817, a cleric who wrote a life of Milton, and whose outspoken Whig views prevented his advancement in the Church. Symmons's passion for liberty leads him to represent Aeolus' subjugation of the winds in *Aeneid* 1 (a passage which many earlier translators read as a paradigm of regal government) as akin to the restrictive regime of a nineteenth-century madhouse:

> Mad with control, they shake their prison's bounds;
> And the high mountain with their howl resounds.   (1.72)

Symmons lived in the Welsh marches, and his family estate contained the house in which Thomas Phaer, that earlier borderland Virgilian, had translated the *Aeneid*: he is a typical English translator of Virgil, on the boundaries of the country, and politically at odds with his betters.

Virgil in the later eighteenth century was on the cusp between readings which made him into a Miltonic prophet of national liberty, and those which made him, and his translators, more Latin than the original. The world of Borges's 'The Real Quixote', in which an imitator seeks to become so faithful to *Don Quixote* that he rewrites it verbatim, is not far away. In 1855–9 Robert Singleton's *Works of Virgil* illustrates a final odd turn in the cult of accuracy. Renaissance readers of Virgil saw moral precepts embedded in the *Aeneid* (as Sidney put it 'Who readeth Aeneas carrying old Anchises on his back, that wisheth not it were his fortune to perform so excellent an act'[10]). For Singleton, the first warden of Radley, whose fascination with discipline led him to produce a treatise on 'Uncleanness', translating Virgil

---

[9] *Pace* Harrison (1967).   [10] Sidney (1973) 115.

was itself a moral activity, by which his charges would be able 'to acquire accuracy; to lay up stores of knowledge; in a word, to chasten and inform their minds' (p. iii). Not for him the 'indulgence', as he calls it, of Dryden's version. In Singleton's hands Virgil becomes a text which compels school-boys to evacuate themselves of identity, and, in the name of purity, to turn themselves into little Romans. Singleton – another Irish-born Englisher of Virgil, who wrote a primer of the Irish language – marks his own additions and the grammatical necessities of the English language in square brackets; but the authorised language of classical translation, laced with phrases from Shakespeare and Milton, thickly adorns his version.

By 1800 Virgil is so associated with poetical self-denial and with efforts to Latinise English that few poets with a sense of their own mastery would attempt him. Shelley, who preferred the republican Lucan to Virgil, turns Gallus into a Wanderer drifting away from civilisation in his version of Eclogue 10, and was attracted too by the under-sea voyage of Aristaeus in *Georgics* 4. Wordsworth translated *Aeneid* 1–3 into heroic couplets in the early 1820s in a spirit which typifies the era: 'Having been displeased in modern translations with the additions of incongruous matter, I began to translate with a resolve to keep clear of that fault, by adding nothing; but I became convinced that a spirited translation can scarcely be accomplished in the English language without admitting a principle of compensation.'[11] A poet with a sense of his own identity as strong as Wordsworth's would inevitably shrink from a version which 'added nothing'. A degree zero of presence for the translator is unattainable, and a great poet who set out to achieve such perfect non-being would inevitably wince in horror from the void which opened before him: the translator's poetic identity depends upon there being some elusive flavour of selfhood or nationhood slipped into the foreign text as it passes to its new cultural milieu. The unconscious identity of the translator is the one thing which must always be gained in translation, and to attempt to eradicate it is to seek a kind of non-being. Wordsworth cannot 'add nothing', and he cannot escape from the dom-inance of Miltonic vocabulary: Laocoon's serpent ends like the tail of Milton's Sin 'In folds voluminous and vast' (2.275; cf. *Paradise Lost* 2.652). Wordsworth's own poems, too, of memory and guilt colour his Aeneas, a compulsive narrator like Wordsworth's own Solitaries: 'I will attempt the theme though in my breast | Memory recoils and shudders at the test' (2.18–19). Wordsworth's unfinished version is eventually driven to add some 'compensation' for Virgil's effects, despite its wish to render the very word of its original.

---

[11] Wordsworth (1947) 4, 545.

Most Victorian Virgils are influenced by the prevalent belief that the 'primary' epic of Homer was superior to the 'secondary', literary, epic of Virgil. There were attempts to turn Virgil into a folk epic by rendering him in ballad measure (John Conington in 1885), in rhyming hexameters (Charles Bowen in 1887), and in the omni-purpose Germanic-heroic style of William Morris (1876), whose Aeneas sounds as ruggedly Anglo-Saxon as Beowulf: 'Nor less Aeneas, howso'er, hampered by arrow-hurt' (12.745) is deliberately reminiscent of alliterative English heroic narrative. Translating Virgil became the weekend activity (one suspects the chief weekend activity) of many a Victorian parson. A domestic Virgil can result, intended to educate the immediate family of the translator in the ways of ancient Rome. The Rev. J. M. King, rendering Virgil in neo-Popean couplets for his family in 1847, creates an Aeneas who does not think first of his father Anchises after witnessing the death of Priam, but of his entire family: 'My wife, my son, my sire of equal age, | My plunder'd dwelling all my care engage' (2.687–8). Virgil found at last a royal home when Rann and Charles Rann Kennedy (the former a friend of Wordsworth's) dedicated their *Works of Virgil* (1849) to Prince Albert. The muscular examples of Shakespeare and Milton are used to justify their limp blank verse. The chief goal of the translation is to flex the native thew and sinew of English, claim these two Scots: 'These two great Masters have shown, of what the English language is capable, when its masculine strength is properly applied' (p. iv). Virgil is rarely deployed explicitly by Victorian translators to justify the Empire, since such an appropriation would weaken their repeated claims to fidelity, but the vocabulary with which they describe the act of translation shows that they regard the conquest of Virgil as the ultimate display of Anglo-Saxon strength.

And now? Virgil has not found an Ezra Pound (whose Cantos show an evident preference for Douglas's translation over Virgil's original) or a Christopher Logue to wrench him into modernity. Translators still work in the shadow of the schoolroom. David Slavitt's effort in 1971 to turn the *Eclogues* and the *Georgics* into exercises in literary self-consciousness often collapses into a parody of someone who is haunted by the voices of dead schoolmasters:

> The beautiful shepherd, Corydon *ardebat* –
> ardently loved. '*Ardeo* here acquires
> a transitive signification and takes the accusative.' (p. 7)

It was as a schoolroom text, a glossed and annotated model for rhetoricians, that Virgil first entered the Western canon, and it may yet be that dons and schoolmasters will retire him into the Elysian Fields to sport with Molesworth as he hunts the gerund.

Our legacy from the Virgils of earlier translators is a schizophrenic one, in which there are absolute divides between personal responses to Virgil, sophisticated scholarly accounts of his politics, and the ideal selfless accuracy of the translator. We inherit the idea that translating Virgil with a minimum of intrusions from our own cultural milieu is a good idea; we also inherit the idea that Virgil is politically and emotionally polymorphous. But in the present these Virgils belong to different modes of writing. This is illustrated by the editions in which translations of Virgil are now most readily available. Both the World's Classics *Aeneid* and that in the Everyman's Library present full and poetically uncoloured translations of the poem (that of C. Day Lewis and of Robert Fitzgerald respectively). They also include introductions in which first-rate scholars of Virgil (Griffin and Hardie) outline the political complexity of the poem when read in its historical context. What is profoundly odd about these books is that neither of their respective dust-jackets, nor even their introductions, mentions the fact that the poem which they are introducing is a translation rather than the original. We have so deeply imbibed the notion that translators should be invisible that we have ceased to confess that they are even there; equally we have so completely grasped the idea that Virgil is implicated in the political life of the early Principate that no edition is thinkable which does not learnedly historicise his verse. What one does not find in recent Virgils is any honestly confessed fruitful overlap between the political and historical concerns of the translators and the way in which they translate.

And the myth of the modern translator's transparency is more of a myth than a reality. Even our twentieth-century literalists retain a folk memory that Virgil is a poet for exiles. C. Day Lewis, although the World's Classics edition will not confess as much, turned to the *Georgics* after leaving the Communist Party in 1940 and retiring to Devon, finding in Virgil, as so many of his fellow translators had done, an imaginary version of the community which eluded him in reality. Fitzgerald too confesses that he first read the *Aeneid* in 'the closing months of the Second Great War, when I was stationed on an island in the Western Pacific'. Other kinds of twentieth-century exile have turned to Aeneas for comfort as well. C. H. Sisson's *Aeneid* (1986) is steeped in a post-Eliotean conviction that Culture has departed from the West: his prefatory remark that 'Everyone should know something of the *Aeneid*. Until recently, everybody did' (p. vii) creates an ambience of cultural loss which flavours his entire version. 'Pater Aeneas' is 'our ancestor' for Sisson, reminding his readers – sometimes with a prod

– that for him, as for T. S. Eliot, Virgil is one of the founding texts of a Western civilisation with which the present is losing touch.

The status of Virgil as a classic has made translators feel that they should suppress their own presence in order to allow his voice to emerge; but despite their efforts at self-effacement Virgil remains a writer who appeals to poets who want to re-insert themselves into the centre of a cultural tradition from which they feel displaced. Seamus Heaney's Aeneas (in *Seeing Things*, 1991) is worn by time, aware that his language has been uttered before – that, as Charles Bowen put it in 1887, 'Hundreds of Virgil's lines are for most of us familiar quotations, which linger in our memory, and round which our literary associations cluster and hang, just as religious feeling clings to well-known texts or passages from Scripture':

> No ordeal, O Priestess,
> That you can imagine would ever surprise me
> For already I have foreseen and foresuffered all.   (p. 1)

Aeneas' weariness was anticipated by T. S. Eliot: 'And I Tiresias have fore-suffered all | Enacted on the same divan or bed' (*The Waste Land*, 234–5), and Heaney's translation of Virgil is part of a consistent project late in his career to insinuate himself into an Eliotean–European line of poetry, which links Dante and Virgil and Eliot in one tradition. And Heaney, of course, like so many earlier translators of Virgil, is no spokesman for an English Empire, but an Irishman.

In his attack on 'The cult of Virgil', Robert Graves remarked sourly that 'Whenever a golden age of stable government, full churches, and expanding wealth dawns among the Western nations, Virgil always returns to supreme favour.'[12] Virgil has indeed often appealed in the modern era to conservatives who wish to resist what they see as the cultural decline around them.[13] But when he is translated into English, he more usually gives a voice to those who feel that they are on the outside of a dominant culture. Those who, like Fanshawe or Dryden, are longing to occupy a world which no longer exists, or who, like Chaucer or Heaney, wish to drag themselves across the threshold of an English House of Fame – these poets have turned to Virgil for support. And which of these many translations should one read? A simple answer: Dryden's. His is the only English Virgil to be consciously founded on the idea that it is right for a translator to bring his own experience to bear on his original, and his is the only English translation to take fire from the delicious friction between the translator's concerns and those of his original.

---

[12] Graves (1962) 13.   [13] Ziolkowski (1993).

FURTHER READING

Primary

Chaucer, Geoffrey (3rd edn, 1987) *The Riverside Chaucer*, ed. Larry D. Benson *et al.* Boston

Douglas, Gavin (4 vols. 1957–64) *Virgil's Aeneid Translated into Scottish Verse*, ed. David F. C. Coldwell. Edinburgh and London

Dryden, John (1987) *The Works of Virgil in English: Works, Volumes V and VI*, ed. William Frost and Vinton A. Dearing. Berkeley, Los Angeles and London

Gransden, K. W., ed. (1996) *Virgil in English*. Harmondsworth

Poole, Adrian, and Maule, Jeremy, eds. (1995) *The Oxford Book of Classical Verse in Translation*. Oxford

Secondary

Baswell, Christopher (1995) *Virgil in Medieval England*. Cambridge

Frost, William (1982) 'Translating Virgil, Douglas to Dryden: some general considerations', in Maynard Mack and George deForest Lord, eds. *Poetic Traditions of the English Renaissance*. New Haven and London, pp. 271–86

Harrison, T. W. (1967) 'English Virgil: the *Aeneid* in the XVIII century', *Philologica Pragensia* 10: 1–11 and 80–91

Martindale, Charles, ed. (1984) *Virgil and his Influence*. Bristol

Steiner, T. R. (1975) *English Translation Theory 1650–1800*. Amsterdam and Assen

Ziolkowski, Theodore (1993) *Virgil and the Moderns*. Princeton, NJ

3

DUNCAN F. KENNEDY

Modern receptions and their interpretative implications

To offer a survey of modern receptions of Virgil in this chapter would be to follow, with unequal footsteps and all too close behind, Theodore Ziolkowski's magisterial account in his *Virgil and the Moderns*, which appeared as recently as 1993. Ziolkowski suggests that Virgil's presence in the twentieth century is particularly apparent as a cultural icon and avatar appropriated by poets, novelists, historians and politicians to configure their aspirations and anxieties in the period between the two world wars:

> [T]he response, including the preference for particular works, varied from country to country and from individual to individual, depending upon polit-ical, social and even religious orientation. Virgil's texts, almost like the *sortes Virgilianae* of the Middle Ages, became a mirror in which every reader found what he wished: populism or elitism, fascism or democracy, commitment or escapism.[1]

The status accorded to the text of Virgil in this period was almost scrip-tural, explicitly so for Theodor Haecker, the passionate anti-Nazi whose *Vergil. Vater des Abendlands* of 1931 was one of the most popular works of the period on the poet, and was translated into English in 1934 (as *Virgil. Father of the West*), French and Italian in 1935, Dutch in 1942 and Spanish in 1945. Haecker proclaims:

> Virgil is the only pagan who takes rank with the Jewish and Christian prophets; the *Aeneid* is the only book, apart from Holy Scriptures, to contain sayings that are valid beyond the particular hour and circumstance of their day, prophecies that re-echo from the doors of eternity, whence they first draw their breath ... For whether we like it or not, whether we know it or not, we are all still members of that *Imperium Romanum*, which finally and after terrible errors accepted Christianity *sua sponte*, of its own free will – a Christianity which it could not abandon now without abandoning itself and humanism too.[2]

---

[1] Ziolkowski (1993) 26.   [2] Haecker (1934) 77–8.

Virgil's poetry has, of course, always brought out a strongly proprietorial sense in his readers. Already in the first century AD, the Stoic Seneca was calling him *Vergilius noster* as he cited him as an authority, and for Tertullian in the following century, in a more complex appropriation which has continued to resonate through the poet's reception, he could be referred to as *anima naturaliter Christiana*. From the vantage-point of his own moment, Ziolkowski offers a thoughtful commentary on the depth of the emotional investment involved in their appropriation of Virgil by twentieth-century figures representing ideological perspectives that were often dramatically divergent:

> Although the political readings range from conservative to totalitarian, the religious views from pagan to Christian, and the ethnic stamp from narrowly national to broadly occidental, the response was triggered in every case by the powerful conviction that Virgil in his works offers a message of compelling relevance for the morally chaotic and socially anarchic present *entre deux guerres* – a view that strikes us, in retrospect, as particularly poignant because we know today what followed those hopeful bimillennial appeals to Virgilian *ordo*, *pietas*, and *humanitas*.[3]

It is with such sentiments in mind that Ziolkowski prefaces his study with the statement that 'Virgil is too important to be left to the classicists',[4] signalling and reproducing a distinction between academic and non-academic receptions of the poet which has become entrenched in the twentieth century. In a historical survey of scholarship on the *Aeneid* in the twentieth century written as a preface to a collection of articles reprinted in 1990 as *Oxford Readings in Vergil's Aeneid*, Stephen Harrison characterises the inter-war years thus:

> The *Aeneid* was seen by scholars such as E. K. Rand as a classic, a foretaste of Christianity and a fundamental document of Western civilization, and T. S. Eliot's well-known assertion of this view in *What is a Classic?* (1945) and 'Virgil and the Christian world' (1951) acknowledges a direct debt to the German scholar Haecker, who had presented Vergil as 'Father of the West' in 1931. J. W. Mackail's edition of the *Aeneid* (1930), likewise part of the bimillenary festivities, pursued a similar line. This positive presentation of the *Aeneid* as a classic vindication of the European world-order, happily consonant with Roman imperialism and the achievements and political settlement of Augustus, found few dissenters between the two World Wars.[5]

Eliot's presence in this company of classical scholars is striking, but perhaps also a source of unease. However, this unease, it may be felt, had to

---

[3] Ziolkowski (1993) 56.   [4] Ziolkowski (1993) ix.   [5] Harrison (1990) 3–4.

be negotiated: such is Eliot's cultural authority that some recognition was not to be denied him here, and yet in attempting to accommodate Eliot's writings on Virgil to the preoccupations and goals of classical scholarship, Harrison ends up by implying that anything of substance a classicist might find in them is derived from the work of classical scholars of the time. The consensus is indeed that evidence for Eliot's detailed knowledge of Virgil's works is scant, whether in his poetry ('even the critics who try the hardest to make the case for a "Virgilian" Eliot are able to demonstrate his presence in at most a few lines in some half-dozen poems'[6]) or in his essays on Virgil ('utterly derivative in content'[7]). There is, then, a received distinction between studying 'Virgil' (the business of classicists, it is implied) and his 'reception'. It seems equally clear to Ziolkowski and Harrison on which side Eliot's encounter with Virgil lies, differ though they may in the value they attach to their respective interpretative strategies. Is that the end of the matter, and are the issues finally and definitively settled? At the heart of this question is what is involved in the interpretation of the past and the role of such interpretation in articulating the present, an issue, it could be argued, equally vital in the writings of Virgil and Eliot, and one that can be rendered unusually visible in their interaction.

We may lead into an examination of the implications of Eliot's engagement with Virgil by articulating two different aspects of a term which plays an important role in his thought, 'tradition'. The first could take as its perspective the etymology of the word, the notion of 'handing down': the present is seen as the passive recipient of the texts of the past, or of whatever else constitutes the tradition. The past is viewed as closed and as determining the present, and tradition is a quasi-religious process like apostolic succession. Within this aspect, the means by which those texts came to constitute the tradition, the succession of judgements over the passage of time by which some texts were included in the canon and others excluded, are elided. There are moments in Eliot's writings when this view of tradition can be felt strongly. Thus in his essay of 1919, 'Tradition and the individual talent', he speaks of tradition as involving the historical sense, which in turn involves a 'perception, not only of the pastness of the past, but of its presence; the historical sense compels a man to write not merely with his own generation in his bones, but with a feeling that the whole of the literature of Europe from Homer and within it the whole of the literature of his own country has a simultaneous existence and composes a simultaneous order'.[8] What might be termed the *politics* of tradition are here suppressed (and thus a sense that tradition in this aspect has its own

---

[6] Ziolkowski (1993) 120. [7] Ziolkowski (1993) 133. [8] Eliot (1951) 14.

history). In the word 'simultaneous', the 'pastness of the past' is collapsed and narrative time is compressed into an instantaneous moment experienced in the here-and-now. This notion is presented in the sentence that follows as 'the timeless': 'This historical sense, which is a sense of the timeless as well as the temporal and of the timeless and of the temporal together, is what makes a writer traditional.'[9] The alternative aspect is that what gets called 'tradition', far from being an inheritance handed down from the past, is an active, open process intimately connected with the pursuit of particular interests in the present, the selective appropriation of the past to serve a particular vision of the present and to project that vision into the future. Eliot's formulation is somewhat milder than this. 'Tradition', he says, 'cannot be inherited, and if you want it, you must obtain it by great labour.'[10] This aspect comes out most clearly in the notion of the 'usable past' which Eliot develops in 'Tradition and the individual talent', and criticism of Eliot emphasises this appropriative aspect of tradition when it plots the ways in which Eliot's literary essays themselves select, organise and evaluate past writers in such a way as to underpin and validate his own poetic production.

This ambivalence *within* the term is subtly orchestrated in 'Tradition and the individual talent' in ways which are important for understanding Eliot's approach to Virgil. A gravitation towards one or other of the two aspects could be suggested by highlighting the static 'timelessness' of the first in bold type and the reconfigurating activity involved in the second in italic:

> What happens when a new work of art is created is something that happens simultaneously to all the works of art which preceded it. The **existing monuments form an ideal order** among themselves, which *is modified by the introduction of the new (the really new) work of art* among them. The **existing order is complete** before the new work *arrives*. For **order to persist** after *the supervention of novelty*, the **whole existing order** must be, if ever so slightly, *altered*; and so the relations of each work of art towards the whole are *readjusted*.[11]

In characterising tradition here, the rhetoric of words and phrases such as 'existing order', 'arrives', 'supervention' and the use of passive verbs work to suppress the notion of *agency*. A tension is being constructed within the term 'tradition' which will find its resolution in the notion of the 'individual talent' Eliot is developing. The curiously discomforting associations of appropriation which can be fleetingly felt in the phrase 'usable past' can

[9] Eliot (1951) 14.   [10] Eliot (1951) 14.   [11] Eliot (1951) 15.

be spirited away if the poet can be presented as altering the past, but not of himself. To configure the poet's relation to tradition in terms of appropriation is to emphasise intervention, agency, the force of will, where Eliot's references to the poet's 'continual surrender of himself', or the progress of the artist as 'a continual self-sacrifice, a continual extinction of personality', and the doctrine of 'depersonalization',[12] work to spirit such associations away.

This resistance to what I called earlier the 'politics' of tradition – the process of contested judgement and evaluation, the play of interests which constitute tradition-*making* – can provide a point of transition to Eliot's interpretation of Virgil's *Aeneid* as *the* representative of the classic. For Eliot, as we shall see, a defining feature of the classic is its capacity to transcend the immediate circumstances of its composition. So, at the very beginning of *What is a Classic?*, Eliot moves quickly at the conclusion of the opening paragraph to rid the term 'classic' of some unwanted contemporary associations: 'And finally, I think that the account of the classic which I propose to give here should remove it from the area of antithesis between "classic" and "romantic" – a pair of terms belonging to literary politics, and therefore arousing winds of passion which I ask Aeolus, on this occasion, to contain in the bag.'[13] The elegant allusion to Aeolus, calculated to create a bond of shared intertextual reference with his audience, the Virgil Society, seems sufficient to foreclose discussion of this particular point, and Eliot promptly moves on. However, it is worth enquiring how this bare reference manages to carry such weight and why it might be deemed to be especially appropriate here. If we are to be precise, the bag of Aeolus recalls Homer's *Odyssey* (10.19–20), but in the context of an address to the Virgil Society, it could be argued that the name of Aeolus recalls more potently the incident in *Aeneid* 1 in which the winds, let loose from their cave by Aeolus to force the ships of Aeneas on to the shores of Carthage, are quelled by Neptune, who then drives in state over the pacified seas in his chariot. A simile, the first in the epic and so occupying a position of particular prominence, compares the situation to what is presented as a characteristic – timeless, we might say – outbreak of violence amongst a crowd (1.148–56):

> ac veluti magno in populo cum saepe coorta est
> seditio, saevitque animis ignobile vulgus
> iamque faces et saxa volant, furor arma ministrat;
> tum, pietate gravem et meritis si forte virum quem
> conspexere, silent arrectisque auribus adstant;

---

[12] Eliot (1951) 17.   [13] Eliot (1957) 53–4.

ille regit dictis animos et pectora mulcet:
sic cunctus pelagi cecidit fragor, aequora postquam
prospiciens genitor caeloque invectus aperto
flectit equos curruque volans dat lora secundo.

And as often when unrest brews up in a large crowd, and the common rabble rages angrily and presently firebrands and stones are flying (for fury brings missiles to hand), if at that point they happen to have caught sight of a man who commands their respect by the quality of his character and conduct, they become silent and stand by with attentive ears; he controls their passions with his words and soothes their hearts: just so all the crashing of the sea died down, as soon as Father Neptune gazing over its surface and driving beneath the cloudless sky guides his steeds and, as he flies along, gives rein to his speeding chariot.

The simile works to associate elemental forces with political disorder in such a way as to represent an ideology of social control generated and presided over by the great man. Eliot's reference to Aeolus serves to appropriate this discourse so as to position himself within it: as the unruly rabble of critics takes sides in a dispute over 'classic' versus 'romantic', there comes among them a man who commands their respect by the quality of his character and conduct to control their passions with his words and soothe their hearts, rescuing the idea of the classic for the notion of timelessness, and thus restoring order to the sordidness of literary politics. The mystique of the great man who can calm the crowd finds its counterpart in the realm of the aesthetic in the mystique of the individual talent grounded in a notion of tradition which suppresses that individual's role as an appropriating agent and so part of the fray. The timelessness of the classic in the realm of the aesthetic is being constructed by means of an opposition to the socio-political, the discourse which seeks to ground its explanations in circumstance, in contestation and in use.

The realm of the aesthetic is more overtly characterised in terms of social emplacement when Eliot, in sketching a theory of cultures, turns to discuss what he calls 'maturity of manners':

With maturity of mind I have associated maturity of manners and absence of provinciality. I suppose that, to a modern European suddenly precipitated into the past, the social behaviour of the Romans and Athenians would seem indifferently coarse, barbarous and offensive. But if the poet can portray something superior to contemporary practice, it is not in the way of anticipating some later, and quite different code of behaviour, but by an insight into what the conduct of his own people at his own time might be, at its best.[14]

[14] Eliot (1957) 62.

Note the way in which Eliot at this juncture is projecting the past as *alien*, as *other* than contemporary practice. Things were very different then, the argument goes; be that as it may, Virgil presents us with a picture of what that society might be. Eliot then presents a near-contemporary illustration in which the terms of social emplacement are immediately apparent:

> House parties of the wealthy, in Edwardian England, were not exactly what we read of in the pages of Henry James; but Mr James's society was an idealization, of a kind, of *that* society, and not an anticipation of any other. I think that we are conscious, in Virgil more than in any other poet – for Catullus and Propertius seem ruffians, and Horace somewhat plebeian, by comparison – of a refinement of manners springing from a delicate sensibility, and particularly in that test of manners, private and public conduct between the sexes.

Unlike the uncouth Catullus and Propertius, and the worthy but common Horace, Virgil could be relied upon, it seems, not to do anything embarrassing at a house party, particularly perhaps in his behaviour towards the hostess. Private and public conduct between the sexes is exemplified by Eliot's reading of the story of Dido and Aeneas, and this episode is held to testify for the 'civilized consciousness and conscience' of the whole. 'It will be observed, finally,' he concludes, 'that the behaviour of Virgil's characters (I might except Turnus, the man without a destiny) never appears to be according to some purely local or tribal code of manners: it is in its time, both Roman and European. Virgil certainly, on the plane of manners, is not provincial.'[15] The absence of Turnus I will consider in a moment; but note how the argument has shifted. From being alien or other, Roman manners have now become the same. From presenting the past as different, Eliot has shifted to presenting it as the same: where before the past was constructed as punctuated, discontinuous with the present, now it is continuous. The past is indeed usable, and in more than one way. The assertion of continuity and timelessness within codes of social behaviour slides into an assertion of continuity and timelessness within the realm of the aesthetic, the sameness in the face of change which for Eliot is the defining feature of the classic, realised in the *Aeneid*. Decorum in social behaviour becomes fused with decorum in the aesthetic sphere, and symbolises that which transcends any immediate manifestation.

So, when Eliot develops his notion of the classic, which for him represents the timeless and the universal within the realm of the aesthetic, that realm, ostensibly transcending the socio-political dimension of contestation and use, none the less constantly appeals to it and is realised in its terms.

---

[15] Eliot (1957) 63.

Eliot interprets the *Aeneid* in such a way as to configure certain themes as timeless, and so in Eliot's account serving to make the poem transcend any immediate historical circumstance to which they may refer. In 'Virgil and the Christian world', he asserts that in the *Aeneid*, 'Virgil is concerned with the *imperium romanum*, with the extension and justification of imperial rule', thus affirming that the poem was a product of particular historical circumstance. But he immediately engineers such a shift to the timeless when he goes on to remark that Virgil 'set an ideal for Rome, and for empire in general, which has never been realized in history'.[16] Eliot cites the prophecy of Jupiter in 1.278–9:

> his ego nec metas rerum, nec tempora pono:
> imperium sine fine dedi . . .

For the Romans I set down no boundaries of space or time: power without limit I have given them.

As Frank Kermode has remarked, thus formulated, *imperium sine fine* becomes the paradigm of the classic for Eliot, and figures its essential characteristics: 'a perpetuity, a transcendent entity, however remote its provinces, however extraordinary its temporal vicissitudes'.[17] Eliot's notion of the individual talent, as we have seen, is grounded in a view of tradition which, in suppressing that individual's role as an agent appropriating the past, evokes a sense of the timeless which he then figures in the Virgilian phrase *imperium sine fine*. However, it is always possible to reveal the rhetoric of a text by treating it *as* an interested appropriation, precisely by viewing 'in the aspect of time' what is presented as 'timeless', as I did in the case of Eliot's reference to Aeolus. Thus we might view Eliot's essay not as *the* definition of the classic, but as *a* definition – precisely the imposition of one set of *fines*, discursive boundaries, on the (timeless) notion of the classic. To treat *this* characterisation of the classic *as* an instance of literary politics is to uncover the pretensions, the will to power it encodes: a desire for an *imperium* that will be co-extensive with European culture.

Eliot's allusion to Aeolus configures an episode in the *Aeneid* in such a way as to suggest an archetype of the great man in his poetic manifestation, the individual talent, but this is not the only way in which Virgil's poem functions as a usable past for Eliot. In the terms of his characterisation of Aeneas in *What is a Classic?*, we may just be able to glimpse another figure playing possum:

> Aeneas is himself, from first to last, a 'man in fate', a man who is neither an adventurer nor a schemer, neither a vagabond nor a careerist, a man

---

[16] Eliot (1957) 126.   [17] Kermode (1975) 28.

fulfilling his destiny, not under compulsion or arbitrary decree, and certainly from no stimulus to glory, but by surrendering his will to a higher power behind the gods who would thwart or direct him. He would have preferred to stop in Troy, but he became an exile, and something more significant than any exile; he is exiled for a purpose greater than he can know, but which he recognises; and he is not, in a human sense, a happy or successful man. But he is a symbol of Rome; and, as Aeneas is to Rome, so is ancient Rome to Europe.[18]

Virgilian discourse is appropriated and mobilised not only to negotiate the anxieties involved in the delicate question of Eliot's own social emplacement in his adopted society (unlike Eliot, Turnus is not a man of destiny, and so there is no place for him in polite society), but more importantly to subserve Eliot's vision of European culture and his own perceived role within it. A number of critics have observed that Eliot seems to identify personally with Aeneas, but we may press this issue somewhat further and explore the mechanisms of such identification and the appropriateness of the *Aeneid* in acting as its vehicle.

Eliot speaks of 'the new insight into history' that the *Aeneid* provides.[19] Narratives, and the analyses made of them, characteristically operate by invoking a distinction between 'story', an idealised series of events in a notionally sequential order, and 'narrative', their emplotment in an actual telling. An easy assumption is that 'story' pre-exists its 'emplotment' in 'narrative'; indeed, a word like 'emplotment' presupposes this order. The relationship emerges as more complex, and open to manipulation and re-description for different ends. Virgilian narrative offers itself as the representation, the telling, of a pre-existing story. The famous narrative plunge *in medias res* (the storm which shipwrecks Aeneas on the shores of Carthage seven years after the fall of Troy provides the narrative with its opening incident) and the consequent flashbacks from the narrative's 'present' in the wanderings of Aeneas and his arrival in Italy help to create this sense of the story as already determined, as simply a matter of report, of passive transcription. The narrator's agency is suppressed: the narrative is presented as handed down to the poet rather than as being shaped by him, as is signalled in the poet's appeal to the Muse in 1.8 to 'recount to me the causes' (*Musa, mihi causas memora*). Or, to re-present that in Eliot's terms, the past is presented as though it were *not* usable but an ideal order. In the *Aeneid*, as well as flashbacks such as Aeneas' own account of the fall of Troy, a view 'forwards' from the narrative's 'present' into its 'future' is presented by means of the supernatural, primarily prophecy in various

---

[18] Eliot (1957) 68.   [19] Eliot (1957) 70.

guises. Jupiter's speech to Venus (1.257–96), the parade of Roman heroes as yet unborn in the Underworld (6.756–886) and the scenes depicted on the shield fashioned by Vulcan for Aeneas (8.630–728) look 'forward' from the moment chosen as the narrative's 'present' beyond the incident with which the narrative closes, the death of Turnus, to the age of Augustus as its end, in the sense of both finishing-point and goal, its *telos*. For a character within such a narrative (Aeneas, for example, or 'Eliot' figured in the character sketch of Aeneas in *What is a Classic?*), events will appear contingent, their shape or goal uncertain. No such character can normally see into the future, and for that reason, the view 'forwards' is usually occluded in most narratives (though, as we shall see, we should not make the mistake of believing that it is therefore absent). It is the explicit representation in the person of Jupiter within the narrative of the view 'forwards' (of the 'future' from the narrative's 'present' as *known*, its significance already determined) that has made the *Aeneid* the paradigm of teleological narrative. The association of the view 'forwards' with the god Jupiter makes the view, in the fullest sense of the term, providential. The episodes of the poem are end-determined; the story elements are selected, characterised and arranged so as to exist, in Frank Kermode's phrase, 'under the shadow of the end'.[20] But that end is, of course, the narrator's own time, and it is the narrator who has chosen the story elements and constructed the sequence, its beginning- and end-points and its order of presentation, and thus furnishes the narrative with its view 'forwards'. The view 'forwards' from the *narrative's* 'present' is thus the view 'backwards' from the *narrator's* 'present'. The 'story' which the *Aeneid* purports to narrate emerges as a suprapersonal, providential order of history (History with a capital 'H'), named in the *Aeneid* as *fatum* ('an utterance') and articulated in the utterances of Jupiter. It is thus no less possible to view Fate or History (and, indeed, history) as an *effect* of narrative and the narrator's agency, than, as the poem seeks to suggest, its *cause*. For there to be a 'shape' or 'order' to history, the 'future' (seen from whatever constitutes the narrative's 'present') must be, in some way, *known*: we are asked not only to look back to a point in the past, but also to look forward from that point to the *telos* of the here-and-now, the moment which encapsulates the interests and desires which motivate the narrative act, and which the narrative act seeks to satisfy. It is from this shuttle effect, backwards and forwards, that narratives and historical representations derive their sense of closure and fulfilment.

What I have analysed as the view 'backwards' and the view 'forwards' are totally separable only in theory, never in practice. However, if they are

---

[20] Kermode (1966) 5.

ultimately inseparable, interactive components of any narrative act, they are none the less open to manipulation in different ways to different ends. Thus prophecy presents a sequence of events from the narrative's 'present' with the view 'forwards' explicit, but although the view 'backwards' is occluded, the point and perspective, the *end*, from which that sequence is viewed, is necessary to establish it *as* a prophecy rather than, say, a prediction, a conjecture or a guess. For a prophecy to be a prophecy, the significance of the events it narrates must be simultaneously already, but not yet, known. The *Aeneid* may be regarded as a dramatic allegory of the act of narration and of historical understanding. The complex of perspectives involved in any act of historical narration are resolved into, and enacted by, the poem's characters, and Jupiter, the one character who enjoys perspectives both 'forwards' and 'backwards', becomes a figure of the narrator, the epic poet transcribing History – even down to the description of his own articulation of Fate in terms of reading a book already written: 'I will unroll and bring to light the secrets of fate' (*volvens fatorum arcana movebo*, 1.262).

Although it is the explicit representation within the narrative of the perspective 'forwards' in the character of Jupiter that has made the *Aeneid* the model of teleological narrative, the implication of the previous argument is that all narratives, whether they be fictions or histories, can be seen to have a teleological character and a providential aspect by virtue of having a narrator, though generally this will only be apparent if the perspective 'forwards' is in some way rendered explicit. Contrariwise, if this forward perspective is suppressed by various rhetorical means (primarily, as we have seen, by eliding the agency of the narrator in the fashioning of the narrative), both the teleological and the providential aspect will be occluded. This is no less the case in the stories we tell about ourselves, in which we are *both* narrator and character. In such stories, we create a character in a narrative 'present' which is never entirely identical to the narrator's 'present', and whose perspective on events, and hence of their significance, is never quite the same as that of the narrator. If for the character 'Eliot' (be he configured in the 'individual talent' of the essay of 1919 or the terms of the character sketch of Aeneas in *What is a Classic?*), history appears contingent, it is the narrator Eliot who furnishes him with the destiny he cannot know; and if 'Eliot' has inklings of his destiny (also, in Eliot's terms, an *imperium sine fine*, in this case identified as European culture), it is by virtue of a very oblique and subtle appropriation of the figure of Aeneas in the *Aeneid*, who is given glimpses of the future which he cannot fully understand because he cannot view them from the end, the narrator's present. Allusion to, and identification with, the figure of Aeneas in the *Aeneid* provides a way of activating, without explicitly acknowledging, the providential perspective within such a personal narrative.

However, the implications of such an appropriation go further than this. Eliot's account of Virgil and the *Aeneid* is at times explicitly providential and teleological. In *What is a Classic?* he speaks of 'the Roman empire and the Latin language conforming to its destiny' which he then goes on to define as 'a unique destiny in relation to ourselves',[21] and in 'Virgil and the Christian World', Virgil is presented as an adventist Christian and Aeneas as 'the prototype of a Christian hero'.[22] Eliot thus casts his interpretation in an explicitly typological form which will be familiar to readers of the *Aeneid*: Aeneas is already but not yet a Roman of the poet's own time. Some of the implications of this emerge in Frank Kermode's discussion of the phenomenon of typology in *The Classic*:

> Strictly speaking, a type is distinguished from a symbol or allegory in that it is constituted by an historical event or person (as Christ makes Jonah the type of his resurrection, and St. Paul the crossing of the Red Sea by the Israelites a type of baptism). A type can therefore be identified only by its antitype, a later event in a providentially structured history; the Old Covenant is a type of the New.[23]

Thus, seen retrospectively from the narrator's point of view at the end, earlier events or personalities are deemed to prefigure or foreshadow significant aspects of the present: a prospective, providential view is simultaneously operative. Typology is most closely associated with scripture, but not restricted to it, as Kermode's subsequent comments make clear:

> Types are essentially what Auerbach has in mind when he speaks of *figurae*, events or persons that are themselves, but may presage others. Their purpose, to put it too simply, is to accommodate the events and persons of a superseded order of time to a new one.[24]

Such typologies are explicitly precipitated in texts which, as Kermode suggests, project themselves as signalling the advent of a new order (the New Testament, the *Aeneid* or, it can be argued, the literary essays of Eliot) and thus offer a revision of received, 'traditional', interpretations of the past. But it is possible to see such an accommodatory aspect in *any* historical statement or interpretation, whenever 'events or persons that are themselves' are held to 'figure' others, or a text is so 'characterized' as to foreshadow someone or something. Thus typologies are precipitated in the course of any interpretative activity which involves a process of *identification* in any

---

[21] Eliot (1957) 67–8. [22] Eliot (1957) 127–8.
[23] Kermode (1975) 89–90. [24] Kermode (1975) 90.

form, identification *with* (for example, Aeneas with Augustus, or Aeneas with Eliot) and, more subtly, identification *as*, for such identification *as* is as a type, constituted as such 'only when fulfilled by its antitype, a later event in a providentially structured history' as Kermode says. In an essay on Tennyson's *In Memoriam* (1936), Eliot speaks of its poet thus: 'Tennyson is not only a minor Virgil, he is also with Virgil as Dante saw him, a Virgil among the Shades, the saddest of all English poets, among the Great in Limbo, the most instinctive rebel against the society in which he was the most perfect conformist.'[25] Eliot here explicitly identifies Tennyson with Virgil, and in his book *T. S. Eliot: A Virgilian Poet*, Gareth Reeves remarks of this passage that '[u]ndoubtedly this view of Virgil owes much to Eliot's own radical conservatism',[26] thus further identifying Virgil with Eliot in such a way as to suggest, in the terms in which the identification is configured by Reeves, the teleology of Eliot's rhetoric. Identification *with* (as Tennyson with Virgil, or Eliot with Virgil or, to a lesser extent, we may surmise, with that minor Virgil, Tennyson) entails identification *as*, which is revealed in the terms in which the identification is made: 'the most instinctive rebel against the society in which he was the most perfect conformist'. When Eliot is characterised in the title of Reeves's book *as* 'a Virgilian poet', a typology is no less operative. For there to be a 'shape' or 'order' to history, the 'future' (seen from whatever constitutes the narrative's 'present') must be, in some way, *known*: we are asked not only to look back to a point in the past, but also to look forward from that point to the *telos* of the here-and-now. However, the providential aspect of Reeves's historical view is occluded. Eliot is, in this account, a Virgilian poet, but buried in this assertion is the assumption, certainly unspoken and perhaps also unacknowledged, that (in whatever characteristics link the two across time and so are presented as transcendent) Virgil is already, but not yet, an Eliotic poet.

Any interpretation (be it Virgil's of a History already written, Eliot's of Virgil, Reeves's of Eliot or mine of all of these) will thus figure its object, which might equally be a person or a text, as the type of its concerns, so making itself the antitype within its own providential history; and such interpretations, interpreted in turn, will thereby be seen to be accommodated teleologically to their ends – the preoccupations and interests of their interpreters. But, with the passage of time, the end from, and to, which any text is viewed, is always shifting, thus requiring the constant re-interpretation of 'classic' texts and canonical monuments so as to accommodate them to contemporary concerns, so as to make them *modern*. The terms in which

---

[25] Eliot (1951) 337.   [26] Reeves (1989) 88.

the shuttle between past and present, antitype and type, is configured are thereby projected in the interpretation as timeless, transcending their real-isation in any particular historical manifestation. Thus Eliot's interpreta-tion can be seen to configure the *Aeneid* as the type of providential history and of a decorum that is both social and aesthetic, and Jupiter's phrase *imperium sine fine* as the type of the transcendent, all of which have their antitype in Eliot's definition of the classic. Again, description as 'the most instinctive rebel against the society in which he was the most perfect con-formist' projects a set of categories which can embrace Virgil and Tennyson, and Eliot too, and elide the historical distance between them. And, some-times, the appropriation configures text and interpretation, type and anti-type, so deftly as to make the reading seem, more or less, 'appropriate' to both: 'from first to last, a "man in fate", a man who is neither an adven-turer nor a schemer, neither a vagabond nor a careerist ... he became an exile, and something more than an exile; he is exiled for a purpose greater than he can know, but which he recognises; and he is not, in a human sense, a happy or successful man ...' In such cases, the text has been so thoroughly appropriated that we might even speak of possession – not only of but by the text.

Eliot's appropriation of Virgil, for those of his interpreters at least who accept Eliot's version of his own role in relation to European culture, would seem to have worked; but we may also be close to getting some pur-chase on the wariness with which classicists view him and his interpreta-tion of Virgil. Writing in 'Virgil and the Christian world' of the Messianic interpretation of Virgil's Fourth Eclogue and opining that 'whether we con-sider Virgil a Christian prophet will depend on our interpretation of the word "prophecy"', Eliot at first emphasises the traditional perspective of scholarly interpretation and observes its constraints: 'That Virgil himself was consciously concerned only with domestic affairs or with Roman pol-itics I feel sure.'[27] The character Virgil in the narrative present of 40 BC can have no certain knowledge of the future, but in a gesture of sympa-thetic identification which endows his character momentarily with a view forwards over the events to the end from which the narrator looks back, Eliot immediately continues: 'I think that he would have been very much astonished by the career which his fourth Eclogue was to have.' The provi-dential aspect of historical narrative, so often occluded, is laid open to view, but is attributed to the character in a way that distances it from the narrator, who can now offer an interpretation of the word 'prophecy' which continues ostensibly to forswear recourse to overtly providential history:

[27] Eliot (1957) 122.

> If a prophet were by definition a man who understood the full meaning of what he was saying, this would be for me the end of the matter. But if the word 'inspiration' is to have any meaning, it must mean just this, that the speaker or writer is uttering something which he does not wholly understand – or which he may even misinterpret when the inspiration has departed from him ... It seems to me that one can accept whatever explanation of the fourth Eclogue, by a scholar or historian, is the most plausible; because scholars and historians can only be concerned with what Virgil *thought* he was doing. But at the same time, if there is such a thing as inspiration – and we do go on using the word – then it is something which escapes historical research.[28]

We can view the 'historical research' of 'scholars and historians', which seeks to eschew its providential aspect and teleological structure, and Eliot's own history, which allows them to emerge, as two divergent definitions of the notion of history. Eliot's interpretation of Virgil as an adventist Christian is ahistorical only within *one* definition of 'history', the imposition, in the aspect of time, of one set of boundaries (*fines*) on the (timeless) notion of history. Eliot works within the constraints of the 'scholarly' definition here so as to gesture towards something beyond them, not history in the aspect of time, but History, the realm in which not only Prophecy operates, but Destiny and Providence as well, forces beyond human understanding and control whose workings we can glimpse but darkly. Unless, that is, we recuperate them in the aspect of time as 'providential' history, occluded aspects of the human will to understand and to control, where the appropriation of the past to serve present interests is, precisely, rhetorically *disowned*.

We may now move to a consideration of the more general implications of what we have been discussing for the issue of interpretation itself. For the purposes of this chapter, my interpretation has configured the *Aeneid* as a dramatic allegory of the act of historical understanding and of some of the issues involved. Within the narrative of the past the poem constructs, the end of History and the *telos* of the narrative are identified through the narrator's surrogate, Jupiter, as *imperium* without boundaries of space or time. *Imperium* is thus represented as the outcome of linking disparate phenomena across time into a meaningful narrative, figured in the *Aeneid*, as we have seen, not as the result of the agency of the narrator, nor even perhaps of Jupiter himself, but as the transcription of (the book of) History itself. From this perspective, historical understanding, narrative and power are all intimately linked. 'Conversely', as David Quint has argued, 'the ability to construct narratives that join beginnings purposefully to

[28] Eliot (1957) 122–3.

ends is already the sign and dispensation of power.'[29] As Quint goes on to suggest, the *Aeneid* signals its complicity with power by the shape of its narrative, representing the achievement of its goal by its steady advance to reach the ending towards which it has been directed from the beginning, projecting episodes of suspension and indirection in order that it may overcome them and in so doing demonstrate its ultimately teleological form. Rhetorically, the effect of identifying *imperium sine fine* with the fulfilment of narrative form is to give the impression of a cessation of history, a feeling that History, in achieving its goal, has reached its end as well. *Imperium* thus emerges as identical with the capacity to create an order of historical meaning, to impose a unified interpretation upon the past, configuring and accommodating it to the end from, and to, which it is viewed. That end was once Virgil's own time, and the goal of History, *imperium sine fine*, could be felt to be realised in the aspect of time in the principate of Augustus – or, to be more precise, never quite fully realised, thus leaving the moment of complete fulfilment ever a tantalising prospect. But with the passage of time, that end is always shifting and the prospect in the *Aeneid* of *imperium sine fine* is accommodated to fresh circumstance. It becomes, for example, the vehicle for the ideology of *translatio imperii*, in accordance with which the King of the Franks, Charlemagne, could be crowned Holy *Roman* Emperor, and its sibling, *translatio studii*, embodied in the Carolingian scholarly project, indicating how the appropriation of the *Aeneid* is complicit with the institutions of its interpretation. For Camoens in the *Lusiads*, it provides a ratification for the project of Portuguese imperialism, and it legitimises in turn the succession of the Hapsburgs, the last (or the latest, to date) to lay claim to the posterity and inheritance of Aeneas and Augustus.[30] But *imperium sine fine* can come to configure the *telos* of any interpretative act, as Eliot appropriates the *Aeneid* for his vision of European culture and Christianity. It can even, as here, configure the act of interpretation itself, with its pursuit of the tantalising prospect of final meaning.

Any interpretative act can be resolved into, on the one hand, the search for an originary meaning for the text, attributed to it as immanent, and on the other, the accommodation of the text to the particular circumstances in which the reading is produced, which highlights the role of the text in the authorisation of the beliefs and practices which inform the reading. In the timeless aspect of theory, these two constituent elements carry equal weight, but in the aspect of time, in practice and use in different interpretative schemes, privilege will be accorded to one element at the expense of

---

[29] Quint (1993) 45.   [30] See Tanner (1993).

the other in furtherance of some end or other. Thus for E. D. Hirsch in *The Validity of Interpretation*,[31] the 'meaning' of a text is exalted above its 'significance' in order to posit authorial intention as the goal of valid interpretation. The search for an originary, immanent meaning, in seeing history as already determined and simply awaiting discovery and transcription, must marginalise the notion of appropriation (and, in particular, its own appropriative activity) insofar as it suggests that history is an open-ended process, continuing here and now, and will relegate interpretations, such as Eliot's of Virgil, to a secondary sphere of 'reception'. Contrariwise, an interpretative method which is rhetorically weighted towards the notion of appropriation will assert that the meaning of a text cannot be immanent in an original moment of inscription (the author's intentions or the immediate circumstances of composition, as it may be), but lies in the multiplicity of ways it has been interpreted. From this perspective, the meaning of the text *is* its significance, and that will be a story forever open to fresh interpretation as the text is endlessly re-appropriated in different contexts to configure fresh interests and preoccupations. From within such a definition of history, Eliot's interpretation of Virgil as an adventist Christian, far from being ahistorical, becomes essential to the meaning of the text. But such a method will correspondingly marginalise the way in which it attributes immanent meanings to those interpretations, and emplots previous modes of interpretation as episodes within a teleological narrative of 'reception' in such a way as to project 'reception' as the transcendentally true mode of interpretation. Thus the meaning of a text can neither be collapsed into an instantaneous moment of inscription nor reduced to a history, however protracted, of its reception. A meaning can only be attributed to a text when its significance (in whatever terms that is construed, political, aesthetic, personal or whatever) is at some level, however occluded, already known.

Rather than insisting upon a distinction between pairs of opposed terms (tradition/appropriation, text/interpretation, meaning/significance, theory/practice, the timeless/the aspect of time), we might rather meditate upon the way each of these terms forms an essential constituent of the other, which may be repressed but can never be excluded. However much an interpreter may succeed in elevating one term at the expense of marginalising the other, the latter always remains in play and has the potential to undermine not necessarily the 'findings' (for all findings depend on distinctions such as these being operative, and are validated or negated only in terms of the discourse, for example 'historical philology', in which they appear),

---

[31] Hirsch (1967).

but the *pretensions* of the interpretation, its claim to authority as presenting the *final* truth, the 'end of history'. Reading for the repressed term
performs the immediate function of indicating the way in which texts are
appropriated to inform institutions which, by perpetuating particular modes
of interpretation as legitimate or appropriate, attempt to 'turn cultural values
into ideological possessions', as Frank Kermode has put it.[32] We might
rephrase that as 'project ideological possessions as cultural values' so as to
bring under scrutiny in turn the way in which Kermode's use of the term
'cultural values' rhetorically appeals to the realm of the timeless. In the
aspect of time, that emollient phrase 'cultural values', redolent of an ideal
order, covers over the continuing process of interaction and contestation
out of which value emerges and without which the term could have no
meaning. This process inevitably produces winners and losers, and the need
for both to identify their positions and be reconciled to them. To a sense
of the vertiginous contingency of being in history, a situation that cries out
for the reassurance of shape and closure, an *end*, the *Aeneid* has offered
to its readers, and continues to offer to them however they accommodate
it to their own preoccupations, a memorably elaborated and seductively
attractive response: a sense of destiny, an end to history in *imperium* and
the role-complex of authority and submission it offers.

FURTHER READING

Vergil (ed. Craig Kallendorf, The Classical Heritage vol. 2, New York and London,
1993) reprints fourteen essays on various aspects of Virgil's reception, and contains
an extensive bibliographical survey by the editor (reprinted from *Vergilius* 36
(1990) 82–98). Theodor Ziolkowski's *Virgil and the Moderns* (Princeton, 1993)
has immediately established itself as the point of departure for future studies of
Virgil's impact on the literature of the twentieth century. For a brief survey of the
scholarly reception in the twentieth century (with detailed bibliography) see the
editor's introduction to (ed. S. J. Harrison), *Oxford Readings in Vergil's Aeneid*
(Oxford, 1990). An introduction to reception theory and a spirited exploration of
its role in the interpretation of classical texts can be found in Charles Martindale,
Redeeming the Text. Latin Poetry and the Hermeneutics of Reception (Cambridge,
1993); see esp. ch. 2 on Virgil.

[32] Kermode (1990) 26.

4

R. J. TARRANT

Aspects of Virgil's reception in antiquity

I

The celebrity of Virgil's works in the Roman world was immediate and lasting. The *Aeneid* enjoyed the rare distinction of being hailed as a canonical poem while it was still being written: 'something greater than the *Iliad* is being born' (*nescioquid maius nascitur Iliade*), wrote the elegist Propertius in the mid-20s, perhaps with a touch of irony, but anticipating the serious comparisons with Homer that would become conventional.[1] Virgil's first appearance as a school author also dates from the 20s, when his published work still comprised only the *Eclogues* and *Georgics*; in the guise of a 'modern poet' he was lectured on by Q. Caecilius Epirota, a freedman of Cicero's friend Atticus and an intimate of Cornelius Gallus, from whom he may have derived a fondness for neoteric poetry uncommon in a schoolmaster.[2] Caecilius probably knew Virgil, and could have had personal reasons for including him among the authors he read with his students, but his decision looks forward to the central role Virgil was to play in Roman literary education for the rest of Antiquity.

Acclaim by fellow-poets and early embalmment as a school text are not unusual fates for a major Latin poet; as much could be said, for example, of Horace, especially the lyric Horace of the *Odes*. What makes the reception of Virgil unique among Roman poets is the pervasive quality of his influence, which is visible both at the level of popular culture and of official ideology. This broader effect is almost entirely linked to Virgil's authorship of the *Aeneid*. Had Virgil written only the *Eclogues* and the *Georgics*, his place in the front rank of Latin poets would still be assured, but his fame would not have spread as widely as it did beyond cultivated literary circles. Verses and characters from his poetry appear in wall-paintings and graffiti, mosaics and sarcophagi, even the occasional silver spoon, in

---

[1] Prop. 2.34.66.   [2] Kaster (1995) especially 188–9.

locations ranging from Somerset to Halicarnassus.[3] Virgil's place in the development of an Augustan public discourse is harder to make out, but his depiction of Aeneas as a heroic founder-figure almost certainly contributed to the prominence of Aeneas in major Augustan monuments such as the Ara Pacis (planned between 13 and 9 BC) and the Forum of Augustus (completed in 2 BC). In both settings Aeneas occupies a place visually equivalent to that of Romulus, and is no longer presented as a figure with partisan Caesarian overtones but as a national icon (see pl. 16).[4] A close personal connection with Augustus is itself a component of Virgil's image in later times; evocations of one often entail the other, and changes in attitude toward one inevitably affect the interpretation of the other.

The popularity of Virgil's works naturally stimulated lively interest in the person of their author, and that interest is reflected in the relative fullness of the ancient biographical tradition regarding him. The most substantial of the extant lives, formally the work of Virgil's great fourth-century commentator Aelius Donatus, in large part replicates the life published two centuries earlier by Suetonius in his *De poetis*, and Suetonius was able to draw on a substantial body of anecdotal and documentary material. Virtually no component of the biographical tradition, however, is entirely free from the suspicion of being embellished or even invented, and the biographical picture may indeed have been elaborated precisely to compensate for the unhelpful personal reticence of Virgil's writing.[5] Virgilian biography can thus be seen as an aspect of Virgilian reception, especially given the tendency of ancient literary biographers to transform elements of an author's work into episodes of his life.[6] Most of the individual details furnished by the ancient biographies are harmless – some may even be true – but cumulatively they have exerted a subtly distorting influence from which critics of Virgil's work must struggle to remain free.[7]

A similar fascination with the life of the poet helps to account for some of the spurious poems that circulated under Virgil's name in Antiquity.[8]

---

[3] Horsfall (1995) 249–55.

[4] On Aeneas in Augustan state art see Zanker (1988) 201–10. More speculatively, one might see a connection between the design of the Forum of Augustus, in which galleries containing statues of Roman worthies implicitly point toward the greatness of the present, and the teleologically oriented pageants of Roman history in *Aeneid* 6 and 8; cf. Zanker (1988) 212–13.

[5] A properly sceptical discussion of all the ancient biographies by Horsfall (1995) 1–25.

[6] On ancient lives of the Greek poets see Lefkowitz (1981). A corresponding survey on the Latin side is lacking.

[7] For an example see below, p. 169; also Oliensis, below, p. 294.

[8] A selection of such poems is found in modern editions under the conventional title *Appendix Virgiliana*; some of the individual items were mentioned as youthful works of Virgil by late antique commentators, but the set as a whole corresponds closely to the contents of a now lost manuscript described in a ninth-century catalogue of the library of Murbach; see Reeve (1983).

Many of these were written long after Virgil's time and with no conscious intention of passing for his work, but a few present themselves as Virgilian compositions. Among the latter is an 'epyllion' called the *Culex* ('The gnat'), a work of late Augustan or Tiberian date accepted as Virgilian by Lucan, Statius, and Martial; in its proem the poet addresses a youth named Octavius (i.e. the future Augustus before his adoption by Julius Caesar) and offers him this literary trifle, promising in the future to compose poetry in a more serious vein. As Eduard Fraenkel conclusively showed, the author of the *Culex* adopts the persona of the young Virgil to fill an apparent gap in the poet's literary career.[9] Virgil's authentic works described a steady ascent in poetic ambition, from bucolic to didactic to epic; but even the *Eclogues* were obviously the work of a fully mature poet, and ancient conceptions of a poet's development suggested that they must have been preceded by youthful efforts that dimly foretold the greatness to come. Homer had the *Batrachomyomachia* ('Battle of frogs and mice'); Virgil now had the *Culex*.[10]

The analogy with Homer can be more generally pursued, since Homer provides the closest ancient parallel for the combination of literary prestige and popular recognition that characterises Virgil's reputation in Antiquity.[11] Virgil's name was regularly coupled with Homer's, as in the lines of Propertius quoted earlier, which express a nationalistic pride in Rome's having produced a poet worthy to rival Homer. Sober Roman judges admitted that Virgil was not Homer's equal – Quintilian, for example, approvingly cites the dictum of his teacher Domitius Afer that 'Virgil comes second [to Homer], but is closer to first place than to third'[12] – but his standing as *Homerus alter*[13] was unquestioned, and accounts for certain features of his posthumous reception.

One of these is the close attention devoted to Virgil's text by ancient scholars, and the continuity of such scholarly work from Virgil's own time onward. Virgil was the first Roman poet to achieve canonical status after literary scholarship on Alexandrian lines had taken root in Rome, and his poetry quickly received the kind of philological analysis developed in Greek Homeric scholarship and previously accorded older Latin authors such as Plautus; this focused on establishing an authentic text by weighing variant

---

[9] Fraenkel (1964) 181–97.

[10] The underlying assumption is most clearly put by Statius, *Silv.* 1 pr. *sed et Culicem legimus et Batrachomachiam etiam agnoscimus, nec quisquam est inlustrium poetarum qui non aliquid operibus stilo remissiore praeluserit.* Statius' remark is evidently self-serving, see below, p. 68.

[11] Among later writers Dante perhaps comes closest – a highly suitable conjunction.

[12] *Inst.* 10.1.86.   [13] The phrase is Jerome's, cf. *Epist.* 121.10.

readings, explicating difficulties and apparent inconsistencies, and commenting on features of language, especially anomalies. These techniques might seem to have little relevance to criticism of a contemporary poet, but Virgil's early death and the unfinished state of the *Aeneid* opportunely lent his text some of the indefinite quality appropriate to a more remote classic, and fuelled lively discussion (and probably invention) of possible authorial variants for centuries to come.[14]

Virgilian scholarship also aped its Homeric counterpart in its pedantic carping; the connection is made explicitly by Donatus, who remarked that Virgil, like Homer before him, never lacked detractors (*obtrectatores*).[15] One hostile critic, a certain Carvilius Pictor, entitled a treatise *Aeneidomastix* ('The scourge of the *Aeneid*'), echoing the title 'Homeromastix' given to Zoilus of Amphipolis for his obsession with alleged Homeric blunders. The work of these Virgilian *obtrectatores* (most of them shadowy figures even among the ranks of scholiasts) is no indication that his poetic authority was seriously challenged; indeed, the explicit parallel with adverse criticism of Homer is the clearest admission of Virgil's canonical status.[16]

Homer and Virgil, as the most widely familiar poetic texts in their respective cultures, also shared the honour of frequent parody and whimsical quotation. The practice of giving Virgilian phrases a new point by citing them out of context, which began in Virgil's own lifetime, found especially skilled exponents in the Neronian period: Seneca applies *non passibus aequis* (*Aen.* 2.724, the 'unequal steps' of the child Ascanius) to the limping emperor Claudius (*Apocol.* 1.2) and Petronius conflates lines relating to Dido and Nisus and Euryalus into a mock-heroic description of Encolpius' unresponsive penis.[17] Such isolated quotation foreshadows the poetic cento, in which lines or half-lines of a famous poet were stitched together to form a new composition.[18] A Homeric pastiche in a speech by Dio Chrysostom shows an embryonic stage of the genre,[19] but the earliest extant specimens are in Latin and several are based on Virgil. It appears

---

[14] For the philological methods involved cf. Pfeiffer (1968); on Virgilian textual scholarship in Antiquity see Zetzel (1973) and (1981), Timpanaro (1986).

[15] *Vit. Don.* 43 (probably based on Suetonius).

[16] Cf. W. Görler in *Enciclopedia Virgiliana* vol. 3, 807–13.

[17] *Sat.* 132.11 *illa solo fixos oculos aversa tenebat,* | *nec magis incepto vultum sermone movetur* [= *Aen.* 6.469–50] *quam lentae salices lassove papavera collo* [*Ecl.* 5.16 + *Aen.* 9.436].

[18] Cf. O. Crusius, *RE* 3.2.1929–32, R. Lamacchia, *EV* 1.734–7. Homeric rhapsodes may have used analogous techniques (as did Virgil himself in relation to Homer), but the cento proper depends on a fixed text, what Nagy (1996) 110 calls the 'texts as *scripture*' phase of Homeric transmission; Nagy places the beginning of this period at about the middle of the second century BC.

[19] *Or.* 32.82–5, probably delivered during the reign of Vespasian, cf. Jones (1978) 40, 134.

to have been a rule of the game that the text produced should be on a subject that differed entirely from that of the original – sometimes shockingly so, as in the description of sexual intercourse that concludes Ausonius' *Cento nuptialis*. The cento thus gave modestly gifted writers the opportunity for *variatio* in handling a classic text that stronger poets created for themselves. The diversity of subjects also fostered the notion that the original source material had a universal character; Virgil's work thus becomes a sort of 'master poem' containing the seeds of an infinite number of other poems.[20]

II

Works of literature can exert influence in either positive or negative directions. Some create an immediate vogue for similar writings, like Cornelius Gallus' *Amores* and Ovid's *Heroides*. Others deter imitation, either by the weight of their authority or because they appear to exhaust for the moment the possibilities of a given form. To varying degrees each of Virgil's works seems to have had a repelling effect of this kind; while none of the genres involved remained unexplored by later writers, no poetry in those genres directly inspired by his work is known to have appeared for at least two generations (with the partial exception of Ovid's *Ars amatoria*). Even then the imitators are relatively minor figures, such as the Neronian bucolic poets, Calpurnius Siculus[21] and the unknown author of the Einsiedeln *Eclogues*, who took up Virgil's use of pastoral as a framework for dealing with contemporary events, but employed it in a more blatantly panegyrical vein.[22] It is not surprising that the *Georgics* had no immediate followers: Virgil's transformation of the didactic genre, though profound, was less overt than his reshaping of bucolic or epic, and his Greek didactic predecessors Nicander and Aratus continued to serve as models for poets in subsequent generations. The *Aeneid*, on the other hand, may have been too conspicuously innovative to be directly imitated; at any event, Virgil's fusion of mythological epic and poetry on themes from Roman history remained

---

[20] From here it is an intelligible further step to endow his text with the power to predict the future, the origin of the practice of taking the *sortes Virgilianae*. On the Christian view of Virgil as a prophet see below, p. 70.

[21] Calpurnius can still be counted as Neronian, despite the attempt by Champlin (1978) to redate him to the Severan period.

[22] The *Eclogues* found at least one imitator within the Augustan period, but his existence is proved only by a textually obscure reference in one of Ovid's last poems, *Pont.* 4.16.33 *Tityron antiquas †passerque rediret† ad herbas*; the reference to Tityrus and the adjective *antiquus* guarantee direct evocation of Virgil.

essentially unique, and later poets continued to treat these as distinct forms of epic writing.[23]

Virgil's strongest poetic contemporaries, Horace and Propertius, prudently kept their generic distance from him, while registering the disturbance in the literary atmosphere produced by his successively more imposing works. For both poets the publication of the *Aeneid* falls between their first and last published collections of lyric and elegy respectively. The late poems of each are influenced by Virgil's epic in ways that go beyond their explicit references to Aeneas and his story, but that influence is subordinated to other factors in their development, such as Horace's own evolving role as a public poet and consequent handling of Augustan themes, and Propertius' interest in aetiology and in an enlarged conception of elegy's poetic range.

The case is different with Ovid. Born in 43, he was not yet in his teens at the time of Actium, and still in his early twenties when Virgil died. Just as he was the first Roman poet to regard the Augustan principate as an established fact, he was also the first for whom the poetic career of Virgil is a given rather than a gradual discovery, and the first to see it as paradigmatic.[24] His earliest published collection of poems, the elegiac *Amores*, opens with a poem in which Ovid is deflected from epic to elegy when Amor removes a metrical foot from the second line of his work-in-progress. The elegy (and presumably the imagined epic) begins with *arma*, and an allusion to the *Aeneid* seems likely. Since Ovid, unlike other elegists, does not portray himself as unfit for grander themes, and his service as a writer of elegy is from the outset temporary, the Virgilian echo may signal his ambition to emulate Virgil by rising through the genres to epic. Certainly imitation (in parodic form) of the *Georgics* is one of the motivating forces of the mock-didactic *Ars amatoria*, a work of Ovid's mid-career, while his largest and most ambitious work, the *Metamorphoses*, is in several senses a response and counterpart to the *Aeneid*. (Ovid clinches the connection by claiming that he burned a copy – though not, he wryly adds, the only copy – of the *Metamorphoses* when he was sent into exile, a clear reference to Virgil's reported deathbed attempt to destroy the *Aeneid*.[25]) While observing all the stages of the Virgilian *cursus*, Ovid characteristically went several steps further, adding tragedy (the lost *Medea*) and aetiological poetry (*Fasti*), and, with some help from Augustus, creating the genre of exile-poetry.

---

[23] So, for example, the *Heracleid, Posthomerica*, and *Perseid* mentioned by Ovid in *Pont.* 4.16.7, 19, 25 and the historical epics of Rabirius and Cornelius Severus. Lucan's *Bellum civile* is another matter, see below.

[24] Though not the last, see Conte (1994) 289–90.   [25] *Tr.* 1.7.15ff.; cf. *Vit. Don.* 39.

Whatever its genre, Ovid's writing is suffused with Virgilian reminiscence, often paraded rather than concealed. To take a programmatic example, Ovid's lovelorn Echo bids farewell to the dying Narcissus in a line that is itself an echo and an 'improvement' of a line from the *Eclogues*: *Met.* 3.501 *dictoque 'vale' 'vale' inquit et Echo*, cf. *Ecl.* 3.79 *longum 'formose, vale, vale,' inquit, 'Iolla'*. The repeated *vale* (with shifting metrical treatment of the second syllable), a slightly mannered pathetic feature of the Virgilian passage, becomes in Ovid the final word of Narcissus and the last hopeless reply of Echo. The allusion acknowledges Virgil's place as model (casting Ovid in the role of a 'mere' echo) while demonstrating Ovid's originality (thus showing the echo metaphor to be ironic).

Ovid's appropriations of Virgilian language usually contain an element of mischief, often transposing material from solemn contexts to humorous or disreputable settings. Thus the notorious quotation of *hoc opus, hic labor est* ('this is the labour, this the task', *Aen.* 6.129, the Sibyl to Aeneas on returning from the Underworld) to describe the difficulty of sleeping with a woman without having given her presents beforehand (*Ars* 1.453), or the even bolder (and generally unnoticed) appearance of details from Dido's death agony – heavy eyes, futile attempts to rise, leaning on one elbow – in the droll description of Somnus shaking himself awake.[26] Ovid clearly relishes the challenge of stealing Hercules' club,[27] but even his most impish reworkings are at the same time a means of artistic self-assertion; by showing that the most authoritative poetic language (that of Virgil) is at every point open to re-use and re-imagining, he creates the space and the freedom to articulate his own very different vision.

The agonistic quality in Ovid's relation to Virgil becomes more overt when Ovid comes into contact with Virgilian subject matter; here his need to assert poetic equality takes the form of revisionism. Where this entails confronting Virgil directly, as in the letter of Dido to Aeneas (*Heroides* 7), the result is arguably less than successful: Ovid gives Dido a blatantly accusatory and point-scoring approach to a situation for which Virgil had already provided her with powerfully moving rhetoric, and risks seeming merely shallow and strident by comparison.[28] By contrast, Ovid's way of dealing with Aeneas and the *Aeneid* in the *Metamorphoses*, though hardly subtle, is highly effective. Aeneas has an important structural function in

[26] *Aen.* 4.688ff. *illa gravis oculos conata attollere rursus | deficit . . . | ter sese attollens cubitoque adnixa levavit, | ter revoluta toro est*; *Met.* 11.618ff. *tarda . . . gravitate iacentes | vix oculos tollens iterumque iterumque relabens | . . . | excussit tandem sibi se cubitoque levatus* etc.

[27] Allegedly Virgil's own image for taking a line out of Homer, cf. *Vit. Don.* 46, Macrob. *Sat.* 5.23.16.

[28] On the other hand, the ability to provoke such strong negative responses is itself a kind of poetic power.

Ovid's poem, as the hinge that moves the narrative from Troy to Italy in its final books, but Ovid is determined to keep Aeneas a subsidiary or even marginal figure. The thread of his story is constantly interrupted in favour of less familiar (usually erotic) plots, the most famous episodes in his Virgilian career, his affair with Dido and his journey to the Underworld, are each reduced to bald four-line summaries (*Met.* 14.78–81, 116–19), and his climactic battle with Turnus is treated as merely one more instance of wars fought for a stolen bride (*Met.* 14.450–1, cf. 5.10, 12.5). By subsuming Aeneas into the *Metamorphoses* in this way, Ovid subordinates Virgil's epic to his own poem, which can thus claim to be the more truly comprehensive work. This response to the *Aeneid* operates at the ideological as well as at the literary level: just as Aeneas as a character is deprived of the centrality given him by Virgil, the logic of constant change that governs the *Metamorphoses* has no room for the distinctness and permanence forecast for the Roman state by the *Aeneid*.

III

The shifting literary tastes of the mid and late first century AD are naturally reflected in the treatment of Virgil's poetry. Even among 'modernist' Neronians Virgil's canonical standing was not affected, but their different stylistic tastes and their self-confidence made them openly critical of him in a way that has not been seen before. Seneca, for example, accused Virgil of inserting uncouth archaisms in his poetry to please the taste of a public that still idolized Ennius as a model of epic diction.[29] Just as Cicero appeared bland and long-winded to a generation grown accustomed to the pointed declamatory style,[30] Virgil's manner might have struck admirers of Ovidian epigram as ponderous and lacking in polish. By contrast the 'neoclassical' reaction of the Flavian period, as represented by its professorial spokesman Quintilian, firmly placed Virgil at the head of Latin poets, demoted Ovid to the role of gifted but self-indulgent trifler, and singled out Seneca for particular execration.[31] (Quintilian's capsule judgements

---

[29] From one of the lost books of *Epistulae morales*, cited by Aulus Gellius 12.2.10. Seneca's comment appears to be specifically aimed at the hypermetric verses found occasionally in the *Georgics* and the *Aeneid*; oddly enough, no such lines are found in the surviving fragments of Ennius, and Virgil himself accounts for more than half the extant examples in classical Latin. The Flavian epic writers Valerius Flaccus and Silius Italicus each permit themselves one hypermetric line, presumably in deference to Virgil.

[30] As shown by the comments of M. Aper in Tacitus' *Dialogus* 22–3.

[31] *Inst.* 10.1.88 *lascivus quidem in herois quoque* [i.e. in the *Metamorphoses*] *Ovidius et nimium amator ingenii sui, laudandus tamen partibus*. On Seneca cf. 10.1.125–31. In Petronius, *Sat.* 118.5 the poet Eumolpus, deprecating the sententious style (as found, for example, in Lucan), adduces Homer, Virgil, and Horace as models of proper procedure.

have been so often quoted, and approximate so closely to what has long been conventional wisdom, that it is easy to ignore their polemical and tendentious aspects.)

Despite (or, perhaps better, because of) their critical attitude toward Virgil, the Neronian writers' engagement with him is especially intense. As at other periods, this engagement is as much ideological as literary; since Nero was, for a time at least, seen as a new but improved Augustus, the Augustan component of Virgil's poetry in particular offered a stimulus for competitive imitation. The extravagant hopes that attended Nero's accession found a natural poetic outlet in the Golden Age imagery of the Fourth Eclogue, and the writer of the second Einsiedeln Eclogue quotes the words *tuus iam regnat Apollo* ('your Apollo now reigns', *Ecl.* 4.10) while applying them to Nero.[32] The companion-piece to this poem enlists Virgil himself in Nero's praises: when Mantua hears Nero perform his poem on the Fall of Troy, she is moved to destroy her own writings (48–9). Virgil is inextricably bound to Augustus in defining the canon of imperial virtue that Nero is said to surpass.

The most significant poetry of the period, however, Seneca's tragedies and Lucan's *Bellum civile*, responds to Virgil in a grimmer spirit. In Seneca's depictions of extreme emotional states and his horrific portrayal of the destructive power of passion, the darker side of Virgil's view of human nature finds a more hellish and apocalyptic form. The final scene of the *Aeneid* in particular, it has been argued, impressed itself on Seneca's imagination as an archetypal account of *pietas* overwhelmed by *odium* and *ira*.[33] In *Thyestes*, arguably his most powerful tragedy and certainly the most overtly Roman in its atmosphere,[34] Virgilian reminiscence takes on an important thematic function. The play opens with a scene in which the shade of Tantalus is forced by a Fury to infect the home of his descendants. The Virgilian model is the appearance of the Fury Allecto to Turnus in *Aeneid* 7, the starting-point for the conflict between Trojans and Latins that dominates the second half of the epic;[35] by invoking Virgil in this way, Seneca may give his own story of fraternal strife some of the Roman resonance of his source. A later allusion to the same book of the *Aeneid* is still more pointed. The palace of Atreus, in whose innermost recess Thyestes' children are killed and served to their father, is described in terms that

---

[32] Compare the more skilful manipulation of similar material in Seneca's *Apocolocyntosis* 4.1. For a later use of *Ecl.* 4.10 in an imperial context see below, pp. 70–1.

[33] See Putnam (1992) 231–91.

[34] It is also one of the few Senecan plays that can with some confidence be called Neronian in the literal sense, cf. Tarrant (1985) 10–13.

[35] Schiesaro (1994) 200–2.

unmistakably recall the palace of Latinus (*Thy.* 641ff., cf. *Aen.* 7.170ff.). Since Virgil's lines were thought in Antiquity to refer to the house of Augustus on the Palatine, it is tempting to conclude that Seneca is implicitly contrasting the depraved present with the Virgilian ideal of imperial authority.

The use of Virgil (and specifically Virgil as the poetic voice of Augustan ideology) as a means of articulating a contemporary political viewpoint would seem to apply even more fully to Lucan's historical epic. Lucan's impassioned meditation on the civil war between Julius Caesar and Pompey, and the loathing for Caesar and his legacy that becomes more pronounced as the poem proceeds, have traditionally been linked to the opposition to Nero which eventually cost Lucan his life. The connection may indeed be valid, but seeing the *Bellum civile* as merely a literary reflex of Lucan's political activism has had a reductive effect on its interpretation, hindering awareness of the poem's ambiguities and contradictions.[36] Whatever Lucan's own outlook and the relation of his epic to his political views, the *Aeneid* occupies a central place in Lucan's project, and much of his poem constitutes a bitterly disillusioned rewriting of the Virgilian myth of Rome's past and future.

Detailed encounters with Virgil's text pervade the poem, beginning with its prologue, seven lines corresponding exactly in length to the opening of the *Aeneid*:[37]

> Bella per Emathios plus quam civilia campos
> iusque datum sceleri canimus, populumque potentem
> in sua victrici conversum viscera dextra
> cognatasque acies et rupto foedere regni
> certatum totis concussi viribus orbis
> in commune nefas infestisque obvia signis
> signa, pares aquilas et pila minantia pilis.

> Of wars across Emathian plains, worse than civil wars,
> and of legality conferred on crime we sing, and of a mighty people
> attacking its own guts with victorious sword-hand,

---

[36] Masters (1992), (1994). Something comparable has taken place with Virgil, see below, pp. 182–3.

[37] A scholion on this passage (perhaps ultimately derived from Suetonius) amusingly claims that Lucan's poem originally began with 1.8 *quis furor, o cives*, and that the prologue was composed by Seneca (!) after Lucan's death. In a way that might have pleased Lucan, the story conflates two motifs found in the Virgilian biographical tradition, 'poem left unfinished at poet's death and edited by others' and 'original beginning of poem different from standard text' (cf. the 'original' opening of the *Aeneid*, *ille ego qui quondam* etc., deleted by Varius and Tucca; a fiction likewise transmitted by Suetonius). See Conte (1966).

of kin facing kin, and, once the pact of tyranny was broken,
of conflict waged with all the forces of the shaken world
for universal guilt, and of standards ranged in enmity against
standards, of eagles matched and javelins threatening javelins.

(trans. S. Braund)

Arma virumque cano, Troiae qui primus ab oris
Italiam fato profugus Laviniaque venit
litora, multum ille et terris iactatus et alto
vi superum, saevae memorem Iunonis ob iram,
multa quoque et bello passus, dum conderet urbem
inferretque deos Latio; genus unde Latinum
Albanique patres atque altae moenia Romae.

I sing of arms and of a man: his fate
had made him fugitive; he was the first
to journey from the coasts of Troy as far
as Italy and the Lavinian shores.
Across the lands and waters he was battered
beneath the violence of High Ones, for
the savage Juno's unforgetting anger;
and many sufferings were his in war –
until he brought a city into being
and carried in his gods to Latium;
from this have come the Latin race, the lords
of Alba, and the ramparts of high Rome.   (trans. A. Mandelbaum)

Virgil's introduction encapsulates the movement of the poem as a whole
from Troy (1) to Rome (7); the process is difficult and thwarted by Juno's
opposition, but issues in ultimate triumph. Lucan negates any sense of progress, obsessively repeating with variation the single idea of civil war. The
repetitiveness of Lucan's opening, which was criticized in the following
century by Fronto, thus has thematic value, but it also points to Lucan's conscious stylistic distancing from Virgil. In place of Virgil's dense and highly
wrought manner (the result, so the biographers assert, of a painstakingly
slow writing process), Lucan gives the impression of having written at furious speed, relying on emotive language and sharply pointed epigrams to
engage and startle the reader. (The Neronians in general, beginning with
the *princeps* himself, rejected Augustan fastidiousness in favour of brilliance
and lush fertility.) The absence of references to the gods or to a mythic background is, of course, programmatic; Lucan rigorously demystifies Virgil's
conception of Roman history and so denies Caesar the ennobling effects of
a divine origin and Trojan forebears.

Though studiously un-Virgilian in mood and style, Lucan's opening contains a clear echo of the *Aeneid* which illustrates *in nuce* his inversion of Virgil's outlook. The words *populumque potentem | in sua victrici conversum viscera dextra* recall the plea of Anchises in the Underworld to the yet-unborn souls of Caesar and Pompey to refrain from civil war, *ne, pueri, ne tanta animis adsuescite bella | neu patriae validas in viscera vertite viris* ('do not, my sons, make such wars familiar to your minds, nor turn your mighty strength against your country's guts', *Aen.* 6.832–3). Anchises' appeal was, of course, destined to fail; Virgil acknowledges the failure but subsumes it in a larger historical context, while Lucan refuses to see beyond the event and its catastrophic consequences. Revision of this sort on a larger scale animates Lucan's depiction of the Underworld, placed in strict parallelism with Virgil's at the end of the poem's sixth book;[38] there civil strife divides the shades as well, while Catiline, loosed from the eternal punishment to which Virgil had consigned him on the shield of Aeneas, rejoices at the coming victory of the demagogue Caesar.[39]

The most puzzling passage in Lucan's poem, the panegyrical address to Nero that follows the statement of the theme, is a sustained allusion to the invocation of Octavian at the start of the *Georgics*, and some of its problems result from Lucan's use of this model. The appearance in an epic of an invocation in a radically different mode raises questions of generic propriety, and the disastrous subject of the poem which the *princeps* is being called on to inspire makes Nero's involvement more troubling than Octavian's. In the matter of tone, Virgil treats the future divinity of his addressee with friendly irony, while Lucan's far more extravagant portrait of Nero as a god must be read either as straight panegyric or as bitterly sarcastic.[40] However Lucan's proem is understood, it takes Virgil's praise of Octavian as a norm that it characteristically subverts.

In the Flavian period Virgil becomes a monument in the literal sense: Silius Italicus visited the poet's alleged resting-place as if it were a shrine (and apparently purchased the property, as he had one of Cicero's villas), and Statius portrays himself as 'singing by the side of the great master's tomb' (*magni tumulis accanto magistri*).[41] Such reverential gestures helped

---

[38] *BC* 6.777–820, cf. *Aen.* 6.756–859. This structural parallel is one argument for believing that Lucan planned an epic in twelve books. If so, the most probable concluding point would have been the suicide of Cato, an act of self-liberation from Caesarian tyranny corresponding to the killing of Turnus by Aeneas that had made that tyranny possible.

[39] *BC* 6.793–4 *abruptis Catilina minax fractisque catenis | exultat*, cf. *Aen.* 8.668–9 *et te, Catilina, minaci | pendentem scopulo Furiarumque ora trementem*. The verbal echo underscores the changed situation.

[40] The hostile reading is eloquently expounded by Feeney (1991) 298–301.

[41] *Silv.* 4.4.55. For Silius' devotion to Virgil cf. Pliny, *Epist.* 3.7, Martial 11.48 (also *Pun.* 8.596–7).

create an image of Statius, Valerius Flaccus, and Silius Italicus as mere epigones, content (as the penultimate lines of Statius' *Thebaid* put it) to 'follow the *Aeneid* at a distance and worshipfully trace its footsteps'.[42] Recent criticism has revealed in these poets a more active and genuinely emulous form of engagement with Virgil's work,[43] and Statius' concluding reference to the *Aeneid* can now be seen as suggesting the exalted company he wished his poem to keep in posterity's eyes.[44]

Still, by comparison with Ovid and Lucan, the Flavian approach to epic after the *Aeneid* is more accommodating than confrontational; to call any of their poems an 'anti-*Aeneid*' would be wishful exaggeration.[45] By choosing precisely the type of epic subject that Virgil had rejected (the myths of Thebes and the Argonauts, the youthful exploits of Achilles, safely remote Roman history), they avoid directly challenging him and give themselves space within which to work freely. Their relationship to him is nicely figured by a passage in the first book of the *Argonautica*, where Valerius' Jason urges his men on almost in the very words previously used by Aeneas, to do *quae meminisse iuvet nostrisque nepotibus instent* (1.249, cf. *Aen.* 1.203) – a suitable image for these poets' efforts to achieve something memorable after Virgil while using the poetic means that Virgil had fashioned.

Literary influence, however, is hardly ever direct and unmediated, and as Virgil read Homer in the light of Hellenistic poetry and exegesis, the Flavians' evocation of Virgil is filtered through an awareness of Ovid, Seneca, and Lucan. Valerius follows Lucan in addressing the *princeps* as a source of epic inspiration (a motif transposed by Lucan from the *Georgics*), and Statius' announcement of the *Thebaid*'s subject of brotherly strife, *fraternas acies*, is indebted to Lucan both in content and wording.[46] Silius' subject, the Second Punic War, occupies a space between that of the *Aeneid* and the *Bellum civile*: it supplements Virgil by narrating the conflict between Rome and Carthage foretold in Dido's curse (*Aen.* 4.622ff.), and anticipates Lucan by depicting the seeds of that moral decline which was thought to have culminated in the fall of the Republic.[47] Statius offers an especially striking instance of mediated influence in his description of the Fury Tisiphone's appearance in the first book of the *Thebaid*: while recalling Allecto's

---

[42] *Theb.* 12.816–17 *nec tu divinam Aeneida tempta, | sed longe sequere et vestigia semper adora.*

[43] Hardie (1993).

[44] So also at *Theb.* 10.445–8, where he hopes (vainly) that two of his characters will enjoy renown as 'comrades' (*comites*) of the shades of Nisus and Euryalus.

[45] For attempts see Barnes (1995) 276 (Valerius), 281 (Statius (*Thebaid*)), 290 (Silius).

[46] See above, p. 65.   [47] Feeney (1991) 302.

maddening of Turnus in *Aeneid* 7, the scene draws its sense of cosmic disintegration from the prologue of Seneca's *Thyestes*, which is itself strongly shaped by the same episode of the *Aeneid*.[48]

As that example suggests, their post-Neronian perspective on Virgil may help to explain why the Flavians (Statius in particular) seem so often responsive to the darker aspects of the *Aeneid*. In addition, the fact that Virgil admits irrational and chaotic forces into his poem but does not give them free rein makes fuller exploration of this area a natural step for a successor. Contemporary anxieties may have played a part as well, although clear evidence of political subtexts is not easily found. Whatever the cause, the Flavian treatment of Virgil offers further evidence that the ambivalence that much modern criticism finds in Virgil's poetry is also present in the responses of his earliest ancient readers.[49]

One of the most perceptive of those readers was the historian Tacitus; the 'sympathetic assimilation' of Virgil that Tacitus' greatest modern interpreter describes[50] is due at least in part to a sympathy of outlook, since Tacitus is perhaps Virgil's only equal among Roman writers in what Keats called 'negative capability', the capacity for holding contradictory views in tension. Virgilian colouring often heightens and deepens Tacitus' narrative, but it is applied with such skill that specific reference is not usually detectable, still less any crude equation between characters in the respective works.[51] On the rare occasions when Tacitus points to a particular Virgilian passage the effect is correspondingly more powerful: for example, the mordant irony with which Virgil's description of Dido in the Underworld, among those who had wasted away from unhappy love, is evoked by Tiberius' condemnation of his former wife Julia to a lingering death in exile.[52] A yet more complex irony emerges from Tacitus' reworking of *G.* 4.6 *in tenui labor; at tenuis non gloria* into *in arto et inglorius labor* at *Ann.* 4.32.2. Virgil had claimed that the apparently slight subject-matter of this book (i.e. bee-keeping) would yield no slight fame; Tacitus affects to complain that the unappealing topics open to him as a historian of Tiberius' rule cramp his efforts and deny them glory. (It will not have escaped Tacitus' notice that it was the Augustan principate celebrated by Virgil

---

[48] Ibid. 347–8; above, p. 64.

[49] I do not mean to assert that any ancient reader attributed to Virgil himself ambivalence of the sort that many modern critics have claimed to see in his work.

[50] Syme (1957) 357–8.

[51] Baxter (1972) and Bews (1972) are too ready to see such reference; see Goodyear (1981) 200 n. 1, 243–4.

[52] *Ann.* 1.53.2 *inopia ac tabe longa peremit,* cf. *Aen.* 6.442 *hic quos durus amor crudeli tabe peredit.*

which in his own view inaugurated the change he is ostensibly lamenting.) At another level, however, Tacitus sees himself engaged in a task similar to Virgil's, drawing out the larger significance of events that at first sight appear trivial or unmemorable, and so can implicitly forecast a like renown for his work.[53]

IV

In the most famous expression of Christian anxiety about its relation to classical literature, Jerome relates a dream in which he found himself haled before the divine judgement seat to hear the dread accusation *Ciceronianus es, non Christianus.*[54] It is difficult to imagine this scene replayed with Virgil's name replacing Cicero's, and not simply for reasons of assonance. By Jerome's time Virgil had become the common property of pagans and Christians – a situation neatly symbolised by the fact that Jerome himself, like his contemporary Servius, was a student of Virgil's commentator Donatus. This position is only partly due to Virgil's by now customary place at the heart of literary education, as one of the *quadriga* of authors studied most universally, since the other members of that quartet – Terence, Cicero, and Sallust – did not attain the same degree of overt acceptance among Christians. None of those authors, however, could be claimed as a vehicle of divine inspiration, as had been done for Virgil a century before Jerome wrote. Lactantius appears to have been the first writer to see in the wondrous child of the Fourth Eclogue a prophetic announcement of the coming of Jesus, but this reading of the poem received its most explicit statement from the emperor Constantine himself in his 'Speech to the Assembly of the Saints', an extraordinary Good Friday sermon delivered in the early 320s.[55] By its use of Virgil Constantine's speech implicitly acknowledged the place of classical culture in his New Empire, while at the same time clothing his Christianised regime in the prestige of that culture's principal literary exponent. Whether coincidentally or not, Constantine's reign was especially rich in the composition of Christian poetry that takes Virgil as its formal model, including the most ambitious of the Christian Virgilian centos, by the aristocratic lady Proba, and the first biblical epic, Juvencus' *Evangelia.* In his preface Juvencus cites Virgil along with Homer as the epic forerunners destined to be surpassed by his own work;[56] thus begins

---

[53] Syme (1957) 339 n. 2.   [54] *Epist.* 22.30.
[55] For the speech and its date see Barnes (1981) 73–6, who also defends the transmitted text as essentially Constantinian.
[56] *Evang.* pr. 17–18.

a new phase in Virgil's reception, a new stimulus for competitive imitation that was to continue for more than a millennium.

As it happens, the 'Speech to the Assembly of the Saints' was not Constantine's first encounter with the Fourth Eclogue. A dozen years earlier, before his adoption of Christianity, he had been eulogized in strictly classical terms by an orator who attributed to him a vision of Apollo in which he had recognized himself, the youthful saviour and world ruler sung of in the 'divine poems of bards' (*vatum carmina divina*). The discreetly phrased reference is to *Ecl.* 4.10 *tuus iam regnat Apollo*, a text that would shortly be seen as a 'divine poem' in a very different sense.[57] The contrasted citations show Virgil assisting at one of the formative events in the history of the West, and illustrate once more the conjunction of his poetry with imperial ideology that is a recurring feature of his ancient reception.

FURTHER READING

There is currently no modern study of Virgil's ancient reception seen as a whole; the topic forms part of a broader treatment of Virgilian reception now in preparation by Richard Thomas (to be published by Harvard University Press).

In *A Companion to the Study of Virgil*, ed. N. M. Horsfall (*Mnem.* Suppl. 151, Leiden, 1995), Nicholas Horsfall subjects the ancient accounts of Virgil's life to rigorous scrutiny (pp. 1–25) and surveys the non-literary evidence for Virgil's popular reception (pp. 249–55). In the same volume (pp. 257–92) W. R. Barnes provides a well-documented overview of imitations of and responses to Virgil (primarily the *Aeneid*) by epic poets of the following century (Ovid, Lucan, Statius, Valerius Flaccus, Silius), with abundant references to more specialised studies. This area of Virgil's reception is also the subject of Philip Hardie's more analytical and thematically organised discussion in *The Epic Successors of Virgil* (Cambridge, 1993), and figures prominently as well in Denis Feeney's *The Gods in Epic: Poets and Critics of the Classical Tradition* (Oxford, 1991). Studies of individual authors in relation to Virgil are too numerous for even a representative selection to be feasible; I mention just two articles of widely differing focus, E. J. Kenney's 'The style of the *Metamorphoses*', in *Ovid*, ed. J. W. Binns (London, 1973) pp. 116–53, for incisive comments on Ovid's poetic language in relation to Virgil's, and Michael Putnam's 'Virgil's tragic future: Senecan drama and the *Aeneid*', in *La storia, la letteratura e l'arte a Roma da Tiberio a Domiziano: Atti del convegno*, 231–91 (= *Virgil's Aeneid: Interpretation and Influence* (Chapel Hill, 1995) pp. 246–85), on which see above, p. 64.

On the late antique phase of Virgil's influence H. Hagendahl, *The Latin Fathers and the Classics* (Göteborg, 1958) is still useful, though for the *Aeneid* there is a much fuller treatment in P. Courcelle, *Lecteurs païens et lecteurs chrétiens de l'Enéide* (Mémoires de l'Académie des inscriptions et des belles-lettres, n. s. 4, 2 vols., Rome, 1984). Other evidence of Virgil's special place in late antique Latin culture comes from the several ancient manuscripts of his work still at least

---

[57] *Pan. Lat.* 6.(7).21.5, cf. Barnes (1981) 36 and n. 72.

partially extant, described briefly by L. D. Reynolds in *Texts and Transmission*, ed. L. D. Reynolds (Oxford, 1983) pp. 433–6 and in greater detail by Mario Geymonat in the Horsfall *Companion*, pp. 292–312. Virgil's late antique commentators Donatus and Servius are considered by Robert Kaster in *Guardians of Language: the Grammarian and Society in Late Antiquity* (Berkeley, 1988) pp. 169–96. See also the discussion of Servius by D. P. Fowler in chapter 5 of this volume.

5

DON FOWLER

The Virgil commentary of Servius

Servius (called Marius or Maurus Servius Honoratus in MSS from the ninth century onwards) was a grammarian of the fourth century AD, the author of a celebrated commentary on Virgil. This is generally held to be based on a commentary (now lost) by an earlier fourth-century AD commentator, Aelius Donatus (the teacher of St Jerome), and exists in two forms: the longer, known as *Servius Auctus*, *Servius Danielis*, *DServius*, or *DS*, was first published in 1600 by Pierre Daniel, and is thought to be a seventh- to eighth-century expansion of the shorter form on the basis of material from Donatus' commentary not used by Servius himself. We know little about Servius' life, but he appears as a young man in Macrobius' dialogue the *Saturnalia* (dramatic date 383–4, but probably composed later in the fifth century) as a respectful follower of the pagan leader Aurelius Symmachus (*Sat.* 1.2.15).

Servius' commentary comes at the end of a long period of Virgilian commentary, which had begun in the first century BC.[1] The commentary form itself goes back to Hellenistic and earlier Greek scholarship, above all on Homer, and in a sense Servius' work bears the same relationship to Homeric commentary as the *Aeneid* does to the *Iliad* and *Odyssey*. The format is the familiar one of a lemma (one or more words of the text) followed by comments, in the manner of a modern variorum edition: sometimes scholars are named, but more commonly (especially in the shorter version) we have merely expressions like 'some say ... others ...' The text is typically seen as raising a 'problem' (*quaestio*), to which a 'solution' is offered: the methodology goes back to the beginnings of Homeric commentary.[2] From a modern point of view, this means that the tendency is towards the removal of 'difficulties', rather than their incorporation into

---

[1] Cf. H. Nettleship, 'The ancient commentators on Virgil', in his edition with J. Conington, 4th edn (London, 1881).

[2] Cf. Aristotle, *Poetics* ch. 25, with the commentary of D. W. Lucas (Oxford, 1968).

a more complex reading, but the same objection might be made against many modern commentaries.

The range of interest is also similar to that of modern commentaries (unsurprisingly, since modern commentary has been shaped in part by the Servian model), and includes grammatical points, rhetoric and poetics, and general cultural background. The usage of other writers is often compared, but when we can check the data they are not always correct, and statements about lost works need to be used with care. There is a particular interest in the formulae of traditional Roman law and religion, reflecting the contemporary struggle between Christianity and paganism, and Servius is alert to possible impieties. He is concerned, for instance, when in line 4 of the poem Juno is called *saeva*, 'savage', 'cruel':

> saevae: cum a iuvando dicta sit Iuno, quaerunt multi, cur eam dixerit saevam, et putant temporale esse epitheton, quasi *saeva circa Troianos*, nescientes quod *saevam* dicebant veteres *magnam*. sic Ennius 'induta fuit saeva stola'. item Vergilius cum ubique pium inducat Aeneam, ait 'maternis saevus in armis Aeneas', id est magnus.

> savage: since Juno is named from her action of helping (*iuvando*), many ask why he called her 'savage', and they allege that the epithet is a 'temporary' one, meaning as it were 'savage towards the Trojans', unaware that the ancients used to use 'savage' to mean 'great'. So Ennius 'she was clad in a savage dress' [*Sc.* fr. 410]. Similarly, although Virgil always represents Aeneas as pious, he says 'Aeneas savage in his mother's arms' (12.107), that is, 'great'.

That calling Juno 'savage' is disturbing to an ancient pagan is a point modern critics may well want to accommodate in their own readings; the 'solution' of the unnamed 'many', that she is not always savage but just at this point towards the Trojans is an obvious one, though it perhaps underplays the theological problem; but the statement that in the 'ancients' (*veteres*) *saevus* 'savage' can mean *magnus* 'great' is much more dubious. For Servius, it is unthinkable that Juno or Aeneas could be *saevus*, and so he tries to give the word another meaning: the 'solution' is again of a type not unfamiliar in modern commentaries.

The Servian commentaries can be studied from various aspects. They deserve (and are beginning to receive[3]) treatment in their own right, as fourth-century AD writings with an ideology of their own and they are an important document in the history of ancient literary criticism, rhetoric, and education. Most readers of Virgil, however, use them as a heuristic device, a mine of information and views to excavate for use in constructing

---

[3] Cf. Horsfall (1991).

their own readings of the Virgilian texts. They tend to be used opportunistically: quoted if they support an interpretation, ignored if they do not. There is nothing wrong with this approach, so long as it is clear that Servius' authority in itself does not in any way validate a reading. Particularly useful here is the information about rites and formulae of which we would otherwise be unaware. At *Aen.* 2.148, for instance, Aeneas describes how Priam accepts the deceiver Sinon with the words *quisquis es, amissos hinc iam obliviscere Graios* | (*noster eris*), 'whoever you are, forget now the Greeks you have lost: you will be one of us', and Servius comments:

> **quisquis es**: licet hostis sis. et sunt, ut habemus in Livio, imperatoris verba transfugam recipientis in fidem 'quisquis es noster eris'. item 'vigilasne, deum gens' verba sunt, quibus pontifex maximus utitur in pulvinaribus: quia variam scientiam suo inserit carmini.

> **whoever you are**: even though you are an enemy. As attested in Livy, these are the words of a general accepting a runaway into trust, 'whoever you are, you shall be one of us'. Again later 'are you awake, race of the gods?' [*Aen.* 10.228] are the words that the chief priest uses in relation to the ritual couches: because Virgil inserts into his poem a variety of knowledge.

For Servius, these two instances of formulae are part of his view of Virgil as a master of learning who has 'inserted' into the *Aeneid* a mass of arcane matter – similar views were held about Homer – while for a modern critic, they provide possible starting-points for readings of the two passages in question. It is worth noting, however, that the passage of Livy referred to is not extant (it *may* come from a lost book), and a slightly different story is told later about the religious background of the phrase in Book 10: the Servian commentary is a text like any other, not an infallible source of incontestable information.

Servius' 'literary' explication of the text consists in part of elementary explanations of meaning of words and the construction of sentences (often introduced with the phrase *ordo est* ... , meaning 'take the words in the following order':[4] cf. 1.109 *saxa vocant Itali mediis quae in fluctibus aras: ordo est, 'quae saxa in mediis fluctibus Itali aras vocant'*, 'take the words in the order "which rocks in the middle of the waves the Italians call altars"'). There are also, however, more advanced observations on rhetorical figures of thought and speech and on narrative technique. It is this last element which may be most interesting for modern critics. Servius often comments on what he calls *persona*, and what modern narratologists would see as matters of voice and mood (focalisation, 'point of view'). In

---

[4] Cf. H. L. Levy in *TAPhA* 100 (1969) 237.

1.23, for instance, Juno is described as *veteris . . . memor . . . belli*, 'mind-ful of the old war', referring to Troy: but since the Trojan war was not particularly old at the dramatic date of the *Aeneid*, there is a *problema* awaiting a *lysis* or solution. Modern commentators tend to take *veteris* as focalised by Juno, and meaning something like 'past' rather than 'ancient' (with a hint of bitterness), but Servius adopts a different solution:

> **veteris belli**: quantum ad Vergilium pertinet, antiqui; si ad Iunonem referas, diu (DServius id est per decennium) gesti. tunc autem ad personam referendum est, cum ipsa loquitur; quod si nulla persona sit, ad poetam refertur. nunc ergo 'veteris' ex persona poetae intellegendum. sic ipse in alio loco 'mirantur dona Aeneae, mirantur Iulum flagrantesque dei vultus' partem ad se rettulit, partem ad Tyrios, qui deum *eum* esse nesciebant.

> **the old war**: pertaining to Virgil, 'ancient'; if you refer it to Juno, 'fought for a long time' (DServius: that is for ten years). One must refer an expression to the point of view of a character only when he or she speaks; if there is no character speaking, it is referred to the poet. Therefore here 'old' is to be taken as coming from the character of the poet. So Virgil himself in another passage says 'they admire the gifts of Aeneas, they admire Iulus and the blazing face of the god' [*Aen.* 1.709–10], referring in part to himself, in part to the Tyrians, who did not know that he was a god.

Since Virgil speaks in 1.23, Servius is not prepared to accept an embedded focalisation, even though it is a natural one with a phrase like 'mindful of . . .': he therefore says that *veteris* 'old' must 'pertain to Virgil', i.e. repres-ent his point of view rather than Juno's. The example cited within the note is, however, more complicated. When Cupid, disguised as Iulus, goes to the banquet in Dido's palace, he is much admired: the denomination 'Iulus' represents the point of view of the Tyrians, who do not know that it is really Cupid, while 'the blazing face of the god' is clearly from the point of view of the omniscient narrator, who knows his real nature. Despite his explicit statement that 'who sees?' should coincide with 'who speaks?', there-fore, Servius is in fact willing to accept variation in focalisation as a critical tool, and does so elsewhere in his commentary: even where a modern critic might wish to take a different line, the comments are extremely suggestive.

Rhetorical analysis naturally plays an important role throughout. This may consist simply in the labelling of rhetorical figures in the poems, from *aposiopesis* (e.g. 2.100) to *zeugma* (e.g. 1.120), but it may be more extens-ive, especially in the comments on the speeches of characters such as Sinon in Book 2 or Drances in Book 11. The rhetorical tendency to see all speech as performance directed towards an end rather than revelatory of character has in the past seemed antiquated and unhelpful, but now perhaps attracts more respect. One interesting aspect of this approach to rhetoric is the way Servius reads descriptions of speakers' moods in the introduction to speeches.[5] In 1.521, for instance, when Ilioneus speaks to Dido, he is described as beginning to speak *placido ... pectore*, 'with a calm breast', and Servius comments:

> **placido sic pectore coepit**: more suo uno sermone habitum futurae orationis expressit. (DServius bene ergo 'placido', ne timore consternatus videretur, quem ideo aetate maximum et patientem ostendit, ut ei auctoritas et de aetate et de moribus crescat. ergo 'placido' ad placandum apto; et definitio est oratoris, qui talem se debet componere, qualem vult indicem reddere.)

> **thus he began with placid breast**: in his usual fashion, Virgil expresses the tone of the coming speech in one phrase. (DServius: 'placid' is well used, so that he does not seem disturbed by fear. He therefore shows himself of full years and patient, so that his authority is increased by his age and character. Therefore 'placid', as suitable for placating; and it is the definition of an orator, who ought to compose himself in the same way as he wants to render the judge.)

It is not so much that Ilioneus really is calm at this point, as that he speaks calmly, puts on an air of calm. This approach to these introductory phrases may be useful in cases like 12.55, where Amata's speech to Turnus is introduced with the words *ardentem generum moritura tenebat*, 'and she, about to die, was holding back her blazing son-in-law'. The violent prolepsis in *moritura*, 'about to die', has disturbed modern critics, notably Housman: Servius does not comment, but we might say that here too *moritura* represents the tone she adopts, rather than being simply an anticipation of her death. She speaks *as* one about to die, takes on that role. This example also reveals, however, some of the dangers of this rhetorical approach: one would not want to remove all sense of a tragic prolepsis from *moritura*, given the way the participle links Amata to tragic female figures in the poem like Dido.

Apart from their own interest as late antique texts, the Servian commentaries are always worth consulting on passages in Virgil's poems: the more interesting observations are by no means always picked up by modern commentators, even those (such as R. G. Austin) who make an especial point of using the Servian material. They are not an infallible, neutral source of information about Roman customs or lost texts, nor do they embody 'what the ancients thought' about Virgil or anything else: even Servius' knowledge of Latin, as a native speaker, is not necessarily to be preferred to that

---

[5] Cf. Lazzarini (1989) 82–6.

of a modern scholar (he is as far distant in time from Virgil as a modern scholar from Shakespeare). Had the commentaries been written two centuries later, they would have attracted much less attention as containing 'medieval' rather than 'ancient' comment. Even where a critic may wish to disagree, however, the commentaries are always a potentially productive stimulus for criticism.

FURTHER READING

Editions: G. Thilo and H. Hagen (Leipzig, 1881–1902), 'Harvard Servius' (vol. 2 (*Aen.* 1–2) Lancaster, 1946, vol. 3 (*Aen.* 3–5) Oxford, 1965). On the manuscript tradition, see P. K. Marshall in *Texts and Transmission*, ed. L. D. Reynolds (Oxford, 1983) 385–8. For a dissenting view of the relationship of the longer and shorter forms, see D. Daintree, 'The Virgil commentary of Aelius Donatus – black hole or "éminence grise"?', *Greece & Rome* 37 (1990) 65–79.

Index: J. F. Mountford and J. T. Schultz (1930).

Life: *Real-Encyclopädie der Klassischen Altertumswissenschaft* (Stuttgart, 1894–1980) s.v. (P. Wessner); H. Georgii, 'Zur Bestimmung der Zeit des Servius', *Philologus* 71 (1912) 518–28; R. Kaster, 'Macrobius and Servius: *Verecundia* and the grammarian's function', *Harvard Studies in Classical Philo!ogy* 84 (1980) 219–62, and *Guardians of Language: The Grammarian and Society in Late Antiquity* (Berkeley, 1988) 169–97.

General works: E. Thomas, *Essai sur Servius et son commentaire sur Virgile* (1880); A. F. Stocker, 'Servius servus magistrorum', *Vergilius* 9 (1963) 9–15; R. D. Williams, 'Servius, commentator and guide', *Proceedings of the Virgil Society* 6 (1966–7) 50–6; E. Fraenkel, *Kleine Beiträge* (Rome, 1964) 2.339–90; M. Mühmelt, *Griechische Grammatik in der Vergilerklärung* (Munich, 1965); G. P. Goold, 'Servius and the Helen episode', *Harvard Studies in Classical Philology* 74 (1970) 101–68 (cf. C. E. Murgia, *California Studies in Classical Antiquity* 7 (1974) 257–77); J. E. G. Zetzel, *Latin Textual Criticism in Antiquity* (Salem, 1981) 81–147.

Hermeneutics: J. W. J. Jones, 'Allegorical interpretation in Servius', *Classical Journal* 56 (1960–1) 217–26; G. Rosati, 'Punto di vista narrativo e antichi esegeti di Virgilio', *Annali della Scuola Normale Superione di Pisa*, Class. di Lett. e Fil. (1979) 539–62; C. Lazzarini, 'Historia/fabula: forme della costruzione poetica virgiliana nel commento di Servio all'Eneide', *Materiali e Discussioni* 12 (1984) 117–44 (cf. David B. Dietz, 'Historia in the commentary of Servius', *Transactions of the American Philological Association* 125 (1995) 61–97), and 'Elementi di una poetica serviana', *Studi Italiani di Filologia Classica* 82 (1989) 56–109, 240–60.

6

COLIN BURROW

Virgils, from Dante to Milton

A medieval *Companion to Virgil* would not have presented him as the author of a tightly limited canon, nor would it have related his works, as modern scholars do, to the context of political life in the early principate or to their Greek sources. It would probably have reproduced exemplary stories about the poet's life drawn from the biography attributed to Donatus, perhaps augmented with tales, which enjoyed widespread circulation in thirteenth-century Italy, of Virgil the magician (whose feats included ridding Naples of flies with a magic bronze statue).[1] It might well have included discussion of the *Appendix Virgiliana*, the *Culex*, *Ciris* and miscellaneous epigrams, which were widely believed to be Virgilian juvenilia, and it would certainly also have contained a large quantity of allegorical commentary on Virgil's works. The Fourth Eclogue was often read as a prophecy of the birth of Christ, while commentators such as Fulgentius (in the fifth century) established a reading of the first half of the *Aeneid* – which persisted until the sixteenth century – as an allegory of the moral progress of the soul from childish cupidity to maturity. There might have been an updated edition of the *Companion* in 1479, when Politian suggested that early codices read not 'Virgil' but 'Vergil', and after Petrarch had done much to make Virgil a model for a laureate poet's career rather than an allegorical guide to living. There were multiple Virgils in circulation throughout this period – Virgils transformed into vernacular romance, Virgils which included the thirteenth book of the *Aeneid* by Mapheus Vegius in which the hero marries Lavinia, Virgils accompanied by accurate philological annotation, and Virgils who guided poets through their lives and their careers.[2] Not 'Virgil from Dante to Milton', then, but Virgil*s*.

---

[1] Comparetti (1966) 259.
[2] Baswell (1996). For reasons of space this essay will concentrate on the reception of the *Aeneid*. On the *Georgics*, see Chalker (1969) and Low (1985); on the *Eclogues* see Patterson (1988) and Cooper (1977).

There are, however, some recurrent features in the ways in which writers read Virgil across this long period. Most see him as not quite a Christian, and this could be taken in a positive sense – he leads the way to the Christian era – or a negative one – he presents a secular vision of imperial power which a Christian reader must seek to leave behind. These responses, however, are seldom simply antithetical, as writers find it impossible entirely to discard or overgo Virgil's influence. St Augustine rebukes himself in the *Confessions* for weeping over the abandoned Dido in a way that is explicitly anti-Virgilian: 'For what can be more miserable than a wretch that pities not himself; one bemoaning Dido's death, caused by loving of Aeneas, and yet not lamenting his own death, caused by not loving of thee, O God.'[3] But Augustine's abandonment of his literary pity for Dido in favour of spiritual advancement has clear Virgilian precedent: it is a spiritualised version of Aeneas' departure from Dido for an imperial future. Even in trying to transcend Virgil writers remain structurally indebted to him.

Virgil is often invoked at moments of personal or historical transition, and the reason for this is not hard to find. The most literal-minded reading of the *Aeneid* would see it as a poem centrally concerned with relocation, and perhaps too with constructive departure: it tells how one society moves from one place to another, and how that society reconstructs a set of values by which to live. The poem also itself enacts a process of translation (in the literal sense of 'moving across') in the way it adapts material from the Homeric poems and their Hellenistic offshoots to suit a Roman setting. Every level of the poem testifies to the strain of moving between worlds: Aeneas endures the literal hardships of a wanderer and the deeper forms of unease created by entering a world governed by conventions which are not quite those of Troy. Virgil himself shows the efforts to reconcile innovation and indebtedness required of one who is attempting to transpose an old genre into a new place. As a poet of inauguration and renovation (as the Fourth Eclogue says, 'the great sequence of centuries is born anew', 5) Virgil invites renovation himself.

Dante is the most sophisticated medieval renovator of Virgil. His Statius says when he meets Virgil in Purgatory: 'You first set me on the way to Parnassus to drink in its waters, and you first set me on fire towards God ... Through you I was a poet, through you a Christian' (*Purgatorio* 22.64–73). This praise is apparently the highest which Statius could offer, attributing both his poetic and religious advancement to his master. But it is also carefully qualified: Virgil directs him on the way *towards* God, rather than actually leading him directly to the beatific vision. Dante's view of Virgil

---

[3] Augustine (1912) vol. I, 39. See Watkins (1995) 34–8.

is of a guide who cannot himself complete the course towards which he points his imitators, and who needs the benevolent reinterpretations of later readers to complete what in him is only suggested. Virgil directs Dante the wayfarer throughout the *Inferno* and *Purgatorio*, carrying him in his bosom like a child, or laying down footsteps in which his imitator can follow. The *Commedia* maintains a continual delicate counterpoint between the actions of the character Virgil and allusions to his poems, in which the two Virgils, the man and the text, sustain or comment ruefully on each other.[4] Often when the character Virgil stumbles, Dante the poet graciously acknowledges his debt to his master by an allusion to his writing, as though picking him up from a fall; equally too when Dante's Virgil is made a silent witness of the inaccuracy of his own poem the wayfarer's responses to his guide grow in emotional intensity. Like Augustine, Dante is unable to keep Virgil from his mind even when he is renouncing or transforming his predecessor's vision. When the wayfarer first encounters Beatrice, who is to be his guide through Paradise, he turns to Virgil to exclaim 'conosco i segni de l'antica fiamma' (30.48), but finds as he turns that Virgil is no longer beside him. The allusion to *Aeneid* 4.23, when Dido says to Anna that because of Aeneas' arrival she 'recognises the signs of ancient passion', transfigures Virgil – Dante's love for Beatrice is not a distraction from empire but a means towards God – but also indicates that for Dante Virgil's influence grows in intensity as he is abandoned. The words of this 'dolcissimo padre', sweetest father, guide the wayfarer on to a new era, while Virgil himself is left behind like his own Dido.[5]

Critics can write heavy-handedly when they consider the sense of cultural superiority which Christianity brings: all writers who had a rhetorical training – and up to 1700 that was all writers – knew that their style was immeasurably indebted to the works of pagan antiquity. Dante by no means simply triumphs over Virgil, and in one particular respect he saw Virgil as having enjoyed a more complete world than his own. When he wrote the *Commedia* Dante had been exiled from Florence. From around 1310 (scholars are not agreed over the chronology) he became convinced that the solution to the chaos of Italy was to reverse the effects of the Donation of Constantine, which had ceded secular authority over the western empire to the Pope, and to re-establish an empire under a ruler who enjoyed absolute sway over temporal affairs.[6] Dante derived this vision partly from his reading of Virgil, whom he came to idealise as a poet who enjoyed a

---

[4] Barolini (1984) 188–256. On Dante's Virgil see Foster (1977) 156–253; Consoli and Ronconi (1976).

[5] See Hawkins (1991) and Watkins (1995).

[6] For a summary of debates about the chronology of Dante's works see Davis (1993).

perfect political state: the *imperium* of Augustan Rome, he believed, guaranteed the universal peace into which Christ was born (*De Monarchia* 1.xvi and *Paradiso* 6.80–1). Measured against this grand political example Dante's own Italy was an enfeebled relic of a Roman past, and Virgil was not a benighted pagan but the poet of an ideal polity. So in *Paradiso* 15–16 when Dante's great-great-great-grandfather Cacciaguida describes the origins of the Florentine state he does so in an impoverished, backward-looking version of Anchises' prophetic visions of Rome's future in *Aeneid* 6. Cacciaguida's description of Florence has affinities too with Aeneas' tour around the kingdom of Evander in *Aeneid* 8, but it pointedly lacks Virgil's continual glances towards the future greatness of Rome. For Dante the ideal Florence lies in the past, not the future, and his poem, written by an exiled, disappointed imperialist, can only limp after the confident strides of Virgil.

The weakness of Dante's own imperial vision, however, does prompt him to pick out moments in the *Aeneid* which intimate frailties within the Roman imperial dynasty. In *Paradiso* 30 he describes an empty imperial chair in heaven which awaits the arrival of the Emperor Henry VII, who promised in 1310 to re-establish the power of the Holy Roman Empire in Italy. By the time Dante wrote the latter part of the *Paradiso*, however, Henry was dead, having failed entirely in his Italian expedition. When Dante sees that empty throne it is impossible to exclude a reminiscence of Virgil's Marcellus, the dead heir to Augustus described at the end of *Aeneid* 6. At such moments the incompleteness of Virgil's historical vision – which does not dare to extend itself into the future after Augustus – enables Dante to find a comforting shared vulnerability in Virgil. Dante's imperialism often expresses itself in excitedly apocalyptic prophecy; but both the *Commedia* and the *Aeneid* reluctantly confess the fragility of imperial ambitions.

In many respects the *Divina Commedia* is unlike subsequent imitations of Virgil. It shows little interest in reduplicating the narrative structure or the densely compacted style of Virgil's poem, and Dante himself did not seek to follow what came to be regarded as the 'Virgilian' progression of genres from pastoral to georgic and epic (indeed his Neo-Latin eclogues, which echo Virgil's, were written right at the end of his life). Commentaries concentrate through the fifteenth century less on the life of Virgil and the allegorical significance of his poems than on their language and style; accordingly Virgil generally ceases to be represented as a real person, and his authority is experienced by poets more as a set of formal and stylistic pressures than as direct moral admonition. One feature of Dante's Virgil, though, does anticipate Renaissance responses to Virgil. Dante's guide tells his charge not to waste pity on the damned, and by the end of the *Inferno* Virgil has enabled the wayfarer to feel righteous anger towards the souls he sees in hell. This progression from pity to just anger became central to the development of the epic genre in the sixteenth century, as poets are guided by Virgil to emerge out of a world of romance into a poetic realm of formal unity and ethical rigour. Throughout the fifteenth century imitations of Virgil tended to be founded on the belief that Virgil's *pietas* – familial and religious duty – meant something like 'pity' (the word did give rise to both our 'pity' and our 'piety'). This interpretation was brought about by a complex interplay between semantic change, shifts in ethical priorities, and readings of Virgil.[7] It intensifies a problem raised by the *Aeneid* itself, in which the strength of devotion to divine command is often registered by the way that it forces characters to act against their emotional instincts, which grow with resistance to them. Aeneas does groan as he leaves Dido and pities her spirit as it flees from him in Book 6. But if one believes that *pius Aeneas* means no more than 'pitiful Aeneas' then several of the hero's actions become not just agonising but inexplicable: how can a hero who is adequately characterised as 'pitiful' leave Dido behind him, or execute Turnus after only a brief pause? For many medieval readers Aeneas' killing of Turnus was an outrage against compassion – Lactantius vehemently cries 'Where then was your *pietas* (pity)?' when he discusses the episode. The way to resolve this problem was to revise the poem, giving the more or less unconscious ethical transposition of Aeneas' character deliberate structural consequences: an Aeneas who is primarily motivated by pity does not leave Dido or kill Turnus; instead he acts on his instincts, wanders after distressed women, and spares suppliant antagonists. In the hybrids of vernacular romance and classically influenced epic which developed in late fifteenth- and early sixteenth-century Italy this transformation of Aeneas into a man of pity generated poems which have both local debts to the *Aeneid* and an overall indebtedness to the reading of the poem as one steeped in pity, or *pietà*. Ariosto's *Orlando furioso* (1516–32) wanders with the pitying instincts of its many heroes, digressing as they encounter unfortunate women, and often actually reviving characters in the *Aeneid* who meet a pitiful end. When Ariosto imitates the episode of Nisus and Euryalus in *Aeneid* 9 his equivalent of Euryalus (a squire called Medoro) does not die pathetically. He is left apparently for dead, and is then cured by the pagan princess Angelica, whom he subsequently marries. A reading of Virgil which attaches primary significance to his compassion for the victims of empire produces a potentially endless work. Characters are not sacrificed to an emerging imperial design, but live on, spared by the pity of the poem's heroes or by their authors' misprision of the *Aeneid*.

---

[7] See Ball (1991) and Burrow (1993).

Ariosto's poem, however, concludes with the single combat of Ruggiero and his irascible pagan adversary Rodomonte in an episode which is unmistakably modelled on the encounter between Aeneas and Turnus which ends the *Aeneid*. In the course of writing *Orlando furioso* Ariosto came increasingly to curb his digressive, pity-centred reading of Virgil, and to impose upon it both the austere narrative structure of the *Aeneid* and an appreciation of the harshness to which Virgil's *pietas* can lead. This reflects, and in part anticipates, increasing concern among literary critics in sixteenth-century Italy to establish formal unity in the epic, in which Virgil, allied with Aristotle, comes to take on a new role as a structural guide to composition. Virgil is not a character within *Orlando furioso* who rebukes Ariosto for his inappropriate compassion for vanquished pagans as Dante's Virgil does; but the text of the *Aeneid* becomes as it were the superego of the mode of romance, urging it to renounce the indulgence of digressions in order to return to the austere imperial outline of the *Aeneid*. In Torquato Tasso's *Gerusalemme liberata* (1581) Virgil becomes not just a poet who writes of the self-denials necessary to imperial expansion, but one whose example compels his imitators to curb their own imaginations to the shape of his. Tasso's poem is scattered with the mournful deaths of youths, who are ruthlessly slain by irascible heroes and then lamented by their compassionate author. At the climax of the poem his main hero Tancred has to perform a symbolic exorcism of the spirit of fantastical romance digressions from his poem: in an enchanted forest a tree talks to him with the voice of his pagan love Clorinda. With a just disdain Tancred destroys this delusion, which appeals for pity in a vain echo of Virgil's Polydorus, whom Aeneas piously inters in *Aeneid* 3. Tasso's version of the episode has moral, political, and formal significance: it suggests that renouncing pity is a precondition for achieving epic unity, and that it is the means by which Tancred is able to return to the government of his ruler 'pio Goffredo' – and 'pio' there means pious rather than pitiful. The episode also implies that by 1570 a 'Virgilian' conception of formal restraint was beginning to turn against Virgil himself. Neo-classical critics wrote increasingly against the 'marvellous' episodes in the *Aeneid*, such as the Polydorus episode and the metamorphosis of the Trojan ships to nymphs in *Aeneid* 9. Epic poets came consciously to seek to drive such Ovidian metamorphic excesses from the epic tradition (Tasso extensively revised his poem), and they did so in the name of Virgil. Virgil's influence as a regulator of the Renaissance epic tradition became so rigorous by the late sixteenth century that even his own poems could not live up to the critical precepts extracted from them. The poet of Empire became the poet of formal and political unity and of poetical self-suppression.

Dante's fascination with Virgil's politics, and particularly with the traces of vulnerability which attend Virgil's imperialism, also anticipates later imitations. Renaissance epics tended to be gestures of national self-definition, which praised the dynasty of their ruling house, and illustrated the potential of their own vernacular tongue to rival the achievements of Virgil. Since epic was also regarded as the highest of the genres, writing a heroic poem became the most effective means by which poets could win the patronage of a ruler. For these reasons the panegyric and prophetic elements in the *Aeneid* became definitional elements in the genre by the later sixteenth century. Poets such as Ariosto and Tasso, however, who wrote for the Estense, the ruling dynasty of Ferrara, confronted the central problem of Renaissance epic: that in comparison with the example of Virgil their state was provincial, and their celebrations of a relatively minor *signoria* in Northern Italy could in no sense match the imperial authority which underwrote the poems of Virgil.[8] For Ariosto the lack of fit between his city state and the imperial city of Rome becomes a source of continual and very deliberate irony. The blood-line of Ippolito d'Este which he praises is simply not equivalent to its Virgilian prototype, and frequently Ariosto signals this fact by the awkwardness with which he inserts prophetic and encomiastic material into his poem. Ariosto's heroine Bradamante, who is to bring forth the blood-line of the Estense, receives a prophecy of her family's future not, like Aeneas, after being gravely conducted to the underworld by the Sibyl, but after falling into a pit. Ariosto's own relationship with his patron was uneasy, and he spent the latter part of his career in miserable exile as governor of Garfagnana, a military outpost on the edges of the Ferrarese *signoria*. He was no Virgil reciting historical prophecies to the ruler of the greater part of the world, and he repeatedly reminds his readers of this fact. The result is a poem which jokily augments the qualifications which Virgil writes into his imperialism.

Virgil can give to poets after Dante a vision of an ideal imperial state against which their own political world is found wanting; but frequently their sense of inferiority to the *Aeneid* leads them to respond with eager sympathy to moments when Virgil implies less than total confidence in the *imperium sine fine* which Jove promises to the Trojan exiles. Edmund Spenser was another would-be author of an imperial epic, who, like Dante and Ariosto, was a heroic poet in exile: the majority of his adult life was spent in Ireland. He began his poetic career in good Virgilian fashion by endenizening the Virgilian pastoral into the English idiom in *The Shepheardes Calender* (1579), and was also to translate the *Culex* as *Virgils*

---

[8] See Quint (1993) 213–47.

Gnat. His *Faerie Queene* (1590–6), dedicated to Elizabeth I, is an epic romance in the line of Ariosto and Tasso which re-enacts their fraught struggles between the urge pitifully to wander and the desire dutifully to complete a heroic task. Implicit in every stage of *The Faerie Queene* too is an imprisoning nostalgia, which locates in the ideal world of Faerie-land a moral and political ideal which pointedly cannot be related to the poet's own present. The poem, dedicated to the childless and ageing Elizabeth I, attempts to extend its dynastic vision back into a Virgilian past and on into an Elizabethan Protestant future in which London becomes Troynovant, ruled over by an imperial virgin. Spenser, however, is often unable to bridge the gap between mythical past and the present, and his vision of the future is, like Virgil's, scarred by anxieties about the future succession. In Book III the heroine Britomart receives a prophecy of her dynastic future from Merlin, and the moment is carefully signalled as a Virgilian one: Britomart descends into an underworld as Aeneas does in *Aeneid 6* (here Spenser both recalls Ariosto's mildly ironised imitation of the episode in *Orlando furioso* and seeks to remind his readers of the Virgilian original), and the immediately preceding narrative alludes very closely to the pseudo-Virgilian *Ciris*, which Spenser believed was by Virgil. The prophecy of Britain's future which Britomart receives serves a structurally Virgilian effect: it transforms her from being a passionately obsessed girl like the heroine of the *Ciris* into a purposive dynastic heroine. But Merlin's triumphant vision of England's future breaks off, like Anchises' prophecy in *Aeneid 6*, before it can extend from the time of its composition into the future – and it does so with a stark rupture which recalls Virgil's uncertainties about imperial succession. Merlin predicts the accession of Elizabeth ('Then shall a royall virgin raine'), and then stops on the brink of the future as though by 'ghastly spectacle dismayd' (III.iii.50). Virgin Queens cannot be expected to have children, and their empires consequently cannot last for ever. Spenser's Virgilianism is sporadic, and is often hybridised with influences from other authors; but the greatest thing which he learnt from Virgil was that an epic which appears to praise an imperial ruler need not do so in an unqualified way. Prophecy is a two-edged sword, at once promising a glorious future for a nation, and at the same time drawing attention to features of the present which might make the emergence of that future in practice impossible. Virgil gave to the Renaissance the concept of an encomiastic epic, which praises a nation state and its ruler and which seeks to manifest the strengths of a vernacular tongue. He also gave to the period a precedent for poems which accommodate political unease within their praise, in which prophecies seem to emerge from the gates of ivory like false dreams.

John Milton stands at the end of this line of sceptical responses to Virgil. Through the 1630s he composed pastorals which show his early efforts to shape a Virgilian career for himself. His 'Epitaphium Damonis' adapts with extreme delicacy the language and concerns of Virgil's *Eclogues* to a Christian purpose; in 'Lycidas' Virgil's lament for Daphnis fuses with an apocalyptic zeal for the violent reconstruction of the English Church in a radical Protestant Virgilian *renovatio*. Milton's later works also allude to the Virgilian career structure: *Paradise Regained* begins by echoing the pseudo-Virgilian opening to the *Aeneid* ('I who erewhile the happy Garden sung'), and has been seen as a georgic poem, in which a hero works to cultivate a wilderness.[9] But in *Paradise Lost* (1667) Milton deliberately resists much of the received image of Virgil which had grown up over the previous three centuries. By 1660 Virgil had been thoroughly assimilated into the tradition of Christian epic. Girolamo Vida's neo-Latin *Christiad* (1535) had used a richly Virgilian style to recount the life of Christ and the prophetic hopes which it released. Virgil had also acquired clear political colours: the imperial conquests of Aeneas had provided a model for fables of national expansion (to which Milton preferred the cultivation of godliness at home) under absolute monarchies (to which Milton was constitutionally averse). Fracastoro's neo-Latin *Syphilis* relates the discovery of a cure for the French disease by Spaniards venturing into the new world; Camoens' *Lusiads* (1572) praises, with insistent allusion to the empire-building of Aeneas, the heroic expansion of Portugal. These Catholic and absolutist epics were matched by the Virgils produced by the majority of seventeenth-century English translators. As chapter 2 shows, Virgilian dreams of *imperium sine fine* consoled many a disappointed royalist in the English civil war, who hoped that the future would bring back the monarchy which they had lost in 1649. At the Restoration innumerable panegyrists alluded to Virgil's Fourth Eclogue in order to voice their hope that English would enjoy a glorious renewal under Charles II. This background, when combined with Milton's defeated but still resistant republicanism, and welded to the growing association of Virgil with self-restraint and self-suppression, gives us *Paradise Lost*, which is in many ways the most anti-Virgilian epic ever written. Conquest and imperial voyaging are consistently associated in the poem with Satanic fraudulence, and empire is always shown to be a divine prerogative alone. At 4.159–65 Satan is compared to a voyager seeking booty in a new world; later he claims to seek 'Honour and empire with revenge enlarged' by making Adam and Eve fall. There is, though, no final victory of an imperial hero in Milton's poem; indeed the most

---

[9] See Low (1985) 296–352.

remarkable feature of *Paradise Lost* is its combination of an enormous chronological span, stretching from the creation to the apocalypse, with a great bashfulness about indulging in Christian triumphalism. It ends with the fallen Adam and Eve venturing out of paradise 'with wandering steps and slow' in victorious defeat, consoled not by the reassuring shape of an imperial prophecy stretching out before them, but by the Archangel Michael's narration of a tortuous and often bloody Biblical history. During the previous century Virgil had become associated with imperial destiny and resistance to the charms of women, and had increasingly come to embody a stylistic ideal to which poets aspired at the expense of their own poetic identity. Milton's poem militantly opposes these features of his Virgil: his hero, Adam, falls because of his sympathetic bond with Eve, and his only searcher after an empire is the devil himself.

Running through the reception of Virgil is a continual oscillation between received readings of the poet and direct responses to his works. The strongest means of resisting a received reading is to return to the works themselves in order to show that the received image of them is partial or misleading. Milton's anti-Virgilianism is of this type. It often entails a predatory inflation of the negative elements that lie within Virgil's portrayal of Aeneas in order to express Milton's hostility to human aspirations to imperial dominion. So when Satan emerges from hell on a fitful, chancy voyage through Chaos, Milton is thinking of Aeneas' storm-tossed voyage from Troy; but he sets the action of his hero within a sublimely vast space which shrinks him to the scale of a feather:

> At last his Sail-broad Vanns
> He spreads for flight, and in the surging smoke
> Uplifted spurns the ground, thence many a League
> As in a cloudy Chair ascending rides
> Audacious, but that seat soon failing, meets
> A vast vacuitie: all unawares
> Fluttering his pennons vain plumb down he drops
> Ten thousand fadom deep, and to this hour
> Down had been falling, had not by ill chance
> The strong rebuff of som tumultuous cloud
> Instinct with Fire and Nitre hurried him
> As many miles aloft.   (2.927–38)

All of time ('to this hour') and all the chaotic extent of the cosmos swirl around and nearly swamp the audacious activity of Satan. This is not simply a sublime overgoing on a cosmic scale of Aeneas' storm-tossed journey. Satan's desperate tumbling through a disordered cosmos develops Virgil's hints that part of Aeneas' heroism lies in his inability to control his fate – his ship is, after all, left rudderless after the death of Palinurus, and we first meet him when he is tossed on a storm at sea. By pressing on the heroic powerlessness, or *amechania*, which Virgil's hero derives from Apollonius Rhodius' Jason, Milton transforms Aeneas' heroic incapacity to know the structure of the imperial plot in which he acts into Satan's vain aspiration to achieve some heroic conquest within the providential framework established by Milton's omniscient deity. That is a provocative transformation of Virgil's poem, because it entails substituting a willing acceptance of the providential unfolding of God's will for Aeneas' self-abnegating acceptance of his place in an imperial design. But it is a *reading* of the *Aeneid*, rather than a dismissive violation of its ethos. Virgil writes with sufficient complexity to enable even his enemies to learn from his methods. Milton mines like a destructive virus into his uncertainties, and wrests from them a Christian transcendence of his imperial predecessor.

Paradise Lost is in one respect a profoundly Virgilian poem. It uses allusions to the earlier epic tradition both to show debts and to signal radical departures from that tradition in a way which would have been impossible without Virgil, and without the post-Virgilian epicists such as Lucan who learnt from their master how best to signal their differences from him. At the end of Book 4, a third of the way through his poem, Milton alludes to the death of Turnus with which Virgil's poem ends. A squadron of angels discover Satan 'squat like a toad' as he attempts to seduce Eve's sleeping imagination to his cause. He blazes like a comet as he prepares for battle with the heavenly hosts, then sees God's scales ('Wherein all things created first he weighd, | The pendulous round Earth with ballanc't Aire | In counterpoise', 4.999–1001) in the sky tip against him. The allusion to *Aeneid* 12.725–7 is clear; so too is its aggressive inversion. Satan's imminent defeat is indicated by his scale going up, rather than down, as Milton recalls Daniel 5.27, 'Thou art weighed in the balance and found wanting.' When Jove's scales sink under the weight of Turnus' fate the Iliadic hero barely looks at them, but leaps into battle (*emicat hic*), and at the end of the poem his 'indignant soul flees beneath the shadows' of death; when Satan sees the future running against him, however, he just gives up the fight and runs:

> The Fiend lookd up and knew
> His mounted scale aloft: nor more; but fled
> Murmuring, and with him fled the shades of night.
>
> (4.1013–15)

The hint of dawn with which Milton's imitation concludes, together with its biblical readjustment of the heavenly balances, is just the sort of

indebted reversal which Virgil performs on his sources. One way, and perhaps the most powerful way, of imitating a predecessor is to imitate his
methods of imitation, and to treat his text as he had treated his own
sources. This is what Milton does with Virgil, and in doing so he makes
full use of the growing awareness in seventeenth-century commentaries of
the radical delicacy with which Virgil had transformed Homer. Virgil's techniques for shifting the ethical mood of an episode from the Homeric poems,
or of combining them with allusions to their Hellenistic offshoots, feed
directly into Milton's poem. In *Paradise Lost* allusions to Virgil resound
backwards to Homer, or give faint echoes of Italian imitations of Virgil's
original. Virgil becomes in Milton's works not a moral guide but a model
of how to insinuate one's poem into the complex of intertextual relations
within which epic poems make their significance. Virgil was by 1667 so
associated with poetic, emotional and political self-suppression that it is
entirely appropriate that Milton all but suppresses his presence in *Paradise
Lost*. But although Virgil was no longer the sustaining guide who could lift
the struggling Dante onto his bosom and carry him over the ramparts of
Hell, he remained embedded in the epic tradition as the master of how to
allude, of how to impose a new epic poem and a new poetic and political
form onto an existing tradition of writing.

FURTHER READING

Barolini, Teodolinda (1984) *Dante's Poets: Textuality and Truth in the Comedy.*
    Princeton, NJ
Baswell, Christopher (1995) *Virgil in Medieval England.* Cambridge
Burrow, Colin (1993) *Epic Romance: Homer to Milton.* Oxford
Chalker, J. (1969) *The English Georgic.* London
Comparetti, D. (1966) *Virgil in the Middle Ages*, trans. E. F. M. Benecke, 2nd edn.
    London
Cooper, Helen (1977) *Pastoral: Mediaeval into Renaissance.* Ipswich
Foster, Kenelm (1977) *The Two Dantes and other Studies.* London
Griffin, Jasper (1992) 'Virgil', in Richard Jenkyns, ed., *The Legacy of Rome: A
    New Appraisal*, pp. 125–50. Oxford
Jacoff, Rachel, and Schnapp, Jeffrey T., eds. (1991) *The Poetry of Allusion: Virgil
    and Ovid in Dante's Commedia.* Stanford
Kermode, Frank (1975) *The Classic.* London
Low, Anthony (1985) *The Georgic Revolution.* Princeton
Martindale, Charles, ed. (1984) *Virgil and his Influence.* Bristol
Patterson, Annabel M. (1988) *Pastoral and Ideology: Virgil to Valéry.* Oxford
Quint, David (1993) *Epic and Empire.* Princeton
Watkins, John (1995) *The Specter of Dido: Spenser and Virgilian Epic.* New
    Haven and London

7

M. J. H. LIVERSIDGE

Virgil in art

Of all the classical authors it is Virgil whose visual legacy is the most difficult to define. With most other writers, artists were mainly concerned with illustrating their works, though the choice of subject represented and its interpretation or intended reading by the viewer may be inflected by the time and context in which it occurs. So, for example, while allegorical meanings were sometimes imparted to otherwise literally rendered episodes from writers like Homer and Ovid, or some historical event described by Plutarch or Livy could be used to express an ideal of exemplary action or to point a moral, on the whole the iconographies associated with particular authors predominantly fall into the category of illustration. Virgil is different because his influence on artists is so varied in its content and interpretation.

There are, of course, a great many works of art which individually or in series draw their subjects directly from what he wrote and which very accurately reproduce his words – indeed, only Ovid has been more frequently or more exhaustively illustrated – but Virgil's presence in art goes much further than the process of translating texts into images. He has a visual existence that extends beyond the illustration of his own works. Any complete account of how artists have responded to Virgil must necessarily include other topics as well: their representations of the poet himself, both as an ideal of literary inspiration and as a figure within the accepted canon of literature; the pictures associated with his legendary reputation in the Middle Ages and the stories that became part of his apocryphal biography, as well as some more credible scenes from his life taken from the account written by Donatus in the fourth century; his significance for the development of landscape in art from the Renaissance to eighteenth-century English gardens and beyond; and, in the context of Renaissance and later artistic theory, the part that visual interpretations of his work played in defining the relationship of poetry to painting (the *ut pictura poesis* question which was central to so much theoretical debate from the sixteenth to the eighteenth centuries) and demonstrating the supremacy of history (intellectually and morally elevating subjects) as the pre-eminent genre in art. And there is also the Virgil of Dante's visionary imagination who appears in paintings from Botticelli to the nineteenth-century Romantics. All of which requires the book which has yet to be written about Virgil and the visual arts.

The first works of art inspired by Virgil may have appeared during his own lifetime. At any rate the popularity and wide circulation his books quickly achieved are reflected in the rapid spread of what can be regarded as a Virgilian iconography which became part of the Roman artistic tradition generally and extended across the empire. It is not, though, always possible to be certain that an artist or craftsman has consciously illustrated a particular subject from the actual text. Sometimes it must have been the case that a pattern or convention was created and carried on independently simply because the story or theme had become generally familiar, but the fact that it would have been easily recognised and understood is in itself evidence of how Virgil was assimilated into Roman visual culture. An example is provided by the fourth-century mosaic from Low Ham Villa in Somerset (pl. 2a) which depicts four scenes from the story of Dido and Aeneas around a central panel of Venus with two cupids. The narrative panels show the meeting of Dido and Aeneas with Venus and Cupid disguised as Ascanius between them, the arrival of the Trojan ships from one of which Achates collects gifts for Dido, the hunt scene, and finally Aeneas with Dido. The first two subjects are taken from the *Aeneid* Book 1 and the other two from Book 4, but as each episode is so abbreviated it is difficult to say more than that it must be generally informed by the appreciation of the *Aeneid*.

There are two late Roman illuminated manuscripts that do provide certain evidence of how Virgil was interpreted visually in antiquity. Both date from the first quarter of the fifth century. The Roman Virgil ('Vergilius Romanus', Vatican Library, Rome: Codex Vat. Lat. 3867) has a portrait of the poet (pl. 2b) showing him seated beside his desk holding his book in what is probably a late copy taken from an earlier version. The same may be true of the illustrations of which nineteen survive, ten from the *Aeneid* and two from the *Georgics*, all full-page, with seven from the *Eclogues*. However, as they are in a robustly provincial style which is probably a degenerate imitation of earlier Roman painting, they give only a rather crude impression of the tradition which the codex follows. Those for the *Aeneid* and *Georgics*, though, are painted in a full range of colours and give some idea of how luxurious the finest early manuscripts must have been. The miniatures represent single episodes rather than a continuous narrative with more than one scene from a particular story: the illustration of Dido and Aeneas sheltering in the cave from the storm (*Aen.* 4.160–72: fol. 108r) does, however, allude to the events leading up to what is happening in the picture by showing the trees of the forest where they had been hunting, their saddled horses, and the comical detail of Ascanius taking cover from the rain beneath his shield (pl. *3a*). The other codex, the Vatican Virgil ('Vergilius Vaticanus', Vatican Library, Rome: Codex Vat. Lat. 3225) is more complete, with forty-one *Aeneid* miniatures and nine of the *Georgics*. A few of the illustrations are full-page, but most are inserted into the text. The narration is more ambitious than in the Roman Virgil in that within a single frame successive events are shown: the Laocoön story, for example, is told visually in three episodes (*Aen.* 2.340–82: fol. 18v), the priest sacrificing in front of a temple, the serpents coming from the sea towards the Trojan coast, and Laocoön and his sons strangled by the serpents (pl. *3b*). The Vatican Virgil illustrations are generally thought to have been copied from an earlier model, perhaps of the second or third century, and as they are more refined than those of the Roman Virgil the book is probably more representative of the fine quality and narrative style of the best Virgil manuscripts produced in Rome in the first centuries of the imperial period. As the only reliably authentic classical examples, between them the two Vatican codices provide at least a partial insight into how in Roman times a specifically Virgilian iconography evolved and was circulated.

From late antiquity until the fifteenth century Virgil's visual existence almost completely disappeared, at least as far as illustrations of his own works are concerned. Finely scripted copies were still made of his books, but other than an occasional portrait in an opening initial, or the odd medieval manuscript with some historiated letters incorporating a figure or two at the beginnings of different books, there is almost nothing for nearly a thousand years.[1] Pictures of some of the stories about the fall of Troy adapted from the *Aeneid* and other sources can still be found illustrating manuscripts of a popular medieval romance, the *Roman de Troie* by Benoît de Sainte-Maure dating from the 1160s. These are similar to the illuminated chivalric chronicles that were fashionable in courtly circles from the twelfth century, and they were important for the literary and visual transmission of Virgil's epic in the medieval world. There are echoes of them in some of the narrative scenes by the early Renaissance painters and

---

[1] The point is made by Panofsky (1939), where he cites only two 'really illustrated' Virgil manuscripts for the middle ages, a tenth-century book in Naples (Bibl. Nazionale, Cod. olim Vienna 58) and a fourteenth-century example in Rome (Vatican Library, Cod. Vat. Lat. 2761), and one other of the fourteenth-century with historiated initials (Oxford, Bodleian Library, MS Can. Class. Lat. 52). See the reprinted article in E. Panofsky, *Meaning in the Visual Arts* (Harmondsworth, 1970) 74 (n. 20).

illuminators who revived Virgilian illustration in quattrocento Italy. Another comparable derivative from Virgil was the *Roman d'Eneas* (imitated in the *Eneit*, a German version composed by Heinrich von Veldeke around 1160, of which there is a copy in Berlin with seventy-one whole-page illustrations[2]), which recounts the stories of Dido and Aeneas and of Aeneas and Lavinia from Books 1, 4 and 7 in the style of courtly love romances. Similarly, the visual tradition of representing landscape and agriculture that might have been carried on in pictures accompanying the *Eclogues* and *Georgics* developed independently in the labours-of-the-months iconography of medieval calendar illustrations, which in their turn also influenced the Renaissance treatment of Virgil's descriptions of pastoral and country life.

Without a continuous tradition of illustration to draw on, Renaissance artists had to reinvent appropriate iconographical programmes for Virgil's books. The renewed demand for classical texts which the new humanist culture had generated resulted in a dramatic increase in the production of illuminated copies of all the major Latin authors, especially at the luxury end of the market. From the fifteenth century the way that artists interpreted Virgil changed to accommodate allegorising readings of mythology and the view of the Aeneas epic as an exemplar of the triumph of heroic virtue, sacrifice and resolute endeavour over passion and human frailty. An influential source, especially for the sixteenth and seventeenth centuries, was Cristoforo Landino, whose 1474 *Disputationes Camuldulenses* constructed a consistently moralising exegesis of the *Aeneid* which interprets the story metaphorically as representing spiritual achievement through the performance of great actions. Landino's ideal image of Aeneas profoundly influenced subsequent commentators whose works were, in their turn, consulted by artists who portrayed subjects from the *Aeneid* for exemplary purposes in contexts that make it clear an allegorical meaning is intended, such as in a monumental decorative cycle like Pietro da Cortona's great gallery in the Palazzo Pamphili in Rome (1651–3).[3] Equally, smaller private rooms might be decorated with *Aeneid* scenes for the edification by example of a nobleman or ruler, as happened with Alfonso d'Este's *camerino* in the ducal palace at Ferrara (a frieze of ten panels by Dosso Dossi, 1520–1) and Count Giulio Boiardo's *gabinetto* in the castle of Scandiano (twelve frescoes, one for each book of the *Aeneid*, by Nicolò dell'Abate, early 1540s).[4] In a general sense, too, the Renaissance concept of the ancient world's legendary past as a 'golden age' of ideal harmony encouraged the vision of

[2] Berlin, Staatsbibliotek, MS germ. fol. 282.
[3] For a full survey of allegorical interpretations of the *Aeneid* see Allen (1970) 135–62.
[4] Hope (1971) 641–50 for Dossi; Langmuir (1976) 158–70 for dell'Abate.

an idyllic past which was re-created in the pastoral images that were evolved to illustrate the *Eclogues*. Virgil's Fourth Eclogue predicts the return of a new golden age, a theme which could be introduced into pictorial allegories to add a contemporary political resonance to compliment a ruler: there is an example in Pietro da Cortona's Sala della Stufa frescoes in the Pitti Palace in Florence, carried out for Grand Duke Ferdinand II de Medici between 1637 and 1641, where Virgilian references are incorporated with Ovid's Four Ages of Man (Gold, Silver, Bronze and Iron) to convey the idea of a dawning revival under the Prince's enlightened governance.[5]

The origins of this kind of visual adaptation of Virgil can be found in Italian Renaissance manuscripts and related paintings from the late 1450s onwards. The earlier ones record the beginnings of the new pictorial approach. Typical of the animated style of illustration and vividly imaginative response to the text are the miniatures in the complete *Eclogues, Georgics, Aeneid* which belonged to the Venetian nobleman Leonardo Sanudo (1458–9; pl. 4*a*).[6] As the scene of the storm and shipwreck of the Trojan fleet off the North African coast shows, they are in a lively narrative idiom which, page by page, relates visually the lines of verse above each miniature: there is no attempt to render the subjects classically or 'historically', however, and the contemporary details make the manuscript, as Jonathan Alexander has observed, one of 'the most vivid documentary accounts of Italian Renaissance civilisation'. The style continues until the end of the quattrocento, but from the late 1460s onwards there are other Virgils that are more consciously classicising, if not always consistently so. A Paduan manuscript of about 1490 attributed to Bartolomeo Sanvito demonstrates this development, framing its pages with devices made up of classical ornaments and making more of an attempt to show the principal figures of the *Aeneid* illustrations in antique costume (pl. 4*b*).[7] The opening page of Book 2 is not as architectural as some, but the miniature of the Trojan Horse is set in a frame surrounded by cornucopiae, and the design and Roman-style humanist script are intended to give it the 'feel' of an antique book. More evidently classicising are the costumes and details like the horse itself, clearly modelled on the antique bronze horses of St Mark's in Venice. The main scene together with the pictorial initial provide a visual summary of Aeneas' account of the fall of Troy in an unfolding narrative, with the horse entering the city, Troy burning in the background, and Aeneas escaping carrying Anchises and with Ascanius beside him in the initial-letter

---

[5] Campbell (1977) 31–5, 41–7.   [6] Alexander (1994) 109.
[7] Alexander (1994) 110–11.

illumination. Sometimes a manuscript was produced that was deliberately made *all'antica* to look like a Roman book with pages dyed green or purple imitating antique *codices purpurei*. A Virgil in this fashion is the manuscript illustrated by the Paduan artist Marco Zoppo about 1466–8.[8]

Simultaneously with the earlier quattrocento manuscripts *Aeneid* scenes began appearing on *cassoni*, marriage chests with painted panels to the front and sides. These usually had mythological, legendary, religious or classical history subjects considered worthy of emulation – often themes exemplary of heroic virtue in men and appropriate submission in women. The presence of the Aeneas story on a number of these reflects the Renaissance reading of the story in terms of its moral interpretation. Thus Dido and Aeneas represent the dangers of illicit love (for the bride especially) and the pursuit of manly duty; Lavinia and Aeneas is the model to follow. The history of Aeneas (for such it was popularly regarded, rather than legend) was appropriate for another reason: his heroic deeds had led to the foundation of Rome and, since it was a commonplace among Renaissance Italy's élite to claim descent from noble Romans and their heroic Trojan precursors, he had, as Ellen Callman has shown, the status of an ancestor whose 'glorious line was to be continued by the young couple about to be married'.[9] Several particularly fine cassone panels of composite *Aeneid* scenes in continuous narrative have survived from the workshop of the Florentine painter Apollonio di Giovanni, who died in 1465. The pair at Yale combine a sequence of episodes, from Juno's descent to ask Aeolus to unleash the winds to cause the storm and shipwreck of Aeneas' fleet (*Aen.* 1.50–2, 65–75) to the vision of Rome (*Aen.* 3.388–93) and the feast after the Trojans land at Latium (*Aen.* 5.166). Noticeably, only certain Dido and Aeneas scenes occur, such as the banquet when he tells the tale of Troy in the hall with murals of the story (*Aen.* 1.455–94) – but there is no meeting and no passionate encounter in the cave, so as to avoid the embarrassment of an awkward liaison on a marriage chest. Since, however, Venus is actively involved in the whole story, the eventual triumph of love and the divine ordination of events are allegorically appropriate to the occasion the cassoni commemorate (pl. 6).[10] Apollonio di Giovanni also painted the miniatures in one of the finest of all fifteenth-century manuscripts, the Riccardiana Virgil in Florence.[11] Like his cassone panels, the illuminations show his mastery of the narrative art of summarising in a single picture a sequence of episodes (or, for the *Eclogues* and *Georgics*, whole passages with multiple references) in a way that enables the reader

---

[8] Bibliothèque Nationale, Paris, MS Latin 11309. Alexander (1969); Alexander (1994) 154–5.
[9] Callman (1974) 40.   [10] Callman (1974) 54–5.   [11] Callman (1974) 7–11, 55–6.

to follow the essentials of the text (pl. 5). Virgil subjects quickly spread from books and decorative painting into the whole range of Renaissance fine and applied art. By the middle of the sixteenth century individual pictures of single episodes were commonly incorporated into decorative schemes alongside other historical, literary or mythological subjects, usually as part of a symbolic programme. So, for example, Perino del Vaga painted a *Shipwreck of Aeneas* for the Palazzo Doria in Genoa to allude to Andrea Doria's achievements as commander of the Genoese navy. Increasingly Virgil was used for political, allegorical and symbolic purposes: a reference made to Aeneas within a decorative programme would often serve a double purpose, as a model of exemplary conduct meant to inspire and also as a representation to the viewer of the patron's virtues. From the sixteenth to the eighteenth centuries references to Aeneas constantly recur serving one kind of propaganda function or another to signify military prowess, nobility, wisdom, divine destiny, undeviating faith and so forth, adapted to the specific circumstances of the commission. In mid-sixteenth-century Counter-Reformation Rome, for instance, the story of Aeneas could be used to express Catholic ideals, as it was in the Sala de Enea in the Palazzo Spada, where the programme emphasises heavenly providence and the messianic predestination of Rome, presenting its hero as the instrument of divine will.[12] In Pietro da Cortona's vast baroque scheme for the gallery of the Palazzo Pamphili (Rome, Piazza Navona) the emphasis is different, principally secular though with religious connotations. Painted between 1651 and 1654 during the pontificate of the Pamphili Pope Innocent XI, the entire programme exploits the *Aeneid* to celebrate the papal family by emphasising their *romanitas* as descendants of the nation's founders and their divinely ordained authority as Rome's temporal and spiritual rulers.[13] Pietro da Cortona's gallery was by no means the last great decorative scheme to use Virgilian themes for contemporary propaganda, but it does represent the artistic climax on the grandest scale and in the most exuberantly rhetorical style of an iconographic tradition that is especially important to any discussion of Virgil in art.

History painting supplies many more examples of artists drawing on Virgil for inspiration. As one of the sources of elevated subject matter regularly recommended by writers on art theory from the Renaissance onwards, he became enshrined in the repertoire of the academies. History painting of the highest order demanded more than simply an illustration of a particular subject or text in literal terms. Above all it required the artist to respond in an inspired way to capture the expressive content of

[12] *Virgilio nell'arte e nella cultura europea* (1981) 144.   [13] Preimesberger (1976).

the subject, demonstrating imagination and invention. History painting was meant to elevate and instruct, but also to animate the mind through mastery of an aesthetic ideal which was usually defined by the rules of classical art or what in the eighteenth century Joshua Reynolds termed 'the great style'. The range of dramatic events, emotions and intellectual ideas that could be culled from Virgil's poetry made him a primary source for artists concerned with historical themes. A single image, however, had to convey not just a momentary action but a sense of its significance and its place within a larger narrative. How this was attempted can be seen in a sculpted group by Gianlorenzo Bernini of *Aeneas, Anchises and Ascanius Fleeing Troy* from 1619 (pl. 8). It accurately follows Virgil's text (*Aen.* 2.707–14) describing the escape from Troy, but in choosing the subject Bernini also suggests the idea of the epic journey beginning, the hero's virtues, and with the three ages of man the sense of past and future that the *Aeneid* projects. For early seventeenth-century Rome there is a contemporary relevance in the themes of piety (Anchises with the house-gods) and faith triumphing over adversity which reflect Counter Reformation ideals. In a completely contrasting mood, Salvator Rosa's *Dream of Aeneas* (pl. 9) painted in the 1660s is an imaginatively forceful rendering of the moment when the river god Tiber appears to Aeneas after his arrival in Latium and directs him for aid to King Evander, whose city Pallanteum will eventually be the site for Rome (*Aen.* 8.26–34). The romantically charged atmosphere of the picture effectively evokes the mysterious mood of the passage, and again the artist chooses a subject which suggests the past (Aeneas' exhaustion from his journey) and the future (Tiber's gesture, pointing onwards to the ultimate goal).

That artists working in the academic and classical tradition thought deeply about how Virgil could be translated visually is evident from a letter written in 1647 by the French painter Nicolas Poussin to his friend and patron, Paul Fréart de Chantelou. In it he explains how he formulated his theory of style by which the subject determined the way a picture was conceived and the expressive idiom he selected, citing Virgil's use of language as a model.

> Good poets have used great diligence and marvellous artifice in adapting their choice of words ... and metre according to the propriety of speech, as Virgil has observed throughout his poem, because to all three manners of speech he adjusts the sound of the verse so skilfully that he seems to set before our eyes by the sound of the words the things he represents. So that, when he speaks of love he artfully chooses such words as are gentle, pleasing and very delightful to hear; elsewhere, where he sings of a feat of arms, or describes a naval battle or accident at sea, he has chosen words that are

hard, harsh and dissonant so that when they are heard or spoken they provoke fear.[14]

Poussin is making a general point from his reference to Virgil, but none the less it is revealing about the poet's influence on the aesthetics of art. In his *Landscape with Hercules and Cacus* Poussin demonstrates visually how a specific text informs his pictorial realisation of it (pl. 10). The painting is based on Virgil's dramatic description of the ferocious events which led to the slaying of Cacus (*Aen.* 8.190–270), reproducing the sombre atmosphere and wild scenery in which the story is set. Above all, it is through the dark brooding tones he uses that he communicates the sensations Virgil's words evoke.

Virgil's influence on landscape art has been one of his most enduring legacies. The imaginary pastoral world of the *Eclogues* (often conflated with the Renaissance vision of Arcadia), the observation of country life in the *Georgics,* and the vividly described Italian scenery in which he set the events of the *Aeneid* have each been a major source of inspiration to artists from the Renaissance to the nineteenth century. The illustrations added to the *Eclogues* and *Georgics* in fifteenth-century manuscripts are one of the principal starting-points for landscape painting as an independent genre in European art (pl. 6), and the pastoral poetry of Theocritus, Virgil and their Renaissance imitators played a significant role in creating a new pictorial language for interpreting nature. Ultimately the idealised vision and classical landscapes of painters like Poussin and his contemporary Claude Lorrain derive from this tradition. The idyllic enchantment and poetic feeling for landscape and atmosphere expressed in Claude's *Landscape with a Goatherd and Goats* painted from nature around 1636 immediately bring to mind the sentiment of Virgil in the *Eclogues* (pl. 12a). In his later landscapes with mythological and literary subjects, several of them depicting episodes from the *Aeneid* (pl. 11), he often introduced classical buildings and picturesque antiquities, creating a paradigm which became the standard convention for ideal landscape.[15] It served as a model throughout the eighteenth century, especially in England where his paintings were avidly collected.

The *Georgics,* too, had their own distinctive influence, providing a suitable classical precedent for another kind of landscape painting which depicted the supposedly real world of the working countryside. Here was a literary prototype that conferred respectability on what was otherwise regarded as an inferior subject, merely concerned with the topography of toil and the menial tasks of those who lived by tending livestock and

[14] The full text is given with a translation in Blunt (1967) 367–70. [15] Kitson (1960).

cultivating the land. Where the *Eclogues* present an idealised vision of Arcadian nature and leisure, the *Georgics* are about the laborious business of agriculture. One of the images they conjure up is of the countryside as a socially ordered place where nature and man are controlled by the productive rural economy. This was precisely what many seventeenth-century Dutch and Flemish painters portrayed in their landscapes and rural scenes with country labourers, following on from the tradition inaugurated by Pieter Bruegel the Elder in his series of *Labours of the Months* (1565; Kunsthistorisches Museum, Vienna) which have been specifically related to Virgil's *Georgics*.[16] Much later, John Constable was to identify the landscapes he painted of his native Suffolk as 'georgic' by inference when he reproduced a selection of them in his book *English Landscape Scenery* (1832), a set of mezzotint engravings which carried a quotation from Virgil on the title page. By then landscape art had moved on to a new romantic perception of nature in which subjective feeling and sensation are the prevailing preoccupations of painters, but still Virgil could inspire and affect the way an artist imagined a subject or responded to a specific scene. In English painting examples are to be found in Turner's Claudean treatment of *Aeneid* subjects, and in Samuel Palmer's etchings illustrating his own translation of the *Eclogues* which appeared in 1883 (pl. 12*b*).

Claude's influence on the way that Virgil's landscapes were perceived and imagined was not confined to painting. It was also present in landscape gardens. The eighteenth-century English classical garden is redolent of Claude's pictorial values and was intended to evoke associations with Italy and antiquity. In some there are specific references to Virgil. One example is Stourhead in Wiltshire, where the London banker Henry Hoare created in the 1740s and 1750s a landscape with a programme contrived in part around allusions to Aeneas (pl. 13*a*). Taking the prescribed circuit around the lake, the visitor is prepared for the garden's theme by an inscription over the entrance to the first of the classical temples: *Procul, o procul este profani* ('Begone, you that are uninitiated, begone') – the words of the Cumaean Sibyl to Aeneas immediately before they enter the Underworld where Rome's future history is revealed to him (*Aen.* 6.258). Further on, over the entrance to the grotto, there was originally an inscription referring to the nymphs' cave where Aeneas landed on the coast of North Africa, and inside at the exit is a river god statue recognisably derived from Salvator Rosa's Tiber figure (pl. 9), which an educated eighteenth-century visitor might have been expected to know from an etching by the artist, or at least could identify from the iconographic type and gesture which

---

[16] Gibson (1977) 156–8.

correspond to Virgil's description. The next feature in the landscape is the Temple of Hercules (now called the Pantheon): the sequence follows the journey of Aeneas, who, following Tiber's instructions, sets out to find the Arcadian king, and joins him at an altar dedicated to Hercules. The symbolic meaning of it all is made clear in a letter Henry Hoare wrote to his daughter in which he refers to an improvement he made to the path leading into the grotto which, he says, 'will make it easier of access facilis descensus Averno', quoting the words spoken by the Cumaean Sibyl, 'The descent to Avernus is easy ... but to retrace your steps and pass back to the air above, that is the task, this is the endeavour' (Aen. 6.126–9). Clearly the classical references are meant to convey a moral by analogy with Aeneas, and the landscape itself participates in revealing the message because aesthetically it is recognisably Virgilian.[17] Other gardens also referred to Virgil, for example William Shenstone's at The Leasowes in Shropshire where by 1748 there was a 'Virgil's Grove' (pl. 13b). As Douglas Chambers has recently shown, landscape gardeners were consciously responding to Virgil in the way they planted and laid out their designs, and in doing so they were also looking to the pictorial tradition that they associated with the poet.[18]

To Joshua Reynolds writing in the late eighteenth century an artist who 'warms his imagination with the best productions of ancient and modern poetry' will find thereby the means of attaining that 'nobleness of conception' which all great art must possess (Discourse III, 1770). On another occasion he makes a passing reference comparing the painter Titian to Virgil to demonstrate the point that an artist who represents nature and human actions in the same elevated spirit that the poet does belongs in the same class of sublime genius. As he puts it, 'What was said of Virgil, that he threw even the dung about the ground with an air of dignity, may be applied to Titian: whatever he touched, however naturally mean, and habitually familiar, by a kind of magick he invested with grandeur and importance' (Discourse XI, 1781).

Reynolds gives a practical demonstration of what he means by noble conception inspired by the imaginative force of poetry in his *Death of Dido* (pl. 14b) in which he successfully conjures from a picture of the tragic conclusion to the story all the passion and drama of what has gone before. It is also a picture that reveals a great deal about the different kinds of inspiration and imaginative experience that artists have continually discovered and redefined in Virgil's poetry. For Reynolds, as a classical painter and the leading spokesman for the academic tradition in England, Virgil

---

[17] Woodbridge (1970).   [18] Chambers (1993).

represented the authority of the classical canon in all the arts; his poetry was ordered by reason, but it also had an emotional and sensational charge that fired the imagination. The classical canon in Greek and Roman art consisted of two complementary components: ideal beauty and eloquent expression. The first is intellectually contrived and rationally perceived, but the second is more subjective and communicates feeling. To someone like Reynolds Virgil's poetry must have exhibited precisely the same aesthetic and expressive qualities that distinguished the acknowledged masterpieces of classical art and the works of those artists from the Renaissance onwards who exemplified his concept of the 'great style' or grand manner. In this he was following a long tradition, one in which art and literature, especially painting and poetry, were regarded as sister arts – hence the whole theory of painting that derived from Horace's famous analogy *ut pictura poesis*, 'as is painting so is poetry' (*Ars poetica*, 361).[19] This is the key to explaining why so many artists found Virgil such a compelling source of inspiration. But what also becomes apparent from their responses to him is that there were in a sense two Virgils they could give expression to – one we might call 'classical', the other 'romantic'. These contrasting but still compatible interpretations are reflected in the images of the poet himself by which artists of very different temperaments have represented their perceptions of him. Whether it is Poussin's iconic treatment of him as the epitome of classical intellect, gravitas and heavenly inspiration (pl. 16*a*), or Ribera's romantic figure of passionate feeling caught up in an intense agony of imaginative creation and vision (pl. 16*b*), each conveys a vivid impression of why Virgil's has been such an enduring and richly varied visual legacy.

FURTHER READING

For a subject which has such an important place in the iconography of western art from Roman times to the modern period there is surprisingly little literature other than specialised studies of particular works or selected themes derived from Virgil sources. The only general discussion of the topic in English is a stimulating essay by Nigel Llewellyn on 'Virgil and the visual arts' in Charles Martindale (ed.), *Virgil and his Influence* (Bristol, 1984) which primarily focuses on artists' ways of translating poetic into pictorial narratives. For Virgil in Roman and late antique art there is David H. Wright's monograph, *The Vatican Vergil. A Masterpiece of Late Antique Art* (Princeton, 1993). The medieval reception of Virgil and his reputation as a magician is comprehensively covered by Domenico Comparetti in *Vergil in the Middle Ages* (New York, 1895), with many references to pictorial evidence but no illustrations. Virgil's influence on landscape art is covered by Annabel Patterson in *Pastoral and Ideology. Virgil to Valéry* (Oxford, 1988), though the book is mainly

[19] Lee (1967).

about literary forms. For the eighteenth-century classical garden in England and the transmission of Virgil's inspiration through landscape design Douglas D. C. Chambers, *The Planters of the English Landscape Garden: Botany, Trees and the Georgics* (London and New Haven, 1993) is particularly interesting. Otherwise the reader must rely on individual monographs on different artists who have been influenced by or illustrated subjects from Virgil, but these usually do little more than refer rather generally to the literary source; an exception is Humphrey Wine's *Claude: The Poetic Landscape* (London, 1994). The one extensive treatment of Virgil in art is to be found in an elusive Italian exhibition catalogue, *Virgilio nell'arte e nella cultura europea*, Biblioteca Nazionale Centrale (Rome, 1981), which has the fullest bibliography of the article literature (mostly not in English). Taken as a whole, the subject still awaits the treatment it undoubtedly deserves.

2

GENRE AND POETIC CAREER

8

CHARLES MARTINDALE

Green politics: the *Eclogues*

It may have been at the suggestion of his patron Asinius Pollio, aristocratic promoter of the new poetics which began with the generation of Catullus, that Virgil undertook to become the Roman Theocritus.[1] At all events his decision to imitate a collection of sophisticated Hellenistic literary experiments, and in the process to 'pastoralise' them (only a minority of the *Idylls* have a rustic setting), was to have important and unexpected consequences. Without the *Eclogues* pastoral might never have become one of the major, exemplary genres of European poetry. E. R. Curtius declared that anyone unfamiliar with the First Eclogue 'lacks one key to the literary tradition of Europe'; while for Paul Alpers the collection constitutes 'probably the single most important document in the history of poetry'.[2] Moreover Virgil's canonical status and the eventual shape of his poetic career as it appeared in retrospect, with its apparently purposeful upward march through the genres, meant that pastoral became an appropriate *point d'appui* for a youthful poet with aspirations for immortality; both Spenser and Milton, for example, consciously shaped their artistic lives to the Virgilian example.

There are many precedents one could cite for Theocritus' green world (leaving aside the possibility that he was inspired by actual shepherd songs): pastoral elements in the *Iliad* and *Odyssey* (the similes, the shield of Achilles which includes a vignette of music at a grape harvest, Calypso's island, the gardens of Alcinous, rustic scenes and characters in Ithaca); Hippolytus' virgin meadow in Euripides' play; the enchanted landscape setting at the opening of Plato's *Phaedrus* that has nothing to teach Socrates, lover of the city. But Theocritus is normally credited with the 'invention' of pastoral as a literary genre. David Halperin (1983) argues that to do this is to read history backwards, and that the *Idylls* were designed as a species

---

[1] Cf. *Ecl.* 8.11–2 (*accipe iussis | carmina coepta tuis*), assuming, as do the majority of scholars, that these lines are addressed to Pollio, not Octavian.

[2] Curtius (1953) 190; Alpers (1979) 1.

of avant-garde, modernist epic;[3] this accounts for the metre (hexameters) and the complex intertextual relationship with Homer (e.g. the appearance of the Cyclops). That Theocritus wrote what he himself called 'bucolic (cowherd's) song' (so the refrain in Idyll 1), a term used also by ancient critics which Halperin is at pains to differentiate from the later conception of pastoral, does not mean that there was a separate bucolic genre. Quintilian, for whom metre was a key defining element of genre, classifies the *Eclogues* too as epic; no classical theorist clearly recognises a pastoral genre as such. Pastoral in anything like the modern sense was, in this historicising account, the invention of late antiquity or even (in Halperin's view) of the Renaissance. The situation is complicated by the fact that between Theocritus and Virgil a separate collection may have been made of the rustic idylls (if so, does the selector have a claim to be the true 'inventor' of pastoral?). Or are we to say that Virgil, almost by accident as it were, invented pastoral when he chose to unify his Theocritean book by making shepherds and the countryside central to it? One could argue that it is precisely such a process of concentration and selection which makes a genre; according to the elder Scaliger, one of the Renaissance's most influential theorists of literature, 'pastoral works continually draw back material of every kind to a rural character' (*pastoralia ... cuiuscumque generis negotium semper retrahunt ad agrorum naturam*).[4] Within a generation Ovid could evoke with a few deft touches the defining hallmarks of what thus must already have become to a degree 'a closed and self-sufficient discourse';[5] during the story of Io (*Met.* 1.674ff.) Mercury, to assume the role of a shepherd, takes off his usual accoutrements save his staff (*virga*) which immediately functions as a discursive marker plunging us into a bucolic world (*pastor, per devia rura, capellas, structis avenis*). But, although Virgil had a Neronian imitator (Calpurnius Siculus), there was no outbreak of such writing in antiquity as there was to be in the Renaissance. Or can a single great work on its own constitute a genre, albeit one that had yet to receive its name?

The failure to find a clear validating point of origin, or even any authoritative ancient account, for what is often considered an unusually normative genre is itself instructive. It might suggest that genres are best thought of as processes; not as essences or ontological entities, things, but as discursive formations, contested, fluid, resisting even while inviting definition (Derrida famously asked in 'The Law of Genre' whether there might not be 'lodged within the heart of the law itself, a law of impurity or a principle

---

[3] For a critique of this view see Cameron (1995) ch. 16 'Theocritus'.
[4] Quoted Conte (1994b) 116.   [5] Conte (1994b) 116.

of contamination'[6]). Scholars often employ, like the ancients themselves, the rhetoric of invention and discovery (so a celebrated essay by Bruno Snell begins with the claim that Virgil 'discovered' Arcadia); post-structuralists prefer a counter-rhetoric of betweenness – genres are not discovered, but, in so far as they 'exist' at all, are always already there. And genres are historical not only in the sense that they operate within history but in the sense that they have a history. A historicist can argue that Virgil did not suppose himself to be writing pastoral but rather a form of neoteric *epos* in imitation of Theocritus. One possible reply is that history always involves reading backwards, and that the *Eclogues* must unavoidably be read in relation to the pastoral tradition within which they have been inscribed. Even if not conceived as pastoral (any more than the *Iliad* was conceived as epic), they are pastoral *now*.

The title of this chapter is contrivedly ambiguous. The colour green, a colour of complex signification (its English meanings include 'simple', 'innocent', 'naïve', 'lovesick', 'jealous'), came to be an emblem of pastoral, as in Spenser's 'green cabinet' from the December Eclogue of his *Shepherd's Calendar* which Thomas Rosenmeyer (1969) appropriated for the title of a famous study of the Theocritean tradition (Spenser himself plucked the phrase from an earlier pastoralist Clément Marot, pastoral being in general self-consciously imitative, traditional, and intertextual). In 'The Garden' Marvell famously colour-codes the contrast between erotic and pastoral discourse to suggest the latter's paradoxically greater sexual allure: 'Nor white nor red was ever seen | so am'rous as this lovely green'. A later stanza praises the garden for 'Annihilating all that's made | To a green thought in a green shade', where 'green shade' translates Virgil's *viridis umbra*. (*Viridis* occurs 11 times in the *Eclogues*, while grass is an unsurprising staple ingredient of the Virgilian landscape, but *umbra* and *silva* are more clearly used metonymically as bucolic markers.)

Pastoral politics might mean the politics, or political themes, to be found *in* pastoral, and indeed it is commonplace to say that, in comparison with Theocritus, Virgil politicises pastoral space by admitting elements of the wider world, including the world of high politics, into his green one. Or it might mean the politics *of* pastoral, with the poems treated as political through and through, as constituting in fact a potent ideological vehicle. And green politics also hints at the modern environmental movement, whose prescriptions for the good life, designed to counter ever-encroaching urbanism and the rape of nature, might be construed as another modern version of pastoral (if one generally lacking the self-reflexiveness and ironic

---

[6] Derrida (1981) 204.

sense of play to be found in Theocritus or Virgil). Indeed the allegorisations of the *Eclogues* favoured by modern scholarship include some of a rather evidently environmentalist hue; so according to A. J. Boyle the poems investigate 'the psychological chaos and spiritual impoverishment which Virgil sees as the city's legacy and *the corollary of technological growth*' (italics mine).[7] And in general, at least since Schiller's *On Naïve and Sentimental Poetry*, Virgil's green places have been constituted as a privileged site of the harmonious co-operation between Man and Nature.[8]

This chapter will explore the relationship between the political and the aesthetic both within the *Eclogues* themselves and within writing about them (indeed my contention would be that, because of the importance of reception in the making of meanings, this distinction between text and commentary can, and should, be partially collapsed). The poetry of third-century BC Alexandria to which the *Idylls* belong is in general often seen as comparatively 'pure' and autonomous, art mainly for art's sake, at least in comparison with the earlier 'political' poetry of classical Athens, the poetry of the polis. There is an obvious paradox here. Callimachus, the most important and innovative writer of the period, held an official post under the ruling Ptolemies and composed poems in their praise. Artists – in this at least like academics – have a necessary complicity with the political systems they work under, whatever claims to purity they may make or have made for them. The *Eclogues* likewise are often presented as inhabiting a charmed enclosure, a comparatively self-contained aesthetic sphere. When Paul Veyne argues that Roman love elegy is a kind of literary game bearing little relation to any social realities he calls it pastoral in city clothes; elegy for him takes place 'outside the world, just like bucolic poetry'.[9] The *Eclogues* in other words are an *unproblematic* instance of evidently aesthetic play; whereas many have been misled by elegy, 'such pastoral fiction never fooled anyone'. In what is perhaps the most influential account of the *Eclogues* written by a classicist in this century, 'Arcadia: the discovery of a spiritual landscape', Bruno Snell argued that they are set, not in any actual Mediterranean countryside, but in 'a far-away land overlaid with the golden haze of unreality'.[10] Although Virgil allowed political matters to intrude into his Arcadia, in this departing from Theocritean precedent, he converted them into myth, being indeed 'always careful not to get involved in the slippery problems of political action; in fact one may presume that they never even penetrated to his dreaming ear'. And, like Veyne, Snell stresses the poetic autonomy of the *Eclogues*, which 'represent the first

---

[7] Boyle (1986) 15.   [8] See Halperin (1983) 42–9.

[9] Veyne (1988) 101. For a critique of Veyne's general approach see Kennedy (1993) 95–100.

[10] Snell (1953) 282; the two subsequent quotations are from pp. 294 and 308.

1*a*. Mosaic from Hadrumetum in Africa, *Virgil seated between the Muses of History and Tragedy*. (Bardo Museum, Tunis.)

1*b*. Roman relief, *Aeneas sacrificing*: fragment of the frieze from the Ara Pacis (Altar of Augustan Peace), 13–9 BC. (Ara Pacis Museum, Rome.)

2a. *Dido and Aeneas*: mosaic pavement from Low Ham Villa, Somerset, fourth century. (Somerset County Museum, Taunton.)

2b. *Portrait of Virgil*: miniature from the Roman Virgil, early fifth century. (Vatican Library, Rome; Cod. Vat. Lat. 3867, fol. 3v.)

3a. Dido and Aeneas sheltering from the storm: miniature from the Roman Virgil,
early fifth century. (Vatican Library, Rome; Cod. Vat. Lat. 3867, fol. 108r.)

3b. Laocoön: miniature from the Vatican Virgil, early fifth century. (Vatican Library,
Rome; Cod. Vat. Lat. 3225, fol. 18v.)

4a. The storm with Aeneas shipwrecked off the coast of North Africa: miniature from *Eclogues, Georgics, Aeneid*, 1458–9 (illuminated by Guglielmo Giraldi), fol. 60r. (Bibliothèque Nationale, Paris; MS Latin 7939A.)

4b. Aeneid Book 2 Title-page: The Trojan Horse and Aeneas, Anchises and Ascanius: from *Eclogues, Georgics, Aeneid, c.* 1490 (attributed to Bartolomeus Sanvito). (The British Library, London; Kings MS 24, fol. 73v.)

PRAEFATIO LIBRORVM GEORGICO
RVM INCIPIT FOELICITER
Qid faciat letaf fegetef :quo fidere ferner·
Agricola .ut facilem terram pfemdat aratrif·
Semina que tacienda / modof cultuiſq locorum
e docuit .meſſef magno olim fenore reddi .

LIBER PRIMVS GEORGICORVM IN
CIPIT FOELICITER.
Qid faciat letaf fegetef :quo
fidere terram
Sertere mecennaf :ulmifq
adiungere uitef
Conuemat :que cura boum
quif cultuf habendo
Sit pecori apibuf quanta
experienta paraf·
Hnc canere incipiam .Vof o
clariſſim i mundi
I umina Libentem qlo que ducatif annum
L iber et alma cerf. ueftro fi munere tellus
c halonam pingui glandem mutauit ariſta·
P oculaq inuentif acheloia mifcuit uuif
e t uof agreftum prefentia numina telluf faum
F erte fimul faunique pedem : druadefq puellſ
M unera ueftra cano: tuq o cui prima frementem

5. Apollonio di Giovanni: *Georgics Book 1*, c. 1460, from Codex Riccardiana. (Biblioteca
Riccardiana, Florence; MS 492, fol. 18r.)

6. Apollonio di Giovanni, *Scenes from Virgil's Aeneid*: cassone panels, c. 1460. (Yale University Art Gallery, New Haven (Jarves Collection).)

7. Sandro Botticelli, illustration to Dante's *Inferno*, Canto XVIII, 1490–7: from an illuminated manuscript of Dante's *Divine Comedy*. (Staatliche Museen Preussischer Kulturbesitz, Berlin.)

8. Gianlorenzo Bernini, *Aeneas, Anchises and Ascanius fleeing Troy*, 1619. (Galleria Borghese, Rome.)

9. Salvator Rosa, *The Dream of Aeneas*, c. 1660–5. (Metropolitan Museum of Art, New York (Rogers Fund, 1965).)

10. Nicolas Poussin, *Landscape with Hercules and Cacus*, c. 1660. (Pushkin Museum of Fine Arts, Moscow.)

11. Claude Lorrain, *The Arrival of Aeneas at Pallanteum*, 1675. (The National Trust, Anglesey Abbey (Lord Fairhaven Collection).)

12*a*. Claude Lorrain, detail from *Landscape with a Goatherd and Goats, c.* 1636. (National Gallery, London.)

12*b*. Samuel Palmer, *Eclogue 8: Opening the Fold,* 1880: etching from *The Eclogues of Virgil: An English Version,* 1883.

13*a*. Stourhead, Wiltshire. The Lake and Pantheon (originally Temple of Hercules): watercolour by Francis Nicholson, 1813. (British Museum, London.)

13*b*. The Leasowes, Shropshire. Virgil's Grove: engraving after Thomas Smith, 1748.

14a. Giambattista Tiepolo, *The Apotheosis of Aeneas*, 1763–4: study for the painted ceiling of the Guard Room in the Royal Palace, Madrid. (Fogg Art Museum, Cambridge, MA.)

14b. Sir Joshua Reynolds, *The Death of Dido*, 1781. (The Royal Collection.)

15a. Pietro da Cortona, detail from *Virgil reading to the Emperor Augustus*, 1642: fresco. (Sala di Apollo, Palazzo Pitti, Florence.)

15b. Jean Auguste Dominique Ingres, *Virgil reading the Aeneid to the Emperor Augustus*, 1812. (Musée des Augustins, Toulouse.)

16b. Jusepe Ribera, *The Poet* (*Virgil*): etching, 1621–5. (Metropolitan Museum of Art, New York.)

16a. Nicolas Poussin, *Virgil*: engraved by Claude Mellan, 1641. (The British Library, London.)

serious attempt in literature to mould the Greek motifs into self-contained forms of beauty whose reality lies within themselves'; as a result, for the first time, 'art became "symbol"'. The New Historicist Louis Montrose has observed how theories of pastoral have a way of becoming theories of literature, and certainly many of those who have been drawn to pastoral seem anxious to clear a space for the aesthetic uncontaminated by more banausic discourses in what can itself be seen as 'an exemplary pastoral process'; in Montrose's words, 'to write *about* pastoral may be a way of displacing and simplifying the discontents of the latter-day humanist in an increasingly technocratic academy and society'.[11] The pastoral world can readily function as an emblem for the academic world.

It is easy to find elements in the *Eclogues* to support such an aestheticising reading. Pastoral is, in general, unusually self-conscious about its own status as art, to the extent that critics sometimes claim that this is what the genre is fundamentally 'about'; for example the literary theorist Wolfgang Iser finds in the invented world of the *Eclogues* not so much Snell's landscape of the mind as 'a work of art that thematizes art itself',[12] one indeed that largely frees itself from the traditional referential function of poetry as mimesis articulated by Plato and Aristotle. Certainly Eclogue 6 is now normally read metapoetically, as a poem about poem-making, one that constitutes a poetics relevant to Virgil's whole project. Significantly although the piece has some bucolic colour its principal matter is mythology, not the rustic world. It opens with what in modern times has been termed a *recusatio*, a refusal enjoined by Apollo to write about kings and battles, which is a close imitation, seemingly the first in Latin, of a passage from the *Aetia* prologue where Callimachus answers his critics and defends his poetic practice. We are often told that Virgil here rejects epic for pastoral; in view of what has been said above, we might say rather that Virgil justifies writing Theocritean bucolic *epos* by appealing to Callimachus' aesthetic credo, his championing of stylistic refinement, *leptotes* (as Theocritus himself had already done in Idyll 7).[13] Apollo had told Callimachus 'poet, feed your offering as fat as possible, but keep the muse lean (*leptaleen*)'. With witty appropriateness Virgil gives the Callimachean imagery a more specifically pastoral turn. Tityrus is instructed to feed his sheep fat, but the song of the Theocritean poet, troped as a shepherd, is to be fine-spun (*deductum carmen*); the resonant figure of the shepherd-poet can be traced back to

---

[11] Montrose (1983) 415. [12] Iser (1993) 34.

[13] For Callimachus' text and a list of Latin texts derived from it see Hopkinson (1988). Cameron (1995) has recently challenged many of the orthodoxies about Callimachus, particularly the view that the *Aetia* prologue is an attack on traditional narrative epic. If his views are accepted, Latin literary history will need to be modified accordingly.

farmer Hesiod's meeting with the Muses on Helicon while tending his flocks (*Theogony* 21–34), a passage imitated subsequently in the poem. Virgil's muse will display *tenuitas* (*tenuis* is used of the shepherd's reed-pipe both literally and with reference to the poetry associated with it), and will be a species of play, *lusus*, far from the gloom of traditional martial themes (*tristia bella*). The song of Silenus which follows, a catalogue of mythological tales, might almost be a blueprint for Ovid's *Metamorphoses*, the work that in so many ways can be seen as the climax of Roman Alexandrianism. It begins with a tiny cosmology, in the style of Hesiod (a poet also evoked by Callimachus in the Aetia prologue[14]) and with Lucretian echoes, and continues with abbreviated narrations of various myths, several of them involving metamorphosis or love or both. At its centre is a mini-epyllion, a miniaturisation of the miniature epic that Catullus and his fellow modernists favoured. It tells, obliquely and with a sort of hyper-refined lyricism, of Pasiphae's perverse desire for the bull, and it even includes, in the manner of some other epyllia including Catullus 64, an inset-narrative (the story of the Proetides who imagined they had become cows). The writer projects himself empathetically into his story, and consoles (*solatur*) the victim for her pathological condition. This is the sort of writing that, in both content and preciosity of style, traditionalists, ancient and modern, might stigmatise as 'decadent' (Jasper Griffin compares it to Wilde's *Salome*[15]). Silenus' song also compliments a second-generation neoteric, Virgil's friend Gaius Cornelius Gallus, who composes a poem in imitation of Euphorion, another Alexandrian of ostentatious obscurity, and becomes Hesiod's successor, receiving the pipes with which, like Orpheus, Hesiod used to bring down (*deducere*) the trees from the mountains. And in all this we have both a poetics of eros and an erotics of poetry (Silenus recalls songs Apollo sang by the river Eurotas after killing his lover, the beautiful and beautifully named boy Hyacinthus), together with a heralding of the Orphic and Apollonian powers of poetry; poets create the world of myth, create that is their own kind of reality, one far from the tedium and *tristitia* of high politics, and one in which they are sovereign. From a different perspective, of course, one could call this escapism.

Veyne's conception of aesthetic play is consonant both with the importance of singing contests in Theocritus and Virgil and with the characterisation of the *Eclogues* by one of their most intelligent early readers. The poet Horace contrasts the martial poetry of 'fierce' Varius with what may be rendered 'the sensitive and witty *epos* that the Italian Muses who rejoice in the countryside have bestowed on Virgil': (*epos*) *molle atque facetum* |

---

[14] But see now Cameron (1995) ch. 13 'Hesiodic elegy'.   [15] Griffin (1986) 32.

Vergilio adnuerunt gaudentes rure Camenae (*Satires* 1.10.44–5).[16] The sophisticated, at times whimsical, wit of the *Eclogues* is something that much
modern criticism (eager to stress the 'serious', even dark, side of the poems,
in an understandable anxiety to free them from any imputations of triviality) frequently underplays. The Tenth Eclogue, for example, is one of
which rather heavy critical weather has been made; the poem is widely
read as acknowledging the failure of pastoral (already threatened in Eclogue
9 by the irruptions of politics and war), since the world of the shepherds
proves impotent to assuage the passional dolours of Gallus who, in a con-
cretisation of a common erotic trope, is literally dying of love (*amore per-
ibat*, 10). The poem is seen as staging a debate about literary modes, the
deficiencies and limitations of pastoral leading in the end to its abandonment by Virgil. Certainly Eclogue 10 explicitly presents itself as closural,
the last of the collection (*extremum laborem*, 1), and the shadows of evening fall across its close:[17]

> Haec sat erit, divae, vestrum cecinisse poetam,
> dum sedet et gracili fiscellam texit hibisco ...
> surgamus: solet esse gravis cantantibus umbra,
> iuniperi gravis umbra; nocent et frugibus umbrae.
> ite domum saturae, venit Hesperus, ite capellae.

> To have sung these things, goddesses, while he sat and wove
> A frail of thin hibiscus, will suffice your poet ...
> Let us arise: for singers heavy is the shade,
> Heavy the shade of juniper; and shade harms fruit.
> Go, little she-goats, Hesper comes, go home replete.　　(Guy Lee)

Umbra, shade, is readily taken as a figure for bucolic writing (the beginning of the First Eclogue saw Tityrus reclining *lentus in umbra*), while
surgamus might imply, allegorically, that the writer will proceed to other,
perhaps 'higher' poetic forms (already in the Fourth Eclogue he had assayed
paulo maiora, a slightly grander, panegyrical theme[18]). Virgil tropes himself as an inhabitant of his bucolic world, himself sitting at ease while
Gallus pours forth his passionate complaint, and weaving his slender hibis-
cus basket (which could stand for the poem itself and its stylistic *gracilitas*
or for the whole now-completed eclogue book – weaving had been used
as a metaphor for writing poetry by Catullus and others); this passage

---

[16] I follow here the interpretation of Halperin (1983) 213–14; editors usually take the adjectives adverbially.
[17] See further the chapter by Elena Theodorakopoulos in this volume.
[18] For some possible resonances of *maiora* see Cameron (1995) 470–1.

evidently elides being a shepherd and writing Theocritean verse. There is a sense of completion: the poet has sung enough (*sat*), the flocks are fed full (*saturae*) – the sheep are fat, though the bucolic muse must remain lean. The lines thus constitute a sort of *sphragis* or seal for the entire collection (designed as an artistically satisfying whole), which introduces, or reintroduces, its author. The poem fuses with wit and virtuosity material from two literary models, themselves both probably indebted to Callimachus' thin-spun verse, Theocritus (especially the First Idyll, in which the shepherd hero Daphnis dies) and Gallus, where the object of imitation was in a different metre (elegiac couplets). Since, according to Servius, *Amores* was the title Gallus gave his elegies, *sollicitos Galli dicamus amores* (6) could be translated either 'let me describe Gallus' troubled feelings of love / love affair', or 'let me speak of Gallus' poems the *Amores* with their depiction of troubled love'; the line punningly collapses the distinction between love as an emotion and its literary expression in a text. Although Gallus' love-poetry is lost, except for a fragment recently recovered in Egypt,[19] there are pretty clearly reminiscences of it in his lament, which constitutes a song within a song (the performance element is strong here as throughout the *Eclogues*). At one point in Servius' commentary we read that 'all these verses of Gallus have been transferred from his own poems', while surviving love-elegy provides close parallels for the mood and *topoi* of the speech together with the dramatic situation it presupposes (Lycoris, Gallus' mistress, is away with a rival, like Cynthia in Propertius 1.8). *Omnia vincit amor* (69) could be a quotation from Gallus since it constitutes half of a pentameter, while the threefold exclamatory *a* (47–9) reproduces a mannerism Gallus must have shared with other neoterics. But none of this means that Virgil is solemnly debating the merits and demerits of different genres, let alone acknowledging the failure of his own bucolic art, including its failure to deal with the vicissitudes of erotic passion (there is anyway no clear distinction between bucolic and elegiac love, which share many of the same tropes). Virgil has to compose verses to honour or to help his friend for Lycoris herself to read: *pauca meo Gallo, sed quae legat ipsa Lycoris,* | *carmina sunt dicenda* (2–3 – from the new fragment we now know that these lines too echo Gallus: *carmina . . .* | *quae possem domina dicere digna mea*). We could say that Virgil is expressing poetic and erotic solidarity with Gallus, with consummate art is helping him court his *docta puella*. Virgil himself is a lover of Gallus (*cuius amor . . . mihi crescit in horas*, 73), so is perhaps humorously presenting himself as Lycoris' rival in erotics. There is an undertow of (often pleasing) melancholy about much

---

[19] For the text see Anderson et al. (1979) 138ff.

pastoral writing, but it is easier to read this comparatively sprightly, poised poem as primarily an exercise in wit, *facetiae* (Horace, as we have seen, found the *Eclogues* 'sensitive and witty'). Veyne is quite insistent:

> I do not for an instant believe that . . . Virgil meant to deliver a 'message' to us, to draw melancholy conclusions about 'the final failure of poetry, unable to purge the passions'. What reader would think of taking a poetic fiction for some moralist's guidebook, drawing such a clear lesson from it? This epilogue merely signifies that, the pastiche being ended, the two poets again become what eternity will change them into . . . The confusion of genres was only a momentary game, the flock can reenter its fold.[20]

One may contrast the stress on aesthetic autonomy we encounter in Veyne or Snell with some of the uses the *Eclogues* have been put to in our century. In 1917 John H. Finley, commissioner of education for New York State and president of the State University, in his poem 'Virgil's First Eclogue remembered' appropriated the piece to argue for US intervention in the First World War. In 'Build soil: a political pastoral' the conservative Robert Frost used the same poem to criticise Roosevelt's liberal agricultural policies, while in Latin America, from a different point in the political spectrum, Eclogues 1 and 9 could serve to provide oblique support for land reform.[21] In the Renaissance, when the fashion for pastoral poetry on the Virgilian model was at its height, critics underlined the political subtexts of the *Eclogues*. Thus Sidney wrote in his *Apology for Poetry* (published 1595), 'Is the poor pipe [i.e. pastoral poetry] disdained, which sometimes out of Meliboeus' mouth can show the misery of people under hard lords or ravening soldiers, and again, by Tityrus, what blessedness is derived to them that lie lowest from the goodness of them that sit highest?'; while George Puttenham in *The Art of English Poetry* (1589) sees the eclogue as a late and oblique form of poetry devised 'not of purpose to counterfeit or represent the rustical manner of loves and communication, but under the veil of homely persons and in rude speeches to insinuate and glance at greater matters, and such as perchance had not been safe to have been disclosed in any other sort, which may be perceived by the *Eclogues* of Virgil, in which are treated by figure matters of greater importance than the loves of Tityrus and Corydon'.[22] Renaissance texts of the *Eclogues* often featured the ancient commentary of Servius, which presented the poems as intermittently allegorical (Puttenham's 'by figure'), in contrast to Theocritus' *Idylls*, supposedly written on one level (*simpliciter*); Donatus had been of the

---

[20] Veyne (1988) 103–4; see too Conte (1994b) 120–1.
[21] See for these details Ziolkowski (1993) 156–63, 21–2.
[22] Loughrey (1984) 33–4 (texts modernised).

same opinion, stating that there is a certain amount of figurative allegorical discourse 'neither nowhere nor everywhere' (*neque nusquam neque
ubique aliquid figurate dici, hoc est per allegoriam*). Such scraps of evidence as we possess might suggest that the *Eclogues* were read allegorically
throughout antiquity. Quintilian (8.6.46), citing lines from Eclogue 9 to
illustrate a particular type of allegory, assumes that Menalcas in this poem
is to be understood as Virgil. Apuleius (*Apology* 10) tells that through the
masks of Corydon and Alexis Virgil is expressing his love for a slave boy
of Pollio's. Despite their continual appeals to the supposed responses of
ancient readers, modern scholars reject the story (while accepting Apuleius'
identifications in the same passage of the various women in love elegy),
although something like it seems already assumed in one of Martial's epigrams (8.56) and elsewhere; it might suggest a possible reading of Eclogue
2 as a witty coterie piece.

'Where he [Servius] goes most astray is in allegorizing the *Eclogues*';
Richard Jenkyns' comment is typical enough of modern scholarship[23] (actually it would be easy to configure all interpretations, scholarly or otherwise,
as allegory, a saying of the text in other words which involves appropriation to current concerns). By contrast Annabel Patterson argues that such
hostility to what she calls 'the Servian hermeneutic' can be seen as an occlus-
ive attempt to depoliticise the *Eclogues*, to represent them as comparatively
pure art untainted by ideology, whereas to both Servius and those poets
influenced by the Servian tradition they were the loci of social and political
concerns as much as of artistic ones. As Patterson puts it (thereby herself
becoming a modern shepherd-scholar):

> Among the competing ideologies proleptically displayed in the *Eclogues* are
> Roman republicanism, the classic statement of the claims of the many to
> equal consideration; the counter-claim of the privileged few to special treat-
> ment on the grounds of special talent; the hegemonic needs of the holders of
> power for cultural authentication; the responsibility of the intellectual for pro-
> viding that authentication, in the interests of stability; the value of political
> or social stability in nurturing the arts; the responsibility of the intellectual
> for telling the whole truth, in the interests of social justice; the intellectual's
> claim to personal autonomy.[24]

And she rightly observes that any appeal to ideological purity can itself be
construed as ideological. Classicists, in a way that can be related to romantic and post-romantic aesthetic preferences, are happier with symbolism, a
mode of fusion which implies wholeness, than with allegory which works

---

[23] Jenkyns (1992) 155.   [24] Patterson (1988) 8.

by fragmentation and discontinuity. Thus it is frequently argued that Tityrus in Eclogue 1 cannot stand for Virgil, because he is an elderly man and an ex-slave; but it is *because* Tityrus is different from Virgil (or Daphnis in Eclogue 5 from Julius Caesar) that he can be (as Servius supposed) an allegory of him – allegory is precisely a figure of disjunction. Significantly it is only with poetic allegory that modern criticism seems much at home; the poems are acknowledged to be self-reflexive, allegorising their own writing. We have seen how commentators are happy to discuss the possibility that the end of Eclogue 10 is a farewell to pastoral, with *umbra* figuring bucolic poetry, whereas they would not even think to cite Servius Danielis' gloss on *in umbra* in Eclogue 1 'under Augustus' protection' *allegorice sub tutela Imperatoris Augusti* (though a glance at the dictionary will show the political connotations of shade). Jasper Griffin comments that if Virgil did lose his farm, or have one restored to him, 'this series of transactions . . . was . . . inherently unpoetical'[25] (a stress on aesthetic autonomy always tends to narrow the range of what poetry can treat); while he regards Eclogue 4 as not so much 'a response to a political settlement' (the poem may be a celebration of the peace of Brundisium and a sort of epithalamium for the marriage of Antony and Octavia) as a poetic fantasy. Yet Eclogue 4 has continually been evoked in precise political circumstance; Dryden, for example, echoes it in connection with the Restoration of Charles II in *Astraea Redux*. The poem, of course, became the subject of the most famous of all allegorisations of the *Eclogues*, and one whose resonance has lasted well into our century, as being 'about' the birth of Christ. In *Purgatorio* 22, in a notable piece of fiction-making, Dante has Statius tell 'the poet of the bucolic songs' that he was first drawn to Christianity by reading the Fourth Eclogue; this is not mere historical naïvety (Dante knows perfectly well that the *virgo* of line 6 is the goddess Astraea, not the Virgin Mary), but rather a matter of different reading habits.

Politicising accounts of the *Eclogues* may take both admiring and hostile forms. The poems may be praised for articulating a desire for simplicity (though always from the perspective of the sophisticated), and constituting a protest, sometimes overt, more often implied, against the evils of the city, even an implicit pacifism. Thus Servius claims that Eclogue 1 not only thanks Octavian for restoring the poet's farm, but also criticises him over the sufferings of the dispossessed (his note on *impius miles* in 70 begins *hic Vergilius Octavianum Augustum laesit*). Or they may be criticised for concealing the realities and oppressions of rural life, in a way that serves the interests of the ruling class. Thus the editors of *The Penguin Book of*

---

[25] Griffin (1986) 24; the subsequent quotation is from p. 29.

English Pastoral, writing in the Marxising tradition of Raymond Williams' *The Country and the City*, argue that the genre is 'a way of *not* looking at the countryside': 'For the pastoral vision is, at base, a false vision positing a simplistic, unhistorical relationship between the ruling, landowning class – the poet's patrons and often the poet himself – and the workers on the land; as such its function is to mystify and to obscure the harshness of actual social and economic organization.'[26] One response to such criticism is to say that it rests on a naïve representational realism. There is no unmediated way of representing the countryside; any representation is, in the words of Simon Schama, 'the product of culture's craving and culture's framing' (his *Landscape and Memory* argues that 'landscapes are culture before they are nature; constructs of the imagination projected onto wood and water and rock', texts 'on which generations write their recurring obsessions').[27] Or one could say that no reader anyway ever mistook the pastoral world for the real countryside, while there are, in C. S. Lewis' words, 'many causes (reasons too) that have led humanity to symbolise by rural scenes a region in the mind which does exist and which should be visited often'.[28] But the argument that pastoral never fooled anyone sits uneasily, perhaps, with the memory of Marie Antoinette and her courtiers playing at shepherds as the poor starved and the old order began to crumble. Certainly anti-pastoralists like the poet George Crabbe found the Virgilian tradition an oppressive one: 'From Truth and Nature shall we widely stray | Where fancy leads, or Virgil led the way' (*The Village*, 1783).[29] At the very least one must recognise that Virgil's green spaces are somewhat 'lordly possessions'.[30] Virgil shapes his rustic world into a form that allows him and his friends and patrons to make their own appearance there without embarrassment alongside the shepherds. Corydon in Eclogue 2 is said to produce artless verses (*incondita*); but his song is decked out with obtruded artistry (what Crabbe would call 'the tinsel trappings of poetic pride'), including the notorious line *Amphion Dircaeus in Actaeo Aracyntho* (24), mannered, allusive, Graecising (it can be turned into a Greek hexameter with the lightest of adjustments). For all the supposed rusticity of the bucolic style, its 'lowness', the *Eclogues* belong rather evidently to 'high' culture; as one feminist scholar puts it, 'access to the pastoral speaking position is determined by cultural possessions – of specific educational, class, gender, and racial identities', while 'the lowly are not

---

[26] Barrell and Bull (1974) 4.   [27] Schama (1995) 7, 61, 12.

[28] Loughrey (1984) 142 (from *The Allegory of Love*, 1936, ch. 7).

[29] See Raymond Williams in Loughrey (1984) 155–7; Dr Johnson persuaded Crabbe to emend the second line of the quotation to 'Where Virgil, not where Fancy, leads the way'.

[30] Schama (1995) 546.

assigned a subjectivity of their own'.[31] To Montrose and his fellow New Historicists the question is not what pastoral is, but what it does;[32] and what it does is to mediate social relations and cultural exchanges among the elite. Such 'demystifying' ('remystifying'?) political readings tend to become exact mirror images of the mystified aesthetic readings they seek to displace. A recent critic of pastoral makes the point well: 'What is occurring here is a kind of aesthetic scapegoating: the creation of a stable category of pure, "empty", idyllic formalism allows for the simultaneous creation of a category of pure, "full" political meaning, of an unmediated real uncontaminated by "the mirror of art".'[33]

The argument partly revolves round both *what* the *Eclogues* represent (if indeed they are referential) and *how* they represent. Iser insists that they are not mimetic in any traditional sense; in his view the tendency to treat them as such vitiates Snell's account, in which the pastoral world serves to represent an internal landscape, as much as any other. The green cabinet is a cabinet of tropes, but there is no straightforwardly 'proper' sense to which those tropes can be reduced (this is a familiar poststructuralist position about textuality in general). Signified and signifier float free, so that the signs 'no longer denote given positions or substances; instead, they insinuate links, unfold directions, and adumbrate realizations in order to reveal what cannot be denoted'.[34] The poems do not imitate politics, instead politics are inscribed within poetry that has become its own concern.[35] This is a subtle reading, not least because it respects the self-imitation of the eclogue world without making that self-imitation autonomous, but it still assumes that the text is subject to a single account. However, one could argue for an intermittent mimetic element in the *Eclogues*; in antiquity some of the poems (which indeed are indebted to mime and display some interest in characterisation) were performed on stage as miniature dramas. Perhaps then, just as the *Eclogues* may be discontinuously allegorical (Servius comments that Tityrus should be understood as Virgil, but not everywhere, only where reason requires, *ubi exigit ratio*), so they are discontinuously mimetic. This fits well enough with the landscape setting, which critics so frequently describe as Arcadian and idealised. It is true that the depiction (like any representation of nature) involves selection but what seems most distinctive is not the element of idealisation (one should not forget the bare rock and bog that surround Tityrus' farm in 1.48–9) but again the discontinuity and disjunction. The landscape is a composite of Theocritus' Sicily and various Italian scenes and indeed Arcadia (perhaps

[31] Smith (1993) 170–1. [32] So Montrose (1983) 416.
[33] Haber (1994) 5. [34] Iser (1993) 31. [35] Iser (1993) 34.

out of Gallus' poetry[36]); but one element in this mix is a precision of visualisation which involves a form of mimesis, like the picture of the goats Meliboeus used to watch hang (*pendere*) on the hills around his farm (1.76) that Wordsworth so admired.[37]

In general the modern critical stress on the structural unity of the collection may serve to conceal the considerable variousness of its contents – the title it was in all probability given by later editors 'Selections' (Virgil's was *Bucolica*) serves to suggest that, certainly in comparison with the *Georgics* or *Aeneid*, it is fragmented as much as unified, composed at it were of chips from the writer's block. Indeed Eclogue 9 operates with what might be termed a poetics of fragmentation as, amid the chaos brought by the land confiscations, the two farmers on their way to town recall snatches of the songs of Menalcas (as we have seen, taken in antiquity to be a mask for Virgil himself); these Virgilian bucolic fragments, two closely imitated from Theocritus, two recalling Roman political life (Caesar's comet, the land confiscations), are in turn framed by a bucolic dialogue which imitates and inverts Theocritus' celebratory Idyll 7, proclaiming, in lines that particularly caught the imagination of Renaissance readers, the impotence of poetry amid the weapons of war (11–13). We could say that what is shown here is precisely the impossibility of creating an enclosed self-sustaining aesthetic domain, but to take this as the final 'message' of the whole book would be to privilege this poem at the expense of, say, Eclogue 6.

'Alternate singing is proper to a Pastoral' (so Rapin, the leading neoclassical theorist of the genre, in 1659).[38] One can imagine a pastoral dialogue debating the issue of aesthetics versus politics (Renaissance writers used the mode to stage religious debates as well as to explore the role of the intellectual in society).[39] The two singing contests, Eclogues 3 and 7, provide different models of dialogue, one ending in compromise and harmony, the other in victory for one party, both agonistic, competitive, the second more abrasively so. Such *amoebaean* poems (as they are called) rarely involve any substantive engagement at the level of content – engagement is rather primarily formal, in terms of rhetorical organisation and sentence structure. In an analogous way the two kinds of critic treated in this chapter seem often to be talking past each other. Yet aesthetics and politics (in this like genres) may be thought of as differential terms rather than ontological entities, in which case each term is necessarily present

---

[36] So Kennedy (1987).   [37] For the reference see the note of Clausen (1994) *ad loc.*
[38] Loughrey (1984) 41 (Thomas Creech's translation of 1684).
[39] Auden's distinction between the Arcadian and the Utopian has a bearing on this dispute; see Loughrey (1984) 90–2 (from *The Dyer's Hand and Other Essays*, 1962) and the poem 'Vespers' from *The Shield of Achilles*.

within the other, at however occluded a level. And more pragmatically we can say that we need both discourses, and the *Eclogues* seem to acknowledge that need. Seamus Heaney, in a series of essays that compose yet another apology for poetry, observes that we want poems to be 'a source of truth and at the same time a vehicle for harmony'.[40] Heaney, whose writing continually reflects the troubles in Ireland, seeks himself 'to affirm that within our individual selves we can reconcile two orders of knowledge which we might call the practical and the poetic; to affirm also that each form of knowledge redresses the other and that the frontier between them is there for the crossing'. If we can find that frontier and recover the Renaissance's sense of the *Eclogues* as both a refined artistic enclosure and an oblique mode of addressing and redressing a variety of worldly concerns, then these ten short poems that for so long were one of the cornerstones of the Western canon may again speak forcefully to our condition.

> Ah me! this many a year
> My pipe is lost, my shepherd's holiday!
> Needs must I lose them, needs with heavy heart
> Into the world and wave of men depart.[41]

Pastoral is often said to be dead or dying. Since 1800 there has been the occasional pastoral deliberately conceived after the ancient model (Matthew Arnold's 'Thyrsis' and 'Scholar Gypsy' for instance), but nothing like the widespread production of earlier centuries. Some would say that the pastoral impulse has simply transferred itself to other forms, the literature of childhood say, like *Cider With Rosie* or Dylan Thomas' 'Fern Hill'. Each such attempt to define an abstracted and essentialised 'spirit' of pastoral – whether as a mode of nostalgia or as putting the complex into the simple (so William Empson, *Some Versions of Pastoral*, 1935) or as 'the recognition of a contrast, implicit or expressed, between pastoral life and some more complex type of civilisation' (W. W. Greg, *Pastoral Poetry and Pastoral Drama*, 1906)[42] – will involve privileging different passages from Virgil and his successors in support of the definition that is proposed. Again we see at work that desire and need to produce a unified account which lies within the very notion of genre, and which indeed, along with the attendant failure of that desire, is, one can argue, thematised *within* pastoral. Thus those who see a connection between pastoral and infancy (including the childhood of the world, recalled in representations of the Golden Age)

---

[40] Heaney (1995) 193, 203.   [41] Arnold, 'Thyrsis' 36–9.
[42] Loughrey (1984) 79, 21.

will inevitably cite the wistful lines in Eclogue 8 (37–41) – so admired by Macaulay who thought them 'the finest ... in the Latin language'[43] – which intertwine the loss of innocence and the end of childhood and the first experience of sexuality:

> saepibus in nostris parvam te roscida mala
> (dux ego vester eram) vidi cum matre legentem.
> alter ab undecimo tum me iam acceperat annus,
> iam fragilis poteram a terra contingere ramos:
> ut vidi, ut perii, ut me malus abstulit error!

> Inside our fence I saw you, as a little girl
> (I was your guide) with mother, picking dewy apples.
> I had just entered upon my thirteenth year,
> And could just reach the brittle branches from the ground.
> I looked and I was lost. How fantasy misled me!   (Guy Lee)

Whether the current preoccupation with the environment and the greening of politics will turn poets back to the *Eclogues* remains to be seen. The editors of the Penguin anthology end their introduction by proclaiming, eloquently, the end of pastoral:

> The separation of life in the town and in the country that the Pastoral demands is now almost devoid of any meaning ... As the countryside becomes ever more efficiently a dormitory for a managerial and executive *elite* ... so the last sad remains of the Pastoral are parcelled up and auctioned off in semi-detached lots. The purchasers of such pastoral remains look around in vain for the Arcadian shepherd or shepherdess to reassure them that they, too, are in Arcadia; but for them, much as for Sidney and Pope, the shepherds are invisible, and now for the simplest of reasons – that there are no shepherds left ... The Pastoral vision might still have some life elsewhere – in the Third World, or in North America perhaps ... but now and in England, the Pastoral, occasional twitches notwithstanding, is a lifeless form, of service only to decorate the shelves of tasteful cottages, 'modernized to a high standard'.[44]

But paradoxically this very denial might itself be seen as a piece of modern pastoral, even a version of Virgil's First Eclogue, a lament for a lost harmony projected onto a past which is timeless but haunted by a sense of temporality, and for an authentic nature free from the discontents and vulgarities of the life of the modern city.

---

[43] See Page's note *ad loc*.   [44] Barrell and Bull (1974) 432–3.

Let us arise, for singers heavy is the shade,
Go, little she-goats, Hesper comes, go home replete.[45]

FURTHER READING

The best modern commentary in English is by Wendell Clausen: *A Commentary on Virgil Eclogues* (Oxford, 1994). Clausen's approach is philological and formalist, with a particular stress on Hellenistic parallels and on the formal artistry of individual poems; cf. his essay 'Theocritus and Virgil', in E. J. Kenney and W. V. Clausen, eds., *The Cambridge History of Classical Literature*: II *Latin Literature* (Cambridge, 1982) pp. 301–19. The earlier commentary by Robert Coleman (Cambridge, 1977) is still worth consulting. The excellent Penguin translation by Guy Lee (Harmondsworth, 1984) contains the Latin text of Mynors, a helpful introduction and brief notes.

Bruno Snell's 'Arcadia: the discovery of a spiritual landscape' is part of his celebrated book *The Discovery of the Mind*, trs. T. G. Rosenmeyer (Cambridge, MA, 1953) 281–309. Perhaps the best modern introduction to the genre is now Paul Alpers, *What Is Pastoral?* (Chicago and London, 1996).

There are several book-length studies of the *Eclogues* in English, of which the best is probably Paul Alpers, *The Singer of the Eclogues* (Berkeley, 1979); others include Michael Putnam, *Virgil's Pastoral Art: Studies in the Eclogues* (Princeton, 1970), and Eleanor Winsor Leach, *Vergil's Eclogues: Landscapes of Experience* (Ithaca, 1974). A representative collection of essays is A. J. Boyle, *Ancient Pastoral* (Victoria, 1975). All this work has a predominantly New Critical flavour.

The poems have been worked over in detail by classicists: for a bibliography 1927–77 see W. W. Briggs in H. Temporini and W. Haase, eds., *Aufstieg und Niedergang der Römischen Welt* II, 31.2 (Berlin, 1981) 1267–1357. There are important extended discussions of individual eclogues by I. M. Le M. DuQuesnay: 'Vergil's First Eclogue', in F. Cairns, ed., *Papers of the Liverpool Latin Seminar* (Liverpool, 1981) 29–182 and 'From Polyphemus to Corydon', in D. A. West and A. J. Woodman, eds., *Creative Imitation and Latin Literature* (Cambridge, 1979) 35–69 (on Eclogue 2). A number of the poems are well discussed in Gordon Williams, *Tradition and Originality in Roman Poetry* (Oxford, 1968).

Much of the most innovative work on pastoral has been done by non-classicists: among the most influential studies are William Empson, *Some Versions of Pastoral* (London, 1935) and Renato Poggioli, *The Oaten Flute: Essays on Pastoral Poetry and the Pastoral Ideal* (Cambridge, MA, 1975). See too the chapter 'Renaissance pastoralism as a paradigm of literary fictionality', in Wolfgang Iser, *The Fictive and the Imaginary: Charting Literary Anthropology* (Baltimore and London, 1993).

For political approaches to pastoral see Raymond Williams, *The Country and the City* (London, 1973); the general introduction and section introductions in John Barrell and John Bull, eds., *The Penguin Book of English Pastoral Verse* (London, 1974); Louis Montrose, 'Of gentlemen and shepherds: the politics of Elizabethan pastoral form', *English Literary History* 50 (1983) 415–59; Annabel

---

[45] I would like to thank Susanna Morton Braund, Catharine Edwards and Duncan Kennedy for help with this chapter.

Patterson, *Pastoral and Ideology: Virgil to Valéry* (Oxford, 1988), a fine study unfortunately marred by inaccuracies and mistranslations.

For genre and the *Eclogues* see especially David M. Halperin, *Before Pastoral: Theocritus and the Ancient Tradition of Bucolic Poetry* (New Haven and London, 1983), and Gian Biagio Conte, *The Rhetoric of Imitation: Genre and Poetic Memory in Virgil and Other Latin Poets* (Ithaca and London, 1986) and *Genres and Readers* (Baltimore and London, 1994).

The *fable convenue* about the place of the *Eclogues* in Latin literary history, as formulated by Clausen and others, may now need to be modified in the light of Alan Cameron's iconoclastic study *Callimachus and His Critics* (Princeton, NJ, 1995).

For the influence and critical reception of the *Eclogues* and the history of pastoral see the essay 'Pastoral' by the editor in Richard Jenkyns, ed., *The Legacy of Rome: A New Appraisal* (London, 1992) pp. 151–75; also Halperin, *Before Pastoral*, pt 1. Brian Loughrey's useful *The Pastoral Mode: a Casebook* (London 1984) contains a collection of early criticism until 1818 together with a representative selection of twentieth-century studies.

9

WILLIAM BATSTONE

Virgilian didaxis: value and meaning in the *Georgics*

The best poem by the best poet.
Dryden

Despite the innumerable labours of many critics, Virgil's *Georgics* remains one of the most fundamentally intractable works of ancient literature.[1] In recent years, most interpreters have agreed that the poem does not really tell us about farming[2] but about ourselves and our world:[3] 'didacticism about agriculture proves metaphor for didacticism about man'.[4] While this consensus may result in part from a modern distaste for and unfamiliarity with agriculture, it has yielded a diversity of compelling interpretations that cannot be wholly explained by changing cultural needs.[5] If we are to understand more fully what this poem does, we need to abandon the interpretive paradigm that seeks some authoritative discursive unity without taking refuge in mere relativism (*quot homines, tot sententiae*). I would like to argue that the diversity of compelling interpretations is part of the *Georgics*' larger value and meaning.

We do not need to choose between a poem about dirt and dung and a poem about metaphysics, because this poem addresses the great abstracts (knowledge, history, power, psychology, ethics, art, death) in the way our lives do: by 'contact' with things, by fictions and interpretations, by witty and elegant postures, and ultimately by the failure of projects and systems. The poem captures a double movement: particulars serve as allegories of human problems and values, while allegories are inhabited by things with their particular tasks, objects, and (sometimes colliding) perspectives. There is interdependence and discontinuity in both the object and the

---

[1] Wilkinson (1969) 3 identified the problem as one of genre: 'What kind of poem is it?' His own answer was that the poem is 'descriptive'. See also Wilkinson (1950) and Otis (1972).

[2] For a positive assessment of Virgil's understanding of agriculture, see Spurr (1986).

[3] 'A handbook showing us ourselves', Putnam (1980) 15; a political–philosophical dialectic, Miles (1980); the poet's truth, Perkell (1989). For a view of the poem as 'a means for examining and calling into question the fundamental assumptions on which all didactic poetry is based' see Kromer (1979).

[4] Boyle (1979); the quotation comes from p. 37.   [5] See 'Further reading' below.

interpretation,[6] and here we find the space which the poem opens for thought and feeling as its tensions, contradictions, and mysteries impinge on the project of knowing-and-doing which seems to underwrite didaxis and exegesis.[7] Here, where the ordinary is not ordinary, where the true becomes untrue and material excess meets interpretive inadequacy, I find the opening for meaning and the value of the poem.[8]

Orpheus and Aristaeus

> This multiplicity of possible interpretations does not discredit the strictness of the thought content. For all true thought remains open to more than one interpretation – and this by reason of its nature.
>
> Heidegger

The end of Book 4 is exemplary of the poem's interdependencies and discontinuities.[9] Here, two obvious fictions interweave their threads: the story of Aristaeus ending in his discovery of *bougonia* and the inserted story of Orpheus and Eurydice ending in both of their deaths. The tales are carefully linked in that Aristaeus sets in motion the events that destroy Orpheus and Eurydice (he attempts to rape her) while Orpheus sets in motion the

---

[6] Supplementarity by which readers, as they perform texts, create poems by filling the 'gaps' of signification and appropriating the text for new circumstances is lucidly discussed and richly applied as a hermeneutic concept by Martindale (1993a) 11–18, 37–9. I am emphasising here another aspect of the situation, namely the way in which a collection of signs may create an excess of signification (contradiction, tension, polyphony). This requires a discounting of elements, the opposite of 'gap-filling'. In both cases readers are at stake and appropriate (by addition or subtraction) the poems they perform. In this double movement the reader conceals and discloses in a fashion precisely complementary to the work's disclosures and concealments.

[7] In this regard I am trying to move beyond the unresolved oppositions which Perkell (1989) so sensitively elaborates (see e.g. 139–45). Her 'oppositions' require reified and distinct entities which I believe the poem ultimately does not support: in other words, we do not find victor opposed to vanquished, profit to art, or past to future, nor do we have the elements of these oppositions (e.g. of precept and myth) hierarchically arranged (see e.g. 177 and Perkell's argument for the poet's truth as higher than the farmer's knowledge); rather, we find one inhabiting, becoming, concealing, and revealing, the other.

[8] Cf. Heidegger's notion of *Lichtung* as the function of *Stelle* and of the nature of truth as unconcealedness. 'At bottom, the ordinary is not ordinary; it is extra-ordinary, uncanny. The nature of truth, that is, of unconcealedness, is dominated throughout by denial ... Truth, in its nature, is un-truth. We put the matter this way in order to serve notice with a possibly surprising trenchancy, that denial in the manner of concealment belongs to unconcealedness as clearing. The proposition, "the nature of truth is untruth", is not, however, intended to state that truth is at bottom falsehood' (Heidegger (1971) esp. pages 50–6).

[9] It has accordingly produced an exemplary number of interpretations: Griffin (1979) 61 reviews seventeen interpretations within the period of 1967–79.

events that lead to Aristaeus' discovery of *bougonia* (he destroys Aristaeus' bees). Critics attempt to unravel and account for these tales by posing polar oppositions: Aristaeus is heroic, effective, capable of learning, while Orpheus is ineffective, forgetful and victimised; Aristaeus is the public man, arrogant, self-assertive, indifferent to his guilt, while Orpheus is the poet, the sympathetic and passionate figure of love and human values; Aristaeus is Iron Age man interested in exchange value and the future, while Orpheus values the individual, the irreplaceable and the past.

There is always some truth to these articulations, but in the end they are partial and founder. The figures merge as they separate: both are passionate, self-absorbed, and destructive of others; both destroy Eurydice but remain indifferent to guilt.[10] If the greatness (and seductiveness) of Orpheus' passion gains our sympathy, its self-indulgence (which cannot be separated from his backward glance) is shared by Aristaeus, who lusts for Eurydice and longs for new bees. Both recall the farmer, staving off the backward pull of entropy (see 1.199–203). Both seek to dominate nature and death. They are the victims of their own capacities – and these capacities are both remarkably similar and inextricably linked to their greatness.

The conceptual closure that would categorise them as symbolic abstracts fails even more radically when those abstracts are located in the contextually lived lives of the characters. Orpheus' grief is excessive, as is his desire for vengeance (*haudquaquam ob meritum poenas*, 4.455): but is this a transference of self-hatred? He did fail both Eurydice and himself. If so, the heroic beauty of his song derives its subject from loss and its depth from denial and guilt. On the other hand, Aristaeus' benefaction was originally a religious ritual (*modus orandi*, 4.537) performed as an act of atonement: he is an accidental hero, a chance symbol. Another example: Orpheus values the human and irreplaceable (Eurydice), Aristaeus desires economy, a replacement. But the bee's lack of individuality supports Virgil's thematics of the communal hive, and it is an experiential fact to the extent that we do not keep pet bees. It would be ridiculous for Aristaeus to want exactly the same bees back. Thus, Orpheus and Aristaeus exceed the polar oppositions by which we know them with an uncanny likeness and they elude those same constructs by virtue of particular circumstances. This is what makes them hard to think and necessary to rethink.

Interpretive decisions to identify, align and evaluate the elements of the text in one way or another disambiguate the poem at the expense of denying other identifications and alignments. The poem addresses this

---

[10] Perkell (1989) 69, calls them 'elaborately parallel'; my observations extend some of her observations and contest some of the differences she sees.

dilemma: it ends with a story of interpretation which becomes part of the labyrinth of thought. Aristaeus is sent to Proteus to learn the cause and remedy for his loss. Proteus gives only the cause (Orpheus); Cyrene interprets the remedy, but she adds new causes: the Nymphs and Eurydice. Thus she points to both the excess and the gap in Proteus' story, but in doing so raises other questions: Did she know all along or is she just being careful not to forget an offended *numen*? Is the ritual she prescribes different from the Egyptian *bougonia* because it was really the Egyptians who turned a religious act into an economic remedy? In fact, her interpretation is contingent and practical, and so it cannot be ours: she forgets the blame that belongs to Orpheus and the matrons who tear Orpheus limb from limb. Cyrene as a figure of practical disambiguation represents the problems of praxis and disambiguation: they must add, subtract, and are always local.

The book and the poem ends, then, with a vignette in which victims and heroes are similar, interdependent and inconsistent, where passion rescues and destroys, where destruction meets vengeance ... or not, where divine benefactions are the accidental outcomes of supplements and precarious interpretations, where beauty derives its energy from loss and self-loathing, and where interpretation is precarious and practical. In these combinations we approach something of the *Georgics'* inarticulate strength: it is the gathering of the discrepancies and harmonies of our presence in the world into word and thought.

Of course, the poem does not end with Cyrene's interpretation. After the *bougonia* is enacted and the bees appear – really some kind of 'drone-fly' – they swirl like a storm cloud and hang from the pliant boughs like a cluster of grapes. It is Proteus' world again, where (drone-flies are) bees are a cloud is a cluster of grapes, where the promise and fantasy of agricultural ease is composed with the dangers of storms. But even this suspense and closure is not the end. For the poem ends again, with another storm cloud as Caesar thunders in the east and another image of ease as Virgil recalls his ignoble leisure and Tityrus reclining in the shade – an ease which is itself protected and threatened by Caesar.

The poem ends circling back to the grapes of Book 2 and the invocation to Caesar in Book 1. Outside the poem, I may believe in success or Caesar or entropy or order; I inevitably make (and unmake) decisions about guilt and innocence, about the practical or economic worth of *bougonia* or the spiritual value of myth; I decide what to do. This poem cannot rescue me from those precarious inevitabilities. But it provides a place where conflicting realities coexist and inhabit each other. Here, readers may move, be moved and linger – they may experience in complex figures the violence of success, the beautiful pathos of failure, and the contingency of 'knowing'. This I take as the value of the *Georgics* and I find it more bracing than a univocal message. We forget that whatever we see depends on what we do not see. The *Georgics* keeps reminding us of what we do not see. For truth is always the undoing of truth: this is the nature of truth as untruth. 'Nor does it mean that truth is never itself but, viewed dialectically, is always also its opposite.'[11] 'And when man no longer sees the one side as *one* side, he has lost sight of the other side as well.'[12]

In what follows, I will try to show that Virgil continually presses the resources of didaxis in the direction of multiplicity and, from the discursive point of view, excess. In formal and in substantive matters the poem fragments as it unifies the reader's perspective and creates a simultaneous sense of continuity, discontinuity and interdependence. It is my implicit argument that this 'failure of message' can enrich our lives even as it exceeds our grasp. It is what must be thought.

Generic features

Although ancient critics seem to treat didaxis not as a genre, but as a particular mode of *epos*, modern readers reasonably identify a set of practices and goals in which 'didactic poets' participate. A brief discussion of three formal elements – the statement of subject matter, the invocation, and the addressee[13] – will suggest how Virgil places his poem within these norms at the same time that he is modifying and manipulating them in specific and typical ways.

Beginning with the subject matter

But does the tree stand 'in our consciousness', or does it stand on the meadow? Does the meadow lie in the soul, as experience, or is it spread out there on earth? Is the earth in our head? Or do we stand on earth?
Heidegger

Beginnings present distinct problems. Epic poetry boldly stated the subject matter in the first word of the poem as a noun: anger, a hero, and so on. Virgil in the *Aeneid* designated his subject with two nouns, 'arms and the man', and so drew attention to a dynamic relationship, rather than a thing. Didactic epos follows epic: the poet begins either with the name of the god

---

[11] Heidegger (1971) 54; see also the discussion of Halliburton (1981) 42–5.
[12] Heidegger (1968) 43.
[13] Ancient critics identify only the addressee as necessary to didaxis: 'so he [Virgil] writes to Maecenas as Hesiod to Perses, Lucretius to Memmius' (Servius, *praefatio in G.*).

he invokes (Hesiod, Aratus, Lucretius) or his nominal subject (Nicander). And the poets who begin invoking a god later transit to the body of the didaxis with the name of their subject.

In this context the beginning of the *Georgics* is extraordinary (I offer an overly literal translation which at the obvious expense of elegance tries to preserve the order of ideas within Virgil's lines and the resonance of at least some of the particular terms):

> What makes the fields happy, beneath what star,
> Maecenas, would it be proper to turn the land, to join vines
> to elms, what should be the concern for cattle, what regimen for keeping
> a herd, for the thrifty bees how much experience –
> from here I begin to sing.

Critics and scholiasts have labelled this 'a table of contents': four subjects (crops, vines, herds and bees) in four lines representing the four books of the *Georgics*. Such a summary, however, makes tidy and secure a literary experience which is anything but tidy and secure. The subject is articulated as (at least) five questions, some elliptical, most enjambed. The language designates the particular things (field, land, vine, elm, cattle, herd, bees) at the same time that it points to qualities – happiness, concern (or passion), regimen (or culture), thrift, experience – that inform a life. As a result, abstract issues of human life join agricultural particulars and suggest the inextricable interpenetration of the practical and the spiritual, the objective and subjective, the material earth and the inhabited world. This interpenetration is actually richer and more elusive in the Latin than the English translation suggests.

'What makes the fields happy?' The term for 'happy', *laetas*, may in Latin designate an objective quality of the land ('teeming' or 'rich', cognate with the Latin term for 'dung', *laetamen*), or the way success makes us feel ('happy', *laetitia*). The term *segetes*, 'fields', may refer to the land where you plant corn, to the ploughed and fertilised field, or to the standing corn crop. The adjective–noun unit, which we know was a farmer's idiom, gives only nominal stability to a process that drifts from cow manure to human joy. While the words make the precise reference elusive, they point to the coinherence of earth and dung, the world of economic success (which will mean hard work and even unhappiness), and human happiness.

Similarly throughout these lines, Virgil's language sets forth his subject as a gathering of coinherent elements. The caretaker's 'concern' joins the erotic passion of his bulls in *cura boum*; the bees' thrift either informs human knowledge or is protected by human experience. Only by *fiat* can we make Virgil's opening mean something didactively singular and secure.

And whenever we do that, our rejected readings return in the poem: bulls do fall in love in Book 3, and the experience of bees seems to offer lessons to humans in Book 4. The fact is that the poem's language makes accessible an indeterminacy about the distinction between 'the farm' as something we control and act upon for our purposes and as something that gathers us into its control and power. The introduction's diction, syntax and structure gather round the reader an unruly conflict of things and images, a world at once precarious and full. There is nothing like this in ancient didaxis or ancient epos.

Beginning again: invocation

Virgil's invocation is similarly complex, and similarly shifty and opaque. Typically, a didactic poet invokes a single god before turning to his subject. Virgil invokes an indeterminate number of gods. His model was Varro's *Res rusticae*, a prose treatise on agriculture, which first invoked an 'agricultural pantheon' (including Mildew, Moisture and Good Luck). Varro secured and negotiated his expanded invocation by good humour and explicit directorial statements. 'First I will invoke the gods ... those twelve gods who are especially helpful to farmers' (1.1.4–5) and 'Therefore, having summoned the gods ...' (1.1.7). Virgil's concatenation takes Varro several steps further. First, he abandons directorial statement and, in the middle of line 5, he recontextualises his multiple subjects: 'You, O clearest lights of the heaven.' This allows what began in the Nicanderian secular mode to switch mid-line to the Aratean and Hesiodic mode. We are reoriented, but as we move from dirt and bees to the gods and the heavens, we find the 'lights of heaven', a reference to the same powers at work in line 1, 'beneath what star to turn the earth'. Beginning again, then, we arrive at a new place, only to discover that we were already there. In this way, Virgil makes the very beginning of his poem address what we might call 'the problem of beginning', namely that one is always beginning and that one's beginnings are always already in another context. Not coincidentally, this 'problem' is the very one occluded by the typical didactic opening: for example, 'Venus, mother of Rome. ... Be with me as I explain the nature of things.'

A close examination of the details of Virgil's invocation will reveal similar poetic gestures throughout: these 'clearest lights' may be the sun and the moon, or the next two gods, *Liber et alma Ceres* (who have themselves been identified with the sun and the moon), or the twelve constellations. Thus, by an elegant irony, the 'clearest lights' violate Varronian clarity at the very moment they are called 'clearest lights', but, on the other hand, it is this very lack of clarity which creates the blurred boundary of numinous power which is part of the experience of knowing the deities that oversee and inhabit the agricultural world. As the invocation proceeds, we find ourselves in a movement from the Roman gods Liber and Ceres backwards to Grecian myths and suggestions of chaotic origins and forward again to wheatfields, water, and wine. We are caught in the web of progress and cultural syncretism, of Alexandrian learning and artifice, as well as the forces that inhabit the wheat and the grapes.

Virgil invokes and evokes not only the divine forces that play around and within the fields but the various traditions of thought and feeling within which we conceptualise their immanence. Even Virgil's closure, 'O gods and goddesses all, whose care looks over the fields' (1.21), suggests that we have here only a representative selection from a larger pantheon. But this closural gesture is not the end: Virgil calls finally on Octavian, the future Augustus, a 34-year-old young man in whom Rome found its greatest hopes and fears. He is, of course, another example of polyvalent and precarious potential.

Praeceptor and addressee[14]

Ancient didaxis retained through its addressee a personal orientation and a mimetic potential.[15] The tradition offers a great range of addressees. Perses helps Hesiod to articulate the danger of injustice which sets brother against brother. Memmius helps Lucretius set Epicurean values in a Roman world of war. Even Aratus' impersonal 'you' becomes the context of Zeus's general beneficence and the measure of Zeus as 'Great wonder, great benefit to men' (15). Virgil's addressees are unique in range and conception.

The first addressee is Maecenas, friend of Octavian and member of the power elite in Rome, literary patron, and self-indulgent *litteratus*. Virgil could hardly have found a more suggestive addressee. This potential is protected in two ways. First, he does not need instruction; in fact, he suggested the poem (3.41). Second, no particular aspect of his life or influence is specified. He is Virgil's moral support and the force that gives the project depth and breadth (3.42, 2.41), but his presence also suggests the poem's vulnerable position before other powers. He seems to mediate between Caesar's heroic accomplishments and the *tenuis labor* of Virgil's Callimachean project (2.41, 44). Because he straddles so many worlds and yet is

---

[14] The discussion here quotes and paraphrases from my dissertation, Batstone (1984) 17–41, esp. 31–8. See now all the contributors to Schiesaro et al. (1993), esp. Schiesaro's own contribution to that volume.

[15] See Mitsis (1993) 123–4: 'Didactic epic, by its very nature, calls to our attention the process of instruction. Moreover, it does so by positing an internal addressee to receive the poet's instruction. In effect, when we are reading the poem, the poet allows us to witness him in a therapeutic session with his addressee.'

not precisely defined, he becomes part of the fullness which inhabits both Virgil's subject and his audience. He is an equally congenial recipient of political allegory, philosophical allegory, Hellenistic poetasting, or agricultural practicality.

There are other addressees. Caesar, always at a distance, consistently associated with war and political life, is asked to join Virgil's project (1.40–2). The reader is now singular, now plural, sometimes addressed as a farmer, sometimes assumed to be a *litteratus*, sometimes a contemporary and patriotic Roman. One may add as addressees objects of praise, improvisatory apostrophes, and the sympathetic you.[16] They are all part of the multiplicity of Virgil's subject and help create the many voices and perspectives of Virgil's praeceptor. Thus, in a single brief passage (1.276–82), Virgil translates Hesiodic superstition with Catonic brevity, 'Flee the fifth [day of the month]!'; he then proceeds with a learned mistranslation of Hesiod in which 'Oath' (Greek, *Horkos*) has become 'Pale Orcus', while 'Earth', the material subject of Book 1, is creating monsters who conspire to threaten the structure of heaven. This mythic danger, however, becomes Virgil's Olympic moment, the opportunity to contest Homer's version of the same event: 'Ossa on Olympus, and leafy Pelion on Ossa' (Homer, *Od.* 11.304–5) becomes 'to pile Ossa on Pelion, indeed, and to roll leafy Olympus on Ossa'. Writing like this creates a space without direction – where life's practical urgency and the shadowy dangers of myth are foil to and foiled by the elegant verse and its learned pretensions. In seven lines we find that (1) trouble in the world is deeper and more mysterious than Hesiod allowed; (2) we need simple and direct action; (3) superstition gives habitation to real fears; and (4) play, distraction, literary elegance and competition are part of how we make it through. This is rather like the systems analysed in chaos theory: balance is maintained by a continually changing centre. In Virgil, the clash of perspectives remains unresolved, not just because life is chaotic, but because balance is as well.

This polyphony is an extension of didactic resources, especially those exploited by Varro.[17] In the first book of the *Res rusticae*, Varro brings on his conversants, a random collection who meet at the temple of Tellus. As the conversation turns to Italy, the Socratic (or perhaps scholiastic) Agrius discourses on the world as divided into its zones by Eratosthenes. Fundanius, however, is more interested in his midday nap. But when the conversation turns to the praise of Italy, he too has a store of authorities: Pacuvius,

---

[16] See Oksala (1978) 56.

[17] On Hesiod and Aratus, see Griffith (1983); Clay (1993) 23–34; Bing (1993) 99–129; and Gagarin (1990) 173–84, esp. 181.

Homer, Cato. Finally, the group sees Stolo and Scrofa arriving and admits that these are the men who speak with authority on the subject. Their ancestral and personal connections with farming and government produce allusions to the Licinian Law, to Roman progress, to Campanian land divisions. Thus Varro uses his *personae* and their personal and family connections as well as their chance activities (like looking at a map of Italy) to touch upon many of the connections and significances that agriculture had for a Roman. The variety of characters allows the different perspectives to arise naturally and the reader is co-opted into sharing them, into seeing agriculture in the broad physical terms of Agrius, the broad historical terms of Fundanius, the narrow, practical and Aristotelian terms of Scrofa and, finally, in terms of the contemporary Roman context as Varro's first book ends with news of a riot and a murder. That the reader of Varro gathers in these different perspectives (and the list is not complete) is important. The Varronian dialogue, unlike the Platonic dialogue, does not move through dialectic to a conclusion; it re-creates the voices of individuals as it protects the camaraderie of the group it vivifies.[18]

It is my suggestion that Virgil, beginning in some sense with the addressees, contexts and complex ambiguities of Hesiod, took the multiple perspectives of Varro's conversants as a model for his own multivalent voice in the *Georgics*, a voice that is never bound or defined by Merula's practical, day-to-day apiculture, or Appius' praise of their incredible apian nature and their *civitates*, by Claudius' antique frugality or by Axius' contemporary luxury. Virgil realised that it was, at least for him, a fiction of limited value to separate our many ways of thinking and knowing into different persons speaking with separate voices. The full life of mind and feeling requires the continual impingement from within of, say, the voice of Axius upon the voice of Claudius – not, of course, without some Callimachean flourishes. In this way, the leisurely values of urbane literary play may meet the need for timely labour, the sympathy of man for nature and her losses can confront the indifferent press of necessity and chance, an allegorical and philosophically expansive worldliness may founder on the stubborn factitude of the material earth of the poem, and the objective system with its precise precepts may be informed by the subjective experience of actors in contexts. As the poem explores the demands of action and knowledge, it creates a deeply contextualised and lyricised sense of the complex and conflicting variety in what things are. This is

---

[18] See, for instance, the disagreements about *pastio* and their 'resolution' in 1.2.21 and 2.1.11, and the discussion of modern *luxuria* and *avaritia* as it pertains to the profitable aviary in 3.4.1. The discussion of Bakhtin (1984) 112–20, and his view of dialogism are also relevant to Varro's handling of his agricultural dialogue, *Res rusticae*.

what allows the poem to ponder its mundane and practical subject matter as well as the powerful allegories and metaphors that arise from the soil, and the limits and failures of those allegories and of didaxis itself.

Georgic didaxis: examples

Knowing will never know what thinking is doing.
Hannah Arendt

Didaxis should be about knowing, and practical didaxis especially should be about knowing things, what to do with things, and when. Meaning in the *Georgics*, however, is so difficult to name because the epistemological certainty presupposed by didaxis is exactly what the poem puts in question. The heterogeneity of being is what provokes thought. In the *Georgics* this experience is in large part a function of discontinuity and contradiction held together by the simultaneous presence of continuity and harmony. While the poem's dynamic or temporal process moves the reader from one centre of value and meaning to another,[19] a standing polyphony (the function of slippage in the sign and the signified as well as of interpretive memory) makes diverse and sometimes contradictory meanings simultaneously accessible. The result is that, while readers move from centre to centre, they are always in a field whose potential exceeds their grasp but whose resonance is familiar: they are always in the middle. A few examples will illustrate.

In mediis rebus

Virgil's beginnings put us in the midst of things. Even the beginning of didaxis catches the reader in a collision between description and precept: 'In the new spring, when the chilly water melts on the white mountains and Zephyr loosens the crumbling clod, then let the bull already groan at the deep-pressed plough' (1.43–5). Here the impulse to enjoy spring (cf. the happy fields) meets the need for immediate labour. But with the adverb 'already' and the precondition that the plough is pressed into the ground, the order to make the bull groan requires that both the reader and the farmer must in a sense catch up after chasing breezes. The celebration of spring will be postponed to the middle of Book 2 (the 'Praise of spring', 315–45), but the very next lines revel in the beaming land and the gleaming plough. Virgil created this complexity in part by ignoring tradition: in agricultural didaxis neither spring nor the calendar comes first because

---

[19] For a dialectical interpretation, see Miles (1980); for a reader-response interpretation, see Batstone (1988).

there are preliminaries to labour (location, crops, tools and so on). Virgil, of course, knows this and in a few lines he advises, 'and before we cleave the unknown plain ... care should be taken first to learn the winds and weather ...' (50–2). For a second time, the reader is conceptually behind. This verse gathers round the contingencies of engaged agency.

The middle requires knowledge of the past and our surroundings, but also of the process we are part of. In Book 1, Virgil's military metaphors for farming develop into the self-destructive civil war that destroys the field. Something at work in our labour destroys our labour, but when did it appear? Critics tell us that the military metaphor begins at line 99:[20] 'the farmer commands the fields'. But the poem has already spoken of 'breaking through' (98), of 'shattering' (94), of the 'hard race of men' (63) and nature's 'eternal treaties' (60), of the 'palms' of victory (59), crops that do not require 'orders' (55), of 'cutting the main with steel' (50), 'lust for domination' (37) and the march of stars in the sky (6). The language of violence and control is part of the poem's diction. When military destruction becomes ineluctable, one realises that it was there all along, growing from seeds of order and violence, power and victory, since the poem began, since before the poem began, and the poem catches the reader within the developing force of the metaphor. Military language and metaphors just like many military virtues (and vices) grew out of the Roman experience with the land and their ideology of that experience.[21] It was part of the web in which their lives were woven, and this web is rewoven (and to that extent unwoven) in the *Georgics* itself.

Our prior implication of the forces that threaten or destroy appears in the metaphors by which we construct our lives and weave together our hopes and fears, our strengths and weaknesses. A brief example will illustrate the density of Virgil's imagination.

> That cornfield finally answers the prayer of the greedy
> farmer, which twice has felt the sun, twice the cool.
> That one's granary the great harvest bursts. (1.47–9)

'The greedy farmer' who prays and labours is an ethically ambivalent image. If the pious virtues of agricultural success demand a morally suspect affect, what we customarily blame is demanded by our practical life. This ambivalence is further complicated by line 49: practical success depends on a practically suspect desire. With the oxymoron of 'pious avarice' and the hyperbole of 'burst granaries' the reader must negotiate contradiction by

---

[20] See, e.g. Thomas (1988) *ad loc.*   [21] See Miles (1980) 1–63.

denial and the boundary between success and excess by the restraint of
hyperbole (verbal excess). In the web in which our lives are woven, reading
mimes action in untangling and restraining the figures of our thought.

System and context

> Do I contradict myself? Very well, then, I contradict
> myself. I am large and contain multitudes.
> Walt Whitman

Virgil's didaxis returns us to the vulnerability of our engaged selves, not
to closure or an imagined, objective security. The objective, mechanistic
certainty of signs that end Book 1 is a good example of this process:
they hold together man's hope and man's despair. 'We are able to predict
storms in an uncertain sky', Virgil assures the farmer. But, as the language
stresses greater certainty, there is a growing and inevitable sense of vulnerability. The 'surest signs' foretell destructive storms (439–60) and civil war
(465–6), and when war comes, the sun's pity signals more war (489–90).
Our only protection is, in fact, our ignorance and the hope that the signs
we rely upon are false. In the midst of this civil chaos Virgil imagines a
diminutive post-bellum farmer still hacking clods in the field where the
great bones of his ancestors amaze him. This curious return both to the
middle and to humour is immediately followed by an appeal to Caesar. In
a continuous movement, then, we find science and hope and certainty leading to fear and failure, ignorance, guilt and prayer. But it is a prayer that
returns us to the invocation (soliciting pity), back to the middle, and, since
prayer is a form of hope, back to our resources and our resourcelessness.

Another passage is more richly complex and compact. Probably no lines
in Virgil have received more commentary per word than the conclusion
of the 'Theodicy': 'then came the various *artes*. Labour conquered everything, damnable labour, and lack pressing on in the midst of hardship'
(1.145–6). Critics have debated whether the *labor* Virgil imagines is successful (labour conquers all hardships) or has failed (everywhere labour
was needed). I suggest that these lines compose the divergent and discordant being of *labor*: simultaneously victory and defeat, effort and the need
for effort, artifice and the failure of artifice. The Jovian dispensation had
promised *artes*, and *artes* we got: navigation, astrology, hunting, fishing,
and tools. But as the Jovian age moves forward toward the present, *labor*
itself expands its scope and ethical implications: from planting and count-
ing stars (134 and 137) to 'lashing the rivers' (141) and 'dragging the sea'
(142). The delicate balance and epigrammatic closure of *tum variae venere
artes. labor omnia vicit* (145) comes in the midst of this movement. The

form promises gnomic resolution,[22] but *omnia* is hyperbolic, and the past tense ('has conquered') is false to experience. The line flirts with our hopes at the very moment that it undermines its own epigrammatic certainty. It seems to be about arrival, victory, and closure, but we are not arriving. We are already moving on, out of the variety of the *artes*, back to the intention of Jupiter, back to *labor* and lack and uncertainty.

Commentators say that *labor*'s epithet, *improbus*, comes as a surprise.[23] It's no surprise: we knew it was coming since before the fisherman was lashing the stream. We regret getting where we were going all along. Sifted by the Jovian dispensation and the progress of history, *labor* turns out to be as various as the *artes* which stand both as memorials of past *labor* and as promises of future *labor*. A few victories, inevitable failures; we are left with dangers and hopes. Since we must endure *labor*, we should not forget the many things it is and our many feelings about it. To gather together this essentially human complexity and then to return to weeding, shooing off birds, pruning overgrowth and prayer is an extraordinary evocation of the human condition, and for the reader, any reader, to be able to do it in the space of these verses is a valuable spiritual achievement. It may be something that we can only do within the confines and luxuries of art. But that makes it no less valuable than the charity we have only in prayer.

Extended implications

> There is no 'the truth', 'a truth' – truth is not one thing or even a
> system. It is an increasing complexity.
> Adrienne Rich

If beginnings are always in the middle and middles are multiply contextualised, then one should expect to find projects imbricated with projects just as one finds innocent beginnings extending into unforeseen conclusions. In Book 3 Virgil explores the complex dynamic of *eros*. A herd requires breeding, *eros* must be controlled and focused, while its hunger (and fullness) must be cultivated and increased. The farmer is playing with fire, but he must, and one of the things that Book 3 does is to set our dreams of control and victory in the context of the *eros* that drives those dreams. The selection of horses is our example. Virgil begins with a line from Ennius, adapting the crane's jerky motions to the gawky movement of a foal (76). But soon both the prizes of poetic primacy and the passions of historical epic are at work: the foal boldly sets forth on this path like the Callimachean

---

[22] Cf. Sallust, *B.C.* 7.6 *virtus omnia domuerat.* [23] See Perkell (1986).

poet (77), then, like Iron Age man, he tries the rivers and the sea (77–8). Soon he hears the empty sound of war (79) and then the sound of war itself (83). His hoof responds with its resounding ring (88) and we enter the realm of Greek poets (90), of the chariots of Mars and Achilles (91), and of Saturn, disguised as a horse, fleeing discovery by Rhea when he tried to seduce Philyra. As he flees, he fills Pelion with the sound of his whinny (94). The passage is a *tour de force* of energies spilling over, of physical and literary boundaries being crossed, of something in the air, on the wind, a sound from afar calling.

The very energies that the farmer must direct (out of his own 'love of praise') are energies that will not stand still, that burst barriers, cross rivers and mountains.[24] In the chariot race, driver and horse merge as their fiery emotions burn the axles of the car. These are the energies of Virgil's poem: 'but we have crossed the unmeasured spaces of the plain and now it is time to unyoke the smoking necks of our steeds' (2.541–2), and the energies that fuel civil war: 'just so the chariots stream forth from their pens. . . .' (1.512–14). The opportunity to improve the present and to fulfil dreams derives from *eros*' capacity to exceed, to drive mad, and to create violence and destruction in the world. This joins man and beast, or god and beast and woman, or Greek and Latin, or poet and tradition in the boundary-crossing, pen-bursting drive for life. The didaxis is not simply about what controls are useful or necessary, but about the necessary and hyperbolic force that drives our dreams, our passions and our poetry, and fuels civil war.

Symbolic coherence

I have just been thinking, and I have come to a very important decision.
These are the wrong sort of bees.
A. A. Milne

Before closing Book 4 with Orpheus and Aristaeus, Virgil meditates on bees and community. Virgil's bees have a rich society with home, father-land, ancestral gods, and so on. They are devoted to law and country; their life is impersonal, collective, motivated by a love of possessions, a love of flowers and the glory of honey-making. These 'virtues' have tempted critics to see in the hive a model for human communities or, at least, a reflection of traditional Roman values, and Varro shows that such a view was tra-ditional. But there is another side to the bees: they are a negative model for Romans. They inhabit their finely wrought homes and indulge their

---

[24] See Miles (1975) 177–97 (still the best overall discussion) and Gale (1991).

fickle spirits in play. They display an Oriental devotion to their king, and this devotion is the very cause of civil destruction, both when there are two kings and when there is no king.

But the bees never were a human allegory: they do not (according to Virgil) reproduce sexually. Within the economy of the poem, this is the nominal solution to the disruptive power of sexual love, but, as a solution, it simultaneously destroys the human analogy and requires the human invention of *bougonia*. At the same time, it does not free the bee community of the essential problem inherent in the erotic energies of life: the bees have their loves, 'love of possession', and their glory, 'glory of honey-making'. They also have their bee-wars with trembling hearts, sounds in the air, and the bursting gates. In fact, bee-wars elucidate the impossibility of a bee-model. When the keeper ends the battle with a handful of dust, it may be a poignant reminder that human battles, too, end in a handful of dust, but the problem is that there is no human keeper to cast the dust. Similarly, the beekeeper is told to examine the warring kings and kill the inferior one: was this the way to choose between Antony and Octavian? There is no principle of human governance here. The model fails precisely when it is needed and precisely because the allegory does not work for men. Instead, it recontextualises human problems and imagines human vulnerability without offering an apian solution.

The failure of allegory, however, is not without wit and humour. In a recapitulation of the major themes of 'plague' and 'signs', the beekeeper is advised to look for 'unambiguous signs' of disease in his population. Varro had already remarked that fuzzy bees were a bad sign, and then he described what a fuzzy bee would look like: 'dusty' (3.16.20). Virgil takes this relatively sensible and realistic description one step further: the beekeeper is to examine the tiny bee faces and if they are thin and deformed with bristly hair, the bee is sick. Virgil's contribution is a change that presses credulity – *tenuis labor*, indeed – as it emphasises the incommensurability of men and bees.

How then should we see what Virgil is doing here? Clearly the bees represent many real virtues, but they also represent the impossibility of projecting our world onto nature. They allow us to contemplate a kind of utopian society, with its admirable qualities, the reality upon which it must exist, the necessary consequences of assumptions like asexual reproduction, as well as the impracticality and impossibility of human stability on those terms. The allegory does not work, both because the bees are continually becoming or remaining bees and because they are themselves a multiple allegory: of what to be, of what not to be, of what we cannot be. It's not that they are real bees in one passage and an allegory in another;

rather, they continually resonate with all the ramifications of their potential, including their contradictory allegorical potential – they are a model, a bad model, a failed model, a hilarious example, a problem, and a model for how models fail us. Here is the space for thought where the poem's excess creates interpretive inadequacy.

Shifting the conceptual centre

The *Georgics'* four books divide the work of the farm into four general areas: ploughing and field crops; trees and vines; large and small herd animals; and bees. It has long been recognised that this material organisation corresponds to two other movements. One in which the outcomes of man's labour result alternately in failure (war), success (harvest), failure (destructive passion) and success (the restoration of the hive); another in which man's relationship to agricultural reality changes from the combative to the educative to the controlling to the protective. How these movements hold together is a significant question for critics of the poem.

It is my view that, in an important sense, they do not hold together: life modelled on or from the perspective of a vineyard is importantly discontinuous with life modelled on a stable. As the poem explores the implications of its different material centres and the metaphors that arise from them, we find that the world changes, that we change, and that our dreams and fears change. It is not that one view is more right than another, or that we must decide whether Virgil is optimistic or pessimistic; rather the poem's movement and organisation allows us to explore the particular implications of our contact with particular things and then, as our material object shifts, to find a different centre. None of these material relationships is ideal or sufficient to model our more complex relationships with ourselves and the world, but neither are they simplistic irrelevancies; as things, as metaphors and allegories, as contexts, they are the stuff of our contact with the world.

The desire to totalise the *Georgics* is not, however, unfounded. It is part of the poem's movement, as indeed it seems to be part of life, that when the centre shifts we uncannily find ourselves either back where we already were or part of a movement that has its own specific rhythm. I would like here to characterise from the broadest perspective the overall movement of the poem in a way that suggests its shifting centres. Book 1 takes its bearings from the harrowing labour of the field and man's militaristic dominance over nature; what develops is the intrusion of the real, on the one hand, of wars we never meant to fight as we set out to plough the land and, on the other, of forces with which we were complicitous. We cannot escape labour, in part because we are the cause of our labour. Then, Book

2 begins, 'So far, cultivation of fields and the stars of the sky', as if we could set aside the civil war and get back to work – which we can, which the diminished future farmer of Book 1 had already done. This new book imagines man's co-operation with nature and nature's response. Labour reappears, and weather to be feared (2.397–419). The vineyard stretches before the eye straight and orderly like a legion deployed in columns in the field; the land gleams with the flash of swords (2.273–87). The new centre does not change the world or man (though it is where Virgil imagines impossible grafts of fruit trees); it recomposes them in new configurations. But nature is, finally, not commensurate with our aspirations until contaminated by our artifice and filled with our fictions. By the end of Book 2, those aspirations fade into the dreams they always were, located in a past that draws us on.

Book 3 explores the other side of the same coin: if not grafted to nature or dominating it, then controlling it. But we cannot be separate from nature because we are ineluctably a part of it: human passion infects horse and chariot, and human artifice becomes nature's way of spreading the plague from animal to man. In Book 4 the centre shifts again as the poem imagines community and the benevolent care of bees. The keeper cultivates an allegory which, like the hive, eventually fails. The understanding we may gain from contemplating the bees (and there is some to be gained) is no more sufficient for our human projects and human passions than the world and labour of Book 1, the dreams of Book 2, or the cultivation and care of Book 3. The poem ends with isolated, self-pitying heroes, images of what is great in man inextricably tied to what destroys us. The various centres of this story (practical success, mythic narrative, personal passions, impractical song, community and isolation, interpretive coherence) recycle the conceptual problems of the poem.

Conclusion

Both art and life desire to lighten their respective burdens; for it is, after all, easier to create without answering to life, and easier to live without answering to art.
Bakhtin

Critics have generally looked to the *Georgics* for some determinate meaning or unified attitude toward the world. I have tried to challenge this endeavour by describing the poem as a field or a dynamic. Rather than create security, clarity, univocity, the poem complicates our feelings and confounds our paradigms. It offers an excess of thought and feeling which, while true to the life of the mind, exceeds both the propositions by which we try to secure our understanding and the determinations upon which we must and do act. We may take directions from the poem (for planting or for governing), but the poem will also always remind us that our understanding is larger than these pressing necessities and that the contingencies of life have already implicated us in failure and greatness. This means that the value of the *Georgics* lies not in knowing or in the virtues of action, but in reading, in revising, in becoming larger than we thought we were and in imagining ourselves larger than we are. The poem offers a place where we can experience what we are and can be, as well as what we are not, where we can know that truth is always also its opposite, and feel the pressure of things in our lives, both our intellectual and emotional lives, and our practical lives. The *Georgics* most assuredly does not tell us what to do – but it reminds us of where we are and could be as we inevitably undertake the tasks which are as urgent as gerunds, as slippery as time, and as formative as the metaphors we live by.

FURTHER READING

The best modern, scholarly commentary in English on the *Georgics* is by R. A. B. Mynors: *Virgil, Georgics* (Oxford, 1990). The standard commentary for students is by Richard F. Thomas: *Virgil, Georgics*, 2 vols. (Cambridge, 1988). Thomas emphasises the highly allusive nature of the poem; cf. his important and influential article 'Virgil's *Georgics* and the art of reference', *Harvard Studies in Classical Philology* 90 (1986) 171–98. His interpretation, often polemical and consistently pessimistic, has greatly influenced recent discussion of the poem.

The discussion of the *Georgics* has been shaped by two debates. Early in this century, the poem was read as a poeticised agricultural treatise whose technical lore allowed the poet to celebrate the Italian countryside and whose digressions served the aesthetic ends of variety and description. The most prominent advocate of that position was L. P. Wilkinson: *The Georgics of Virgil: A Critical Survey* (Cambridge, 1969); cf. his article 'The intention of Virgil's *Georgics*', *Greece & Rome* 19 (1950) 19–28. Almost half a century later, much in his book remains valuable. Wilkinson's kind of reading, however, had already been challenged by German critics, who argued for the symbolic coherence of the whole poem: see Erich Burck, 'Die Komposition von Vergils *Georgika*', *Hermes* 64 (1929) 279–321, followed by F. Klinger, *Vergil's Georgica* (Zurich–Stuttgart, 1963). Today, the 'symbolic' approach dominates discussions in English: cf. the review essay of Wilkinson by Brooks Otis, 'A new study of the *Georgics*', *Phoenix* 26 (1972) 40–62.

In recent years another polarity has shaped debate: some readers, like Brooks Otis, *Virgil: A Study in Civilized Poetry* (Cambridge, 1964), have seen in the poem an optimistic, even redemptive image of political and moral rebirth, while others, like Richard Thomas, have emphasised the poem's darker, more pessimistic message; cf. the more extreme, but stimulating and provocative work of David Ross, *Virgil's Elements: Physics and Poetry in the Georgics* (Princeton, 1987).

Two important books have tried to recognise the poem's tragic and pessimistic aspects without succumbing to an unrelentingly pessimistic analysis. M. C. J. Putnam,

Vergil's Poem of the Earth: Studies in the Georgics (Princeton, 1979) offers a subtle and thorough New Critical reading, and Gary B. Miles, *Virgil's Georgics: A New Interpretation* (Berkeley, 1980) finds in the poem's formal structure a dialectical movement between idealised and inadequate versions of rustic life and Roman civilisation.

The most important recent effort to mediate between optimistic and pessimistic readings of the poem has been Christine Perkell, *The Poet's Truth: A Study of the Poet in Virgil's Georgics* (Berkeley, 1989). Her approach is New Critical and formalistic and her emphasis on the poem as meditative, rather than as strictly 'didactic' or allegorical, attempts to locate its value in ambiguity, ambivalence and mystery.

Other studies focus on particular aspects of the poem. Their titles are self-explanatory: Patricia Johnston, *Vergil's Agricultural Golden Age: A Study of the Georgics*, Mnemosyne Supp. 60 (Leiden, 1980); Edward W. Spofford, *The Social Poetry of the Georgics* (Salem, NH, 1981); Joseph Farrell, *Vergil's Georgics and the Traditions of Ancient Epic: The Art of Allusion in Literary History* (Oxford, 1991).

Among non-classicists useful discussions of the *Georgics* and agricultural literature can be found in: Michael J. K. O'Loughlin, *The Garlands of Repose: Studies in the Literary Representation of Civic and Retired Leisure* (Chicago, 1978) and Raymond Williams, *The Country and the City* (New York, 1973).

10

DUNCAN F. KENNEDY

Virgilian epic

In retrospect, the career of Virgil seems to trace out an inevitable progression. Working within a tradition which defined poetry composed in dactylic hexameter verse as *epos* (connoting 'word' or 'utterance'), the poet of the *Eclogues*, through the figure of the shepherd-singer Tityrus, recalls how his earliest poetic production involved a rejection of martial themes (*reges et proelia*, 'kings and battles', *Ecl.* 6.3) in favour of a pastoral mode, avowedly lowly and humble (cf. *Ecl.* 4.1–2), which looked back to the 'Syracusan verse' of Theocritus (*Ecl.* 6.1–2). Taking leave of this mode at the end of the final poem of the collection, the shepherd-singer, in his characteristic pose recumbent in the shade of a tree, announces his intention to *rise* (*surgamus*, *Ecl.* 10.75), presaging the composition of the Hesiodic *Georgics*. He thereby attributes to that poem a more elevated stylistic level, reiterates a hierarchy within the received types of *epos*, and begins to map an upward trajectory through those types on to the poet's life-cycle. In the opening lines of the Third Georgic, a further move upwards is envisaged (G. 3.8–9):

> temptanda via est, qua me quoque possim
> tollere humo victorque virum volitare per ora.

I must attempt a way, whereby I too may raise myself from the ground and victorious fly through the mouths of men.

'I too' suggests a desired affiliation to an existing tradition, and allusion to the epitaph of Ennius (fr. 46 Courtney), who in the early second century BC was the first Roman poet to adapt to Latin the Greek quantitative hexameter, points perhaps to the kind of Roman historical themes and the fusion of epic form and nationalist ideology which Ennius fashioned in his *Annals*. The poet explicitly promises that 'in time to come, I shall gird myself to sing of the burning battles of Caesar [Octavian] and carry his name in celebration through as many years as Caesar is distant from the first origin of Tithonus [brother of Priam]' (G. 3.46–8):

mox tamen ardentis accingar dicere pugnas
Caesaris et nomen fama tot ferre per annos
Tithoni prima quot abest ab origine Caesar.

However, the opening words of the poem which was eventually to transpire (*arma virumque cano*, 'I sing of arms and the man', *Aen.* 1.1) famously signal a return to Homer and a combination within a single poem of the themes of the *Iliad* and the *Odyssey*. None the less, the centrality of Caesar promised in the *Georgics* (*in medio mihi Caesar erit*, 'in the middle I will have Caesar', *G.* 3.16), as well as the extravagant time-scale stretching back to Trojan times, is realised as the *Aeneid* emplots the story of Aeneas as the first stage in the destined rise of the Romans towards universal dominion as it has evolved up to the poet's own day under the direction of the posterity of Aeneas, the house of Caesar (cf. *Aen.* 1.1–7). However, rather than looking back from the age of Augustus to Troy, the poem takes as its narrative 'present' events in the aftermath of the fall of Troy and insistently looks 'forward' from there to the age of Augustus, though not explicitly through the agency of the poet. The poem's supernatural machinery looks beyond the incident with which the narrative ends, the death of Turnus, to the events and personalities of the poet's own time – and even beyond, for the prophecy of Jupiter sees the outcome of the events narrated as empire without limits of space or time for the Romans (*his ego nec metas rerum nec tempora pono:* | *imperium sine fine dedi*, *Aen.* 1.278–9).

At a number of levels, the notion of repetition can be a useful way of exploring issues in the interpretation of Virgilian epic. In his book *Reading for the Plot*, Peter Brooks has remarked of narrative that

> [it] must ever present itself as a repetition of events that have already happened, and within this postulate of a generalized repetition it must make use of specific, perceptible repetition in order to create plot, that is, to show us a significant interconnection of events. An event gains meaning by its repetition, which is both the recall of an earlier moment and a variation of it: the concept of repetition hovers ambiguously between the idea of reproduction and that of change, forward and backward movement.[1]

In a response to Brooks's observations, David Quint has explored the way the plot of the *Aeneid* is structured around, and achieves some of its most notable effects through, a series of such perceptible repetitions. In what is often termed the 'Odyssean' half of the poem (Books 1–6), the wandering

---

[1] Brooks (1985) 99.

Trojans, instructed to 'seek out their ancient mother' (*Aen.* 3.96), visit, in a series of regressive repetitions as they try to recover what they have lost, a 'parade of replica Troys'.[2] The Sibyl's prophecy to Aeneas (*Aen.* 6.83–97) explicitly figures the action of the second half of the *Aeneid* as a reprise of the action of the Trojan war, familiar from the *Iliad*, but in contrast with the first half of the poem, repetition now involves not regression but reversal as previous failures are re-run as successes, notably in Aeneas' climactic duel with Turnus in Book 12: the details recall Aeneas' ignoble encounters on the battlefield with Diomedes and Achilles in *Iliad* Books 5 and 20, except that now the roles are reversed and it is Aeneas who emerges as victor. Repetition is thus not a matter of identity, but involves an interplay of perceived similarities and differences and must, in one way or another, be signalled or recognised as such for its significance to emerge. Repetition in emplotment thus underlies effects on the one hand of frustration, anticipation and tension, and on the other of progress towards fulfilment and closure. For a plot (whether of a fable or a historical account) to have a shape or order, its events must have a beginning, a middle and an *end*; but some slippage between 'end' as 'stopping-point' and as 'goal' (*telos*) is both unavoidable and open to manipulation to different effect. Quint suggests that it is such considerations that distinguish the open-endedly repetitious, circular narrative form characteristic of romance from the linear, teleological narrative of epic, and that the *Aeneid* incorporates the former in the latter so as ultimately to transcend it and all the more clearly signal the triumph of the poem's teleological form.[3] In her distressed response to what appears to her as the latest in a meaningless sequence of reversals to her son Aeneas, his shipwreck on the shores of Carthage, Venus challenges her father Jupiter who, she asserts, as king of the gods is in control of events (*Aen.* 1.229–30), 'What *end* do you set to these troubles?' (*quem das finem . . . laborum?*, *Aen.* 1.241). Significantly, he responds with a *narrative*, a prophecy about the posterity of Aeneas down to the time of Augustus, which identifies that 'end', that *telos*, as empire without boundaries of time and space for the Romans. The *disclosure* of the full meaning of these events lies, it can be seen, in the possibility of their narrative *completion*, and Quint has observed that this identification of the *telos* of the poem serves to associate its epic form with imperialist victory and so to figure its pretensions:[4] totalising and terminable, narrative structure works to answer the questions it raises in the course of its elaboration and to provide a closure in which the events it embraces, however remote in time or place, are displayed in their full intentional and

---

[2] Quint (1993) 61.   [3] Quint (1993) 31–41.   [4] Quint (1993) 45–6.

consequential significance. *Sic placitum* ('thus it has seemed good', *Aen.* 1.283), Jupiter remarks of his master narrative.

'Telling the story' thus offers the possibility of coming to terms with or being reconciled with the past and with the present which is seen to be its outcome, and narrative closure in turn depends on the satisfaction of the desire to discover the full dramatic significance of events. 'Muse, recount to me the causes' (*Musa, mihi causas memora, Aen.* 1.8), the poet appeals: the narrative of the *Aeneid* is from the very start figured as a telling, a report, a transcription. Narratives, whether they call themselves 'history' or 'fiction', necessarily characterise themselves as repeating what has happened, a structure that is mirrored in the analysis of narrative, which operates by invoking a distinction between 'story', an idealised sequence of events, and their 'emplotment' in an actual narrative which invests them with their significance. Paul Ricoeur has remarked of the writing of history that it 'repeats action in the figure of the memorable',[5] and this is a particularly pronounced feature of the history that epic 'recounts'. Homeric epic is thematised as *klea andrōn*, 'the famous deeds of men' (cf. *Iliad* 9.189), and in a rare apostrophe of his characters, the narrator of the *Aeneid* promises Nisus and Euryalus that, if his poem has any power, no age will take them from the memory of time, so long as Rome retains her *imperium* (9.446–9; for all the formal depersonalisation of the epic narrator, his fame remains an important part of the process of memorialisation, as *G.* 3.8–9, quoted above, suggests). More emphatically than other types of narrative, epic appeals to what Hannah Arendt has called the capacity for 'remembrance', by which the lasting significance of events is affirmed in and through a narrative felt to be satisfactory and complete and in which the past, however distant, is presented as available, and comprehensible, in terms of qualities, good or bad, uplifting or sorrowful, which are transcendentally attached to human achievement or suffering. Arendt sees Odysseus shedding tears at the Phaeacian court as he listens to the song of Demodocus (*Od.* 8.84–92) as paradigmatic of such cathartic remembrance.[6] The past thus celebrated becomes, for those capable of such remembrance, an *inheritance* with which they feel themselves entrusted, and this posture in turn serves to valorise claims made on the basis of a past so presented. In Mikhail Bakhtin's definition, a feature that distinguishes epic from other forms of narrative is that it presents a picture of a valorised 'absolute past' that accounts for the present specifically through ' "beginnings" and "peak times" in the national history, a world of fathers and of founders of families, a

[5] Ricoeur (1991) 115. [6] Arendt (1961) 45.

world of "firsts" and "bests"'.[7] In the memorialisation epic proposes, the act of telling is importantly situated in relation to the account of the past it offers: 'an absolute epic distance separates the epic world from contemporary reality, that is from the time in which the singer (the author and his audience) lives' and 'the authorial position immanent in the epic and constitutive for it (that is, the position of the one who utters the epic word) is the environment of a man speaking about a past that is to him inaccessible, the reverent point of view of a descendant'.[8] Though the narrator of the *Aeneid* poses as just such a reverent descendant, the passive recipient of the Muses' account, this serves to occlude a subtle manipulation of the relationship of story to emplotment in the poem. In analytical terms, the events of Roman history from the fall of Troy to the Augustan Age form the 'story' the *Aeneid* 'emplots'. But as we have seen, the supernatural machinery of the poem offers a prospective account of Rome's history to the 'time in which the singer lives', so that the impression left by the poem is that 'history' repeats the narrative of the *Aeneid*, thus giving 'history' the sense of being the fulfilment of what has been pre-ordained and destined. This sense of destiny is referred to in the poem as *fatum* ('an utterance'), and is identified with the utterances of Jupiter, who thus crucially takes on the responsibility of the 'one who utters the epic word' for the 'providential' aspects of the narrative and becomes a surrogate for the epic poet. A sense of inevitability is so marked a feature of the *Aeneid* that we might even see *fatum* self-reflexively characterised thereby as a distinctively Virgilian calque on the generic term *epos*. Whilst it is this perspective 'forwards' to 'the time in which the singer (the author and his audience) lives' which gives to the *Aeneid* its overtly teleological character, the singer's agency and perspective 'backwards' from the end, the point of fulfilment, is an integral, if occluded, part of an effect which is in no way restricted to the *Aeneid*, but open to narrative in general. We might compare the account of Virgil's career with which I began. Virgil's on-going pronouncements are so organised as to construct prospectively a *telos* of his career's fulfilment in the composition of epic; from the perspective of the realisation of the *telos* ('in retrospect'), they take on the guise of prophecy and their realisation a sense of inevitability. This Virgilian meditation on 'utterance' raises the possibility that any attempt to order the past in relation to the present, to say 'this is how it was', by virtue of its narrative structure incorporates, albeit at a level that may escape our attention, the claim 'this is how it was-to-be'.

---

[7] Bakhtin (1981) 13.   [8] Bakhtin (1981) 13.

Jupiter's role as surrogate narrator of a history of predetermined things-going-to-happen further implies that not only the *Aeneid* but 'history' too, rather than being a contingent series of things-that-happened, has a *plot*, a shape and structure, with a beginning and an end (to which it looks forward), and is thus no less analysable in terms of the sort of significant repetition we have been looking at. And so, to recall Brooks's comments quoted above, an event in 'history' will gain its meaning by its repetition, 'which is both the recall of an earlier moment and a variation of it'. Such a pattern is present in typological readings of the poem which assert, for example, that Aeneas is a 'figure' of Augustus, implying not an identity (for 'both the recall of an earlier moment and a variation of it' are at work) but rather that Aeneas is the 'type', manifesting, however imperfectly, particular idealized, historically transcendent qualities (most famously *pietas*), which within this overtly providential account find later manifestation, their 'antitype', in Augustus. And their fulfilment? Proponents of 'optimistic' and 'pessimistic' readings of the poem will both have their say, for, as we have seen, 'the concept of repetition hovers ambiguously between the idea of reproduction and that of change'.

These considerations can be extended to issues of literary history and interpretation as well. Epic seems to be a tradition that is always already at an end, its monuments firmly in place. For example, Philip Hardie's recent book *The Epic Successors of Virgil*, which argues that post-Virgilian epic 'may in some ways be understood better through a forward rather than a backward glance, to the epics of the Middle Ages and Renaissance' (and so explicitly promises to explain 'how it was' as 'how it was-to-be'), speaks of '[g]lancing forward to *the end of the tradition*, in *Paradise Lost* . . .'[9] In the words of Bakhtin, 'we come upon epic when it is already completely finished',[10] and within narratives of literary history, epic as a genre seems to belong to a Bakhtinian 'absolute past' which itself is a world of ' "beginnings" and "peak times" . . . of fathers and founders of families . . . of "firsts" and "bests" ', in which the place of Homer seems enshrined once and for all. Affiliation to a tradition that seems so closed is an object of desire and anxiety for Roman poets; Virgil's pronouncements in the *Eclogues* and *Georgics* are part of a complex discourse in Augustan poetry which appeals to the precedent of Callimachus to keep Homeric epic in view, but at a distance. Ennius' solution at the beginning of the *Annals* had been to present himself as a reincarnation of Homer;[11] we could plot a Virgilian strategy along the following lines. In the *Iliad*, Hector at the

[9] Hardie (1993) 89; emphasis mine. [10] Bakhtin (1981) 14.
[11] Cf. Skutsch (1985) 147–67.

Scaean Gate had prophesied: 'There will come a day when the holy city of Troy will fall' (6.448). What in the *Iliad* is a prophetic future finds its fulfilment in the *Aeneid* in the lament of the priest Panthus on the night the city is sacked: *venit summa dies et ineluctabile tempus | Dardaniae* ('Troy's final day and its inevitable hour has come', *Aen.* 2.324–5). The event which signals the 'end' in one emplotment becomes transformed into the 'beginning' in another, the repetition serving to open a previous closure, disclosing the previous story as but one element in a grander narrative. Repetition not only underlies narrative emplotment but is involved in notions of citation, imitation, allusion and intertextuality as well, and it is in the act of relating the *Aeneid* to the Homeric poems that such patterning and its significance particularly emerge. Genre, it has been remarked, is allusion on a massive scale, an intertextual frame which 'constitutes a field of reference within which, by means of comparisons and contrasts, the author can direct the specificity of his texts and the addressee can recognise it'.[12] For the ancient commentators on Homer, the *Odyssey* was the *anaplerosis*, the completion or fulfilment, of the *Iliad*, not merely its narrative continuation. Through an extraordinarily complex web of verbal repetitions such as this, the *Aeneid* not only establishes its identity as an epic but offers itself in turn as the *anaplerosis*, generic no less than narrative, of the Homeric poems. Much recent criticism of Virgil has seen the *Aeneid* as seeking to open out any closure, of narrative, of national and cultural identity, of genre or literary history, which the Homeric poems imposed; and in turn, the criticism of post-Virgilian epic has seen the epic successors of Virgil as attempting to question and challenge the various such closures the *Aeneid* may be thought to have imposed.

Such interpretations suggest that the text supports a multiplicity of interacting meanings, that, for example, what is read as a narrative theme can self-reflexively (a critical notion that invokes repetition once more) thematise generic issues as well, or that a character in the narrative (Tityrus in the *Eclogues* or Jupiter in the *Aeneid*, for example) can 'figure' authorial – or interpretative – preoccupations (the structure of such arguments is typological in the sense explored above). Thus, if legitimacy of succession is identified as a narrative theme of the *Aeneid*, such a theme can also be seen self-reflexively as its literary concern as well. From some perspectives, Aeneas comes to Italy as an interloper. His rights are valorised by presenting his presence there as a return, specifically metaphorised, in the words of the prophecy ('seek out your ancestral mother'), in terms of familial succession. Metapoetically, the citation of the openings of the *Iliad*

---

[12] Conte (1994a) 4.

and the *Odyssey* in the first words of the *Aeneid* can be seen to set in motion a literary-historical emplotment of the *Aeneid* as the successor of the Homeric poems. G. B. Conte has said of the generic significance of such citations that the opening of a poem 'is the place where all the signals point to the originality of the work or to its position within literary production . . . It classifies the genre so that the new text enters the literary system as a literary work, *as though* by hereditary right.'[13] The qualification is important, for the language of hereditary right is fully apropos only if literary systems are regarded as closed 'traditions' in which the poet is the passive recipient of 'what is handed down' to him, as Conte elsewhere remarks: 'If literary genres were merely closed structures . . . then [the] dialogue between texts would only take the form of direct patrilinear succession: in each instance, the patriarch, the author-inventor, would stand at the beginning of the family, and after him would follow a pure-blooded genealogy.'[14] The language of hereditary right and affiliation, of coming rightfully into one's inheritance, in the case of Virgil no less than that of Aeneas (or of Augustus, for that matter), occludes the actively appropriative and agonistic role each plays in relation to the past. The *telos* of the *Aeneid* in Jupiter's speech is 'empire without boundaries of time and space', suggesting the absorption into one unit of territories previously viewed as discrete and autonomous, and the significance of this for the poem's epic form has already been remarked upon. The citation of the *Iliad* and the *Odyssey* in the opening words of the *Aeneid* can be seen to offer a literary-historical emplotment for the poem as not merely succeeding but superseding the Homeric poems, and embracing both in a gesture of totalising imperialism. The ancient Homeric commentators saw Homer as the source of all subsequent genres, and critics have recently paid considerable attention to the way Virgilian epic in turn seems to incorporate within it a wide variety of generic forms: cosmological poetry, elegy, lyric and tragedy have all been the subject of extended discussions. But more than that. Genre (*genus*) implies 'type', and all generic criticism, even that which would deny that any one work can ever fully exemplify a generic norm, still relies on and invokes the concept of the norm. Any attempt, by poet or literary historian, to conceptualise genre by narrativising it, by offering a historical overview, will inevitably offer a framework teleologically directed by and towards a particular characterising, typifying work (e.g. a 'martial' tradition of epic characterised by Homer or an aetiological tradition characterised by Ovid's *Metamorphoses*). Just as Jupiter's vision of empire seeks to

---

[13] Conte (1986) 76, 82; emphasis mine.   [14] Conte (1994a) 5–6.

place it beyond the boundaries (the *fines*) of space and time and thus give it a transcendent status beyond the contingencies of history as the 'type' of empire, so we might conceive of the *Aeneid* as attempting generically to transcend any definition, any closures, that might be imposed upon it, so as to arrogate for itself the role of norm or type of epic, and thus to assert for itself a privileged position in the structure of literary history analogous to that of Rome's *imperium* within the 'history' the narrative of the poem constructs. Similarly, if the *Aeneid* is viewed from the perspective of its reception (historical, ideological, poetical or whatever), the theme of legitimacy of succession becomes that of *translatio imperii*.

Finally, if we think about the (history of the) interpretation of a text such as the *Aeneid* in terms of repetition, two possible, though not distinct, models come to mind. A 'romance' model would see any interpretation of the text (including the author's) as one in an endless series of readings (none of which has a more privileged status than any other *per se*) which make of the text a configuration or allegory of the interpreter's concerns. An 'epic' model would similarly see previous readings as allegories, but within a teleological structure that would foreground the present interpretation as the truth. In the words of Philip Hardie, '[t]he epic strives for totality and completion, yet is at the same time driven obsessively to repetition and reworking'.[15] However, in so far as any interpretation makes its totalising claim to truth, to be the last word, it will be a version of *epos*.

FURTHER READING

Richard Heinze's *Vergils epische Technik* (3rd edn, Leipzig and Berlin, 1915) underlies much of the scholarly work done on Virgilian epic during this century and is now belatedly available in an English translation (*Virgil's Epic Technique*, trans. Hazel and David Harvey and Fred Robertson, London, 1993). The issues of narrative and tradition treated above are explored at length in two excellent recent books, *Epic and Empire* by David Quint (Princeton, 1993) and *The Epic Successors of Virgil: A Study in the Dynamic of a Tradition* by Philip Hardie (Cambridge, 1993); see also ch. 3 above. The basic treatment of the relationship of the *Aeneid* to the Homeric poems remains G. N. Knauer, *Die Aeneis und Homer* (Gottingen, 1964); for a summary, in English, of his conclusions see 'Vergil's *Aeneid* and Homer', *Greek, Roman and Byzantine Studies* 5 (1964) 61–84 (= (ed. S. J. Harrison) *Oxford Readings in Vergil's Aeneid* (Oxford, 1990) 390–412). *Epic in Republican Rome* by Sander M. Goldberg (Oxford, 1995) offers many stimulating observations on Virgil's Roman epic predecessors; see also D. C. Feeney, *The Gods in Epic: Poets and Critics of the Classical Tradition* (Oxford, 1991) ch. 3. Feeney is

---

[15] Hardie (1993) 1.

the best guide on the poem's supernatural machinery (see esp. ch. 4), and has many pertinent remarks to make on the ancient exegetical tradition. On the generic inclusivity of the *Aeneid* see Francis Cairns, *Virgil's Augustan Epic* (Cambridge, 1987) chs. 6 and 7, and Hardie's chapter in this volume. Theoretical issues of genre are explored by G. B. Conte, *Genres and Readers* (Baltimore and London, 1994) chs. 4 and 5.

11

ELENA THEODORAKOPOULOS

Closure: the Book of Virgil

The Virgilian *Vitae* impose on the poet's life a strong pattern of linear development, a teleology which constructs the *Aeneid* as the simultaneous closure – ideological and narrative – of Virgil's life and his writings.[1] Within this pattern, which distinguishes Virgil from his contemporaries and makes of him a paradigm for his successors, the *Eclogues*, the *Georgics*, and the *Aeneid* become part of one text, which we might call 'the Book of Virgil', or (referring to the development from the relatively modest beginning in the short *Eclogues* to the final project of the *Aeneid*) 'the poetic career'. In the Middle Ages for instance, the biographical sequence found in the *Vitae*, which links the heroic epic with its bucolic and didactic predecessors, is mapped onto a hierarchy not only of literary genres but also of social rank: the *Rota Virgilii* (the 'Wheel of Virgil').[2] Here, the triadic career is pictured in the form of concentric circles, a quasi-cosmic image, in which the texts of Virgil come to stand for all possible forms of human life and expression. The notion of the career, a triadic biography to match the triadic *œuvre*, may also be found in the well-known epitaph quoted by Donatus:

> Mantua me genuit, Calabri rapuere, tenet nunc
> Parthenope; cecini pascua rura duces.

> Mantua bore me, Calabria took me away, and now Parthenope holds me.
> I sang of pastures, agriculture, and of leaders.　　　　　(*Vita Donati* 36)

But the limitations of literary biography become apparent when the early years of our own century, with the renewed interest in the *Appendix Virgiliana*, herald a new figure of the poet, who is no longer the paradigmatic hero of a teleological narrative of progress. With the publication

---

[1] On the 'Lives' of Virgil see Ziolkowksi (1993) 27–56; Suerbaum (1981) 1157–1262.
[2] The image is shown in Faral (1924) 87. See Curtius (1953) 232 and 201 n. 35; Laugesen (1962); and Suerbaum (1981) 1226 n. 112.

of Skutsch's *Aus Vergil's Frühzeit* (1901), Virgil's biography ceases to be the portrait of the artist as he presented himself through the works which became part of his *cursus honorum*. The 'new Virgil' was greeted with enthusiasm by some:

> From it all there has been born a new Vergil ... a Vergil who, like many another tiro in poetry, tried his prentice hand at parody and skit, wrote rakish verses of which he may afterwards have been ashamed – a new Vergil and a more human Vergil.[3]

One of my concerns in this chapter is to show how we may read the three canonical works as one poetic space, both in terms of the linear development of the career but also in terms of an aesthetic and thematic coherence which unites them. I want to show how the sense of closure which unites the works is achieved, and what role is played by the figure of the author in unifying the works, stylistically or formally, and themat-ically. One modern critic at least has been concerned with the interac-tion between the career-progress and the teleological shape of the Virgilian *œuvre*: '*Eclogues, Georgics, Aeneid* – these three works, and these only, belong to the *cursus honorum* that Virgil pursued (even the *Aeneid* may qualify against its author's will). Together they complete a "wheel" or pattern.'[4] Because Virgil's poetic boundaries are stretched to include his entire life's work from the *Eclogues* onwards, and because the *Aeneid* comes to an end when its author dies, the sense of a totalising teleology within the *œuvre* really is stronger here than in any other ancient poet.[5] Moreover, the explicitly self-referential passages in which Virgil presents himself as author involved in the shaping of his text may point us towards an understanding of the symbiotic relationship between the poet and his poems, which may indeed be closer than we think to the allegorical and literary biographies of antiquity.[6]

But the narrative or linear type of closure we find mirrored in the *Vitae*, and in which the three texts are united in the striving for the generic and political climax of the *Aeneid*, is not the only way in which Virgil achieves his Book, or his poetic enclosure. The linear and teleological impulse is often fought against throughout the three texts, and especially in the *Georgics* and in the *Aeneid*. Both of these texts ostensibly celebrate the achievements of Octavian/Augustus, both therefore ostensibly share a sense of ideological

---

[3] Stuart (1922) 30.

[4] Lipking (1981) 77; see also xi on how Virgil provides the paradigm for the poetic career for later poets. Most (1987) 208–9 shows that the structure of the *Culex* also mirrors the triadic career.

[5] See Hardie (1993) 102 on post-Virgilian imitations of this.

[6] See Hardie (1993) 99 and 101–2 on the symbiosis of poets and their heroes (and poems).

closure. Yet recent interpretations have shown that neither text has to be read as ultimately committing itself to the empire. The *Aeneid* in particular struggles violently against the linear and seemingly inevitable progress of epic teleology,[7] and this struggle may be read also as the poet's own struggle against the inevitable closure of his Book. In delaying and disrupting the closure of the epic, Virgil repeatedly takes his reader back to an alternative poetic space, the imaginary lands of the *Eclogues* and *Georgics*, which he appears only reluctantly to have left behind. As the political ambivalence of the *Aeneid* becomes part of the dynamic of the Book of Virgil, the poet's resistance to epic and empire also structures his resistance to his own para-digmatic career-progress. This anti-teleological struggle may be read as a more circular paradigm of closure to counter the linear closure of the *Vitae*: the Book of Virgil need not be merely about reading forwards towards the satisfaction of the desire for narrative closure, it may offer the reader the pleasures of re-reading, or repetition, which are functions of the internal intertextualities (we could term them intratextualities) that interweave the three texts.

In this circular enclosure the world of the *Eclogues* with its small-scale songs of love and exile becomes part of the 'private voice' of the *Aeneid*, which in the midst of empire and ideology may take us back to an Ital-ian landscape which is not yet part of the public world of epic. So, for instance, the images of Italy evoked in *Aeneid* 7 and 8, linked as they are with the youth and innocence of the Arcadian boy Pallas and the pastoral huntress Camilla, not only create a universe of grief and sorrow for the victims of empire, but take the reader of the Book of Virgil back to an alternative poetic world. In other words, the *Eclogues* and *Georgics* are not left behind in the author's poetic progress, but retain a strong presence in the *Aeneid*, and through this intratextuality they invite the reader repeatedly to look back at those parts of the Book she may consider finished and to integrate them into what she can then perceive as a coherent whole. In order, then, to escape from the linear path which the *Vitae* ask us to take in reading the Book of Virgil, it is important to look closely at the ways in which the texts may offer the reader the sensation of closure, without necessarily coercing her into the end-directedness of the linear narrative of progress.

In her influential study of poetic closure Barbara Herrnstein Smith shows clearly that, as she puts it, 'the perception of closure is a function of the perception of structure'.[8] This, evidently, is what happens when we look

---

[7] See Quint (1993) 50–96.
[8] Smith (1968) 2. Fowler (1989) offers a useful survey of classicists' use of Smith's work.

back over the Virgilian *œuvre*, having reached the end of the *Aeneid*, and are able to perceive, in retrospect, the three texts as forming the canonical triad. But it might also happen when we merely read 'around' in the three texts, perusing the Book of Virgil without adhering to the linearity pre-scribed by the *Vita*. So, while we may experience a sense of closure when the textual end or *telos* coincides with a sense of structural stability or coherence, it is also possible to experience closure outside a chronological or linear sequence. Smith draws a useful comparison with visual art, when she says that closure 'is not always a matter of endings'. She continues by referring to the use of the term 'closure' by psychologists, to describe forms which are visually perceived as clear or coherent:

> In such forms no particular point is experienced as the last one; and although one can speak of closure in works of spatial art it is obviously inappropriate to speak of it there as a quality of finality or conclusiveness.[9]

In other words, it is important to discover where and how closure is per-ceived, when it is not at the end of a text, or when it does not offer the ideological and narrative stopping-point. We are seeking then a sense of completeness or coherence that may hold the three texts of Virgil together, even as we recognise that the teleological narrative we might have relied on to do this is racked with tensions and ruptures, and its linearity crinkled with repetition and digression. Smith's study shows how we may perceive the completeness and integrity of a poem much as we might perceive that of a piece of music or a picture, through the implicit frame the artistic expression draws around itself:

> A passage of music frames itself, so to speak, by being more highly organised than anything else in the environment of sound or silence ... Similarly, a painting is framed not so much by the piece of wood around its borders as by the borders implied by its own internal structure.[10]

Similarly, beyond the narrative and teleological completeness of the career, the Book of Virgil appears to 'frame itself' by being more 'Virgilian' than anything else around it, and the three texts form a sense of coherence by being more like each other than they are like anything else (this is, evid-ently, why minor works such as the *Catalepton* cannot have a place in the Book of Virgil). One way in which this likeness, and the sense of conti-nuity, become manifest is in Virgil's consistent use of the hexameter. Other Augustan poets also organise their work to a model of progress.[11] For

---

[9] Smith (1968) 2.   [10] Smith (1968) 23–4.
[11] See Zetzel (1983b); and compare Sharrock (1994) 1–2. See Porter (1987) 3–13 on Horace. See also *Arethusa* 13 (1980) no. 1, an entire volume devoted to the ancient poetry book.

instance Horace 'graduates' from the *Satires* and *Epodes* to the *Odes*, and finally to the *Ars poetica*, and Ovid appears to imitate the Virgilian career by placing the didactic *Ars amatoria* between the small-scale love-poems of the *Amores* and *Heroides*, and the epic *Metamorphoses* and *Fasti*. But both Horace and Ovid separate the various stages of their work by working in different metres. Only Virgil stays with the hexameter throughout, as though to make it quite clear that all three texts are part of his *epos*, literally his utterance.[12]

One aspect of Virgil's ownership, or authority, involves the intertextuality of his works, which has often served to underline the separateness of the three texts by dividing them as imitations of Theocritus, Hesiod, and Homer.[13] The tripartition of the models serves to reinforce the sense of hierarchy which helps to form the teleological narrative of the 'poetic career', but which also segregates and categorises the texts in such a way that the Book of Virgil becomes not one coherent creative utterance, but three separate dialogues with three separate predecessors. Amongst other factors, the recognition of Callimachus' presence throughout the three texts (and not merely in the explicitly Callimachean *Eclogues*) has helped to create a better picture of the intricacies of Virgil's intertextualities, and a recent book on the *Georgics* has shown the complexity and individual nature of Virgil's intertextuality in that text as going well beyond the imitation of Hesiod.[14] We can also see the same models echoing throughout, for instance Catullus 64 and Apollonius in both Eclogue 4 and *Aeneid* 8. Alternatively, the Book of Virgil creates its own intratextualities, for instance in the pattern of allusions which govern *Georgics* 4 and *Aeneid* 2 and 9.[15] R. F. Thomas has shown how the programmatic Eclogue 6 is linked with the 'proem in the middle' of *Aeneid* 7,[16] in a continuous development of the Callimachean intertext, and he has referred to these intratextualities as a 'network' which shapes within the texts a sense of the poetic career.[17] Both of these intensely allusive passages are also intensely self-referential and absolutely preoccupied with authorship and originality. So the intertexts are bound into a cohesive whole, which spans across the three texts by one 'controlling intelligence',[18] which in turn is always reflecting on its own progress and authority. Virgil is no stranger to the anxiety of influence (the anecdote from the *Vita* in which he defends himself against charges of

---

[12] See Zetzel (1983b) 101: 'all three works taken together create a poetic universe united by the mastery of one poetic voice'.

[13] See Servius' preface to the *Georgics*.   [14] Farrell (1991).

[15] See Austin (1964) 285–9; and Hardie (1994) 142–4.

[16] Thomas (1983b) and (1986a). See Conte (1992) for 'proems in the middle'.

[17] Thomas (1986a) 71.   [18] See Lyas (1992) for the formulation.

plagiarism by saying that it would be easier to steal his club from Hercules than even one word from Homer may well be read as a statement about Virgil's own authority), and he weaves a web of intertextualities so tight and so controlled by his selection and invention that the reader (even the post-modern one) might almost be fooled into thinking that this poet has imposed closure on the perpetual dialogue of intertextuality.

Donatus' *Vita* offers an oddly appropriate reflection on how Virgilian self-reference, and literary autobiography, and the closure of the Book of Virgil might be linked. Donatus quotes the so-called *ille ego* opening of the *Aeneid*, which, he says, Varius (one of the two men entrusted with Virgil's literary estate after his death) excised in favour of the now canonical *arma virumque*:[19]

Ille ego qui quondam gracili modulatus avena
carmen et egressus silvis vicina coegi
ut quamvis avido parerent arva colono,
gratum opus agricolis, at nunc horrentia Martis
arma virumque cano

That man am I who having once played his song upon a slender reed, emerging from the woods compelled neighbouring fields to submit even to the greediest farmer, a work welcome to husbandmen, but now Mars's bristling Arms and the Man I sing.

In a short summary of the poetic career we see the clear tripartition, familiar from the epitaph (quoted above), and we see an attempt, however clumsy, to link the three works together in a narrative of poetic creativity. One important effect of this opening is that it links the *Aeneid*, at its beginning, to the literary biography, so that the epic grows out of the two previous works, and not, like the *Iliad* or the *Odyssey*, out of silence interrupted by divine inspiration.[20] This effect is of course achieved through *cano* in *Aen.* 1.1 alone, which links this opening to every other important opening in the *œuvre*. And yet *ille ego*, a mere elaboration on *cano*, makes an important point, because it offers a reading of the *Aeneid* as a part of a continuous Virgilian utterance, and because it shows that in the heroic *epos* as in the didactic it is the poet who speaks, in his own right, and not

---

[19] But see Henry (1873–92) who condemns *arma virumque* as 'turgid and abrupt' (5–7). He defends *ille ego*, interestingly, because it is more like the openings of Eclogues 4 and 6 (7–10). However, most modern scholars agree in rejecting the authenticity of these lines. See for instance Austin (1968).

[20] See Nuttall (1992) ch. 1 and 207–8.

as an instrument of god.[21] The intratexts form a connection between *cano* and other, crucial, occurrences of first-person forms of that verb, assertions of authority and personal responsibility at strategic or programmatic points, which link the poet inextricably to his work and which help to unite the works as one.[22] The *Georgics* opens with such an assertion, *G.* 1.5 *canere incipiam* ('I will begin to sing'), which is followed by *canam* in 2.2, and *canemus* in 3.1. The *sphragis* (a type of signature-passage after an Alexandrian convention in which the poet closes a collection of poems by asserting his authorship) at the end of Book 4 is framed by two forms of *cano: canebam* in 4.559, and *cecini* in 4.566, the final line of the poem. In Eclogues 4, 6, and 10 the poet reflects on his poetic ambitions, and on the limitations of his genre. Eclogue 4 opens with *canamus*, and Eclogue 6, a poem which reworks Callimachus' two highly influential tropes of beginning with a personal biographical statement, the two *Aetia* prologues (*Ecl.* 6.3–5, and *Ecl.* 6.64–73), has *canerem* in the third line.[23] In the last Eclogue the poet takes his leave of pastoral by referring one last time to his authorship in *Ecl.* 10.70, *haec sat erit, divae, vestrum cecinisse poetam* ('Goddesses, may this be enough for your poet to have sung'). The *ille ego* opening maps the poetic self-references, which play a huge part in the shaping of the Book of Virgil, onto the poetic career and makes of that literary autobiography the beginning of the *Aeneid*.

As a gesture, the *ille ego* opening also interprets other crucial Virgilian openings, and, perhaps most directly, the explicitly autobiographical *sphragis* which concludes the *Georgics*.[24] And the self-referential passages together with the *sphragis* do lend to the Book of Virgil a sense of closure through the narrative of creation and authority which runs through the three texts. A rare, but emphatic, authorial intervention in the *Aeneid* quite explicitly links a sense of closure and authoritative stability with the self-referential mode. In the address to Nisus and Euryalus in *Aeneid* 9.446–9 the narrator speaks of the power of his poetry, and compares its longevity with that of the Capitoline rock. Virgil's pride in his creation and his confidence in its power have two close relations, one in Horace, *Odes* 3.30, the other in Ovid, *Metamorphoses* 15.871–9. Both are explicitly self-referential, both tie the permanence and stability of poetry to the physical and political

---

[21] Austin (1968) 109 objects to *ille ego* because the personal voice of didactic is incompatible with heroic epic.

[22] See the discussion of Smith (1968) by Hamon (1975) 496 with a list of such *lieux stratégiques*, usually boundaries or transitional passages, all of which are as much connected with the idea of closure as the endings of complete texts.

[23] See Clausen (1994) 174–7, 179–80, 199–201.

[24] See Fowler (1989) 82–4, on 'supertextual closure', especially on the link between *Georgics* and *Eclogues* achieved with the *sphragis*.

power of Rome, and both are closural passages, variations on the Alexandrian *sphragis*. Virgil's only version of the closural-signature motif in the
Aeneid is linked to his invention of two minor characters, whose tragedy
is their failure as heroes of epic. Perhaps it is not altogether surprising,
then, that the authorial intervention, for all its apparent confidence in the
stability of the Capitoline rock and the power of the Roman empire, reworks, in the qualified assertion of the power of song, *Aen.* 9.446 *si quid
mea carmina possunt* ('if my songs have any power'), one of the most
pessimistic passages from the *Eclogues* (*Ecl.* 9.11–13) in which the power
of poetry in the midst of empire is less than certain.[25]

As strategic points in the Book of Virgil, we must look also at the endings of the three texts, and at the story of closure they tell. All of Virgil's
endings tend to look back to the final line of the First Eclogue, which is
a version of the beginning of Virgilian poetry with Tityrus' leisure in the
shade (*Ecl.* 1.4 *lentus in umbra*). Within its 83 lines Eclogue 1 is a microcosm of the entire Eclogue collection. This first poem contains the transformation of shade from a peaceful enclosure or shelter into a menacing
darkness which envelops the landscape completely in *Ecl.* 1.83 *maioresque
cadunt altis de montibus umbrae* ('larger now the shadows are falling from
the high mountains'). It contains also the destruction of pastoral innocence
and the compensation offered by Rome and civilisation. In the figure of
Meliboeus, the poem contains exile and the end of poetry in *Ecl.* 1.77
carmina nulla canam ('I will sing no more songs'). As a microcosm of the
Eclogue book, Eclogue 1 is also a microcosm of the Book of Virgil, which
mirrors the development from light to darkness, the loss of pastoral innocence, and the final goal of Roman civilisation. Eclogue 1 is the beginning
of the end, and the shadows that fall from its closure reach out over the
entire corpus of Virgil's poetry. When we read the last words of the *Aeneid*,
the death of Turnus and his descent *sub umbras* ('under the shadows'),
the Book of Virgil has ended in darkness, just like Eclogue 1. In the final
lines of Eclogue 10 evening falls again, this time to end the collection.
Tityrus' shade is now rejected as harmful to both singers and crops, and
so the poet demands that singers (and readers) should rise up from its
shelter (*Ecl.* 10.75 *surgamus*). Previously, the poet has taken his leave of
the Muses, and made it clear that the desire for Bucolic song is now
saturated, so that the rise from the humility and the leisure of the shade
towards the didactic toils of the *Georgics* is well prepared for.[26] The exhortation *surgamus* is striking in a closing passage, where we might expect a

---

[25] On Nisus and Euryalus see Hardie (1994) 153–5. See also Feeney (1991) 184–7 on the
poet's command over his text.
[26] See Kennedy (1983).

downwards movement, to illustrate the sense of ending, as for instance the First Eclogue gives us *cadunt* as a closural image.[27] But the rising implies quite strongly a beginning, leaving behind the past, and in a sense closing it, but at the same time an awareness of the new opening.[28] The end of Eclogue 10 shows how easily an end may become a beginning, within a larger intratextual structure.[29] The didactic poem is not entirely separate because it shares with its humble predecessor the author's voice. That voice asserts its presence when the *sphragis* of *Georgics* 4 reverts to a notion of the shade as *locus amoenus* which the end of Eclogue 10 had abandoned. Within the larger structure of the Book of Virgil, the dynamic of closure and continuation tells of a career and of the formation of a coherent and mature authorial voice, which may not be entirely committed to the model of progress offered by the hierarchy of genre.

The final line of the *Aeneid* returns to a different and darker *umbra*: 12.952 *vitaque cum gemitu fugit indignata sub umbras* ('and life fled with a groan, indignant, to the shadows'). On a first reading, *umbras* here must refer to the ghosts of the dead in the Underworld, not to shadows or darkness. But the ramifications of this word are prepared not only through the development in the *Eclogues*, but again in the *Aeneid* itself, and particularly in *Aeneid* 6. Here, *umbra* is often used to refer to the human ghosts, the *simulacra* which populate the Underworld in lines such as 6.294 *frustra ferro diverberet umbras* ('he would have attacked shades, vainly, with his sword'). But *Aeneid* 6 covers a range of meanings of *umbra*, using it to denote the darkness of the Underworld, for instance in 6.268 *ibant obscuri sola sub nocte per umbram* ('obscured they walked, through the darkness in the desolate night'), or in 6.340 *vix multa maestum cognovit in umbra* ('he hardly recognised him, sorrowful, in the thick shadow'). In some instances the distinction between ghosts and darkness is almost impossible to draw, as indeed the ghosts themselves often are almost indiscernible to Aeneas' eye in the murky darkness of the Underworld. Most poignantly Aeneas sees, or thinks he sees, Dido in the dark woods of the Grieving Fields, *Aen* 6.452–3 *per umbras | obscuram* ('obscured by the shades'). The figure of Dido is obscured by darkness, but she is also one of a crowd of other ghosts who fill the woods, so that Aeneas' difficulty in seeing her depends precisely on the difficulty of distinguishing between shadows and shades. Dido is like Aeneas when he first entered the Underworld with the Sibyl (*Aen.* 6.268), but the sense of confusion

---

[27] See Smith (1968) 172–82 for 'closural allusions'.

[28] Compare the end of *Aeneid* 2, with *surgebat*. See the discussion in Nagle (1983) *passim*.

[29] See Hardie (1993) 13 for epic endings which are also beginnings, and Fowler (1989) 82 for 'supertextual groupings'.

and of the erosion of difference between darkness and human shades in the later passage is heightened by the absence of an 'objective' narrator's voice which might help to determine the differences and to separate the *umbra* of darkness from the *umbra* of shades perceived by Aeneas.[30] But it is at the end of the *Georgics*, with Orpheus' descent to hell, that pastoral shade and its darker, Underworldly versions meet and almost become one. First, *umbrae* are the ghosts, or images of the dead (*G.* 4.472). Then, when Orpheus loses Eurydice for the second time, *G.* 4.501 *prensantem nequiquam umbras* ('vainly clasping the shadows'), Eurydice's image becomes one with the darkness which swallows it. After his loss, Orpheus in his endless grief is compared in a simile to the nightingale, singing in the shade of a tree, at night. This night-time shade is both the *locus amoenus* of bucolic song and the cold shades of night, which fall at the end of Eclogue 10 and Eclogue 1. So, the *Georgics* ends by reworking the development of *umbra* from song to silence, from light to darkness, and by introducing the new deathly dimension of the shade which will end the *Aeneid* with Turnus' descent.

Through the development of shade and darkness, the Book of Virgil tells a story which appears to run entirely opposite to the teleology of both the empire and the career-progress of its poet. Perhaps it is significant that Aeneas, at the last moment, hands over the responsibility for his act of closure to Pallas, the dead Arcadian boy. The killing of Turnus is an act of memory, and this memory is not merely that of the character Aeneas, but also that of the reader, and of the poet, who twice repeats the name of the Arcadian (*Aen.* 12.848–9 *Pallas te hoc vulnere, Pallas | immolat*), just as, near the end of Eclogue 10, he repeats the name of Gallus, who tried and failed to become an Arcadian (*Ecl.* 10.72–3 *vos haec facietis maxima Gallo, | Gallo*). Virgil's last words, *sub umbras*, recall at the same time the death of an ideal 'Arcadian' Italy and the darkness which puts an end to all singing. *Sub umbras* is both a version of Tityrus' shelter under the beech tree and of the shadows of the night which end the First Eclogue. Through the intratextual echoing which shapes the Book of Virgil the final lines of the *Aeneid* return to the impossible pastoral of the first and the last Eclogues, at the very moment when we might expect the triumph of epic and empire.

FURTHER READING

Arethusa 13 (1980) no. 1, 'Augustan poetry books'

Brooks, P. (1984) *Reading for the Plot: Design and Intention in Narrative*. New York and London

[30] Compare Austin (1964) 277 on a similar use of *umbra* in *Aeneid* 2.768–72.

Fowler, D. P. (1989) 'First thoughts on closure: problems and prospects', *Materiali e Discussioni* 22: 75–122

Hardie, P. R. (1993) *The Epic Successors of Virgil: A Study in the Dynamics of a Tradition*. Cambridge

Kermode, F. (1966) *The Sense of an Ending*. New York and Oxford

Lipking, L. (1981) *The Life of the Poet: Beginning and Ending Poetic Careers*. Chicago and London

Nuttall, A. D. (1992) *Openings: Narrative Beginnings from the Epic to the Novel*. Oxford

Smith, B. H. (1968) *Poetic Closure: A Study of How Poems End*. Chicago

3
CONTEXTS OF PRODUCTION

12

R. J. TARRANT

Poetry and power: Virgil's poetry in contemporary context

Virgil is at first sight an unlikely prospect as a politically engaged writer. As depicted by his ancient biographers, he is a retiring, even reclusive type, of a philosophic rather than an active nature, uncomfortable in Rome and eager to leave it. By comparison, his fellow-poet Horace, who fought at Philippi and may have witnessed Actium, assumes an almost Hemingway-esque air of bravado. But the ancient Lives also insist on Virgil's proximity to figures of power throughout his literary career, from Asinius Pollio to Maecenas and ultimately to Augustus himself, and repeatedly trace connections between those personal contacts and the prominence of contemporary history in Virgil's poetry. Thus the First Eclogue, in which the shepherd Tityrus relates how he was forced to give up his property but regained it in Rome through the intervention of a godlike youth, was soon read as a *poème à clef* with Tityrus representing Virgil and the youth Octavian. We are told that the *Georgics*, which contains in the proem to Book 3 clear references to the triple triumph of 29 celebrating victory over the forces of Antony and Cleopatra, was read by Virgil to Octavian on his return to Italy from the East in the summer of that year. Contemporary events figure even more explicitly in the *Aeneid*: Actium and its aftermath occupy pride of place on the shield of Aeneas, the title 'Augustus' twice appears, and Aeneas' journey to his father Anchises in the Underworld ends, remarkably, with a lament for the loss of Augustus' nephew Marcellus, dead at an early age in 23. At the same time the relationship between poet and *princeps* as presented in the ancient Lives grows ever closer: Augustus corresponds with Virgil when away from Rome, inquiring after the progress of the epic; he and his sister Octavia hear selected books read by the poet, to Octavia's acute distress when her son's demise is touched on; and finally it is Augustus who secures the *Aeneid*'s survival by overruling Virgil's dying impulse to have the text burned.

Disentangling truth from invention in these biographical accounts is an ultimately impossible task, although one that cannot be entirely avoided.[1] For present purposes, though, the ancient Lives may be more helpfully viewed as a sort of myth of Virgil, not in the sense of being fictional, but by analogy with the way myth gives narrative expression to certain fundamental beliefs or experiences. In that light the two aspects of Virgil highlighted in his biographies can be read as pointing to a dichotomy in his work. Virgil's poetry is indeed remarkable for the degree to which it engages seriously with the political realities of his time, but also, it can be argued, for the distance that it maintains from those realities, and for what many recent critics have called the consistently ambivalent or multivocal viewpoint that it adopts toward them.

That Virgil wrote poetry with political overtones is not in itself cause for surprise; it would have been astonishing had he not done so, given his literary stature and circumstances. But those same factors also help to explain why he chose not to compose straightforward political panegyric or invective. The traditional Roman attitude toward poetry, as toward most activities practised with distinction by the Greeks, had been one of tolerance coloured by suspicion; the strongest defence against the charge of triviality or waste of talent lay in celebrating the achievements of individual Romans and of the Roman people generally, of which the most illustrious example before Virgil's time was Ennius' historical epic, the *Annales*, composed between about 185 and 169 BC. Cicero's speech *In Defence of Archias*, delivered in 62, contains the fullest extant statement of the value of such civically oriented poetry. Cicero's arguments are shaped by the circumstances of the case he is pleading; specifically, his aim is to counteract xenophobic feelings toward a Greek client-poet by playing up the value for Rome and Romans of poetry Archias had written to honour his patrons, the Luculli. But for that very reason it is likely that he stresses the considerations that would have been most effective in influencing a Roman jury's opinion.

At the time of Cicero's speech, however, a very different view of the purpose and form of poetry was gaining currency in Rome. Its only surviving early exponent is Catullus, but Catullus saw himself as one of a circle of writers with shared tastes and aims, 'the new poets', as Cicero called them with more than a touch of disdain.[2] These poets consciously

[1] My own tendency is toward scepticism, see above, p. 57. It *might* be true that the reading of the *Georgics* to Octavian was spread out over four days, and that Maecenas took over from Virgil when the poet's voice occasionally gave out, but such behind-the-scenes details are just the sort of thing that might be devised to satisfy curiosity about so eminent, yet unforthcoming, a figure as Virgil.
[2] Clausen (1986).

cultivated the manner of Hellenistic Greek writers, Callimachus in particular, and thus strove for subtle learning and exquisite refinement, claiming to scorn popular taste and to write only for a discerning elite. While nothing in the pronouncements of Callimachus or Catullus singled out political poetry for disapproval, and it may be coincidental that the butt of Catullus' abuse was the *Annales* of a certain Volusius,[3] the literary values espoused by the 'new poets' would have made the writing of poetry on public themes more challenging and problematic.[4] Virgil probably came to Rome shortly after Catullus' death, and soon entered this modernist literary milieu:[5] the first patron figure in his poetry, Asinius Pollio, is mentioned in a poem of Catullus as a young man of refined tastes, and Virgil himself first appeared in the curriculum of a Roman school as a 'new poet'.[6] The influence of neoteric views of poetry is especially strong in the *Eclogues*, which contains at its mid-point a near-translation into pastoral terms of a famous passage of Callimachus. Virgil claims adherence to Callimachean poetic values for what may have been a new purpose, to explain his refusal to celebrate the military victories of a prominent contemporary, Alfenus Varus; he thus declines for literary reasons to take on the sort of commission that Cicero's Archias had been only too willing to accept. It is worth recalling that from the perspective of Virgil's early poetry the writing of the *Aeneid* – which looks so inevitable in retrospect – would have seemed unlikely if not impossible.[7]

Catullus' poetry voiced mocking contempt for contemporary politics and for its leading figures, Julius Caesar and Pompey. But Catullus' attitude may not have been fully shared by other members of his circle, and as the rivalry of the 50s led to open conflict in the next decade, even poets of the new school would have found it difficult to maintain a non-partisan stance. The effects of these new conditions can be seen, if dimly, in the work of two prominent writers of the 40s spoken of admiringly in the *Eclogues*, L. Varius Rufus and Cornelius Gallus.

Gallus figures in Eclogue 6 as the writer of learned poetry in the Alexandrian mode, in Eclogue 10 as a love-poet mourning the loss of his mistress Lycoris to a soldier-rival. On the basis of these appearances (which until recently comprised almost all the direct evidence for Gallus' poetic activity), Gallus might seem to have adopted a detached or escapist attitude

---

[3] Poems 36, 95 (on the latter cf. Courtney (1993) 230–1).

[4] It is often said that Callimachus rejected epic-style treatment of political themes, but Cameron (1995) argues that there is little evidence of such poetry from the period immediately preceding Callimachus, and that his criticism was based on judgements of quality rather than genre or topic.

[5] Clausen (1987) 1–14.   [6] Above, p. 56.   [7] Thomas (1985).

toward contemporary politics, prefiguring the pose of non-involvement assumed by his elegiac successors Propertius, Tibullus, and Ovid in the years after Actium. That impression was shown to be incorrect, however, when a papyrus containing several previously unknown elegiac verses and plausibly attributed to Gallus was published in 1979.[8] Alongside reproaches to Lycoris and satisfied reflections on his own poetry, the new lines contain a four-line epigram praising a 'Caesar' and predicting his triumphal return from a campaign; the addressee is probably Julius Caesar and the campaign in question the Parthian expedition Caesar was meditating at the time of his assassination. The panegyrical tone appears free of irony (though Gallus' words were subsequently echoed in an ironic spirit by Propertius), and Gallus' persona as a love-poet apparently did not prevent him from expressing Caesarian sentiments.[9]

Gallus' poetic activity may not have extended much beyond the 40s. He drops out of sight for most of the next decade, reappearing as one of Octavian's lieutenants in the Egyptian campaign; in a brilliant but brief tenure as first Prefect of Egypt, his self-aggrandising incurred the displeasure of Augustus and he died by his own hand in 27 or 26. By contrast, Varius enjoyed a long and untroubled career as a supporter of Octavian, and lived to be one of Virgil's literary executors (thus, in all likelihood, the person responsible for the text of the *Aeneid* in its published form). In the 20s he was highly esteemed as an epic poet and tragedian (his *Thyestes* graced Octavian's victory celebrations of 29), but he had won recognition a generation earlier with a poem intriguingly entitled *De morte*, to which Virgil paid the high tribute of allusion or even direct quotation in all three of his works. In it Varius seems to have combined an Epicurean denunciation of the fear of death with topical polemic, conspicuously against Antony; in both places where Virgil echoes such passages he characteristically mutes

---

[8] Anderson, Parsons and Nisbet (1979).

[9] There are other indications that erotic poetry, which in the 20s became almost the emblem of an apolitical poetic stance, was previously not thought incompatible with political engagement or politically oriented poetry. One of Julius Caesar's assassins, Cassius of Parma, a supporter of Antony executed after Actium, was the author of works that Horace teasingly suggests Tibullus might attempt to surpass (*Epist.* 1.4.3), probably therefore love elegies. Virgil's self-depreciation *vis-à-vis* Varius and Cinna, 'a goose honking amid swans' (*Ecl.* 9.35–6 *videor ... argutos inter strepere anser olores*), was explained by Servius as a jibe at a poet named Anser, an adherent and panegyrist of Antony; as Clausen (1994) *ad loc.* notes, what might be suspected as scholiastic invention is supported by Ovid's reference to Anser, in company with Cinna, as the author of love poetry (*Tr.* 2.435), and by Cicero's mention in the *Philippics* (13.11) of 'Ansers' (perhaps brothers) as allies of Antony. Varro of Atax wrote both erotic elegies and an epic treatment of Caesar's campaign against the Sequani, but probably at different periods in his life, cf. Courtney (1993) 236–7.

the *ad hominem* aspect of the description and focuses on moral failing rather than on political invective.[10]

Against this background the distinctness of Virgil's handling of political issues becomes all the more striking. Each of his major works engages with contemporary political reality in a serious and sustained way, rather than constructing a poetic world that excludes or trivialises politics. Yet each also creates the means of preventing Virgil or his poetry from becoming simply a vehicle of political comment.[11] Avoiding the more blatant forms of partisan poetry was surely in part a question of aesthetic judgement, a means of escaping the poetic limitations of panegyric or invective. But a Callimachean aversion to bombast and banality cannot be the only motive: Callimachus, after all, was a court poet, and Virgil was familiar with his panegyrics on Ptolemy and his wife Berenice. Virgil's early association with Asinius Pollio may have some relevance: Pollio's political allegiances were always tempered by a strong sense of his own importance, and in the final struggle between Antony and Octavian he declared neutrality, reportedly describing himself as the prize that would go to the victor.[12] But any effect of Pollio on Virgil's political outlook would only help to account for the *Eclogues* (and even there only in part), whereas the treatment of political themes in his work shows a remarkable consistency. In the end allowance must be made for an authorial cast of mind, one that not only shies away from reductively simple attitudes but gravitates toward antithesis and contradiction as a preferred mode of expression.

The *Eclogues* are paradoxically both the work in which contemporary events are most pervasively present and the one in which they are most thoroughly transformed to subordinate them to a poetic context.[13] The poems allude to the assassination of Julius Caesar in 44 (5) and his deification in the following year (9), to the Italian land confiscations of 41 following the defeat of Caesar's assassins at Philippi (1, 9), to the consulship of Pollio and the pact of Brundisium between Antony and Octavian in 40 (4), and probably to Pollio's Illyrian triumph of 39 (8). Yet each of these events is translated into pastoral terms that soften and distance their topical quality, and that defeat efforts to see direct equivalents between

---

[10] G. 2.505ff., *Aen.* 6.621ff., connected to lines of Varius by Macrobius, *Sat.* 6.1.39–40.

[11] Virgil's closest analogue in this respect is Horace, the other major poet traditionally viewed as an 'Augustan' and the other principal member of the circle of Maecenas. One wonders whether their growing proximity to Augustus gave them added stimulus to devise this kind of artistic strategy. On Horace's strategies for preserving independence cf. Lyne (1995) – though his rhetoric of 'subversion' seems to me unhelpful.

[12] Velleius Paterculus 2.86.3.

[13] Cf. Martindale above, esp. p. 119: 'the [*Eclogues*] do not imitate politics, rather politics are inscribed within poetry that has become its own concern'.

pastoral figures and historic persons (which is not to say that such efforts were not made by Virgil's ancient readers).[14] The Daphnis whose death is lamented in Eclogue 5 is described in terms that inescapably evoke Julius Caesar, but Daphnis is not simply Caesar by another name. Even the Roman contemporaries mentioned by name – Pollio, Varus, Cinna, Varius, above all Gallus – are drawn into the bucolic context and viewed according to its values.

One result of this carefully distanced approach is that nothing as clear-cut as a political stance can be made out. The poet's Caesarian allegiance is obvious, but after Philippi that would hardly have been controversial. More noteworthy is the absence of any expression of partisan adherence to Octavian or Antony: the opening poem strongly suggests gratitude and devotion to Octavian in the guise of the beneficent *iuvenis*,[15] and its place at the head of the book discreetly hints at the transition Virgil had made during its composition from the sphere of Asinius Pollio (which might have entailed at least qualified support of Antony) to that of Octavian, but nothing is said in disparagement of the other. Instead the book's clearest political statement – itself far from explicit – is the utopian vision of the Fourth Eclogue, embodying the hopes produced by the agreement between Antony and Octavian that Pollio had helped to bring about.

Those hopes were soon disappointed, and even if the *Eclogues* were published as a collection in 39, it must have been already apparent that peace between the two dominant triumvirs was fragile. Virgil allows the optimistic vision of Eclogue 4 to remain, but qualified by its position within the book, which is framed by poems (1 and 9) relating to an earlier and less happy state of affairs, the displacement of farmers in northern Italy to accommodate the soldiers of Antony and Octavian after Philippi. Virgil's treatment of this episode illustrates his capacity for a multivocal response to complex situations. In both poems misfortune falls unevenly and with no obvious relation to merit: Tityrus in 1 and Lycidas in 9 are allowed to continue their accustomed lives, Tityrus after a successful appeal in Rome and Lycidas, apparently, through sheer luck; on the other hand, their neighbours Meliboeus (1) and Moeris and Menalcas (9) are forcibly

---

[14] The relationship of the *Eclogues* to political events would become even more oblique on the later dating initiated by Bowersock (1971), with reference to Eclogue 8, and elaborated by Clausen (1972), (1994), which places their composition in 38–35 rather than 42–40/ 39, but that view has not yet won wide acceptance.

[15] *Ecl.* 1.42; the same term is used explicitly of Octavian at the end of *Georgics* 1 (500). Octavian's youth (he was 19 when Julius Caesar was killed) was for some time his salient characteristic.

evicted, and not even the poetry of Menalcas can stave off disaster.[16] In each case Virgil evokes sympathy for the losers – more so, arguably, than for the somewhat complacent survivors. The placement of the two poems also generates multiple reactions. The mood of 9 is noticeably darker than that of 1, and its position might suggest that it is the poet's despairing final word on this theme; but it would be equally legitimate to infer that the gloomy tone of 9 is offset by the partial optimism of 1, that the godlike young man in Rome offers some reassurance against the feeling that blind chance rules (*fors omnia versat*, *Ecl.* 9.5). The absence of a linear 'plot' in the *Eclogues* permits both readings to coexist and to affect each other, a structurally sustained tension with counterparts in Virgil's later work.

If writing a history of the civil wars from the perspective of the 20s was to walk on ashes with fire still smouldering beneath them, as Horace wrote in an ode to Pollio, the challenge Virgil faced in composing the *Georgics* was still more severe. The poem occupied him for much of the 30s, years of almost constant strife in which the enmity between Antony and Octavian grew ever more embittered and at last took the form of declared war. If contemporary events were to be touched on at all, a non-partisan position was no longer possible; and as the dedication of the poem shows, Virgil was now firmly in the circle of Maecenas, and thus a declared adherent of Octavian. Furthermore, as the external world became harder to accommodate, the genre of this poem offered no built-in method of gaining distance from it. In the *Eclogues*, as later in the *Aeneid*, the generic framework is predominantly Greek, and therefore provides a setting for Roman material that is itself transformative and distancing. In the *Georgics*, despite references to Hesiod as the didactic role-model and the more pervasive Callimachean–Hellenistic flavour of the writing, the Greek element is much less prominent at the generic level, partly because of the proximity of Lucretius as a Roman precursor; and since the didactic form requires the content of the poem to be relevant to actual needs, it positively excludes the sort of removal from the present offered by bucolic or epic.

At the level of explicit comment Virgil meets these challenges by turning away from the painful recent past: the poem says nothing specific about events between the aftermath of Julius Caesar's assassination and

---

[16] In *Ecl.* 9.10–29 the despairing thought that poetry is powerless in a time of war corresponds to the near-breakdown of Virgil's own pastoral framework when Mantua and Cremona are mentioned. This self-referential moment does not imply that Menalcas is 'really' Virgil, but that through Menalcas Virgil explores the place of his own poetry in relation to political realities. (It is relevant that in return for help in retaining his land Menalcas promises Varus the kind of praise that Virgil declines to provide in Eclogue 6.)

the ultimate victory of Octavian. The counterpart to this reticence is an openly panegyrical attitude to Octavian, who is addressed at key points in terms redolent of court poetry (and which are indeed influenced by Callimachus' praises of Ptolemy and Berenice in the *Aetia*): he is appealed to as a god-to-be in the opening proem and in the framing passage that ends Book 1, and as a triumphing victor in the proem to Book 3 and the concluding *envoi* (4.560–2).[17] In the latter passages the emphasis falls on victories over foreign opponents, an early example of the Augustan tendency to treat Octavian's campaign against Antony and Cleopatra as a struggle between Rome and Egypt rather than as a civil conflict.

It might appear that Virgil has abandoned the delicate ambiguity of the *Eclogues* for a much more direct and committed attitude of support for Octavian, but that conclusion takes account of only one aspect of the connection between poem and setting. The *Georgics* also contains a more implicit and comprehensive mode of comment: in a way that looks forward to the *Aeneid*, the entire poem can be read as a troubled reflection on its historical context. Even in the framing passages of Book 1, the places where Octavian is spoken of as a god-to-be, the mood is coloured by uncertainty. In the proem, the ironic indecision Virgil affects about the precise divine role Octavian will play can be read as a metaphor for the political situation of the post-Actium period, in which it was obvious that Octavian was now the most powerful figure in the state but not yet clear how he would choose to exercise that power. When the notion of Octavian as incipient divinity reappears at the end of the book, it is given an overtly pessimistic gloss. It was said that in the early days of the world the gods had walked openly among mortals, until the growing corruption of human behaviour had driven them in disgust to the heavens. Virgil implies that Octavian, like his fellow-deities, may not be able to endure Rome in its present depraved condition.

In its professedly didactic passages as well, the poem can be taken as responding to contemporary events. The choice of agriculture as a subject offered a poetic setting at once closer to the real world than the Arcadian landscape of the *Eclogues* and also more remote from it, since connections made at this level are metaphorical rather than literal. (There is no reason to believe that the topic of the poem was imposed on Virgil by Maecenas to generate support for Octavian's agicultural policy,[18] but even if Maecenas encouraged the project, Virgil's execution of it was his own.)

---

[17] The structural place occupied by Octavian is alone sufficient to disprove the story related by Servius that the fourth book originally ended with a panegyric to Cornelius Gallus, for which after Gallus' disgrace Virgil substituted the Aristaeus episode.

[18] White (1993) 135–6.

In this context the most interesting feature of Virgil's treatment is the extreme contrast built into his depiction of the farmer's world, which at times appears one of spontaneous abundance and at others of unremitting and potentially futile toil. The tension between these views remains characteristically unresolved, but the positive elements in the poem are themselves usually muted and qualified, while the negative elements are far darker than anything Virgil had written before. The gloom generated by the poem's grimmer passages may reflect the despair over the apparently endless cycle of bloodshed that surfaces elsewhere in these years, for example, in Horace's Epodes 7 and 16. The latter poem, probably Horace's disillusioned response to the Fourth Eclogue, places the Golden Age not in Rome but at the ends of the earth.[19] Much in the *Georgics* can be understood as Virgil's own rewriting of that optimistic vision in the light of bitter experience.

In the proem to *Georgics* 3, Virgil seems to anticipate writing the sort of epic he had refused to compose at the time of the *Eclogues*, a poem centring on Octavian (*in medio mihi Caesar erit*, 16) and celebrating his victories, with retrospective glances at his legendary Trojan ancestors (34–6). The *Aeneid* fulfilled this promise in a complex and unexpected way. At one level the poem Virgil actually wrote might seem to be the mirror image of the one he had described, an epic focused on the Trojan hero Aeneas and with 'Caesar' (now in his enhanced position as Augustus) occupying the centre only in the literal sense that one of his explicit appearances occurs near the actual mid-point of the poem.[20] But at another level the *Aeneid* more completely carries out the promise made in the *Georgics*, since the entire poem constitutes an oblique reflection on the great political fact of its time, the creation of the principate.

The oblique angle of this reflection is primarily secured through the poem's intricate temporal perspective. The action of the poem is set in the heroic past but is narrated from the viewpoint of the present; in addition, at three points a prophetic vision reveals events that lie far in Aeneas' future but which belonged to the past or present for Virgil's audience.[21] One effect of this interplay of temporal planes is to permit significant connections to be made between the heroic and the Augustan spheres. Thus the protagonist Aeneas, a youthful hero chosen by the gods to assume the leadership of a people facing ruin, both prefigures his descendant Augustus and confers legitimacy on the position of unquestioned pre-eminence he had recently assumed. More specific links are suggested in the prophetic

---

[19] The relative chronology of Epode 16 and Eclogue 4 is disputed; for a discussion favoring the priority of Horace see Clausen (1994) 147–54.

[20] *Aen.* 6.791–805. [21] *Aen.* 1.257–96, 6.756–854, 8.626–728.

passages just mentioned: thus, for example, the climactic place given to Augustus in the parade of Republican heroes in the Underworld is the poetic counterpart to the Augustan claim that the principate had brought about the restoration and fulfilment of the Republic. In this way Virgil can be said to have fashioned a literary myth to support the political myth of the principate.

These moments of prophecy, however, also illustrate a technique Virgil employs to incorporate an Augustan outlook without making it appear simply his own. In all three episodes the future is foretold by other voices or seen through other eyes: Jupiter, Anchises, Vulcan. One result, to be sure, is to invest the predictions with greater authority: Jupiter as a prophet of peace and unlimited empire carries far more weight than Virgil himself. But another consequence is that these explicitly Augustan passages are marked out as sharing a distinctive outlook and mode of presentation, which are in some respects at odds with those of the poem proper. This effect is most evident in the depiction of Roman history on Vulcan's shield, which displays the reductively didactic approach typical of a commissioned work of state art.[22] It is also significant that all three predictions have a hortatory function within the narrative, being directly or indirectly meant to shore up Aeneas' confidence in the ultimate success of his mission. This purpose helps to account for the partial and selective nature of these visions, which might appear merely propagandistic outside their poetic context.

In a similar way the integrity of the heroic narrative and its characters protects the poem from straightforward allegory. However strongly Aeneas may at times be assimilated to Augustus, he never becomes simply his heroic equivalent. Virgil therefore remains free to intimate connections between the two that are more effective for being left inexplicit. For example, Aeneas' affair with Dido, in which (as it appears from the divine perspective) he abandons his obligations to his people and subjects himself shamefully to a foreign queen, could remind some readers of Antony's involvement with Cleopatra. One might say (in blunter terms than Virgil's) that Aeneas is tempted to play the part of a reckless Antony, but is at last made to see that his destiny is as a dutiful Octavian.[23] Aeneas' status as an independent

---

[22] For example, it contains the fullest surviving example of the slanted presentation of Actium as a contest between Rome and Egypt. On the prophetic passages see also Zetzel below, p. 196, who places more weight than I might do on internal evidence of contradiction or undercutting. See also Gurval (1995).

[23] A parallel can also be suggested between the aspects of Aeneas that have left many readers cold and Octavian's notorious want of spontaneous feeling – 'a cool head, an unfeeling heart, and a cowardly disposition', in Gibbon's phrase (D&F I, ch. 3). Whether or not he was aware of the potential comparison, Virgil takes pains to show that Aeneas does not lack courage or feeling but that he has learned the necessity of self-control.

character and not merely a reflection of his descendant also allows for complex treatment of their shared qualities. Thus Aeneas' salient virtue, the respect for duty and authority denoted by the term *pietas*, corresponds to Octavian's vaunted devotion to his adoptive father Julius; but Virgil explores the workings of *pietas* in ways far removed from the sloganeering of political discourse.

A multiple perspective also operates at the larger level of plot, particularly in Books 7–12, which, although less familiar to modern – and perhaps ancient – readers than the first six books, were designated by Virgil himself as the weightier half of the poem.[24] The war between the Trojans and the Latins is explicitly presented in a Homeric light as Virgil's counterpart to the *Iliad*, a re-enactment of the Trojan War in which the outcome is reversed and the Trojans are destined to prevail. But since the combatants are in future to form a single people, and since the war divides the inhabitants of Italy into opposing camps, the conflict is also portrayed in terms that evoke Rome's civil wars and imply Virgil's reflections on that conflict.

Those reflections are remarkable for the complete absence of triumphal emotions. Instead the poem is permeated by revulsion at a war that should never have happened, whose cause is placed outside the human sphere, and located in the implacable and unreasoning hostility of Juno to the Trojans.[25] The losses on both sides, especially of the young, are treated with a sympathy more overtly poignant than the pathos of Homer. Aeneas himself participates to a disturbing degree in the hatred generated by the fighting. When Pallas, a young ally for whom he has assumed quasi-parental responsibility, is brutally killed by the enemy leader Turnus, Aeneas responds with inhuman savagery, collecting captives to be offered as living victims on Pallas' funeral pyre.[26] (Since Octavian was rumoured to have sacrificed human victims to the shades of Julius Caesar after the siege of Perusia, the incident takes on an additional chilling resonance.) Finally, the last image in the poem is not a victory celebration or peace agreement but the furious rage in which Aeneas exacts vengeance for Pallas' death, killing Turnus as he kneels before him wounded and pleading for mercy.

The compassion with which Virgil depicts the war's human cost has long been recognised by critics; it has indeed been a staple element in the image of Virgil as the poet of refined melancholy, of 'the infinite pity of things'. The phrase is that of J. W. Mackail, a prolific Latinist of the late

---

[24] *Aen.* 7.45 *maius opus moveo.*

[25] A similar explanation of the civil war as the product of divine hatred for Rome appears in Horace's ode to Pollio (2.1), arguably his most powerful treatment of the subject.

[26] *Aen.* 10.517–20.

nineteenth and early twentieth century whose edition of the *Aeneid* was published in 1930.[27] Mackail's note on the last lines of the poem is also worth quoting: 'thus in the final cadence of the *Aeneid* ... Virgil's perpetual sense of pity is touched with indignation that the Powers who control life should themselves be so pitiless, and that their purposes are only wrought out through so much human suffering'.[28]

Since the 1950s, however, this strain in Virgilian criticism has taken on a darker hue. Instead of a bitter but ultimately successful struggle to found a city and an empire, Virgil's view of Roman history has been interpreted (in the memorable words of Wendell Clausen) as 'a long Pyrrhic victory of the human spirit',[29] in which the cost is so high and the means so dreadful that success loses its meaning. Though sometimes loosely described as 'anti-Augustan', this reading of the poem does not ascribe to Virgil any form of political opposition. Rather what is attributed to him is a sense of quiet despair, a private lack of faith in the positive vision of Rome and its future that the epic's public voice seems to project.[30] In 1976 Ralph Johnson christened this critical position 'pessimism', and while the term is disclaimed by many of the scholars to whom it has been applied, since then debate over the import of the *Aeneid* (and to an increasing extent the *Georgics*) has often been characterised as an argument between optimists and pessimists.[31]

That discussion continues to be vigorous, stimulating closer study of the poem's relation to its Augustan context. Thanks to the eloquence with which the pessimist viewpoint has been stated, it is no longer possible to read the *Aeneid* as straightforwardly panegyrical – though a full survey of critical responses would show that it has in fact rarely been so read. At the same time, pessimism in the true sense of the word seems a partial and one-sided reaction to the poem. A more adequate description of Virgil's outlook might be ambivalence,[32] but only if that term is understood neither as a gentler name for pessimism nor as a diluted compromise between strong positions, but as a powerful and continuing tension of opposites.

---

[27] Mackail (1930) xxxii.   [28] *Ibid.* 511.   [29] Clausen (1964a) 146.

[30] Thus the 'two voices' distinguished by Parry 1963 and the 'further voices' of Lyne (1987).

[31] Johnson (1976) 1–22. Johnson further qualified the opposing views as 'the essentially optimistic European school' (p. 9) and 'the somewhat pessimistic Harvard school' (p. 11). The link between pessimism and Harvard (however plausible intuitively) proves to be largely coincidental, as Clausen observed in Horsfall (1995) 313–14, but it is true that most European critics of Virgil have taken an optimistic view of the *Aeneid* and have indeed regarded the pessimist interpretation as something of a curiosity.

[32] Thomas (1990).

In the poem's final scene, for example, the focus of the sharpest disagreements in recent criticism, it would be reductive to insist either that Aeneas is justified in killing Turnus or that his action violates his father's precept to 'spare the conquered' and is thus to be condemned. In avenging Pallas' death, Aeneas acts in response to his deepest and best loyalties, yet the deed is presented as an irruption of fury (Aeneas is 'ablaze with furious anger', *furiis accensus et ira*) and a perversion of piety (he claims that Turnus is being 'immolated' by the dead Pallas).[33] One may conclude that Aeneas did what was required of him (and in that sense did the 'right' thing), but still be appalled at the fact that it *was* required and at the effect of doing the 'right' thing on the one who does it. In so far as Aeneas here brings to mind Augustus, Virgil's text can be read as a reflection in advance on Augustus' words in the *Res gestae*: 'those who slaughtered my parent I drove into exile, avenging their crime through legally established tribunals; and afterwards, when they waged war against the republic, I defeated them twice in battle'.[34] The motive for revenge is the same for both, the pressing claims of *pietas*. But where the imperial propagandist views crime, bloodshed, and violation of piety as exclusively the work of the enemy, while describing his own actions in antiseptically unemotive terms, such comforting polarities are pointedly denied the actors of Virgil's poem.

In philosophical terms – and Virgil was a serious student of philosophy, though not an adherent of any single school – Virgil's viewpoint combines an Aristotelian acceptance of anger as justified in certain conditions with a Stoic's horror of the emotion itself and of its effects on the person who acts under its influence. Both views are able to coexist because they are situated within a Platonic conception of human nature as intrinsically divided, the model explicitly set forth by Anchises in speaking to his son in the Underworld:[35]

> igneus est ollis vigor et caelestis origo
> seminibus, quantum non noxia corpora tardant
> terrenique hebetant artus moribundaque membra.
> hinc metuunt cupiuntque dolent gaudentque, neque auras
> dispiciunt clausae tenebris et carcere caeco.

---

[33] The interpretation of these phrases is highly controversial; for a detailed study see Horsfall (1995) 192–216.

[34] *RG* 2 *qui parentem meum trucidaverunt* [*necaverunt* vel sim.], *eos in exilium expuli iudiciis legitimis ultus eorum facinus, et postea bellum inferentis rei publicae vici bis acie.*

[35] *Aen.* 6.730–4. For another view of the ending in a philosophical perspective see Braund below, pp. 214–16.

> Fiery energy
> is in these seeds, their source is heavenly;
> but they are dulled by harmful bodies, blunted
> by their own earthly limbs, their mortal members.
> Because of these, they fear and long, and sorrow
> and joy, they do not see the light of heaven;
> they are dungeoned in their darkness and blind prison.
>
> (trans. A. Mandelbaum)

This doctrine of moral entropy in which the stirrings of the spirit are forever hampered, but never extinguished, by the downward pull of the flesh provides the context for the recurringly ambivalent view of human action in Virgil's poem. For creatures so composed, all striving will be in some way thwarted, all victories partial and compromised – though not necessarily Pyrrhic.

Even an ambivalent Virgil is so much at odds with his traditional image as to prompt suspicion: are we not recasting the poet in a form more congenial to modern tastes, specifically to liberal views of the proper attitude of a writer toward autocratic power? The question is legitimate and useful, since attempting to answer it shows that the picture of Virgil as Augustan poet is itself shaped by historically conditioned assumptions, both ancient and modern.

The most fundamental of these assumptions arises from the circumstantial evidence of the poet's biography. Virgil belonged to the circle of Maecenas; he was also believed to be on close terms with Augustus, and it was said that on the poet's death Augustus himself took a hand in bringing out his *magnum opus*. Whether the latter two items are genuine or invented, they belong to an early image of the poet that coheres seamlessly with the fact that both the *Georgics* and the *Aeneid* openly praise the *princeps*. The poet's life and his work can thus be construed in a mutually reinforcing way as straightforwardly 'Augustan'.[36] (The lack of complexity in this view is typical of most recorded ancient – and especially Roman – statements about literary texts, which tend to focus on their literal sense and rarely show awareness of irony or implicit meaning.)

Though found in ancient sources, this view represents in several ways a misreading of historical conditions. In particular the depiction of Virgil as a 'client' of Maecenas or of Augustus himself, and therefore as saying only what accorded with their wishes and interests, employs a model of

---

[36] Something similar has happened in the case of Lucan: since he is known to have taken part in a conspiracy against Nero, his epic on the civil war has often been read as the poetic counterpart of his political activism, with less notice taken of elements in the poem that do not fit this interpretation; see above, p. 65.

patron–client relations too simplistic for his situation.[37] No doubt when Archias celebrated the victories of Lucullus, he thought mainly (or only) of pleasing his honorand. This style of patronage was not dead in the 20s – the relationship of the elegist Tibullus to M. Valerius Messalla Corvinus has a good deal in common with it – but Maecenas was a literary patron of a different kind. Though not averse to flattery from the poets he cultivated, he subordinated his own praise to that of Octavian/Augustus and served a mediating function between poets and the *princeps*; the effect (and presumably the intention) was precisely to minimise direct pressure and to allow writers the freedom to express their support in ways congenial to them.[38] Augustus wished to be celebrated only by the best writers, and both he and Maecenas knew that such talents did not respond well to outright dictation. Maecenas even seems to have been willing to take risks on politically unsympathetic writers if they showed sufficient talent, as he did in the case of Propertius, the most gifted poet of the generation after Virgil and Horace. Maecenas' favour utterly failed to turn Propertius into an Augustan panegyrist, but the poet does not appear to have suffered for his nonconformity.

Beginning with Propertius, other Roman poets also played a part in the presentation of Virgil as the quintessential Augustan writer. Their statements, however, must be treated with even greater reserve than those of the biographers: poets do not aim at objectivity in portraying eminent predecessors, but react to them as they impinge on their own work, and most of the poets in question found it useful to construct Virgil in a purely Augustan mould in order to measure their distance from him. So, for example, to the extent that Ovid and Lucan create an 'anti-*Aeneid*' in the *Metamorphoses* and the *Bellum civile*, they do so by isolating those aspects of Virgil's poem – its heroising and celebratory elements – that are most at odds with their own outlook. At the same time, poets are likely to be far more perceptive than other readers in their responses. It is therefore significant that Neronian and, to some degree, Flavian poets seem to have responded with particular intensity to many of the features of the *Aeneid* singled out by 'pessimist' critics.[39]

Finally, an attempt to view the *Aeneid* in its historical context would note the fact that ambivalence of the sort that has been found in the poem is hardly absent from other writing of the 20s, and could even be claimed as one of the distinguishing features of that decade. Writing some years after Actium, Livy begins his massive history with strikingly negative remarks

---

[37] White (1993), arguing generally against the 'mouthpiece' view of patron–client relations.
[38] Griffin (1984).   [39] Above, p. 64.

about the present, a time in which 'we can bear neither our vices nor their remedies'.[40] The tone recalls the end of *Georgics* 1, with its fear that Rome may have become too deeply corrupted for the process to be reversed. That fear recurs in the last of Horace's 'Roman Odes', part of the collection of lyric poetry he published in 23, in which reflections on the corrupt state of contemporary morality lead to a chilling final outburst: 'Our fathers' generation, worse than that of their fathers, has produced us who are more wicked still, and we are doomed to bring forth offspring yet more infected with vice.'[41] These passages fix on the theme, strangely congenial to Roman writers, of debased morality and consequent civic ruin. More directly political comments on the price Romans had paid for an end to civil war are not to be found, and may only have been possible in a less explicit medium, such as that of a mythological epic.[42] But what is common is a thread of precariousness and uncertainty, a sense that while one could hope the future would be better, one could not yet feel confident that it would be so.

To see signs in Virgil of an ambivalent or even a pessimistic outlook is thus not to read him anachronistically. In fact, while explicit interpretation of the *Aeneid* along these lines is a relatively recent development, the aspects of the poem to which an ambivalent or pessimist reading responds can claim to be the most basic and permanent, having their origins in the poem's conception of human nature. An optimistic or Augustan view, on the other hand, highlights elements of the poem that ultimately depend on a contingent set of historical circumstances, the hopes for renewal and stability raised by the leadership of Augustus. In that light what calls for explanation is less that critics in the middle of the twentieth century began to articulate a pessimistic view of the *Aeneid* than that an optimistic consensus prevailed for so long.

Since Virgil's optimism is linked to his pride in Rome and his hopes for its future, a positive view of the *Aeneid*'s import requires a reader who either shares that pride or for whom the concept of Rome carries an equivalently powerful value. In other words, just as the grounds for hope within the poem are historically contingent, so too is the perspective needed to

---

[40] *Praef.* 9 *haec tempora quibus nec vitia nostra nec remedia pati possumus*, on which see Syme (1959) 42–3, 49 (on instability subsisting late into the 20s).

[41] *C.* 3.6.45–48 *damnosa quid non imminuit dies? | aetas parentum peior avis tulit | nos nequiores, mox daturos | progeniem vitiosiorem.* Horace's second and last collection of lyrics, which appeared in 13, conveys a far more settled and satisfied view of the present.

[42] Or possibly a tragedy. Varius' *Thyestes*, now lost, was regarded by later critics as one of the crowning achievements of Latin tragedy; one would give much to know how Varius treated the archetypal myth of fraternal enmity in a play staged in 29 to celebrate Octavian's triumph over Antony and Cleopatra.

read the poem optimistically. Those conditions were most easily met as long as the Roman empire itself was still in being, but even after the empire as a political entity had long ceased to exist, Virgil's vision of Rome under Augustus maintained its hold on the European imagination as a model for the beneficent exercise of power – whether the power in question was that of Charlemagne, the Renaissance papacy, Victorian Britain, or Mussolini's Italy.[43] As recently as the 1960s, in a poem composed to mark the inauguration of John F. Kennedy, Robert Frost could hail the new administration as presaging a 'next Augustan age', hopefully described as 'a golden age of poetry and power'.[44]

But although Virgil was able to endow Rome and Augustus with a remarkably resilient metaphorical value, the Augustan principate remains a historical event, and differing assessments of it in historical terms must sooner or later affect reactions to its treatment by Virgil. In particular, the more positively Augustus is judged, the easier it becomes to construe the *Aeneid* as a celebration of his rule, whereas if Augustus was in fact nothing more than an especially crafty tyrant (as Gibbon had viewed him), Virgil's praise of his regime becomes an embarrassment: either the praise is genuine, and damaging to the credit of the poet, or it is feigned to conceal Virgil's true attitude of disgust or opposition. Both conclusions were drawn, and explicitly in these terms, well before the critical discussions of the past two generations. More than a century ago, W. Y. Sellar spoke in Gibbonian accents of Virgil as 'really the panegyrist of despotism under the delusive disguise of paternal government'[45] and for that reason questioned the *Aeneid*'s claim to the highest rank as a work of art. The anti-Augustan view was urged with passionate intensity in 1935 by Francesco Sforza, who credited Virgil with 'the almost incredible feat of . . . reviling the persons connected with the origin of the Eternal City, while purporting, all the time, superlatively to praise them'.[46] The fact that Sforza was then an exile

---

[43] This enduring metaphorical power is closely related to the link Virgil establishes between Rome's imperial destiny and a divinely sanctioned cosmic order; cf. Hardie (1986).

[44] Frost (1962) 30:

> It makes the prophet in us all presage
> the glory of a next Augustan age, . . .
> a golden age of poetry and power
> of which this noonday's the beginning hour.

(The final lines of the expanded version of 'For John Fitzgerald Kennedy his inauguration' as published in the collection *In the Clearing*; on Frost's contacts with Kennedy before and after the inaugural ceremony cf. Thompson and Winnick (1976) 277–83. The text is also of interest as a specimen of the kind of commemorative poetry that Virgil successfully avoided writing.)

[45] Sellar (1877) 349.   [46] Sforza (1935) 102.

from fascist Italy accounts for the virulence of his attitude toward Augustus (referred to as 'autocrat', 'despot', 'tyrant', and 'the Master'), and also explains his desire to claim the *Aeneid* as a work of covert resistance.[47]

Another product of the 1930s, itself strongly influenced by the politics of the period, is more directly relevant to modern interpretation of Augustus, namely Ronald Syme's *Roman Revolution*, published in 1939. Syme's unforgettable portrait of Octavian as a ruthless party leader and of Augustus as a master manipulator of opinion made belief in the benign *pater patriae* virtually impossible. It is highly probable that this starkly unsentimental view of Augustus, combined with postwar revulsion at autocracy as represented by Hitler, Mussolini, and Stalin, laid the foundation for the anti-imperial strain in criticism of the *Aeneid* that started to emerge in the 1950s. Nor does it seem coincidental that ambivalence has become more prominent in recent Virgilian criticism at the same time as ancient historians have begun to replace Syme's dark image of the *princeps* with more nuanced interpretations.[48]

It is highly appropriate that Augustus, as well as Virgil, should now be seen in an ambivalent light, and in terms foreshadowed by Virgil himself. For Virgil knew very well the bloodstained young man that Octavian had been; but he could also appreciate the very different figure he had chosen to become, and could make of Augustus the instrument of a real, if troubled, hope. As for Augustus, none of Virgil's works, least of all the *Aeneid*, can have been the sort of poem he might have hoped for, but one would like to believe that as a master of propaganda he could distinguish between its comfortable half-truths and the untidy confusion of reality, and that he valued Virgil's praise more highly for the honesty with which it was qualified. Surely he was shrewd enough to know that Virgil's poem would be a far greater and more enduring monument to him than any panegyric, and that he was serving his own interests, as well as those of posterity, in saving the *Aeneid* from the flames.

FURTHER READING

On the literary milieu of late Republican Rome and its influence on Virgil see Wendell Clausen, 'A new poet's education', in *Virgil's Aeneid and the Tradition of Hellenistic Poetry* (Berkeley, 1987) 1–14, which restates and modifies Clausen's influential earlier studies. Alan Cameron's *Callimachus and his Critics* (Princeton, 1995) brings many aspects of Callimachus' influence on Roman poetry into sharper focus.

---

[47] Sforza was presumably aware that at this time Augustus and Virgil's portrayal of him were being exploited for propaganda purposes by the fascist and Nazi dictatorships.

[48] As represented, for example, by several of the papers in Raaflaub and Toher (1990).

The political import of Virgil's work, especially the *Aeneid*, has generated a substantial (and still growing) bibliography; S. J. Harrison provides a helpful overview in 'Some views of the *Aeneid* in the twentieth century', in *Oxford Readings in Vergil's Aeneid*, ed. S. J. Harrison (Oxford, 1990) 1–20. Important statements of the so-called 'pessimist' viewpoint include Adam Parry's 'The two voices of Virgil's *Aeneid*', *Arion* 2 (1963) 66–80, Michael Putnam's *The Poetry of the Aeneid* (Cambridge, MA, 1965), Ralph Johnson's *Darkness Visible: A Study of Vergil's Aeneid* (Berkeley, 1976), and, for the *Georgics*, David Ross's *Virgil's Elements. Physics and Poetry in the Georgics* (Princeton, 1987) and the 2-volume commentary by R. F. Thomas (Cambridge, 1988 (Cambridge Greek and Latin Classics)). The recent resurgence of positive or 'Augustan' readings of the poem has drawn much strength from Philip Hardie's *Virgil's Aeneid: Cosmos and Imperium* (Oxford, 1986); other prominent neo-optimists are Francis Cairns in *Virgil's Augustan Epic* (Cambridge, 1989) and Karl Galinsky, most recently in *Augustan Culture: An Interpretive Introduction* (Princeton, 1996). Nicholas Horsfall offers a penetrating review of the entire debate focused on the end of the poem in *A Companion to the Study of Virgil*, ed. N. M. Horsfall (*Mnem.* Suppl. 151 (Leiden, 1995) 192–216). The links between the *Aeneid* and imperial ideology are viewed in a wider context by David Quint in *Epic and Empire: Politics and Generic Form from Virgil to Milton* (Princeton, 1993).

The elusive phenomenon of Augustan literary patronage, especially in its political aspect, is the subject of a scintillating paper by Jasper Griffin, 'Augustus and the poets: "Caesar qui cogere posset"', in *Caesar Augustus: Seven Aspects*, eds. F. Millar and E. Segal (Oxford, 1984) 189–218, and is more broadly reconsidered by Peter White in *Promised Verse: Poets in the Society of Augustan Rome* (Cambridge, MA, 1993).

Finally, our sense of the larger Augustan cultural context has been enlarged and transformed by Paul Zanker's *The Power of Images in the Age of Augustus*, tr. A. Shapiro (Ann Arbor, 1988).

13

JAMES E. G. ZETZEL

Rome and its traditions

In Book 8 of the *Aeneid*, when Aeneas visits the Arcadian settlement of Pallanteum, he is led by Evander through the site of the future city of Rome. What greets them is a rustic scene: wooded hills, herds of cattle, a simple village of humble immigrants. As Aeneas' ship comes up the Tiber, the waves themselves marvel at the unfamiliar sight of armed men on an oared ship. Virgil's readers might have reacted similarly to the novelty of the scene, a view of Rome before historical Rome existed: a small settlement surrounded by forest near the banks of a river, occupying the place of the buildings and grandeur of Augustan Rome, with the commerce of the Tiber and of the Forum Boarium where Aeneas landed. As the Trojans arrive, the contrast between past and present is made explicit: they see Evander's small village 'which Roman power has now raised to the heavens' (8.99–100). So too, during Aeneas' walk through the future city, Evander is described as 'the founder of the Roman citadel' (313); they pass the gate 'which the Romans call Carmentalis' (338–9); the Capitoline is 'golden now, once bristling with wooded thickets' (348). As they reach Evander's house, they see herds of cattle 'mooing in the Roman Forum and the fashionable Carinae' (361).

Although Book 8 contains Aeneas' first visit to the site of Rome, the Roman future is present from the very beginning of Book 1: the proem ends with a reference to 'the walls of lofty Rome' (1.7), and there are frequent reminders of Rome's history throughout the poem. Even though the action of the *Aeneid* ends with Aeneas' killing of Turnus, it is Rome and its destiny that provide the retrospective justification for Aeneas' actions and sufferings. Although Rome is not founded within the narrative of the poem, the creation of a Roman people and a Roman nation is its goal: 'so great was the effort it took to establish the Roman race', *tantae molis erat Romanam condere gentem* (1.33). Prophecies and the narrator's own comments remind the reader of the aetiologies of particular Roman customs or names and of events between the end of the narrative and the poet's own day: the establishment of a joint settlement of Trojans and Latins at Lavinium, the history of Alba Longa and the foundation of Rome, the deeds of individual Romans and the expansion of Roman power, culminating in the glory of the Augustan age. Book 8 in particular spans the history of Rome, from the ruined cities which Evander shows Aeneas and the thickets on the Capitol which Evander says are inhabited by an unknown god, to the final scene on the shield of Aeneas at the end of the book, in which Augustus celebrates his triple triumph, in August of 29 BC, after the victory over Antony at Actium. From the tiny settlement of Evander on the Palatine, the reader is drawn upward to the golden Capitol of the Augustan age, the centre of both the Roman empire and the universe itself.

The narrative of the *Aeneid* is concerned with (and falls chronologically between) the Homeric epics and the history of the Roman people. Much of the structure of the poem and many episodes within it are derived from the *Iliad* and *Odyssey*; much of the material within that framework involves Rome. The two major dramatic sections of the *Aeneid* – the Dido episode in Books 1–4 and the war between the Trojans and the Latins in Books 9–12 – anticipate the major external and internal crises of Roman history, the Punic Wars of the third and second centuries BC and the civil wars of the first century.[1] The central four books are largely static; through scenes marking Aeneas' gradual approach to the locus of his descendants' history – Sicily in Book 5, Cumae in Book 6, the Tiber mouth and the city of Latinus in Book 7, and Rome itself in Book 8 – they provide a set of descriptions of Rome and Italy past and present that offers an alternative to the narrative chronicle of Aeneas' wars and wanderings. These same books, moreover, gradually abandon the framework of the Homeric world (if not of Homer as a literary model) in favour of Italy and Rome, introducing both Aeneas and the reader to a new future and a different past – to the outcome, in Virgil's own day, of the crises adumbrated in the first and last portions of the epic, and to the background, both ethnographic and mythological, of the Italy which Aeneas now encounters. Rome and Italy, of course, provide the framework for the entire *Aeneid*, and some important details (the catalogue of Etruscans in Book 10, for instance) appear outside the central books; but it is the catalogue of the Italian allies of Latinus in Book 7 and Evander's account of Rome's prehistory in Book 8 that give texture and specificity to Virgil's understanding of Italy, and the catalogue of Romans in Anchises' speech in the Underworld in Book 6 and the shield of Aeneas at the end of Book 8 that create Virgil's interpretation of Rome's history and destiny.

---

[1] See, for example, Williams (1983) 70–5.

The Italy that Aeneas encounters is by no means simple. In the first books of the poem, Jupiter announces (1.263–4, 4.229–31) that Aeneas' destiny is to civilise the warring tribes of Italy, and the Italians are portrayed as fierce, lawless, and savage. The inhabitants seem as primitive as the landscape is uncultivated; but the apparent contrasts between a state of nature and the advanced culture of Augustan Rome, and between civilised Trojans and barbarous Italians, dissolves on closer inspection. In the first place, the *Aeneid* depicts the Trojans themselves both as heroic warriors and as representatives of a decadent and destroyed eastern civilisation; their landing in Italy can be understood as either the destined arrival of law and civilisation, as in Jupiter's prophecies, or the colonising and destructive invasion of a foreign army (cf. 7.38–9).[2] Nor are the Italians a primitive and autochthonous people. Latinus claims descent from Saturn (7.48–9); in his palace is a set of effigies of his ancestors, including both Saturn and Janus (7.180). According to Evander's account of the prehistory of Rome, these same gods had built fortifications on the Capitoline and Janiculum respectively, of which huge ruins remain for Aeneas' inspection (8.355–8). In the catalogue of Italians, Aventinus is a child of Hercules, Caeculus of Vulcan, Messapus of Neptune (7.656, 679, 691); Tiburtus and his brothers are Argive, Halaesus is associated with Agamemnon, and Virbius is the son of Hippolytus (7.672, 723, 761). Aeneas' ally Evander too is no aborigine: he is an immigrant from Arcadia, the oldest region of Greece, and had, in his youth, met Priam himself (8.158–9). Like Aeneas, the inhabitants of Italy had divine ancestors; like him, they are a part of the world of mythic Greece.[3] Conversely, the basis of Aeneas' claim to settle in Italy is the Italian origin of his ancestor Dardanus (3.163–8; 7.205–8, 240–2). By making the Trojans Italian and the Italians Greek, Virgil constructs multiple and overlapping history of the two peoples: they have a shared origin, and neither one is precisely what it seems on first appearance.

In the *Aeneid*, moreover, early Italy has more than one history, more than one truth. In introducing his description of the site of Rome, Evander gives Aeneas a brief history of the populations of Italy (8.314–36).[4] According to his account, the aboriginal inhabitants, contemporary with Fauns

---

[2] On various aspects of the double presentation of the Trojans, cf. Anderson (1957) = Harrison (1990) 239–52; Thomas (1982) 99–100; Lyne (1987) 107–13; O'Hara (1994) 215–17.

[3] *Contra* Otis (1964) 329: 'They are unsophisticated primitives whose courage is put to a very bad use.'

[4] On this passage, cf. Thomas (1982) 95–8; Grandsen (1984) 63; O'Hara (1994) 222–3.

and Nymphs, were sprung from trees, and were completely uncivilised; they were settled in cities and given laws by Saturn when he arrived in flight from Jupiter, and under the reign of Saturn there was a golden age. Subsequently, the Saturnian civilisation degenerated through war and greed, and the invasions of various other peoples followed, including Ausonians, Sicani and, most recently, Evander himself with his Arcadians. The arrival of Aeneas is thus only the last in a long series of foreign invasions. Evander's ethnography is an uneasy combination of two standard accounts of the history of civilisation: he blends a hard-primitive anthropological account, such as is found, for instance, in Lucretius Book 5, according to which humans have gradually risen from primeval savagery, and a soft-primitive mythological one, as found in Hesiod's *Works and Days* or Virgil's *Georgics*, in which human behaviour has declined from the ideal simplicity and ease of a Golden Age. In general, Evander's account is pessimistic: he views the reign of Saturn as only an intermission from continuous fighting and invasions. His interpretation accords with that suggested by Jupiter's prophecies, in which the role of Aeneas and the Trojans is to end discord, impose order, and set Italy on the path to civilisation and glory.

Evander's is not the only account of early Italy. In Book 7, both in Virgil's own introduction of Latinus (7.45–6) and in Latinus' description of his people, the Golden Age has not entirely disappeared.[5] The old king has ruled in peace for a long time; he describes his nation (as in traditional Golden-Age mythology) as being naturally just without the need for laws (7.203). According to this version, it is clear that Aeneas and the Trojans are not saviours, but a disruptive influence in a peaceful and harmonious world. At the same time, the version given by the poet and by Latinus is itself undercut: the effigies of military figures in Latinus' palace, the military exercises of the population, and the fact that the Latins are at war with Evander's Arcadians call this idealistic vision into question.[6] Virgil does not resolve this difficulty, and the fact that a figure within the poem contradicts the narrator's voice discourages belief in an omniscient narrator. The Italians are both warlike and peaceful; simple (or savage) tribesmen and figures of heroic myth; both like the Trojans and unlike them. The tidy polarities of civilisation and barbarism, of progress and decline, of war and peace are carefully disturbed and redistributed throughout Virgil's account of Italy: no tidy and schematic distribution of history into antithetical oppositions can do justice to the complexity of human affairs. And,

---

[5] Cf. Horsfall (1981) = Harrison (1990) 473–4. [6] Cf. Williams (1983) 40–2.

as will be seen below, such contradictions and the resulting uncertainties are central to Virgil's portrayal of both Italy and Rome.[7]

In terms of Virgil's construction of history in general, therefore, the contradictory nature of early Italy makes sense; as noted above, it also provides a suitable mirror for the equally ambivalent portrait of the Trojans themselves. In dramatic terms, moreover, it was also necessary for Virgil to elaborate the history and significance of Italy: it would clearly detract from the significance of the war in the final four books of the poem if Aeneas had no opponent, in Virgil's adaptation of the *Iliad*, worthy either of his own stature or of his literary antecedents. The great emphasis that Virgil places on Italy, however, is more important than that; it plays a major role in the poem as a whole, culminating in Juno's wish, honoured by Jupiter at the end of the poem, that Troy should give way to Rome and to Italy: 'Let Latium exist, let the Alban kings last for generations, let Roman stock be powerful with Italian strength', *sit Latium, sint Albani per saecula reges, | sit Romana potens Itala virtute propago* (12.826–7). In the proem to Book 1, Virgil had outlined the future with the triad of Latium, Alba Longa, and Rome; by the end, that has been expanded to include Italy. Similarly, Augustus at Actium, on the shield in Book 8, is leading not the Romans, but the Italians into battle; that verse reflects the 'Oath of all Italy' sworn to Augustus before the war of Actium, and both poem and oath correspond to the genuine and growing importance of the Italians in Roman society and ideology in the first century BC.[8] The end of the Social War (91–89) between Rome and the Italian confederacy gave Roman citizenship to all Italy south of the Po; members of the local Italian aristocracies became increasingly prominent in Roman society and government. The importance of this stratum of society for the Augustan settlement is exemplified by the career of Publius Ventidius, who as a child was led as a captive in 89 in the triumph of Pompeius Strabo in the Social War, and who lived to celebrate a triumph himself in 38 BC.[9] The hardiness, courage, and virtue of the Italian peasant-soldier – Sabine and Volscian,

---

[7] It is worth noting here (although space does not permit elaboration of the subject) that Virgil's approach to the Roman and Italian pasts is deeply indebted to the narrative techniques of the Alexandrian poets, notably Callimachus, and that the combination of Alexandrian methods and Roman antiquarian learning is central to Virgil's understanding of the contingency of historical truth. For Virgil's debt to Callimachus, see most recently Clausen (1987); for the similar combination of Alexandrian method and early Roman materials in Catullus, cf. Zetzel (1983a).

[8] 8.678; cf. *Res gestae* 25.2. On the role of the Italians, cf. Syme (1939) 284–93; Momigliano (1960) 412–15.

[9] Cf. Syme (1939) 71, 223–4. Detailed documentation of the rise of the Italians in Wiseman (1971).

Marsian and Apulian – is a stock theme of late Republican and Augustan literature; the catalogue of Italians stresses those qualities, as does the speech of Numanus Remulus in Book 9.[10] Virgil expands on this picture of simple virtue to include dignity, distinction, and mythic ancestry: the Italians are worthy not only of their role in the *Aeneid*, but of their place in the Augustan order as well. The war between Trojan and Italian in the second half of the poem is both an analogy to and an anticipation of the historical war fought between Roman and Italian at the beginning of the first century, and, given the outcome, both the mythic and the historical wars become, retrospectively, civil wars, between peoples soon to become a single nation. As with the prehistory of Italy, simple polarities become impossible: there is, from the point of view of the Augustan present, no more difference between Roman and Italian than between Trojan and Italian. At the end of the war in the *Aeneid*, the Trojans are subsumed within the Latin community just as, under Augustus, Rome itself became no more than a part (if a central part) of greater Italy. While the *Aeneid* as a whole provides an aetiological link between Troy and Rome, countless details in Books 7 and 8 connect particular Roman names, customs, buildings and cults to the populations of Italy which Aeneas encounters.

Virgil was not the first to write of primitive Italy or to draw connections between early peoples and present customs. The historical epics of Naevius and Ennius, while concentrating on the events of their own lifetimes, had given due attention to the Trojan origins of Rome, and indeed had made Romulus not just the descendant, but the grandson of Aeneas; the chronological difficulties of this reconstruction resulted in the insertion of the kings of Alba into the later tradition.[11] Individual Roman aristocrats too were proud of their ancestral traditions: a number of families traced their descent from Troy, and one, the Aemilii, claimed descent from Pythagoras.[12] For at least a century before Virgil, Roman writers (and some Greeks) had been interested in Roman antiquities, and in his influential *Origines*, the elder Cato had reported the foundation legends not just of Rome, but of other Italian communities. Assertions of settlement by figures of Homeric myth were not limited to Rome and the genuinely Greek foundations of southern Italy and Sicily: many towns attached themselves not only to Aeneas but to Hercules and Odysseus, figures whose western travels were familiar

---

[10] Cf. Horsfall (1971) = Harrison (1990) 305–15; Thomas (1982) 98–9.

[11] See, for instance, Ogilvie's commentary on Livy 1.3.2.

[12] Three Roman families (other than the Iulii) are mentioned in *Aeneid* 5 (Memmii, Sergii, Cluentii); several others are also attested. The Pythagorean ancestry of the Aemilii is found in Plutarch, *Aemilius Paullus* 1. On family history in this period, cf. Rawson (1985) 231–2.

in the Greek mythological tradition.[13] Roman antiquarians had also sought aetiological explanations for obscure religious, legal, and topographical features of Roman life, and in the decades before Virgil began to write the *Aeneid*, the antiquarian Varro had collected a huge mass of material on such subjects. Although most of the works of Varro and others on Roman antiquities are now lost, it is clear that Virgil read widely in this area, and knew not only the early epics, but the historical works of Cato and other annalists – including the early books (which do survive) of the *Ab urbe condita* of his contemporary Livy – and the many antiquarian collections of Varro.[14]

But although he was necessarily interested in Roman antiquities, Virgil's antiquarianism is a means rather than an end: the *Aeneid* offers not an uncritical assemblage of archaic lore, but a selection that is clearly and deliberately shaped.[15] What is more, Virgil's picture of early Italy involved invention as well as selection. Several figures in the catalogue of Italians are almost certainly Virgil's own creations: not merely some with a significant role in the narrative (Lausus and Camilla), but also the lesser figures Ufens and Umbro, both with names of rivers geographically unconnected with the contingents which they lead.[16] Messapus, who leads the Faliscans in the catalogue, has no connection with them in any other source, but is elsewhere a Euboean attached to the Messapians of southern Italy. Halaesus, normally connected to the Faliscans, is moved to Campania, as is Oebalus, normally a legendary Spartan king associated with the Tarentines, who claimed Spartan ancestry.[17] Among the Etruscan leaders in the catalogue in Book 10, Ocnus and Aulestes, though linked in Virgil with Mantua, are traditionally the founders of Felsina (Bologna) and Perusia, while Massicus, whom Virgil links to Clusium and Cosa, has the name of a mountain in Campania.[18] Even Turnus, the Rutulian leader of Latinus' army, is made the son of Daunus, the eponymous ancestor of the Daunians of Apulia. Two figures in the Italian catalogue, moreover, incorporate elements of early Roman legend. Aventinus, for whom the Aventine hill is named, is normally one of the Alban kings; in Virgil, he is the son by Hercules of a priestess

---

[13] For local history (indigenous and Hellenized) cf. Horsfall (1987) 6–9. The connection with Odysseus is as old as Hesiod, *Theogony* 1011–13, naming Agrios and Latinos as the sons of Kirke and Odysseus.

[14] Horsfall (1981) = Harrison (1990) 466–77 is sceptical about the range of Virgil's antiquarian studies, but is the most valuable treatment of his methods in the use of antiquarian materials.

[15] In addition to Horsfall (1981) = Harrison (1990), cf. also Rehm (1932) 66.

[16] For Camilla cf. Horsfall (1988); for the others Rehm (1932) 92 and Holland (1935) 203, 206.

[17] Rehm (1932) 92–5; Holland (1935) 202–6.   [18] Rehm (1932) 9; Holland (1935) 203–5.

named Rhea, anticipating the legend of the birth of Romulus and Remus.[19] The Sabine leader in the catalogue, Clausus, is an otherwise unknown homonymous ancestor of the traditional founder of the gens Claudia, Attus Clausus, who came from Cures with his followers in the first year of the Republic – but who is strangely said by Virgil to have arrived in Rome during the joint reign of Romulus and Titus Tatius.[20]

Just as in the broader accounts of the peopling of early Italy and the development of civilisation, therefore, so too in the details of early Italian history, particularly in the catalogues, Virgil's version is curiously discordant, and is anything but a scrupulous report of traditional lore. While the geography of the catalogue is for the most part precise and accurate (although there are some invented place names and some which can no longer be identified), it is linked to figures sometimes invented, sometimes transposed from their traditional locations; the detailed ethnographic descriptions in the catalogue of costume and weaponry are often borrowed from accounts of other primitive peoples (including the Germans as described by Julius Caesar) and have little connection with the Roman antiquarian tradition.[21] Through the mythological connections of his Italians, Virgil elevates them into worthy antagonists for Aeneas and the Trojans; through the imaginative use of ethnography, he makes them representative of Rome's contemporary tribal enemies; through the displacement of personal and topographical names, he makes a small war in Latium representative of the length and breadth of Augustan Italy. In terms of what the Romans themselves knew or thought about their national past, it is in no sense an accurate portrait of early Italy; but it is an Italian past that is in complete harmony with the rest of the poem.

At the same time, however, the dramatic coherence of Virgil's Italy is disconcerting, precisely because of the thoroughgoing falseness of its details: the geographical and historical distortions inevitably create a certain uneasiness about the order and development of Roman history itself. That applies not only to the mythical anachronisms concerning Aventinus and Clausus in the catalogue, but even more to the retrojection into the past of Roman names and customs. When Aeneas promises the Sibyl (6.69ff.) to build a temple to Apollo and place the Sibylline oracles in it, he is announcing what was not in fact done until the time of Augustus.[22] The palace of Latinus (described as *augustum*, 7.170) is portrayed in terms that bring to mind many of the public places of Augustan Rome – the

---

[19] Rehm (1932) 94.
[20] The only other clear occurrence of the Romulean date for Clausus' arrival is in Suetonius, *Tiberius* 1.1; cf. Wiseman (1979) 59–60.
[21] Cf. Rehm (1932) 66–71.   [22] Cf. Zetzel (1989) 279.

Curia, the temple of Capitoline Jupiter, the Forum of Augustus (planned, if not yet built at the time the *Aeneid* was written), and the speakers' platform in the Forum itself, decorated with the prows (*rostra*) of captured ships. In the appeal to the Muses which opens the catalogue as (twice) in the description of the numinous thickets of the Capitoline, Virgil uses the phrase *iam tum*, 'already at that time' (7.643, 8.349, 8.350): just as in the double vision of Italian prehistory as a golden age or a period of savagery to be ameliorated by Aeneas, one has a sense both of Roman progress from a lesser past and of the immanence and unchanging quality of eternal Rome.

The same combination of change with permanence, and of surface clarity with discordant details, marks Virgil's account of Rome itself, contained primarily in a series of prophecies in which he outlines the course of Roman history, culminating in the Augustan settlement and the Rome of Virgil's own day. Three passages of the poem are particularly important: Jupiter's prophecy to Venus at 1.257–96; Anchises' revelation to Aeneas in the Underworld of the future heroes of Rome at 6.756–886; and the prophetic shield which Vulcan makes for Aeneas at Venus' request, described at 8.626–728. In terms of their contents, the three prophecies have clear similarities: each draws connections between Romulus and Augustus; each foresees both civil war and its conclusion; each includes a prophecy of Roman universal rule. There are also differences among the three: there is very little overlap in specific content; the focus of each is different; and each is affected by its context within the poem as a whole. Furthermore, although each passage is in some sense panegyrical, each also contains elements that disturb or complicate the smooth course of Roman glory.

In this respect, Jupiter's prophecy to Venus is most striking, as it provides the framework for much that is to appear later on.[23] The speech outlines the future of Aeneas' race: the precise (if mystical) chronology of the 333 years to elapse between the arrival of Aeneas in Italy and the foundation of Rome is followed by Jupiter's proclamation of the universality and eternity of Roman rule.[24] 'I place no limits on them of time or space: I have given them power without bound', *his ego nec metas rerum nec tempora pono: | imperium sine fine dedi* (1.278–9). The particulars of this statement follow: Juno will give up her anger, Rome will triumph over the Greeks who had defeated them (in their Trojan shape) at Troy. A Caesar, descended from Aeneas through Iulus/Ascanius, will extend the empire and become a god, after which eternal peace will return to the

---

[23] Cf. Williams (1983) 138–42; Lyne (1987) 79–81; and particularly O'Hara (1990) 132–63.
[24] On the chronology cf. Horsfall (1974).

world, in which Romulus/Quirinus and Remus will jointly preside, while the gates of war are closed on *Furor* bound and imprisoned within.

Jupiter's account of the Roman future is powerfully simple: the reversal of the result of the Trojan War through Rome's conquest of Greece, the end of Juno's hostility in the Punic Wars, the resolution of discord, and universal peace under the leadership of Venus' Roman descendants. In context, however, the prophecy is designed as a consolation for Venus, who is legitimately worried by Aeneas' present circumstances, shipwrecked on the coast of Africa; its rhetorical purpose leads to distortion and over-simplification. The Alban Kings, we learn from Book 6, are descended not from Ascanius, but from the son of Aeneas and Lavinia; Juno's wrath will take a very long time – until the Hannibalic War – to subside;[25] there is a disturbing uncertainty as to whether the 'Caesar' referred to is Julius Caesar or Augustus; and, above all, the idea that Romulus/Quirinus and Remus will rule together in harmony clearly contradicts the accepted legend of Romulus' murder of Remus. All these details call into question the descriptions of universal rule and universal peace which, from the point of view of Virgil's own day, still lie in the future.

Anchises' speech in the Underworld similarly combines panegyrical proph-ecy with discordant historical allusions.[26] Here, the avowed purpose is both consolatory and protreptic. Aeneas cannot understand why any soul could wish to return to the travails of life on earth; Anchises displays to him the individual greatness of their descendants 'so that you may rejoice with me at the discovery of Italy' (6.718). The main body of Anchises' speech contains two basic groups of figures: on the one hand, the monarchs of Alba Longa and Rome; on the other, the military leaders of the Roman republic. Each group, however, is interrupted by description of figures of Virgil's own lifetime: in the first group Augustus, who is juxtaposed with Romulus, and in the second, unnamed, Julius Caesar and Pompey, placed between the heroes of the early Republic and the military leaders of the third and second centuries BC. The coda of Anchises' speech similarly juxta-poses early and very recent history: the praise of the third-century Marcellus leads Aeneas to ask about the shadowy young man next to him, who turns out to be Augustus' nephew, son-in-law, and prospective heir Marcellus, who died suddenly in 23 BC, while Virgil was writing the *Aeneid*.

As with Jupiter's prophecy, Anchises' speech combines two broad themes, the external military successes of the Roman people – including his fam-ous admonition 'to spare the conquered and subdue the proud' – and the importance of Aeneas' own descendants, particularly Augustus, within the

---

[25] Cf. Feeney (1984) = Harrison (1990) 339–62.   [26] Cf. Feeney (1986).

broader framework of Roman achievement. He gives Augustus credit, as in Book 1, for restoring a golden age and extending Roman power throughout the world, with comparison to the territories covered by Hercules and Dionysus. Augustus, as descendant of Aeneas, is equated with the destiny of the Roman people, divinely ordained and divinely justified. But neither the heroes of Rome nor the descendants of Aeneas are presented with unalloyed panegyric. Virgil records the decline of monarchy into tyranny; Ancus is too much the *popularis*; L. Junius Brutus, the founder of the republic, is described as having a 'haughty spirit' (6.815–18)[27] Some of the names of military heroes have connotations of turmoil and discord: the plural *Drusos* (6.824) may include not only the victor over Hasdrubal at the battle of the Metaurus in 209, but the tribune whose actions and death precipitated the Social War in 91; the reference to 'the race of Gracchus' (6.842) must include not only the military leader of the Second Punic War, but also the turbulent tribunes of the late second century. The references in the three sections of Anchises' speech to the three figures who were awarded the *spolia opima* (Romulus, Cossus, Marcellus) necessarily call to mind the controversial decision of Augustus to deny the same honour to Crassus in 27. Within the family of Aeneas and Augustus itself, the reference to Caesar and Pompey explicitly concerns the Civil War of 49–45, and the final figure of the list, the younger Marcellus, closes the sequence with a reference to failed hopes, early death, and the lack of an obvious successor to Augustus.

The third, and most elaborate of the prophecies, the shield of Aeneas, extends the panegyrical elements of the first two; in its very form, moreover, it makes more explicit the teleological elements found elsewhere in the poem. The description begins with small vignettes from early Roman history: the wolf with the twins Romulus and Remus; the abduction of the Sabine women and the settlement with the Sabines; the dismemberment of the treacherous Mettus Fufetius by Tullus Hostilius; and the siege of Rome by Lars Porsenna with the heroic deeds of Horatius Cocles and Cloelia. These four apparently occupy panels on the left and right of the round shield; at the top is the Capitol, being defended by the sacred geese and Manlius from the attack of the Gauls. Corresponding to this, at the bottom of the shield is the Underworld, in which – unlike the description of the actual Underworld in Book 6 – the roles of chief judge and chief sinner are taken by two first-century Romans, Cato the younger and Catiline. The central portion of the shield contains the battle of Actium and its aftermath, depicted not merely as a military victory, but as a war between the

---

[27] The epithet *superbam* is transferred from the name of the last king, Tarquinius Superbus.

gods and the peoples of East and West; the defeat and flight of Cleopatra
(unnamed, as usual in Augustan poetry) is mirrored by the triumph of
Augustus with its imposition of order and peace on the cacophonous and
unruly barbarians of Asia.[28]

The portrayal of Augustus' victory at Actium and subsequent triumph
is the most explicit version which Virgil gives of the goal enunciated by
Jupiter in Book 1: the establishment of order, peace, and empire. It is the
victory of order over disorder, of West over East, of male over female, of
civilisation over barbarism. As the content and organisation of the shield
show, however, it is more than that: the Olympian divinities, particularly
Augustus' patron god Apollo, take part in the war, which is thus a victory
of cosmic order, reflecting the mythological victory of the gods over the
giants. The placement of the Capitol and the Underworld in corresponding positions on the shield equates Rome with Olympus, and thus Roman
order with divine order. The location of Catiline and Cato as archetypal
figures of sinner and judge in the Underworld makes the equation explicit:
Roman and divine justice are one and the same thing. The victory of
Augustus is not merely the achievement of peace, but the achievement of
order in the cosmos itself, the restoration of a golden age of harmony on
earth and in the universe, the beginning of empire without end.[29] And yet
this prophecy, designed to celebrate Rome's military success and expansion, has its disturbing elements too.[30] The scene of Romulus under the
wolf inevitably recalls his unmentioned – and murdered – twin Remus; the
abduction of the Sabine women is a dubious model of military achievement; the execution of Mettus is barbarous, and was singled out for criticism on that score by Livy (1.28). Furthermore, the presence of Catiline
reminds the reader of the discord of the late Republic, and the presence of
Cato as the emblem of justice recalls that he chose to commit suicide
rather than survive the Republic and live under Caesar's rule. If Augustus
embodies Rome's achievement of mastery over the world, that goal has
not been achieved without brutality, discord, and opposition.

Most of the emphases in Virgil's account of pre-Augustan Roman history are traditional: both Livy and Cicero describe the character and successive contributions of the kings to the creation of Rome; the virtue and
courage of the military leaders of the early and middle Republic are constant themes of earlier historiography; the emphasis on Aeneas, Romulus,
Camillus and Augustus as successive founders or saviours of Rome is found

---

[28] For the structure of the shield, cf. West (1975–6) = Harrison (1990) 295–304.
[29] For the interpretation of the shield, see above all Hardie (1986) 97–110, 346–75; for the
scene of Actium in particular, Quint (1993) 21–31.
[30] Cf. Gurval (1995) 209–47.

in Livy; earlier historiography and rhetoric even recorded the occasional exemplary villains of Roman history, and the equation of Roman justice with the divine order was a feature of Cicero's treatise *De republica*.[31] Where Virgil differs most significantly from earlier historiography and epic in his account is his teleology: in his version, Roman history has a clear and definite goal in the Augustan settlement: in all three prophecies, he links the rule of Augustus with the end of external war and internal discord; he describes the arrival of universal peace under Roman rule, and he heralds the outset of a new golden age.

There is, however, another side to this vision of Rome's glorious destiny. As noted above, all three great prophecies are undercut in one respect or another: they include false or misleading statements; they contain discordant and disturbing elements – references to civil war and to the early death of Marcellus. If Rome has produced in Cato a worthy judge for the Underworld, it has also produced a Catiline. The history of Rome matches that of primitive Italy, which has both improved and degenerated in the course of time: the most recent period of Roman history has produced both good and evil in a high degree – both Cato and Catiline, both the civil wars and the Augustan peace. And the possibility that peace will endure is by no means a certainty. Golden ages had existed in the past, but they had not lasted. In Evander's account, the reign of Saturn was merely a pause in the sequence of invasions, and the golden age that is associated with Latinus' peaceful rule is undercut by our knowledge of the wars in which his people had in fact engaged. Evander's tour of Rome includes the remnants of the fortifications of Saturn and Janus: golden ages, like cities, do not last for ever, and utopian visions, not just of the Augustan age, but of the mythic Italian past in Books 7 and 8, in the Fourth Eclogue, or in the praise of country life in the *Georgics*, are visions, not reality. W. H. Auden in *Secondary Epic* imagined Aeneas in looking at the shield asking 'What next? After this triumph, what portends?' Virgil's is a teleology without an end: 'I have given empire without bound', Jupiter says in Book 1. Neither time nor history comes to a halt.

When Virgil introduces Vulcan's forging of Aeneas' shield, he makes two significant comments. First, he describes the Shield as a *non enarrabile textum*, 'a text that cannot fully be described'; he then says that the shield had on it both Italian and Roman history, including in order (*in ordine*) all the wars fought by Aeneas' descendants. That he then proceeds to describe it, and to give it an order and pattern that clearly do not match his account of Vulcan's own plan, draws attention to the selectivity and

---

[31] Cf. Zetzel (1996).

invention involved in his shaping of Rome.[32] Vulcan's shield is a chronicle, an ordered series of discrete events; Virgil's has a structure and shape that give Roman history a design, leading from Aeneas to Romulus to Augustus. It is a closed and perfect circle, mirroring the universe in its order and balance; and in the static pattern of time it portrays, it is similar to the central four books of the *Aeneid* itself. It is perfectly harmonious; and yet, like the whole portrait of Italian and Roman history, it draws attention to its own arbitrariness and invention.

From what point of view is one to perceive events, or understand history? Virgil's audience can read Aeneas' shield, recognise the events, and interpret what they see; but in concluding Book 8, Virgil makes it clear that interpretation is conditional and sometimes impossible. When Aeneas picks up the shield, 'the fame and fate of his descendants' (8.731), he does not understand what he sees: 'he admires, and rejoices in the image, though ignorant of its content'. As with every ecphrasis in the poem, what the immediate viewer sees is not what the reader sees: comprehension and understanding require time, distance, interpretation.[33] And, Virgil shows in other passages (notably the scenes on the temple of Juno in Book 1), the viewer sees what he or she wants to see. The history of early Italy, it is apparent, is multiple: there is more than one way to understand it; and the same is true of the teleological vision of Rome's destined greatness in Augustan Rome. That does not mean that it is false, merely that its truth is contingent. Virgil's is a relativist vision of history: the understanding of what has happened is conditioned by the present, whether that present be of Evander, or Virgil himself, or of the reader. Discussions of Virgil's view of Rome have tended either to stress the positive and panegyrical elements or to see in the contradictions and discordant undertones a deliberate intention on the poet's part to undermine and even invalidate the praise of Augustus; at best, the inconsistencies in Virgil's history become a sign of ambivalence about the events of his own day. That is, of course, possible; and it would be hard to imagine anyone who lived through the civil wars not having a vivid sense of the cost of the Augustan peace – a peace the precariousness of which is apparent in the *Eclogues* and *Georgics* as well as the *Aeneid*. But Virgil, by his emphasis throughout the *Aeneid* on perspective, on uncertainty, on error, discourages drawing a single conclusion either about Roman history itself or about his own

---

[32] West (1975–6) = Harrison (1990) 295–304 sees the difference between the introduction and the ecphrasis, but does not draw any conclusions from it.

[33] On the problem of ecphrasis in general, see Fowler (1991) with copious bibliography; other valuable discussions (particularly of the paintings on Dido's temple) in Johnson (1976) 104–5, 112–14; Lyne (1987) 207–10; Putnam (forthcoming).

interpretation of it. Although he permits the reader to interpret, he lays no claim to omniscience or to truth: he makes the reader aware that Rome has many histories, that what may be seen as the end of the story now will not be so always. The idea that history has an end is a false consolation; wars to end war are a hope, not a reality. The achievement of peace involves brutality and violence, and those do not simply disappear; the retention of stability requires constant effort, and simple polarities of good and evil do not match the real world. Rome's past, and its future, are what the reader will make of them.

FURTHER READING

1. Antiquarian Italy

The numerous articles of Nicholas Horsfall (there is a selection in the 'List of works cited') are the best introduction to the antiquarian content of the *Aeneid*; the most useful is 'Virgil's conquest of chaos', reprinted in S. J. Harrison, *Oxford Readings in Vergil's Aeneid* (Oxford and New York, 1990); for the ethnographic context see also R. F. Thomas, *Lands and Peoples in Roman Poetry* (Cambridge, 1982) 93–107. The most thorough treatment of the details of Italian landscape and ethnography is that of B. Rehm, *Das geographische Bild des alten Italien in Vergils Aeneis* (Leipzig, 1932), to be supplemented by the articles on particular names and places in the *Enciclopedia Virgiliana*.

2. Specific passages

(*a*) The prophecy of Jupiter in Book 1: J. J. O'Hara, *Death and the Optimistic Prophecy in Vergil's Aeneid* (Princeton, 1990).

(*b*) The so-called 'Parade of Heroes' in Book 6: most recently discussed in detail by D. C. Feeney, 'History and revelation in Vergil's Underworld', *Proceedings of the Cambridge Philological Society* n.s. 32 (1986) 1–24; the commentary of Eduard Norden (5th edn, Stuttgart, 1970) is invaluable.

(*c*) The catalogue of Italians in Book 7: W. Warde Fowler, *Virgil's Gathering of the Clans* (2nd edn, Oxford, 1918); see also E. Fraenkel, 'Aspects of the structure of *Aeneid* 7', reprinted in Harrison, *Oxford Readings*.

(*d*) The visit to the site of Rome and the shield of Aeneas in Book 8: W. Warde Fowler, *Aeneas at the Site of Rome* (2nd edn, Oxford, 1918); G. Binder, *Aeneas und Augustus: Interpretationen zum 8. Buch der Aeneis* (Meisenheim, 1971). See also the commentary of P. T. Eden (Leiden, 1975).

3. General interpretation

Every study of the *Aeneid* that considers its relationship to the Augustan present takes some account of Virgil's presentation of the Roman past. Among recent works in English, there are particularly useful discussions in G. Williams, *Technique and Ideas in the Aeneid* (New Haven and London, 1983) 132–56; P. R. Hardie, *Virgil's*

Aeneid: Cosmos and Imperium (Oxford, 1986); J. J. O'Hara, *Death and the Optimistic Prophecy in Vergil's Aeneid* (Princeton, 1990); D. Quint, *Epic and Empire: Politics and Generic Form from Virgil to Milton* (Princeton, 1993) 21–96; and R. A. Gurval, *Actium and Augustus: The Politics and Emotions of Civil War* (Ann Arbor, 1995) 209–47.

14

SUSANNA MORTON BRAUND

Virgil and the cosmos:
religious and philosophical ideas

Introduction

Virgil's cosmos comprises gods and humans and nature. These are huge topics. In this chapter I shall analyse the complex relationships between these elements by taking a broad view of Virgil's religious and philosophical ideas.

Virgil's gods – especially in the *Aeneid* – have always been a major focus of attention for scholars. Typical is Camps's chapter (1969), 'The higher powers: Fate and the Gods'. A recent, crucial contribution to the subject is Feeney's *The Gods in Epic* (1991) which devotes considerable attention to the *Aeneid* and provides a guide through the massive bibliography on the subject.[1] Feeney's approach constitutes an advance on earlier rationalising or allegorising accounts of Virgil's gods. Instead he insists on the complexities of representation of the gods and explores issues of power in epic as they relate to the characters, human and divine.[2] By contrast, the philosophical flavour of Virgil's views is not explicitly the subject of any single, entire book. Hardie in *Virgil's Aeneid: Cosmos and Imperium* (1986) says much of significance about cosmology, but critics' analysis of Virgil's ethics is mostly subsumed in discussions of character, for example, in articles arguing for or against the Stoic dimension of Aeneas' conduct.

This might suggest that religion and philosophy in Virgil are readily separable. Not so. Such a separation would be artificial from any perspective, ancient or modern. When we consider 'religion' and 'philosophy' in Virgil, we are always talking about how Virgil grapples with and articulates the origins, workings and *telos* (purpose) of the world and the way in which

---

[1] Feeney (1991) 129–87 on the *Aeneid*; important items in English mentioned (129 n. 1) include Thornton (1976), Johnson (1976), Coleman (1982), Hardie (1986), Lyne (1987) 61–99.

[2] Feeney's forthcoming book (1997) on Roman religion and belief will further refine our understanding of Roman systems of belief. I am most grateful to him for showing me the typescript.

human beings fit into that world, particularly in their behaviour as individuals and as members of communities towards other individuals and communities. In other words, gods and morality are inextricably linked. Among recent scholars, it is perhaps Hardie who has made the most impact in bringing the two categories together. I shall build on those foundations and extend the debate to encompass all three of Virgil's poems.

There are key texts in any discussion of Virgil's religious and philosophical views. Crucial passages from the *Aeneid* include Anchises' vision in Book 6, Jupiter's role in the council of the gods in Book 10 and the interplay between the gods and human characters in the story of Aeneas and Dido (Book 4) and the closing scene of the poem (Book 12). From the *Georgics* the Proem, the justification of labour in Book 1, the finale to Book 2 with its praise of country life, and the description of the idealised society of the bees in Book 4 are significant. In the *Eclogues*, the prophecy of the fourth poem and the song of Silenus in the sixth are central. These are the texts which will be scrutinised here.

Virgil 'claimed' for philosophical schools

But first I want to contest the way in which Virgil has been 'claimed' on behalf of various Hellenistic philosophical schools with which Romans of the first century BC were familiar. Since there is little external evidence on this issue, it is largely a matter of interpretation of the poems themselves. Virgil's interest in philosophy is attested by his plans, mentioned by Donatus in his biography, to spend his 'retirement' in Greece and Asia devoted to the study of philosophy. Specifically, Virgil has been seen as an Epicurean or a Stoic or even as someone who changed philosophical allegiance. He certainly spent some time with the Epicurean teachers Philodemus and Siro at their base near Naples.[3] Epicureanism seems to have been particularly prominent at this time, probably because it was the first of the schools to present its ideas in Latin.[4] Moreover, Virgil was clearly deeply familiar with Lucretius' *De rerum natura*, the earliest (extant) articulation of Epicureanism in Latin and (arguably) the greatest poem of the generation prior to Virgil.[5] On the other hand, Virgil moved in the same circle as Areius Didymus, a Stoic philosopher who was a lifelong friend of Augustus.[6] The divine apparatus of the poem can be seen as a manifestation in poetic terms of the Stoic Providence, and Aeneas is read as a proto-Stoic, for

---

[3] G. 4.563–4; *Catalepton* 5, 8; Gell. 6.20; Sedley (1989) 103; Rawson (1985) 23–4.
[4] Griffin (1989) 9.   [5] Hardie (1986) 33–51.
[6] Cairns (1989) 34, although Areius was 'concerned with the scholarly propagation of philosophical doctrines from a wide variety of sources'.

example in the impassivity he shows towards Dido in Book 4 once he has received his divine orders to depart.[7]

This stark, antithetical picture is complicated by interpretations of the morality of the final scene of the *Aeneid*. This has stimulated a debate in which Aeneas' final act of anger in killing Turnus is seen by some as a lapse from the Stoic greatness he has attained earlier in the poem and by others as a legitimate manifestation of anger, between the extremes of excessive anger and absence of anger, on the Aristotelian model of the Peripatos (below). More broadly, the 'two voices' model of interpretation (below) can be linked with a contrast between a Stoic-type advocation of participation in public life involving shouldering duty for the state and the quietism often associated with Epicureanism.

In terms of Virgil's cosmology too, various claims are made. A pseudo-Aristotelian work *About the Cosmos* (*c.* 40 BC) presents a similar view of cosmology to Virgil's and may have influenced him.[8] Elsewhere, Virgil appears to incorporate the language of the mysteries, for example, in his celebration of the man who understands the workings of the universe (*G.* 2.490-2), which may evoke Epicurus, Empedocles and Pythagoras.[9] Eclogue 4 offers elements of neo-Pythagoreanism,[10] Stoicism (the conflagration) and Near-Eastern apocalyptic images (resembling Old Testament images) of the birth of a child: this poem has been dubbed the 'Messianic' Eclogue.[11] Then there is the Platonism of Anchises' speech to Aeneas in Book 6.[12] Finally, Virgil has also been claimed for Christianity, probably thanks to Stoicising readings of the poems (especially Eclogue 4), since so much Stoic ideology feeds into Christian thought. In fact, this whole issue of interpreting Virgil as an adherent or even an advocate of particular philosophical or religious views is closely bound up with the reception of Virgil in different places and different eras.

These conflicting claims may seem to demand a reconciliation. This is not necessary. To assign crude labels to this most complex of authors is of limited usefulness. Servius, the commentator writing around AD 400, saw this with his comment about poets and philosophy: 'poets invariably exploit philosophical sects as required by the essence of the context'.[13]

---

[7] Cf. Austin on 4.449, not denying the ambiguity; on Stoic Aeneas and un-Stoic Turnus see Bowra (1933–4).

[8] Thornton (1976) 31–3.   [9] Hardie (1986) 39.

[10] Carcopino (1930).

[11] See Mayor, Warde Fowler & Conway (1907) with Clausen (1994) 128–9.

[12] Norden (1926).

[13] *Sectis philosophorum poetae pro qualitate negotiorum semper utuntur*, on *Aen.* 10.467, cf. on *Aen.* 1.227 and 6.264 on Virgil's inconsistencies; cf. Donatus 1.6.1–12 Georgii: variable factors include time, character, place, cause (*pro tempore, pro persona, pro loco, pro causa*). This does not conflict with Virgil's later status as a sage.

Instead, we need to consider the intellectual context of elite Romans in the late Republic, a context heavily influenced by strands of Hellenistic thought, doubtless, but in which these strands were adapted to serve specifically Roman needs, both for the individual and for the collective Roman state with its ideal of *Romanitas*. The doctrines of the Hellenistic schools were represented by central texts attributed to the founding 'masters' and by the pronouncements of subsequent teachers.[14] They were articulated in Latin for a wider Roman audience by Cicero and Lucretius and were ultimately absorbed from those sources in what we might call a vernacularised form. Lucretius in particular was hugely important in providing an idiom for philosophical ideas in Latin epic. Ideas from the Hellenistic world are moderated by the quintessentially Roman preoccupation with their practical application. This explains the Roman concern with exemplarity in the education process and in public life, and, too, the persisting strength of tradition, encapsulated in *mos maiorum* – 'the way our ancestors did things'. Factors like these inform Virgil's contemporary context and will be our guide in this enquiry. It is intrinsically unlikely that Virgil viewed himself as a card-carrying Stoic or Epicurean, however much he was drawn to Epicurean ideas. Above all, he was a Roman and he was an Italian, from Mantua in north Italy. At the same time, the desire to see Virgil as freed from those philosophical labels typifies his current reception into our world of agnosticism, in which challenges to sects and creeds are in vogue in scholarship as in the wider intellectual life of western Europeans.

So now we must turn to Virgil's religious and philosophical ideas and relate them to their intellectual context, in what we call the late Republic and the beginnings of the Principate, but which for Virgil (without the benefit of hindsight) must have presented countless uncertainties as the series of civil wars concentrated power in the hands of a few men and finally of one man. His ideas fall into three broad categories: issues of physics and cosmology – how the world works, the human place in the world and how gods and humans relate; ethical issues, comprising morality and politics – how humans do and ought to relate to humans; and eschatology, which draws together cosmology and morality, in its portrayal of what awaits humans after death. I shall deal with each area separately, paying less attention to the narrow questions of Virgil's sources and consistency and instead examining the function of these ideas within their poetic context.

Cosmogony and cosmology

Let's start at the beginning. Once upon a time, there was a great void (*magnum ... inane*). Through that void, there came together particles

---

[14] Sedley (1989) on the tradition of charismatic leadership in the Hellenistic schools.

(*semina*) of earth and air and sea and streaming fire and from these elements (*primis*) came all beginnings (*exordia*) and the young globe of the world solidified. Then the world took on its shape, with land and sea, under the new sun, and with clouds and rain, woods and mountains and living creatures. That's how the satyr Silenus begins his song in Eclogue 6 (lines 31–40); he proceeds to evoke the stories of the origin and development of the human race (41–2) and the myths which form the foundations of the history of humankind (43–81). This is the most explicit cosmogony in Virgil's poems. It is crucial to consider its context.

First, the speaker is Silenus, who is associated with arcane wisdom but is here depicted as a drunken, randy satyr who has to be tricked into singing his song, which may make equivocal Virgil's allegiance to the ideas expressed. Secondly, the song, like the rest of Eclogue 6, abounds with complex literary allusions. Most obviously it is a tribute to the contemporary poet Gallus, heavily influenced by Hellenistic poetry and author of a (fragmentary) aetiological poem about Apollo. The climax of Silenus' song (64–73) is a celebration of Gallus' poetic initiation and achievements, climaxing with the aetiological poem (72–3). Virgil is also acknowledging the early Greek poet Hesiod and the Hellenistic poet Callimachus, who combine an interest in the origins and workings of the world with the organisation and interpretation of mythology.[15] Moreover, Silenus' cosmogony is expressed in language heavily reminiscent of Lucretius' poem *De rerum natura*.[16] Does this make Silenus' song Epicurean? Perhaps. Certainly, *inane*, *primis*, *semina* and *exordia* are words that Lucretius uses of the void, atoms and atomic compounds, and the list of the primary four elements, earth, air, water and fire (32–3), evokes the pluralistic system proposed by the fifth-century philosopher Empedocles, whose philosophy-in-poetry influenced Lucretius. Silenus' song is evidently a reprise of themes and techniques of recent Latin poetry which modelled itself upon learned Hellenistic poetry and earlier poet-philosophers.

Silenus' cosmogony presents a linear sequence: the creation of the world and animals and humankind, then human 'history'. This contrasts with the more complex pattern which emerges from the cosmology of Eclogue 4 and *Aeneid* 6. Eclogue 4 opens by celebrating the arrival of 'the last age of the song of Cumae' (4), referring to the oracles associated with the Sibyl of Cumae. It has been argued that the apocalyptic revelations of Eclogue 4 are derived in form and content from the Sibylline oracles, which were consulted at times of crisis, perhaps as recently as 44 BC with the appearance

---

[15] Legitimate subjects for the poet: Hardie (1986) 17, 67.
[16] See Macrobius 6.2.22–4 and Farrell (1991) 301–14.

of the comet soon after Julius Caesar's assassination. Then, *magnus ab integro saeclorum nascitur ordo* (5: 'the great line of the centuries begins anew') fuses two different views of history. The word 'centuries' (*saeclorum*) may evoke the Etruscan doctrine that a nation's life was ten *saecula* long; the commentator Servius (on *Ecl.* 9.46) says that the Julian comet was interpreted by an Etruscan diviner as heralding Rome's tenth *saeculum*. The phrase 'great sequence' (combined with *magni ... menses*, 'great months', 13) evokes the concept of the 'great year' (*magnus annus*) said to begin again every time the stars returned to the precise position that they occupied at the birth of the universe. This cyclical view of the world was held by the Pythagoreans; the Stoics associated it with the circuit (Greek *periodos*) between the periodic conflagrations which cleansed the world (Cic. *ND* 2.118). Next, Virgil throws history into reverse, with the return of the Virgin goddess and the reign of Saturn (6) and with the iron age giving way to the golden race (8–10), inverting Hesiod's myth of the races in *Works and Days* 109–201. It is not clear whether Virgil envisages a cyclical pattern or simply a backwards sequence; and it is not clear that it matters.[17]

Whatever the origin of the ideas here, it is the political context of the poem which gives them significance. The opening of Eclogue 4 announces that this is political discourse ('worthy of a consul'), in antithesis to the opening of Eclogue 6, where the poem is explicitly pushed into the realm of the 'rustic Muse'. Eclogue 4 celebrates the imminent return of the Golden Age and explicitly connects this with contemporary political events. What, precisely, those political events were has stimulated speculation of the widest imaginable range: the date of composition and publication are contested and there are numerous identifications of the *Wunderkind*, the mysterious child whose birth is celebrated in the poem. Some are plausible, some crazy.[18] What is certain is that this apocalyptic, Golden-Age imagery is throughout classical literature associated with the start of a new reign. It is an expression of optimism.[19]

The idea of the harmony of the world in Eclogue 4 receives fuller expression in *Georgics* 4 and *Aeneid* 6. In the final book of the *Georgics*, Virgil commends bees for their social coherence, which includes voluntary self-sacrifice for the community (4.219–27). This, he says, has given rise to claims that bees participate in the divine intelligence (*divinae mentis*) which rules the world. Strikingly similar language and ideas recur in *Aeneid* 6,

---

[17] On Virgil's syncretism see Nisbet (1995).

[18] Coleman (1977) 150–2 offers seven different suggestions; Clausen (1994) 127 gives fourth- and fifth-century Christian interpretations.

[19] Cf. Sen. *Apoc.* 4.1, in praise of Nero.

when Aeneas meets his father Anchises and asks him for an explanation of the souls waiting beside the river of Lethe (6.703–12). In reply, Anchises describes the cosmic principles of the universe in largely Stoic terms, inspired by Platonism and Pythagoreanism (724–32).[20] Anchises represents the universe in figurative terms familiar from Stoicism as endowed with *spiritus* and *mens* and *artus* and *corpus* with fire privileged above the other elements, yet his language is strongly reminiscent of Lucretius, a remarkable combination.[21] This reinforces my earlier point: Virgil is drawing upon the entire range of ideas and expressions available to him. Here these ideas contribute to the articulation of Anchises' inspiring, patriotic vision of the future race of Rome. The very un-Epicurean Anchises[22] is behaving as the quintessential Roman *paterfamilias* – teaching his son what he needs to know in order to be a Roman. Hence his resoundingly famous lines are addressed not directly to Aeneas but to his quintessential descendant, 'Roman' (*Romane*):

> tu regere imperio populos, Romane, memento
> (hae tibi erunt artes) pacique imponere morem,
> parcere subiectis et debellare superbos.   (6.851–3)

Remember, Roman, to rule the peoples with your power – these shall be your skills – and to combine peace with morality, to spare the conquered and to subdue the proud.

It is tempting to identify the authority of Anchises with that of Virgil speaking as the national poet and producing his patriotic vision for Augustus and the Romans, the ultimate *paterfamilias* and his 'sons'. If this is right, politics trumps the labelling of philosophical ideas in interpretations of Virgil: whatever his inspiration, Virgil weaves his ideas into a fabric laden with significance for his Roman readership.

Gods and humans and nature

What is the role of gods and humans in this cosmos? The universe as described by Anchises in *Aeneid* 6 is in motion and is monistic or pantheistic, with its movement governed by divine mind (*mens*). Earlier, a pluralistic view of the universe is expressed in Helenus' prophecy (3.375–6),

---

[20] Norden (1926) 16–17.
[21] Cic. ND 2.39–41; Long & Sedley (1987) 46 A–P; Lucr. 5.68–9 '. . . established earth, sky, sea, stars, sun and the ball of the moon', 92 'first of all look upon seas, and lands, and sky'.
[22] Contrast Lucr. 5.1127–30.

where Jupiter 'deals out the destinies and rolls the wheel of change; and such is the circling sequence' (*ordo*, cf. *Ecl.* 4.5). Is Virgil's representation of Jupiter's role in the workings of the universe self-contradictory? 'He is both the all-comprehending cosmic divinity and the highest divinity ruling over an, at times, unruly group of gods, spirits, and men.'[23] And he is more (or less) than those things. Jupiter is no longer the Homeric Zeus, a god standing above interstate faction; he enters the epic as 'the national god of the Roman state'. Moreover, Jupiter is the only one powerful enough to bring about the conclusion, which he finally achieves (12.829–40) by compromising his pro-Venus, pro-Trojan position in order to accommodate Juno in a partial reconciliation. 'From the beginning Jupiter is associated with the end.'[24]

Juno is more complex still. She is the Carthaginian goddess Tanit, championing her city against the rival Romans, as portrayed by Ennius in his epic *Annales*. She is the Greek Hera of the Homeric poems, who hates the Trojans. She is the allegorical representation of *aer*, the lower air, the realm of storms. And her association with beginnings (as opposed to endings) links her with anarchy and lack of closure.[25]

Once we accept Feeney's argument for 'the ancients' ability to view deity as a many-sided prism',[26] this liberates us from the stark alternatives often posed in earlier scholarship. Consider, for example, the antithetical interpretations of Jupiter's role in the council of the gods in Book 10 (1–117). Either this scene is a vindication of Jupiter's authority and majesty[27] or it is an exhibition of opacity, disingenuousness and mendacity.[28] Better, Jupiter is 'engaged in a nexus with other characters from which he cannot be extricated'.[29] Jupiter's declaration at the end of the council of the gods, that 'the kingship of Jupiter will be the same for all: the fates will find a way' (10.112–13) is, as Feeney says, 'vague' and 'resists quasi-theological exegesis'. All we can sensibly say is that it is an assertion of absolute power, without any manifesto of how that power actually operates.

In a universe ruled by an autocrat, there seems to be little place for free will. Despite arguments to the contrary, humans seem to be entirely subject to divine will. Take the case of Aeneas' departure from Carthage. We have to resist the temptation to read this naturalistically as Aeneas' sudden realisation that he must leave.[30] It is not. A significant part of Book 4 (lines 196–278) is devoted to the delivery by Mercury of Jupiter's command, a

---

[23] Thornton (1976) 71.   [24] Feeney (1991) 140, 137.
[25] Feeney (1991) 131–4, 137–8.   [26] Feeney (1991) 127.
[27] Klingner (1967) 566–8.   [28] Lyne (1987) 89.
[29] Feeney (1991) 145.   [30] Cf. Feeney (1991) 172–6.

point which is emphasised by the unusual reiteration of the speech (223–37 and 265–76) and reinforced later by yet another visit from Mercury (560–70). Moreover, when Mercury aggressively delivers Jupiter's message (265–76), Aeneas is struck dumb with terror (279–80). There is no monologue of indecision. Aeneas' reaction is instant: he wants to get away (281–2). His only hesitation is over how to achieve this. Even when confronted by Dido (305–30) he experiences no conflict about whether or not to leave, only about whether to give expression to the pain he feels (331–2). This may seem like a novelistic moment of crisis, but Virgil says explicitly that he suppresses his love or pity for Dido (whatever *curam* denotes) through his obedience to Jupiter (*Iovis monitis*).

Yet it is not so surprising that we are tempted into a naturalistic interpretation (as, too, were some ancient readers). Virgil often leaves the balance between divine and human agency obfuscated. Johnson is acute on Dido falling in love: 'Vergil chooses to create a baffling design in which the supernatural and the natural, the physical and the psychological, divine intervention and psychological realism are merged together implausibly – the pattern is baffling and disturbing because we see the action from without and from within at different times and sometimes at the same time.'[31] This is typical of Virgil's narrative technique. His weaving is subtle and complex – and our reading of Virgil brings an overlay derived from novelistic verisimilitude. It takes an effort of will to peel away that layer.

The relationship between humans and the autocratic Jupiter identified in the *Aeneid* has its forerunner in the *Georgics*, specifically in the so-called theodicy (divine justification) of labour in Book 1. Here Virgil, in a passage which evokes both Hesiod and Lucretius, states that Jupiter brought the Golden Age to an end and imposed 'hard work' (*labor*) on humankind (118–46): 'The great father himself has willed that the path of husbandry should not be smooth' (121–2). The words which end the passage, *labor omnia vicit | improbus*, have provoked hot debate. For Thomas, these are the 'most crucial lines of the poem' which reflect its overall pessimism and he translates: 'Insatiable toil occupied all areas of existence', while Wilkinson earlier took a more positive view of Virgil's theodicy of labour.[32] Undoubtedly, Virgil emphasises a negative element of human experience. But is it true that this picture of fallen man condemned to toil all the days of his life (recalling Genesis 3.17) dominates the poem? That is highly debatable.

This pessimistic view of Virgil's portrayal of the human condition has not commanded universal assent. It may even be seen as an essentially late

[31] Johnson (1976) 44; at *Aen.* 9.184–5 Virgil explicitly draws attention to the problem.
[32] Thomas (1988) on 145–6; Wilkinson (1969) 135–41.

twentieth-century phenomenon. While some stress Virgil's dark visions and privilege the negative parts of his poems, others emphasise the optimistic material which they see as counterbalancing or outweighing the negative parts.

Georgics 2 has two such passages, the celebration of the natural resources of Italy (136–76) and the finale of the book, in which Virgil praises country life and the country-dweller (458–542), beginning:

> o fortunatos nimium, sua si bona norint,
> agricolas! quibus ipsa, procul discordibus armis,
> fundit humo facilem victum iustissima tellus.   (458–60)

O happy are the farmers! Too happy, if they fully knew their blessings! For them, far from discordant weapons, the most just Earth spontaneously pours out from her soil an easy living.

The following idealisation of rustic life, another reminder of Virgil's Italian origins, is a celebration of humans living in harmony with a co-operative Nature and enjoying the leisure and treasure she bestows. This evocation of the Golden Age is followed by a *makarismos* (celebration) of the man who understands the workings of the universe (*felix qui potuit rerum cognoscere causas*, 490–2). Not only is this couched in terms taken from a fragment of Empedocles probably praising Pythagoras (B 129, cf. B 132), a passage already echoed by Lucretius in his praise of Epicurus for his universal insight into the nature of things at *DRN* 1.62–78 (with reprises at the start of Books 5 and 6). It also seems to be an expression of Virgil's aspirations for his poem. And the strongly Lucretian language here conveys Virgil's tribute to his predecessor in the genre. After this, the focus returns to the country-dweller, this time seen as in tune with the rustic gods, *fortunatus et ille deos qui novit agrestes* (493). *Georgics* 2, then, ends on a note of co-operation and harmony between the divine, human and natural spheres. And this co-operation and harmony is celebrated in the country-dwellers' rituals (*sacra deum* 473 and libations to Bacchus, 529).[33]

This harmony between humans and cosmos is familiar from the vision of the Golden Age in Eclogue 4. As the miraculous child grows from childhood through adolescence to manhood, the universe grows and matures with him. This harmony is an intense example of the so-called 'pathetic fallacy', a feature of pastoral poetry, in which animate and inanimate nature reflects the emotions of the human actors. When Virgil presents nature in anthropomorphic terms in the *Georgics*, as he does frequently,[34]

---

[33] Hardie (1986) 34. Ritual recurs throughout Virgil, e.g. *Ecl.* 5.65–71, *Aen.* 8.280–369; on ritual and Roman poetry and society generally see Feeney (1997) ch. 4.

[34] Wilkinson (1969) 128.

this suggests a pantheistic view of the universe, which has common features with the Stoic view of 'sympathy' of the different parts of the cosmos.[35] If it is possible to draw any conclusion about Virgil's view of the human place in the universe and of human relationships with divinity, ideas of 'sympathy' and 'harmony' must be central. This is clearly an ideal – and there are many potential sources of disruptions of that ideal. But Virgil's optimism comes through. The peace and stability associated with the concentration of power in Augustus' hands are a necessary precondition of that ideal.

Ethical issues

It is clear that in matters of cosmology, Virgil absorbs ideas from a variety of sources and is much less concerned to produce a coherent synthesis than to integrate his material into its immediate context, often highly politicised. Does the same apply in ethical matters? Here, too, there is always a political dimension, in the broadest sense of the word: morality concerns the individual in the community. One ideal community described by Virgil is that of the bees in *Georgics* 4, which has been interpreted as a representation of an idealised human society.[36] One individual who has been regarded as an ethical ideal is Aeneas. Yet for Virgil there is evidently a tension between individuality and community, between private and public, between the personal and the state.[37]

I propose to focus upon Aeneas' duel with Turnus at the end of Book 12. Critics have produced diametrically opposed interpretations of this episode. Aeneas' killing of Turnus is an act of 'frenzy' (*furor*) or of 'duty' (*pietas*), to be condemned in Stoic terms or approved in Aristotelian terms, and he is either fulfilling or disregarding Anchises' instructions in Book 6 'to spare the conquered and subdue the proud' (6.853).

These disagreements epitomise the fluctuations in the interpretation of the *Aeneid* in the past hundred years or so. Johnson outlines the essence of the debate between an optimistic 'European school' and the pessimistic 'Harvard school'.[38] Critics who wish to see Aeneas as unambiguously good rationalise the end of the *Aeneid* by 'proving' the villainy of Turnus. The counter-reaction is crystallised in the largely dominant 'two voices' line, which emphasises the private voice and the pessimism of the ending.

This debate has recently been taken into the philosophical arena of ancient ethics. Putnam and Galinsky continue to dispute the philosophical

---

[35] Thornton (1976) 30.   [36] Dahlmann (1954).
[37] On tension and balance in Virgil see Griffin (1979).   [38] Johnson (1976) 8–16.

flavour of Aeneas' final act.[39] Putnam argues that 'Aeneas' action is morally dubious': it is an 'un-Stoic course of anger and revenge' and the close is a 'powerfully inconclusive, brilliantly calculated ending' which leaves us pondering the 'open-endedness of anger and hatred'. He relates the *Aeneid* to Cicero's 'intensely Stoic interpretation of anger' in the *Tusculans*, to demonstrate that it is the animal part not the celestial part which governs Aeneas. Moreover, he insists that Aeneas 'scorn[s] his father's command to spare a suppliant' and interprets Aeneas' final act as one of *inclementia* (failure to show mercy) which 'adumbrates the negative side of one-man rule'.[40]

In contrast and in contradiction, Galinsky argues that Aeneas' anger is a fitting closure, which is misread by critics who do not take into account ancient views of anger. He points out that Aeneas is not criticised for his angry killing of Turnus until Christian writers such as Lactantius and St Augustine. Galinsky suggests that Aeneas embodies Aristotle's view of anger: under certain circumstances a good man *ought* to become angry and exact revenge, when an injustice has been committed. Anger is viewed as something rational, the mean between excessive anger and a lack of anger. 'In the Aristotelian sense, then, Aeneas is an example of the morally perfect man.'[41]

A feature underplayed in this philosophical debate is the political element. Hardie, while insisting upon the multivalence of the close, acknowledges Virgil's exploration of imperialist themes. He argues that the duel between Aeneas and Turnus presents four contradictory types of allusion which coexist in tension: (1) to Gigantomachy (basically, a positive portrayal of Aeneas defeating the forces of disorder), (2) to the Homeric duel between Achilles and Hector (an allusion which diminishes the significance of Aeneas' victory by reminding us of its transitory nature), (3) to the conflict between Roman and Gaul (another positive allusion, affirming the rightness of Roman might) and (4) to gladiatorial spectacle (another negative allusion in which the fighter is reduced to non-personhood as a transient spectacle for others).[42] In this pluralist reading of the close of the *Aeneid*, he goes some considerable way to rehabilitating imperialist readings of the poem without sacrificing insights gained from the pessimistic type of reading.

---

[39] Trace the debate in Galinsky (1988), Putnam (1990), Galinsky (1994) and now Putnam (1995).

[40] Putnam (1990), quotations from 15, 16, 39, 22, and (1995) 201–45, quotations from 202, 215.

[41] Galinsky (1988), quotation from 335; for criticism of Aeneas also (1994) 191.

[42] Hardie (1986) 153–4.

The relevance of the political factor is clinched by Cairns, who complements Hardie's emphasis upon Virgil's Romanisation of his material by introducing ancient political philosophy into the debate. His point is that in the final books Virgil portrays Aeneas as a virtuous king. In *On the Good King according to Homer* by Philodemus, the first-century BC Epicurean philosopher, Homeric ideas are closely linked with contemporary Roman politics. Cairns argues that Aeneas' anger (*ira*) is 'not an involuntary or uncontrolled passion' (78) and he uses Cicero, *De officiis* 1.34–5, to illuminate the difficulties of the close of the *Aeneid*. In accordance with Cicero's precepts, Aeneas preserves the 'rights of war' (*iura belli*) and makes war to achieve peace. The *Aeneid*, then, can be set in the context of the ancient debate about kingship, focusing upon the qualities of 'good' and 'bad' rulers. Significantly, the name Turnus comes from the Etruscan version of the Greek word *tyrannos*.[43]

What emerges is the importance of detaching ourselves from automatic naturalistic readings and trying instead to reconstruct the intellectual climate in which Virgil was writing. The Roman elite was open to the ideas of the Hellenistic philosophical schools and to the language in which those ideas were beginning to be framed in Latin. Opinion was affected by early Roman history with its ideology of attaining high achievement through emulation of the fine role-models of the past. Of supreme importance was Homer, the basis of Roman education – and it is no coincidence that the *Iliad* opens with the word 'anger', the issue which Virgil tackles at the close of his *Aeneid*. Rather than label Aeneas a 'Stoic' sage, it is more illuminating, then, to see Aeneas as the Homeric ideal of the 'good king' and as a proto-Roman who sets his duty to the gods and the future Roman state above any personal wishes and desires.

Eschatology

Finally, we come to eschatology, ideas about what happens after death (literally 'last things'). The central passage is Anchises' speech in *Aeneid* 6. Anchises explains to Aeneas that the souls beside the river Lethe are waiting for rebirth: 'They are spirits, fated for second bodies, and at the water of Lethe's stream they drink the soothing draught and long forgetfulness' (713–15; *lethe* is Greek for 'forgetfulness'). He then describes what happens to the soul after death: a process of purification and reincarnation. After death each soul undergoes punishments which match the wrongdoings of the body in its lifetime, a process readily seen as equivalent to the

---

[43] Cairns (1989), esp. ch. 1; Aeneas the virtuous king: 78; Turnus: 67.

Christian Purgatory.[44] Once the 'stain of guilt' is removed, some or all of the souls are sent to Elysium. Virgil's language becomes rather elliptical and mysterious at this point. But what is important is the cyclical view of the universe expressed again. Anchises' language is strongly redolent of Stoicism: *donec longa dies, perfecto temporis orbe | concretam exemit labem purumque relinquit | aetherium sensum atque aurai simplicis ignem* (745–7: 'till the long day, the sequence of time fulfilled, has worn our stains away, leaving clear the etherial perception and the fire of pure spirit') and *mille rotam volvere per annos* (748: 'when they have turned time's wheel a thousand years').

Beyond Stoicism lie Platonism and Pythagoreanism. Any reading of the close of *Aeneid* 6 must be informed by Plato's myth of the afterlife, the 'Myth of Er', which closes his *Republic* (Book 10: 614b–621d). Socrates tells the story of a Pamphylian called Er who was found on the battlefield and assumed to be dead. Twelve days later, as he lay on the funeral pyre, he came back to life and described what happens to the soul after death. Plato seems to combine Orphic ideas such as the image of the body as the dark prison (734 *carcere caeco*) of the soul[45] with Pythagorean beliefs, most notably the idea of the transmigration of souls from one body to another in a continuous process of reincarnation. The heavy influence of Plato on Virgil may explain why Norden, in his classic commentary on Book 6, continually re-expresses Virgil's thought in this section in Greek and not in German.[46]

But Plato is not the only influence here. Anchises' language is strongly reminiscent of Cicero's reworking of the 'Myth of Er' in the 'Dream of Scipio' with which he closes his *Republic*. This text presents the fictional dream of Scipio Aemilianus in which his adoptive grandfather, Scipio Africanus, appears to him and explains how souls escape from the prison of their bodies into the only true life, life after death. Next Scipio's natural father, Aemilius Paullus, appears and explains the relative insignificance of the earth, then Africanus explains the arrangement of the planets and the 'music of the spheres' and emphasises the fragility of earthly glory and of Roman activity in the world, before talking about the immortality of the soul. He closes by urging Scipio that the best life for the soul while on earth is to work for the preservation of one's country. While the cosmology and eschatology are familiar from Plato,[47] the tone of the finale is strongly Roman and patriotic.

[44] Norden (1926) 29; cf. Aug. *Civ. dei* 21.13.   [45] Feeney (1986) n. 13.

[46] E.g. 743 *quisque suos patimur Manes* ('we each suffer our own spirit') is more comprehensible when 'spirit' is seen as the Latin equivalent of Greek *daimon* ('guardian spirit').

[47] Powell (1990) 123.

At first sight, this seems to provide a close analogy for Anchises' speech to Aeneas. Both texts combine cosmology, morality and patriotic exhortation and in both texts the knowledge is imparted by dead ancestor to living descendant. Yet there is a radical divergence between Cicero and Virgil; indeed, 'Vergil's eclecticism is by no means synthetic.'[48] Whereas Scipio is told repeatedly that earthly glory is insignificant, Anchises uses the future glory of Rome to inspire Aeneas with patriotic fervour, capping his eschatology with a stirring vision of the future heroes of Rome (756–886), the climax to Book 6. There is, in fact, a fundamental tension between the Platonic articulation of Anchises' eschatology and his eulogy of the future Roman state and her statesmen – a future which for Virgil's audience has become real in the form of their rousing stories of the Roman past. Feeney is right to conclude that the essence of the meeting between Aeneas and his father is not a religious revelation but 'an image of the nature of Rome and . . . an image of the life of the Roman statesman'.[49]

There is one aspect common to all three eschatologies: the idea of getting just rewards. Eschatology, then, brings together cosmology and morality. In Plato, the 'Myth of Er' is Socrates' response to a question about the rewards of virtue. Cicero has Scipio say, just before the narration of the dream, that because Virtue is divine she longs for rewards of a fresher and more permanent kind than statues and triumphs (Macrobius, *Somnium Scipionis* 1.4.2–3). And in *Aeneid* 6, before the meeting of Aeneas and his father, Virgil indicates that entry to the groves of the blessed in Elysium is open to any who deserve it (6.664). In this way, he departs significantly from Homer's depiction of Elysium, where this privilege is confined to those of divine descent (*Od.* 4.561–9). It is very important that Virgil makes this change. He records as inhabitants of Elysium patriots, priests, prophets, philosophers/scientists and those who deserve a place there, *merendo* (6.660–5; cf. Aug. *Civ. dei* 21.27). This makes imaginable a universe in which the human/divine gulf can be bridged. The person who lives for ever in Elysium or in heaven is very close to being a god.

Which brings me, finally, to those figures in Virgil's poems who, by their deserving conduct, are able to cross the boundary to become divine and who represent a strong source of optimism for humankind. The bees of *Georgics* 4 could do this, but only as a non-individualised community: theirs is a collective form of immortality. Virgil explores this theme for human individuals in Eclogue 5 in the shepherds' songs about the death and deification of the mysterious herdsman Daphnis. He adapts the pastoral motif of lament for a herdsman's death (e.g. Theocritus' Idyll 1) into a

---

[48] Feeney (1986) 2; for further bibliography see Feeney (1986) 19 n. 2, 20 n. 11.
[49] Feeney (1986) 16.

celebration of his deification in terms readily interpreted allegorically of the assassinated Julius Caesar.[50]

More explicit is the celebration of Octavian's future divine status in the proem to the *Georgics*. Virgil opens his poem with an invocation of twelve deities of the countryside, then devotes a passage of the same length to a request for Octavian's approval of his poetic task. This, the climax of the catalogue, in effect makes Octavian a god: 'enter on your worship and learn even now to hearken unto our prayers' (1.42).[51] In the poem's closing words, Octavian is portrayed as fulfilling the terms of Anchises' exhortation at *Aen.* 6.851–3: great Caesar is described as 'thundering in war by deep Euphrates and giving victor's laws to willing nations and venturing the path to Olympus' (4.560–2). His embodiment of Anchises' ideal sets him on a par with divinity.

In presenting the possibility of men becoming gods, Virgil explores issues of absolute power. This is nowhere more explicit than in the portrayal of Hercules in *Aeneid* 8. Hercules wins divine status by destroying the monster Cacus, but in so doing displays a manic violence and frenzy which seems to put him on the same level as the bestial Cacus (185–275). In this Gigantomachic imagery, is he beast, man or god?[52] And what is the significance of the apparent parallelism between Hercules and Augustus? Between Hercules and Aeneas? The picture of Octavian on the shield of Aeneas with which *Aeneid* 8 closes reiterates Hercules' imposition of order on chaos and in both episodes, 'Gigantomachic victory [is] followed by religious celebration and thanksgiving.' Moreover, in his duel with Turnus in Book 12, Aeneas is cast in a Herculean role of Gigantomachic victor, as he confronts a Turnus who has taken his enmity too far.[53] The figure of Hercules seems to encapsulate the potential of absolute, quasi-divine power, for good and for ill. When the absolutely powerful behaves like a god, the result is prosperity under his beneficence. When he behaves with the uncontrollable cruelty of a beast, the result is sheer terror. Hercules is a model fraught with ambivalence, for Aeneas and for Augustus alike.

There is another who crosses that barrier of death to attain a kind of immortality – Orpheus. *Georgics* 4 closes with Proteus' narration of the story of how Orpheus loses his wife Eurydice while he is rescuing her from the Underworld because he disobeys the command not to look round at her. He is devastated by his grief and for seven whole months laments his loss in song. The 'reward' for his devotion is to be attacked by Maenads who tear him to pieces. But as his head floats downstream on the river

[50] Taylor (1934) 227; Weinstock (1971) 370–2 on *Ecl.* 9.47; Otis (1964) 135.
[51] On Roman cult of emperors, Feeney (1997) introduction and ch. 3.
[52] Hardie (1986) 110–18; Feeney (1991) 158–61.
[53] Hardie (1986) 147–54, 176–8, quotation from 118.

Hebrus, his voice and tongue survive dismemberment and death to continue his cry for 'Eurydice!' (4.453–527). If Hercules is a model (however ambivalent) for Augustus, then Orpheus is a model for Virgil. Where Augustus' expectation of immortality derives from his military and political achievements, Virgil's hopes of immortality lie in his songs.

Conclusion

Virgil was not a doctrinaire member of any particular school of thought. I have tried to demonstrate the limited usefulness of attempts to label features of Virgil's poetry as 'Stoic' or 'Epicurean'. He uses different ideas for different purposes in different contexts. Many of the ideas go back to Homer and Hesiod – authors who formed the basis of ancient education, in physics and cosmology as much as ethics. And the moral dimension of the poems is better understood within the broader context of late Republican ethical thought. Certainly, Virgil explores issues and dilemmas central to the Hellenistic philosophical schools, but this is where and because they converge with ideological and ethical concerns of the late Republican élite. Any inquiry about the sources of Virgil's 'philosophy' is more fruitfully directed towards Homer: the view that philosophy was learned from poetry, starting from Homer, was axiomatic in antiquity. One of the clearest expressions of this view is in Horace, *Epistles* 1.2, for example (lines 3–4, 6–8, 11–18):

> The poet shows what is fine and foul, what is advisable, what not,
> more clearly and better than Chrysippus or Crantor ...
> The story, which tells how Greece because of Paris' love
> clashed in weary war with a foreign land,
> is full of the passions of foolish kings and peoples ...
> ... Nestor is anxious to settle
> the dispute between Peleus' son and the son of Atreus,
> the first fired by love and both by anger.
> For every act of royal folly, the Achaeans pay the penalty.
> Faction, deceit, crime, lust and anger –
> it's a story of wrongdoing inside and outside the walls of Troy.
> Again, Homer has set before us an instructive model
> of what goodness and wisdom can do in Ulysses ...

Similarly significant for our understanding of Virgil is the Roman exemplary mode of thought manifested in the Roman education system, which relied heavily upon the use of positive and negative role-models (*exempla*), such as Ulysses in Horace above.[54] Virgil's poems are illuminated when

---

[54] Cf. Horace, *Sat.* 1.4.105–25 and the handbook of 967 *exempla* by Valerius Maximus, *Facta et Dicta Memorabilia* ('Deeds and sayings worthy of record').

viewed not in terms of systems of philosophical thought but as reflecting and participating in the exemplarity central to the formation of the Roman 'man' (*vir*) and Roman 'manhood' (*virtus*). This in turn corresponds to the function of Roman education, which was not to develop free thinkers but to focus the individual's thoughts upon his role as an individual in the state. Virgil's prime allegiance is to Italy and to Rome.[55]

FURTHER READING

Two books stand out as essential reading on Virgil's treatment of the relationship between humankind and the gods and nature: P. Hardie, *Virgil's Aeneid: Cosmos and Imperium* (Oxford, 1986) and D. C. Feeney, *The Gods in Epic* (Oxford, 1991). Between them, they cover all the important aspects of this enormous topic and they provide ample detailed bibliography.

A. Thornton, *The Living Universe. Gods and Men in Virgil's Aeneid* (Leiden, 1976) deals with matters of cosmology, philosophy and the gods. On eschatology see D. C. Feeney, 'History and revelation in Vergil's underworld', *Proceedings of the Cambridge Philological Society* n.s. 32 (1986) 1–24. The hot dispute about the ethical flavour of the end of the *Aeneid*, particularly whether Virgil presents a Stoic or an Aristotelian view of Aeneas' anger, is found most recently in K. Galinsky, 'The anger of Aeneas', *American Journal of Philology* 109 (1988) 321–48; M. Putnam, 'Anger, blindness and insight in Virgil's *Aeneid*', in *The Poetics of Therapy*, ed. M. C. Nussbaum (= *Apeiron* 23 (1990) 7–40); K. Galinsky, 'How to be philosophical about the end of the *Aeneid*', *Illinois Classical Studies* 19 (1994) 191–201; and M. Putnam, *Virgil's Aeneid: Interpretation and Influence* (Chapel Hill and London, 1995) 201–45. The political dimension of the *Aeneid* is brought out by Hardie (above) and by F. Cairns, *Virgil's Augustan Epic* (Cambridge, 1989).

R. G. M. Nisbet, 'Virgil's Fourth *Eclogue*: Easterners and Westerners', in *Collected Papers on Latin Literature*, ed. S. J. Harrison (Oxford, 1995) 47–75 (= *Bulletin of the Institute of Classical Studies* 25 (1978) 59–78) uses the polarities of earlier criticism to illuminate Virgil's syncretism in the *Eclogues*. W. R. Johnson, *Darkness Visible: A Study of Vergil's Aeneid* (Berkeley and Los Angeles, 1976) discusses the conflict between optimistic and pessimistic readings of the *Aeneid*, while J. Griffin, 'The Fourth *Georgic*, Virgil, and Rome', *Greece & Rome* 26 (1979) 61–80 analyses the tension between divinity and mortality in the *Georgics* with the conclusion that this is perhaps the most finely poised of all Virgil's poems.

Denis Feeney's forthcoming book *Literature and Religion at Rome: Cultures, Contexts and Beliefs* provides a broader socio-political and cultural context for our appreciation of Virgil's ideas. Finally, for an overview of the influence of Hellenistic ideas in late Republican Rome see E. Rawson, *Intellectual Life in the Late Roman Republic* (London, 1985) and specifically on philosophy see M. Griffin, 'Philosophy, politics, and politicians at Rome', in M. Griffin and J. Barnes, eds., *Philosophia Togata. Essays on Philosophy and Roman Society* (Oxford, 1989) 1–37.

---

[55] Thanks for their comments to Denis Feeney, Monica Gale, Pauline Hire and Charles Martindale, even where I have persisted in my original views.

15

JOSEPH FARRELL

The Virgilian intertext

The fact that Virgil's poetry exhibits many points of contact with the literature of the past is beyond dispute. What to make of this fact is much less certain. The view taken here is that the poetics of intertextuality is one of Virgil's most powerfully evocative tools for communicating ideas, for establishing his place in the literary canon, and for eliciting the reader's active collaboration in making meaning. In this essay I shall try to suggest something of what attention to the intertext can do to enhance the appreciation of Virgil's poetry.[1]

The phenomenon of 'intertextuality' (or 'allusion', 'imitation', 'reference', etc.) is present in all poetry and, to some extent, in all language. Some poets deliberately cultivate an allusive style, and thus encourage their readers' expectation of seeing through one text to its source or model. Virgil alludes constantly to a wide range of authors, and we are fortunate in possessing complete texts of many of his favourite works, both Greek and Latin. In the case of works now lost, we rely on ancient summaries and modern collections of fragments.[2] In fact much of our knowledge about early Latin poetry derives from ancient students of Virgilian intertextuality, who quote many of the fragments we now possess to illustrate their influence on Virgil.[3]

Thus we probably know more about Virgil's sources and models than about those of any other ancient author. I would also argue that it is probably unwise to assume that the phenomena that we can clearly observe at work in Virgil would be visible in others too, if only we had more evidence.

---

[1] This essay is intended to complement rather than to repeat or replace what I have written in Farrell (1991) ch. 1 'Introduction: on Vergilian intertextuality', pp. 3–25.

[2] One of the first studies of Virgilian intertextuality was Perellius Faustus' uncharitably entitled 'Thefts' (Furta). Octavius Avitus' Ὁμοιότητες filled some eight books (Vita Donati 44–5). The fullest surviving example of this scholarly tradition is found in Books 5 and 6 of Macrobius' Saturnalia.

[3] On this aspect of the relationship between Virgil, his models, and ancient scholarship see Wigodsky (1972) and Jocelyn (1964–5).

Nor would it be fair to conclude that Virgil's extensive cultivation of inter-textual resources marks him as less 'original' than other poets. The truth, I believe, lies between these facile notions and points us towards an entirely different understanding: namely that Virgilian intertextuality shows every sign of being the distinct creation and in many ways the artistic signature of classical antiquity's greatest poetic craftsman.

This is not to say that Virgil invented his style out of nothing. Archaic and classical Greek poets certainly alluded in various ways to one another and especially to Homer. Indeed, most surviving Greek poetry can hardly be read without calling to mind some passage or situation in Homer; and the great masters of Greek tragedy, for example, composed for an audi-ence familiar with Homer and a good deal of other poetry both from formal schooling and from attending frequent public performances, pri-vate symposia, and so forth. So the tradition of allusive poetry is very old. But in the Hellenistic kingdoms of Pergamum and Alexandria, close study of earlier literature increased the capacity of poetry to analyse, comment upon, interpret, and even to correct the poetry of the past.[4] In Pergamum scholarly energy was focused on the interpretation of Homer as a philo-sopher through allegory, symbolic etymology, and similar means. Unfortu-nately little of the poetry that may have reflected this intellectual milieu survives; but enough is known to guarantee that Virgil understood the pro-cedures of interpreting Homer through physical, historical, and moral alle-goresis, and that he followed these procedures in his own adaptations of the *Iliad* and the *Odyssey*.[5] In Alexandria an equal amount of energy was focused on the word and on mastery of Greek culture through the mastery of language. The methods by which this mastery was displayed – if 'displayed' is the right word – were often rather cryptic, and at times downright furtive. Poets like Callimachus refused to write in an obviously Homeric style, but loved using specimens of rare Homeric diction: words that occur only once in all of Homer, or once in Homer even if commonly afterwards, or once in the *Iliad* even if several times in the *Odyssey*; or else unusual variants of dialect, preferred manuscript readings, and other rarities. We need not understand these phenomena as allusions to the Homeric context in which such words occur; often enough the relevant context is the reference works in which the words were listed. But stylistically and intellectually, their presence in a poetic text suggests the author's close familiarity with and worshipful respect for the text that he imitates as well as the high stand-ards of literary and scholarly connoisseurship that he requires of his reader.

---

[4] See in general Pfeiffer (1968); for further and more detailed discussion cf. Porter (1992).
[5] Hardie (1986); cf. Farrell (1991) 253–72.

Virgil's poetry has affinities with both styles of allusion. On the one hand, the reader who knows Virgil's favourite authors even casually will not fail to catch their voices in Virgil's words, or to recognise his imitations of famous Homeric or Sophoclean scenes. On the other hand, those who prize Virgil's ability to arrest their attention with a single word and who savour his sheer command of the Latin language, eventually discover that behind many individual words there is a history, a history that is written in the texts of other authors. The two styles are sometimes thought to be at odds, the former representing a perspective on the literary past as the common property of a cultivated readership, the latter marking out a kind of *pomerium philologiae* to which only initiates can gain access. But the difference between the two styles should not be exaggerated. Both types of allusion serve similar rhetorical ends, drawing the reader into a dialogue that transcends the limits of the individual text and establishing continuity between Virgil's poetry and the work of his great predecessors.

One finds the art of intertextuality at work in almost every syllable Virgil wrote, so that analysis might begin almost anywhere. Book 8 of the *Aeneid* ends with one of Virgil's most obvious allusions: the description of a shield fashioned for Aeneas by Vulcan, which is clearly modelled on Achilles' shield in *Iliad* 18. Any reader who is at all familiar with Homer would recognise the reference. Some would stop there, regarding the allusion as generic in character, i.e. as a mark of the poem's participation in the epic genre. It is possible to stop interpreting at this point, of course, and still to enjoy the passage. By the same token, it is not necessary to understand every facet of fire imagery in the *Aeneid* to be moved by Dido's love, Turnus' lust for battle, and the omens that convince Anchises to leave his conquered city. But as in the case of other poetic effects, Virgilian allusion is never one-dimensional or unrelated to other thematic devices.

Virgil's shield, like Homer's, is on the one hand merely an epic shield; but in earlier antiquity, Homer's shield had been read as something more.[6] Because it is encircled by the stream of Ocean and depicts the sun, moon, and constellations, Homer's shield was interpreted as an emblem of the cosmos, and Virgil's shield may well be informed by this exegetical tradition. Thus the two shields are not only generic markers, but also signifiers of the genre's status as a vehicle of cosmological truth. The differences between the shields support this idea as well. Homer's shield depicts two cities, one at war, one at peace, along with the various activities that take place in each, and for this reason was read in Hellenistic times as an image of the poem. Virgil's shield depicts famous events in Roman history, culminating

---

[6] Hardie (1986) ch. 8, 'The shield of Aeneas: the cosmic icon', 336–76, with further references.

in Augustus' victory at Actium, and thus, like Homer's shield, 'stands for' the poem in which it occurs, while the allegorical nature of the comparison is more pronounced. Again ancient interpretation of Homer seems to have guided Virgil's imagination. Finally, note that these shields involve a double comparison, one between the shield and the subject of the poem in which it appears, and another between the shield (and thus the poem for which it stands) and the cosmos. In the case of the *Aeneid* this double comparison can be read as an interpretation of contemporary political arrangements as reflected both in the events of the mythic past and in the permanent structure of the cosmos. This happens to be one of the most notable characteristics of surviving Pergamene art; and since Pergamum was, as I have noted, a centre of Homeric scholarship in the allegorical tradition, it seems certain that Virgil's dialogue with Homer was moderated by commentary of just this type.

An understanding of ancient scholarship thus expands our understanding of the intertextual relationship in at least one direction; but this example still involves treating the shield episode more or less as a single point of contact between the *Iliad* and the *Aeneid*. Allusion to the *Iliad* or *Odyssey* normally invites the reader to compare the structures of the relevant Virgilian and Homeric narratives. Any reader taking this approach to the shield in Book 8 would correctly interpret it as a sign that Aeneas is becoming another Achilles – a reversal of what the Sibyl's prophecy about 'another Achilles come to light in Latium, himself goddess-born' (6.89–90) seems to mean and of Turnus' contention that he himself is that other Achilles; but the reversal is borne out in the poem's final scene when Aeneas forces Turnus into the role of Hector, taking upon himself the mantle of Achilles.

In the immediate context of *Aeneid* 8, how far does this analogy hold? Few readers bother to trace the earlier episodes of the book to a specific prototype. Nevertheless, there are good reasons to regard Aeneas' visit to Pallanteum as a reworking of several Homeric episodes.[7] Aeneas, absent from the battles taking place around the Trojan encampment, resembles Achilles in this way as well – even if formal similarity emphasises the diference in character between a hero who leaves the fray out of concern for his slighted honour and one who carries out an important diplomatic mission on his people's behalf.[8] But Achilles is not the only model. Aeneas is also a type of Telemachus here, visiting the court of a friendly king; and if Evander's tale about Hercules and Cacus (*Aen.* 8.184–279) stands in for Menelaus' story about Proteus (*Od.* 4.332–592), the Laurentian king's

[7] Knauer (1964a) 239–66; cf. Knauer (1964b) 76–8. See also Wimmel (1973) 50–73.
[8] Anderson (1957) 25; Gransden (1984) 97–8.

advanced age marks him as a type of Nestor, who also hosted Telemachus (*Od.* 3).

These parallels are well supported by analysis of the relevant Virgilian and Homeric narratives; nevertheless, they are far less obvious than the allusion that closes the book and may thus be felt to be unimportant or even illusory. It is unwise, however, especially in Virgil, to measure importance in terms of obvious effect. The most certain allusion in Book 8 besides the description of the shield is perhaps the least obvious. It consists of a single word, *scyphus* (8.278), a word that Virgil uses only here.[9] Why is this significant? Because it is a ἅπαξ λεγόμενον, a word used only once by Homer as well. As I noted above, Alexandrian poets consulted special glossaries of such words and used them to suggest their close, scholarly familiarity with the text of Homer, and this surely explains an aspect of its appearance in the *Aeneid*. But if this is really an allusion, and not just a piece of lexicographical bravado, the Homeric context in which the word appears ought to be relevant too. And so it is: in the *Odyssey* it is Eumaeus the swineherd who receives the hero with hospitality into his humble dwelling and hands him a σκύφος (14.112), just as Evander does here. Thus Evander in this scene 'is' Eumaeus (as well as Nestor), while Aeneas plays the role of Odysseus (as well as those of Telemachus and Achilles).

Before we turn to the meaning of this characterisation, there is more to say about the word itself. Virgil may have got the Homeric ἅπαξ from some Hellenistic word list, but it is equally likely that he became aware of it while involved in an earlier intertextual project. In Eclogue 3, two shepherds compete in a singing contest. They agree to a wager: Menalcas stakes a pair of beautifully carved beechwood cups (*pocula*, 36–43). His loving description of them is clearly borrowed from Theocritus' First Idyll. There the goatherd promises Thyrsis all manner of rustic gifts if he will sing the Daphnis song; among them is an embossed cup, which the goatherd calls by the Homeric word σκύφος – a word that Theocritus uses only here (143). So it seems quite likely that Virgil became aware of Theocritus' learned allusion in his own imitation of a passage from Idyll 1 in Eclogue 3.

Returning to *Aeneid* 8, what sense can we make of what we have learned? How is an obvious allusion to a famous passage from the *Iliad* related to the all-but-undetectable borrowing of a rare word from the *Odyssey* by way of Theocritus? To answer this question, one has to be aware of two facts. First, the description of the cup in Idyll 1 is hardly unrelated to the description of the shield in *Iliad* 18. Second, the rustic setting in which Aeneas receives his divine shield is hardly unrelated either

---

[9] On what follows see Wills (1987).

to the heroic deeds that shield will allow him to perform or to the glorious martial future that the scenes embossed on it predict.

First, the cup. On the one hand, Theocritus' cup 'is' the σκύφος with which Eumaeus entertained Odysseus. But it is well known that Theocritus' description of this consummately bucolic artifact alludes carefully to Homer's description of Achilles' shield.[10] Theocritus' fashioning of a symbol for the world of pastoral poetry out of a weapon carried by the greatest of all epic heroes (and the words of the greatest of all epic poets) is typical of the way in which Alexandrian poets imitated Homer – by reducing Homeric grandeur to a more human level in a way that almost disguises the source, all the while leaving unmistakable (if well hidden) traces that a relationship does in fact exist. Theocritus' calling his pastoral cup a Homeric σκύφος is just such a trace. It is also something more. By borrowing the rare word from a passage in which a Homeric hero is entertained by a humble herdsman in rustic surroundings, Theocritus implicitly claims a distinguished poetic heritage and thus legitimacy for his own world of humble herdsmen in rustic surroundings and for the genre that, with his description of this cup, he in effect invents.

Second, the rustic setting of Pallanteum. Italy in Virgil is on the one hand a place very much like the bucolic world described by Theocritus, even like the earth as it was during the Golden Age: a place of natural abundance, clemency, and peaceful living.[11] But it is simultaneously a breeding-ground of strife and warfare. In Pallanteum these contradictions are at their most intense.[12] When Aeneas arrives there, he finds a peaceful, pastoral community where libations are poured from a Theocritean cup. But the hero has come seeking a military alliance, and he is not disappointed; for the libation poured from that cup is in honour of Hercules, who once pacified the district in anger and by main force. In fact, it is a Homeric cup after all, just as the shield Aeneas receives at Pallanteum is a Homeric shield, and the deeds he will perform with it Homeric deeds.

Like Theocritus, Virgil is playing a game that involves both the theory of genres and the history of literature: just as Theocritus had claimed descent from Homer, so Virgil is justifying the course that his career has taken from the *Eclogues* to the *Aeneid*. But he is doing more. By bringing pastoral and martial themes into such intimate proximity – finding them, in fact, within one another – he raises questions that outline several of the major themes that preoccupied him throughout his career. Can humankind

---

[10] On this relationship see Ott (1969) 99–105; Halperin (1983) 176–81.

[11] On the relationship between the bucolic world and the Golden Age myth in Virgil see Johnston (1980) 41–61.

[12] See Putnam (1965) ch. 3 'History's dream', 105–50 and Wimmel (1973) 43–73.

live in peace? Can that peace be achieved through force? Is any and every peace fated to erupt into violence? By raising such questions he comes close to suggesting that the worlds of the shepherd and of the soldier are in fact one – that for all their apparent differences, the shepherd and the soldier differ very little. One can certainly read Virgil's interpretation of Achilles' shield in just this way; but one sees it no less convincingly and much more succinctly in the quiet but definite gesture embodied in the single word *scyphus*, simultaneously pastoral and heroic, Theocritean and Homeric.

This is the essence of Virgilian intertextuality, in which the covert does not contradict, but greatly enriches (and often complicates) the overt. It is a rhetorical device that encourages close scrutiny not only of Virgil's text, but of the many intertexts with which that text becomes enmeshed. And while an analysis like the one above may seem to proceed on a rather *ad hoc* basis, it actually assumes that the Virgilian intertext works in a few quite definite and systematic ways. The main points to keep in mind about Virgil's intertextual practice are the following.

(1) *It is pervasive.* Understanding this point follows on taking seriously what every beginner knows: that the *Aeneid* 'is' the entire *Iliad* and *Odyssey* rolled into one. Taking this proposition seriously means assuming that every line of the poem potentially alludes to something in Homer, either by direct quotation or by virtue of occurring within an episode 'borrowed' from Homer.

(2) *It is analytical.* Allusions to Homer in the *Aeneid* do not occur at random; rather, they are based on careful analysis and comparison of both Homeric poems. The events of Book 8, in which Aeneas receives his divine armour, presage his entry into battle, just like Achilles' acceptance of divine weapons in *Iliad* 18. But *Aeneid* 8 also gives us the hero as Odysseus in Eumaeus' hut and as Telemachus on his visit to Pylos and Sparta – the episodes during which father and son are both absent from their palace, but are about to return to fight the suitors together. Such coincidences can hardly be due to anything other than careful analysis of the sources involved and the development of an allusive programme on that basis.

(3) *It is thematically motivated.* The previous example illustrates this point as well. That Aeneas on his visit to Pallanteum should 'be' both Odysseus and Telemachus, father and son, demands interpretation. The fact that on this visit Evander recognises Virgil's hero as the son of his friend Anchises, and that Aeneas forms a powerful bond with Evander's young son Pallas, will obviously come into play. Similarly, the modelling of commemorative games for Anchises (*Aen.* 5) on the most cheerful aspects

of the funeral games for Patroclus (*Il.* 23) is systematically and thematically related to the imitation of the rest of Patroclus' funeral – down to
the shocking detail of immolating prisoners of war as offerings to the shade
of the deceased (*Il.* 23.175–6) – in the funeral of Pallas, the 'real' Patroclus
of the *Aeneid* (11.81–2).

(4) *It is not limited to any single source or model.* This is crucially
important. Of course Homer in some sense provides the chief intertext for
the *Aeneid*. But to define the poem's intertextual programme as 'Homer
with occasional reference to others' is to misconstrue the three previous
points and to set up unnecessary obstacles to interpreting the *Eclogues* and
Georgics as well. We understand the Homeric element in Virgil's programme
especially well because it has been since antiquity the most intensively
studied aspect. But the relationship between Virgil and Homer is not unique,
and an understanding of Virgilian intertextuality that does not go beyond
Homer is far from sufficient.

To demonstrate these points, let us begin with the traditional view that
Virgil's epic divides into 'Odyssean' and 'Iliadic' halves. Merely accepting
this idea at face value is to mistake for a destination what Virgil clearly
offered as the starting-point of a long and wondrous journey. The argument I have just presented about Iliadic *and* Odyssean models in Book 8
suggests that the *Aeneid* does not divide so easily into Iliadic and Odyssean
halves. Turning back to the first six books of the poem, we find that the
alleged correspondence between *Aeneid* 1–6 and the Homeric *Odyssey*
invites the reader to pose and to meditate on a number of simple but
urgent questions:

(1) What does it mean for Virgil to have 'shrunk' his Odyssey from
    twenty-four to only six books?
(2) How can he have done this when at least one of these six books
    (5) includes a major episode representing an entire book not of the
    Odyssey, but of the *Iliad*?
(3) What must we make of Servius' remark about Book 4 – he exagger-
    ates here but is not essentially incorrect – that 'this entire book is
    taken over from Book 3 of Apollonius'?[13]
(4) The fall of Troy in *Aeneid* 2 is a story that Homer did not tell in any
    detail; that was left to the poets of the epic cycle and of tragedy. Why
    then does Virgil devote to it an entire book of what we think of as
    his Odyssey?

---

[13] *Apollonius Argonautica scripsit ubi inducit amantem Medeam; inde totus hic liber translatus*
est, de tertio Apollonii (*praef. in Aen.* 4, 247. 1–4 Harv.).

(5) If Virgil means to imitate Homer entirely, why does his Odyssey begin with a storm at sea (i.e. in Book 5 of the Homeric *Odyssey*) and end with a trip to the Underworld (i.e. in Homer's Book 11)?

Such questions by their very specificity strike some readers as out of place; for them the general similarity is enough. But Virgil's style is all about specificity in the service of enriching the reader's experience, and not just where allusion is concerned. The questions I have posed can all be answered in various ways, and the answers that we suggest reveal almost everything about what kind of poem we think the *Aeneid* is, representing what kind of values, proposing what model of heroism, offering what kind of insight into the human condition. And as we have seen, it is characteristic of Virgil to provoke meditation upon the most profound questions by dwelling on what might seem the most insignificant of details.

I have so far focused on the *Aeneid* because it is, in this respect at least, the best understood of Virgil's works. The question remains, how far these lessons apply to the earlier works as well. There is no easy answer. The *Eclogues*, like the *Aeneid*, in their relationship to one model in particular, offer a potential organising principle. Unlike the *Iliad* and the *Odyssey*, however, we do not know in what form Virgil read Theocritus; whatever structural relationship may have existed between the Eclogue book and its putative Theocritean model can only remain hypothetical. As for the *Georgics*, we know that direct imitation of its acknowledged model, Hesiod's *Works* and *Days*, is confined to Book 1; the rest of the poem works through a progression of themes that involve substantial interaction with (*inter alios*) first Lucretius, then Homer.[14] Thus in respect of their general intertextual frameworks, both the *Eclogues* (possibly) and the *Georgics* (certainly) differ from the *Aeneid*.

On the other hand, the allusive texture of both earlier works is not essentially different from what we find in the *Aeneid*. Virgil's means of creating intertextual dialogue in the *Georgics* seem to me identical with what one finds in the *Aeneid*. The even earlier Sixth Eclogue already presents the reader with such a dazzlingly elaborate and densely woven intertextual fabric that it is still only partly understood.[15] Imitation in the *Eclogues* is generally more concentrated on Theocritus alone; but even those poems that draw on Theocritus exclusively, or nearly so, show the same kinds of technical and thematic sophistication that one finds in the *Aeneid*.

---

[14] For details see Farrell 1991.

[15] See Farrell (1991) 291–314 and especially Ross (1975) 18–38, with further references.

The Third Eclogue depicts a singing match, a motif found in several Theocritean Idylls.[16] More broadly, the poem is thematically unified by the motif
of exchange, and it alludes to a number of different Idylls that deal with
this theme in various forms. One is Idyll 4, with whose opening words
Eclogue 3 begins:

MENALCAS	Dic mihi, Damoeta, cuium pecus? an Meliboei?
DAMOETAS	Non, vero Aegonis; nuper mihi tradidit Aegon.
M.	infelix o semper, oves, pecus! ipse Neaeram
	dum fovet ac ne me sibi praeferat illa veretur,
	hic alienus ovis custos bis mulget in hora,
	et sucus pecori et lac subducitur agnis!

MENALCAS	Tell me, Damoetas, whose flock? Are they Meliboeus'?
DAMOETAS	No, Aegon's; Aegon just turned them over to me.
M.	Oh, sheep, you're a sad lot! While your master nuzzles Neaera
	and worries she likes me better, this surrogate shepherd milks
	you twice an hour, drying out the flock and cheating the lambs!
	(*Ecl.* 3.1–6)

Βάττος	Εἰπέ μοι, ὦ Κορύδων, τίνος αἱ βόες; ἦ ῥα Φιλώνδα;
Κορύδων	οὔκ, ἀλλ' Αἴγωνος· βόσκειν δέ μοι αὐτὰς ἔδωκεν.
Β.	ἦ πᾷ ψε κρύβδαν τὰ ποθέσπερα πάσας ἀμέλγες;
	* * *
	δείλαιαί γ' αὖται, τὸν βούκολον ὡς κακὸν εὗρον.

BATTUS	Tell me, Corydon, whose cattle? Are they Philondas'?
CORYDON	No, Aegon's; he gave them to me to watch.
B.	And are you milking them all towards evening on the sly?
	* * *
	Poor things, what a bad herdsman they've got!
	(*Idylls* 4.1–3, 13)

These openings not only dramatise an exchange of banter, however; they
concern a material exchange, the exchange of sheep and cattle, or the
animals' exchange of one herdsman for another. It is no great stretch to
see in the image of this transference a special relevance to Virgil's project
of imitating Theocritus, and to find in Menalcas' acid remark a sardonic
commentary on the suspect position of the imitative poet who, as if by
definition, stands accused of living off another's property. Menalcas' taunt
provokes recrimination and a quarrel, which may be anticipated in the
name of Aegon – the only name in the Theocritean passage that Virgil

---

[16] On what follows see Farrell (1992).

leaves unaltered (and actually utters twice) – where we catch a hint of both the rightful owner's (viz. the earlier poet's) and the exploited animals' (who are δείλαιαί) aggrievement (by a pun with the Latin *aeger*) and of the contest (via the Greek ἀγών) that this eclogue will become.

After such an ominous prelude, the contest itself ends in a draw. The eclogue can thus be read metapoetically as at least a moral victory for the imitative poet. The proemium of *Georgics* 3 is even more self-assertive. Having begun with a definitive expression of literary belatedness (*omnia iam uulgata*, 4), Virgil goes on to assert hegemony over his poetic forebears: he will lead the Muses from Greece to Mantua and build a temple to Caesar on the banks of the Mincius. Far from original, this fantasy owes a great deal to the earlier epinician poetry of Pindar and Callimachus;[17] but here belatedness is transvalued into masterly, victorious appropriation, an all-but-literal triumph over the past. And Virgil was willing to go still further. The memorial games for Anchises in *Aeneid* 5 are, as noted above, a redrafting of Homer's funeral games for Patroclus in *Iliad* 23.[18] The episode on the whole is, as a piece of literary imitation and emulation, one of Virgil's most decisive 'victories' over Homer. Not surprisingly, then, it contains what may be his most prideful vaunt. Virgil's first contest, the boat race, is modelled on Homer's first event, a chariot race. The *Aeneid* passage contains a fascinating simile that looks very much like a metaliterary comment on its relationship with its Homeric model:[19]

> non tam praecipites biiugo certamine campum
> corripuere ruuntque effusi carcere currus,
> nec sic immissis aurigae undantia lora
> concussere iugis pronique in verbera pendent.

Not so swift are chariots that have seized the plain in a contest of yoked teams and rush in a flood from their starting-cage, nor do the drivers so shake their waving thongs at the headlong chargers and hang prone over their blows.   (*Aen.* 5.144–7)

If we read this simile with reference to Homer, we are reminded of Virgil's decision to alter a chariot race into a regatta; and if we read with reference to the intertextual relationship (for chariots and boats, like the sheep of Eclogue 4, are generically appropriate symbols for the poetry in which they appear), we catch Virgil's boast that Homer's race is bested in competition with his own.

---

[17] Pindar: Wilkinson (1970); Callimachus: Thomas (1983b).

[18] The classic pages of Heinze (1915) 145–70, recently translated into English (1993) 121–41, are still worth studying.

[19] Nugent (1992).

But Virgilian contests do not always bear a message that is so comforting to the belated challenger. Eclogue 7 contains an amoebaean contest similar to that of Eclogue 3; but this time Corydon, who sings first, defeats Thyrsis, who follows. The contestants are described as equals (4–5), so that it is merely the order in which they sing that assigns Corydon the role of model, Thyrsis that of the imitator who strives in vain to surpass or at least match his predecessor. Returning to the games of *Aeneid* 5 we find a contest that reverses the outcome of an earlier one. In the boxing match themes of age and priority take prominence as the elder contestant, Entellus, bests Dares, his younger opponent. It is tempting to read this athletic contest as an allegorical poetics of belatedness. Certainly Virgil understood all too well when he wrote this episode that not only Homer, but Apollonius and Theocritus had been there before him.[20] And this is to speak only of the Greeks; for when Entellus sacrifices his prize bull to Hercules in thanksgiving for his victory, the narrator speaks in Ennian tones:[21]

sternitur exanimisque tremens procumbit humi bos

The steer is felled and lies lifeless, trembling on the ground. (*Aen.* 5.481)

It seems impossible for Virgil to tell this tale except in words borrowed from the poets of the past, and irresistible for the reader to view such tokens of belatedness as anything but evidence of the modern poet's anxiety that he will never measure up. Dares' failure to overcome his ancient rival, like Aeneas' unsuccessful attempt by means of these games finally to lay the ghost of his dead father, can easily be taken to reflect the poet's anxiety about his own Homeric *agon* and, more generally, the ever-present theme of Rome's deeply ambivalent relationship with Greek culture.

It is often possible to view intertextuality in this way; but it is not the only useful approach, and the notion of rivalry sometimes seems hopelessly inadequate to explain Virgil's work with the literary past. Consider the passage of *Aeneid* 9 in which Nisus and Euryalus propose their ill-starred mission to the Trojan chiefs. The escapade is modelled mainly on two Iliadic episodes. Aeneas in Book 9 (as noted above apropos of Book 8) is still absent from the scene of battle, and his troops are having the worst of it. The proposed mission of Nisus and Euryalus corresponds in purpose to the embassy of *Iliad* 9: the hero must be brought back to the aid of his comrades. But the mission fails because the two adventurers become enmeshed in the plot of *Iliad* 10, the Doloneia, slaughtering drunk

---

[20] Poliakoff (1985).
[21] On this phenomenon see Thomas (1986b) 180–1; cf. Farrell (1991) 228–9.

and sleepy Rutulians in their beds – but, unlike Diomedes and Odysseus in the *Iliad*, Virgil's pair are surprised by dawn and the arrival of the enemy captain Messapus, and meet their doom.

Virgil's redrafting of Homer's plot says a lot about the heroic values that his epic celebrates. Aeneas, dutiful and energetic, is far different from the selfish Achilles. Not only Nisus and Euryalus, though, but the Trojan leaders as well behave in a way that draws upon and debases the typical desire of Homeric heroes to measure their stature in material possessions. The bribes that Agamemnon offers Achilles if he will return to battle – bribes that Achilles pointedly and contemptuously rejects (*Il.* 9.378–87), – become rewards that Iulus offers Nisus and Euryalus if their mission succeeds (*Aen.* 9.257–80). And when the fatal morning comes, Euryalus is betrayed by a shaft of light glinting off the helmet that he has just taken as booty from the body of a man killed by stealth in his sleep, not in open, heroic combat (*Aen.* 9.359–77). Thus if Aeneas at this point surpasses in moral stature his Homeric prototype, the people on whose behalf he labours – not excluding his son – exhibit some of the worst excesses of the older heroic code.

The Homeric plot of the *Aeneid* is not, however, an isolated or self-sufficient element of the poem's meaning, but is set in a broader philosophical context. In proposing his plan to Euryalus, Nisus first asks the astonishing question:

> dine hunc ardorem mentibus addunt,
> Euryale, an sua cuique deus fit dira cupido?

> Do gods apply this burning to our minds,
> Euryalus, or does each man's dread desire become his god?

> (*Aen.* 9.184–5)

If this hermeneutical conundrum sounds odd in the mouth of a military watchman, it serves to introduce a more specific set of references. Euryalus has been introduced to the reader as one of the 'sons of Aeneas' (*Aeneadum*, 9.180); and Nisus will later address Iulus and the other Trojan captains in the same way (235). Virgil uses the word fairly frequently, and in the fragmentary state of our knowledge about earlier Latin literature, it is difficult to know how common the use of this patronymic was. We actually know of only one occurrence before the *Aeneid*, and in a highly marked context indeed: it is the first word of Lucretius' *De rerum natura*. More Lucretian language attends the introduction of the Trojan war council:

> cetera per terras omnis animalia somno
> laxabant curas et corda oblita laborum:

> ductores Teucrum primi, *delecta* iuventus
> consilium summis regni de rebus habebant,
> quid facerent quisve Aeneae iam nuntius esset.

All other animals throughout all lands were relaxing in sleep their cares and hearts forgetful of toil; but **the foremost leaders of the Trojans, select youth,** were holding council over the highest affairs of state: what action to take, or who might take a message to Aeneas. (*Aen.* 9.224–8)

The reference is to a passage in which Lucretius expresses a very dim view of statesmen and the values they stand for:

> Illud in his rebus vereor, ne forte rearis
> impia te rationis inire elementa viamque
> indugredi sceleris; quod contra saepius illa
> religio peperit scelerosa atque impia facta.
> Aulide quo pacto Triviai virginis aram
> Iphianassai turparunt sanguine foede
> ductores Danaum *delecti*, prima virorum

What I fear in all this is that you may happen to think you are entering wicked lessons in reason and walking a road of crime; whereas in fact, it is religion that has more frequently given birth to wicked, criminal deeds. As for instance at Aulis **the select leaders of the Greeks, first of heroes,** foully polluted the altar of the chaste Trivia with the blood of Iphianassa. (*DRN* 1.80–6)

If we probe these verbal parallels for thematic significance, we quickly see that Virgil's 'sons of Aeneas' are in Lucretian terms blinded by their desire for material gain and worldly power, subject to the superstition that is the Roman state religion, and badly in need of the cure that comes only with a bracing draught of Epicurean *ratio*. And the Virgilian context actually supports this interpretation. Nisus proposes action because his mind is not at rest (*mens agitat mihi nec placida contenta quiete est*, 9.187); likewise the Trojan leaders, in contrast to all other living creatures, are beset by cares. This is as if to say that the 'sons of Aeneas' are suffering from ταραχός, disturbance of the soul, the opposite of ἀταραξία, the spiritual tranquillity produced by Epicurean *sapientia*. Thus the revisions of Homeric plot in this episode are supported by reference to a moral code far removed from that of the archaic warrior, but not so far from that of the contemporary politician.[22]

---

[22] The fact that Virgil's Trojans at this point are living out the experiences of Homer's Greeks is reflected linguistically in the change of Lucretius' *ductores Danaum* to Virgil's *ductores Teucrum*.

The intertextuality of a passage like this supports a crucial element of the poem's rhetorical structure as expressed in terms of time. Virgil's narration of events in the distant past has direct relevance for the cultural milieu of contemporary Rome. Voicing a speculative philosophical problem through the persona of an archaic warrior and voicing it as a question that has far-reaching implications for contemporary religious attitudes (as well as for the interpretation of the 'divine machinery' of the epic genre which the *Aeneid* constantly employs), is one of the ways in which Virgil links the two most important time-frames in which the poem operates. It also establishes an important link between the genres of epic and philosophy. Both of these points are made in other ways as well; but the reference to Lucretius in this famously Homeric context greatly intensifies the delicious sensation of temporal convergence that permeates the poem, while accessing a rich vein of Homeric criticism in the service of addressing the ills of contemporary society.

What this example illustrates is Virgil's ability to make his text part of something greater than itself, as if it were merely an episode within a greater, continuous text of almost unimaginable scope. This tendency is most clearly visible in the presence of a strong narrative current within a highly traditional genre, as in the *Aeneid*, a poem that uses time as a raw material to tremendous literary effect. Here, I believe, there is much work to be done. Existing scholarship has tended to see Virgil as a tyro anxious about meeting the standard set by his teachers, or else as a kind of masterly editor, rewriting the poetic past by the light of his own superior discrimination and scholarship. I have tried to suggest that there is also a Virgil who is sure of his right to stand alongside the greatest poets of the past, yet too worshipful of their achievements to molest them with wilful revisionism. The aim of this poet is to create a text that will knit together any number of cherished 'pre-texts' into a vast, continuous intertext – a project that Virgil did not begin or complete, but that he did much to advance.

This Virgil appears wherever the intertext calls attention to itself as such. When Hercules sheds tears over the impending death of young Pallas (*Aen.* 10.464–5), Jupiter consoles Hercules by 'reminding' him of his own tears over the death of Sarpedon. Jupiter thus establishes both that Pallas 'is' Sarpedon and that the circular movement of epic time that allows for such repetitions also moves on a linear axis: Pallas' death does not merely repeat that of Sarpedon, it succeeds it as well. The *Iliad* is pointedly *not* being rewritten here; it stands emphatically unaltered as a model by which to understand this subsequent event. Jupiter's act of remembrance guarantees that the *Iliad* and the *Aeneid* are related not merely as might be any two epic poems on similar themes representing similar events, but also as 'episodes' within a much greater, continuous epic intertext; and it guarantees further that the relationship between them does not depend exclusively on the perception of the reader, but is actually presupposed within the narrative itself. Indeed, the allusion releases still more metapoetic force. The event that Jupiter recalls stands for the immutability of fate: Homer's Zeus could not save Sarpedon from his fate, nor can Virgil's Jupiter or Hercules save Pallas from his. In a context that recalls a Homeric episode so precisely, and an episode that deals with such a theme, it seems again but a small step to infer a comment on the sanctity and inviolability of the literary past. True, Virgil is not always unwilling to summon forth the past in unfamiliar forms. But a passage such as this may remind us that all is not mere putty in his hands; that the past was, to some extent, simply the given with which he had to work, and to which he willingly adapted himself.

This example gives only an idea of the scope and character of the great intertext within which Virgil's poetry inscribes itself. If passages like this, which assume an Olympian perspective, afford the clearest views, the intertext is nevertheless visible everywhere in the *Eclogues*, *Georgics*, and *Aeneid*. Nor is the interpretation of this intertext a mechanistic process. The conflict between heroic and Epicurean values in the episode of Nisus and Euryalus is not resolved one way or the other by the chronological relationship between Homer and Lucretius. But through such passages the dimensions of the reader's experience expand immeasurably. Rather than a skeleton key that opens up the secrets of the poem, the intertext presents vistas and possibilities that would otherwise remain unglimpsed and inaccessible.

FURTHER READING

Literature on the general theory of intertextuality is vast and complex. Exploration might begin with two articles in A. Preminger and T. V. F. Brogan, eds., *The New Princeton Encyclopedia of Poetry and Poetics* (Princeton, 1993) s.vv. 'Allusion' and 'Intertextuality' and continue with the bibliographical material cited there. Of the many studies that focus on Greek and especially Latin poetry, see especially D. West and T. Woodman, eds., *Creative Imitation and Latin Literature* (Cambridge, 1979); G. B. Conte, *The Rhetoric of Imitation: Genre and Poetic Memory in Virgil and Other Latin Poets* (Ithaca and London, 1986); P. R. Hardie, *The Epic Successors of Virgil: A Study in the Dynamics of a Tradition* (Cambridge, 1993); and J. Wills, *Repetition in Latin Poetry: Figures of Allusion* (Oxford, 1997). S. E. Hinds' forthcoming monograph, *Allusion and Intertext: Dynamics of Appropriation in Roman Poetry*, promises to advance the discussion considerably.

For Virgil no satisfactory general study exists, but the individual works are more or less well served. For the *Eclogues* Sebastian Posch (1969), *Beobachtungen zur*

Theokritnachwirkung bei Vergil, Commentationes Aenipontanae 19, provides a reasonably full collection of parallel passages. D. O. Ross, *Backgrounds to Augustan Poetry: Gallus, Elegy, and Rome* (Cambridge, 1975) subtly analyses Virgil's earliest work in relation to the Neoteric movement. Farrell, 'Literary allusion and cultural poetics in Vergil's *Third Eclogue*', *Vergilius* 38 (1992) 64–71 argues that the allusive style of the *Eclogues* is determined by social and historical as much as by literary relations. For the *Georgics* R. F. Thomas, 'Virgil's *Georgics* and the art of reference', *Harvard Studies in Classical Philology* 90 (1986) 171–98 is particularly good on the various forms of poetic intertextuality, while Thomas, 'Prose into poetry: tradition and meaning in Virgil's *Georgics*', *Harvard Studies in Classical Philology* 91 (1987) 229–60 illuminates Virgil's transformation of apparently unpoetic material. See also Thomas' commentary on the poem, *Virgil, Georgics*, 2 vols. (Cambridge, 1988). For an attempt to discern a pervasive intertextual design in the *Georgics* see J. Farrell, *Vergil's Georgics and the Traditions of Ancient Epic: The Art of Allusion in Literary History* (New York and Oxford, 1991). For the *Aeneid* R. Heinze, *Vergils Epische Technik*, 3rd edn (Leipzig and Berlin, 1915), tr. H. and D. Harvey and F. Robertson as *Vergil's Epic Technique* (Bristol, 1993) remains basic, as does W. S. Anderson, 'Virgil's second *Iliad*', reprinted in S. J. Harrison, ed., *Oxford Readings in Vergil's Aeneid* (Oxford and New York, 1990) 239–52; but for the general shape of Virgil's Homeric programme in the poem as for many points of detail, G. N. Knauer, *Die Aeneis und Homer* (Göttingen, 1964) is the *sine qua non*, featuring detailed discussion (in German) and full comparison of parallel passages in tabular form – his results are conveniently if briefly summarised (in English) by Knauer, 'Vergil's *Aeneid* and Homer', *Greek, Roman and Byzantine Studies* 5 (1964) 61–84. It is true that Knauer approaches his material somewhat mechanistically; but more recent work, especially A. Barchiesi, *La traccia del modello: effetti omerici nella narrazione virgiliana* (Pisa, 1984) treats Virgil's engagement with the literary past in a much more suggestive fashion. For Virgil's relationship to Hellenistic and especially Alexandrian authors, see W. V. Clausen, *Virgil's Aeneid and the Tradition of Hellenistic Poetry* (Berkeley, 1987).

4
CONTENTS AND FORMS

16

JAMES J. O'HARA

Virgil's style

Coleridge's famous question, 'If you take from Virgil his language and metre, what do you leave him?', is often taken to mean there is little but style to praise in Virgil, and Coleridge does speak elsewhere of Virgil's lack of 'deep feeling'. But the remark may have been prompted by Coleridge's reading a month before of Wordsworth's translation of *Aeneid* Book 1, and thus be a comment on how much is lost when Virgil is read only in translation.[1] At the end of the twentieth century, the percentage of readers who encounter Virgil only in translation is much higher than in Coleridge's day (that specific comment comes from his *Table Talk* of 8 May 1824). Further, the tendency for those who do read Virgil in Latin to do so after only a few years of study of the language means that his Latin is not so much 'read' as translated or even 'metathesised', that is to say the Latin words are (at least mentally) rearranged and supplemented to fit some combination of the syntax of the reader's own language and his or her expectations of how a Latin prose sentence should read. At the same time, however, that fewer and fewer people on the planet can read Virgil's Latin either at all, or well, a tiny minority can arguably read the poet's language better than anyone has for several centuries. By 'better' I do not mean with the natural responses of one brought up to use Latin as a living language, but with the trained responses of those familiar with extensive scholarly research on metre, vocabulary, syntax, and everything that one might include under the rubric of style. In this century a number of scholars have done excellent work on the language of Latin poetry. In the last forty years new commentaries on Virgil, especially those from Cambridge and Oxford, have offered such useful remarks on style that a fine recent treatment of

---

[1] For Coleridge's reading of Wordsworth's translation cf. his letters of April 1824, especially one to Wordsworth himself. I am indebted to correspondence on this point from Margaret Graver, Joseph Farrell, and Charles Weiss. For comments on drafts of this essay, some of them quite different from the final product, I thank Nicholas Horsfall, Diane Juffras, Joseph Farrell, my colleague Michael Roberts, and Charles Martindale.

the topic (Horsfall 1995) recommends reading with a good commentary as the best introduction. Most recently, computer-readable texts have made word-searches easier and more reliable, and soon those computer-readable texts will be annotated in a way that facilitates sophisticated searches for syntactical and grammatical phenomena.

This chapter has both a modest and easily attainable goal, and a more ambitious and elusive one. The modest goal is to 'prove', as many have before, that much is lost when Virgil is read only in translation or with insufficient attention to style. The more difficult task is to speak both to those who have little or no knowledge of Virgil's Latin and so want to be informed about some of the basic issues, and to those familiar with advanced work on Virgil's style, whom I might join in examining the process by which basic information is acquired and agreed upon – and briefly discussing what to do next. Both groups, however, must ask why style matters, and what the consequences are of attention to style – must ask not how little we leave to Virgil if we take his style and diction away, but how much is gained when we do approach the poet with an awareness of nuances of metre, style, diction, syntax and rhetoric. This is a vast topic, on which much quite good work has been done, but much still remains to be done, both by using the new tools mentioned above, and by pushing recent detailed work to yield more consequential results. No chapter this size, of course, can provide a thorough introduction to Virgil's style; this chapter will focus on a few ways in which reading Virgil in the original and with significant attention to style can make a difference.

I begin with an aspect of poetic style necessarily erased by translation or metathesis: word-order. Because Latin and Greek are inflected languages in which words' functions are indicated more by their endings than by location, they allow greater freedom in word-order than non-inflected languages. This allows poets, for example, to juxtapose terms that are thematically related or even contrasting, and so to make suggestions that owe nothing to syntax, and thus are impossible to translate (e.g. *genitor natum*, 'father . . . son', *puer, virtutem*, 'boy, . . . manliness'; the appendix to Harrison (1991) offers a useful collection). This freedom also dovetails with poets' desire to sound otherwise than prose, one result of which is their greater tendency to separate nouns from their adjectives (in a type of 'hyperbaton' or violation of normal word-order). Noun–adjective placement is part of how Roman poets respond to the twin heritage of Graeco-Roman oratory (which came into its own in Rome in Virgil's youth) and the Alexandrian poetry of those like Callimachus, Theocritus, and the Roman neoteric Catullus, to whom Virgil looked as models and predecessors, and who sought a delicate, highly polished and at times ornately mannered style. Both rhetoric and Alexandrian poetry associated elegance with balance and proportion; thus when Virgil wants a line to sound elegant rather than plain, each of two nouns may have an adjective, as in *G.* 1.129 *ille **malum virus** **serpentibus** addidit **atris***, 'Jupiter added foul poison to dark snakes', or *G.* 1.7 *Chaoniam **pingui glandem** mutavit **arista***, 'replaced Chaonian acorn with juicy grain'.[2] In 129 the nouns are beside or not far from the adjectives; in 7, more stylised or more poetic, the adjectives come first, with the nouns in the second half of the line, here in the same order as the adjectives, so that the words are interlocked in the pattern ABAB; significant juxtaposition like that mentioned may be one result of such an arrangement. In other lines, as in *Ecl.* 1.70 *impius haec tam **culta novalia** miles habebit*, 'Some godless soldier will have these fields I've tended so well', one noun–adjective pair encloses the other in concentric, or chiastic order (ABBA). An extremely stylised line, called a Golden Line by Dryden although there is no ancient testimony about it, will have two adjectives at the start, with their nouns coming only at the end, and 'a verb betwixt to keep the peace', as in *G.* 1.468 *impiaque **aeternam** timuerunt saecula **noctem***, 'the wicked age feared eternal night'. Two noun–adjective pairs may thus dominate the line, and leave the reader or auditor in suspense ('What things', we must ask, 'will be described as "wicked" and "eternal"?'). Less elaborately, a single pair may frame the line (*Aen.* 8.704 *Actius haec cernens arcum intendebat Apollo*, 'seeing this, Actian Apollo drew his bow'), or appear at the start or finish of each half of the line (*Aen.* 2.215 *implicat et miseros morsu depascitur artus*, 'enfolds and feeds on their pitiful limbs with a bite'). One effect, as Habinek has shown, is to make the unit of thought longer than a few words, and clauses so arranged may be stretched over more than one line (*Aen.* 2.285–6 *quae causa indigna serenos | foedavit vultus?*, 'What unworthy cause has fouled your peaceful face?'; cf. *Aen.* 12.473–4, where *nigra . . . harundo*, 'the black swallow', frames a two-line clause). Highly stylised lines appear more often in the mannered *Eclogues*, and least in the *Aeneid*, but are still used effectively in the *Georgics* and *Aeneid*, sometimes to round off a section or what modern scholars often refer to as a 'paragraph', or to produce pathos or the effect of lush or ornate description. Recognisable variations of such lines appear throughout all the poems; with carefully modulated intensity, the same concern for symmetry, balance and proportion informs all of Virgil's writing. The lengths of clauses and their deployment over the hexameter are both artfully managed, with frequent parallelism of form, pointed antithesis of

---

[2] On noun–adjective pairs see Norden (1981 [1916]) 391–400, Conrad (1965), Pearce (1966), Ross (1969) 132–7, Habinek (1985), Thomas (1993).

thought, and words or clauses often arranged in groups of two, four, or especially three (the 'tricolon' or 'tricolon crescendo' with each element longer than the last). The concern for symmetry works together with an overriding interest in variety, especially in the *Georgics*, where material that might be thought intractable is presented with consummate art, and in the *Aeneid*, where Virgil confronts the enormous challenge of maintaining an Alexandrian standard of polish over the length of an epic.

These hard-won effects of patterning are deployed, as I have mentioned, across the patterns of long and short syllables that make up the dactylic hexameter adapted by Virgil's predecessors from the Greeks.[3] In the hexameter the first five feet may be dactyls (–∪∪) or spondees (––), though in Latin the fifth foot is most often a dactyl, while the last foot is a spondee or a trochee (–∪). Latin offers fewer short syllables than Greek, so Roman poets had to work to find enough dactyls, and were happy to exploit the discoveries of predecessors (e.g. such metrically convenient devices as the use of poetic neuter plurals, or alternative forms of the perfect verb). Ovid's quickly flowing hexameters have more dactyls than Virgil's, but the *Eclogues* have more than the *Aeneid*, probably because of the affinities of the *Eclogues* with Theocritus, and of the *Aeneid* with the early Roman *Annals* of Ennius; the *Aeneid* is therefore also more solemn and 'stately', to use Tennyson's word (actually 'stateliest', from the last line of 'To Virgil'). Both variety and certain expressive effects are achieved in the alternation of spondees and dactyls, as Duckworth's many charts have shown. Long stretches of the *Georgics* or *Aeneid* in English sound monotonous, but the variety of metrical patterns and other factors to be noted below make continuous reading of or listening to the *Georgics* or even the much longer *Aeneid* extremely pleasurable. In individual lines, dactyls will be quick and light, and so appropriate for, e.g. Diana's graceful motion: *illa pharetram | fert umero, gradiensque deas supereminet omnis* (*Aen.* 1.500–1, 'she, with her quiver on her shoulder, as she walks towers over the others'). The slower, heavier spondees may suggest solemnity, as in *olli sedato respondit corde Latinus* (12.18, 'Latinus calmly spoke to him in reply'), or sadness, as in this reference to the death of Marcellus: *o gnate, ingentem luctum ne quaere tuorum* (6.868, 'O son, don't ask about your clan's great grief').

---

[3] Many commentaries have sections or index-entries on metre; the discussion of ictus and accent below, for example, is indebted to Thomas (1988). Many of my examples come from standard works on style cited below in 'Further reading'; cf. esp. Norden (1981 [1916]) 413–34; Jackson Knight (1944) 230–43; Wilkinson (1963) 89–134; Duckworth (1969); Horsfall (1995) 222–4.

Variety and special effects also accrue as hexameter patterns interact with Latin's stress accent. In most Virgilian hexameters, stress accent and the metrical pattern come together in the last two feet (as in 'shave and a hair-cut'), so we have 'coincidence' of accent with 'ictus', ictus being the beat felt in the first long of the foot. The first four feet regularly feature 'clash', achieved mainly by avoiding having foot-boundaries as word-boundaries. Awareness of ictus and accent can produce strikingly emphatic verses, like Meliboeus' cry at *Ecl.* 1.70 *impius haec tam culta novalia miles habebit*, 'Some godless soldier will have these fields I've tended so well', in which each foot begins with a stressed syllable (each foot is 'homodyne'). Lines with much 'clash' ('heterodyne' feet)[4] may suggest the struggle or effort of men swimming from a shipwreck (*Aen.* 1.118 *apparent rari nantes in gurgite vasto*, 'Here and there are seen a few men swimming in the vastness of the sea') or Cyclopes at work as blacksmiths (8.452 *illi inter sese multa vi bracchia tollunt*, 'each of them in turn brings up his arms with great force'). Dido's angry confrontation of Aeneas as he prepares to leave Carthage begins with excited lines with much coincidence, much of it in the fourth foot (*Aen.* 4.305–13). A final single monosyllable produces clash in the preceding word, and so prevents coincidence at line-end; final monosyllables may mark indignation (*Aen.* 4.313: Dido tells Aeneas, 'I beg you by these tears and your right hand', *per ego has lacrimas dextramque tuam te*), a crashing sound (a falling bull at *Aen.* 5.481 *procumbit humi bos*), or a recall of Ennius (*Aen.* 1.65 *divum pater atque hominum rex*, 'father of gods and king of men', 8.679 *magnis dis*, 'great gods').

After these glances at some (and only some) of the devices of word-order and metre used by Virgil, we may consider briefly and in a preliminary way what consequences attention to style may have for one's approach to the poet. Since much of the energy devoted to style recently has involved line-by-line commentary, there has been little occasion for reflection on this point: many commentaries note stylistic points as one would mark in a notebook rare birds spotted by means of binoculars. In this space of course only the briefest remarks can be made; more (but still only preliminary) suggestions will follow below in the context of other stylistic features. First, the elegance and variety of Virgil's style means that these are certainly ἡδυσμένοι λόγοι, 'sweetened or "pleasured-up" words', to use the term from Aristotle, *Poetics* 49b25, or words with the ability to 'delight' (*delectare*) as much as 'be useful' or 'teach' (*prodesse* or *docere*), to use the terms contrasted by both Horace, *Ars poetica* 333 and Seneca, *Epistles*

---

[4] On the terms 'homodyne' and 'heterodyne' see Horsfall (1995) 233.

86.15 (where he specifically mentions the *Georgics*). The reader approaching the poet today either in English or with rusty or immature Latin must keep in mind the enormous extent to which aesthetic pleasure figured in the experience of Virgil's first readers and auditors. Elsewhere in this volume the possibility of an aesthetic rather than cognitive approach to the *Eclogues* is explored (inconclusively, and rightly so), and despite the Roman and other thematic content of those poems and even the *Georgics* and *Aeneid*, many Romans when listening to or reading Virgil may have paid more attention to the sound and beauty of the language than to what was being said. Analogies with music are not inappropriate; in Virgil's youth or young adulthood his friend Philodemus feels compelled to argue against 'euphonists' who have argued that sound is all in poetry, and that 'good poets excel and endure only on account of their sounds'.[5] And yet we have learned at least since Adorno not to overlook the ideological impact of music even in the absence of words. How does Virgil's style interact with content? Both narrow and broader kinds of approaches may be mentioned. On the level of the individual line or sentence, remarks can be made about how style contributes to or even determines meaning in numerous passages; a few of these will come below, although space does not allow many examples here.[6] The neophyte scholar or person approaching Virgil from another field is urged to undertake a complete stylistic analysis of any passage he or she is about to discuss in print, but it must be noted that it is difficult to avoid having one's observations about style confirming one's notions about the ideology of the poems, which are often set in stone before a young reader has developed enough competence to develop ideas about ideology from a stylistically sensitive reading of the poem. More broadly, two contradictory claims might be advanced. One is that the orderliness and 'classical' attention to proportion and balance both reflect and endorse the order now being imposed upon the Roman world by Augustus, or upon the whole world by Rome; older analogies between the supposed orderliness of both the Parthenon and Sophocles might suggest similar claims between the *Ara Pacis* (especially as viewed by Zanker (1988)) and Virgilian *epos*, especially in the *Georgics* and *Aeneid*. Tennyson's notion of Virgil's metre as 'stately' perhaps implies that it is

---

[5] I quote Janko's paraphrase of a damaged portion of Philodemus; see the essays by Janko and others in Obbink (1995) (quotation p. 92) for a convenient introduction to Philodemus, whose discussion of style and content may come to play more of a role in our approach to Virgil's style as we come to understand it better; cf. Obbink's index s.v. 'euphony' for this topic.

[6] Horsfall (1995) 237–48 helpfully ends his chapter on style with twelve pages offering sample analysis of four passages.

state-ly. The other claim is that the melancholy style of the *Georgics* and *Aeneid* directs sympathy away from the values that a more tone-deaf reading of the poem would find central and dominant, and so style mirrors what some have seen in other features of the poem (see, e.g. chapter 13 in this volume). Discussion below of style and emotion will return to this point. Consideration must also be given to the way that style suggests generic affiliation or intertextuality (cf. in this volume the chapters on Bucolic (8), Georgic (9), Epic (10), and Intertextuality (15); the last rightly speaks of an 'allusive style'). I have noted above that certain metrical features may sound Ennian, and certain noun–adjective pairings Alexandrian and mannered: style may suggest epic, or pastoral, or the world of Greek or archaic Roman poetry; above all features of epic style suggest dialogue with the whole epic tradition, as discussed by Conte (1986), Farrell (1991), and others.

I return to specific features of Virgil's style; further broader comments will be sprinkled throughout the rest of the chapter. The Virgilian sentence is rightly regarded as a considerable achievement and a richly rewarding object of study.[7] In Virgil's youth Cicero perfected the 'periodic' style for prose oratory, with sentences about the length of four hexameters, and information arranged in complex 'hypotactic' structures with main and subordinate clauses, and key information held until the end of the sentence. Many of Virgil's sentences are that long, but he prefers a 'paratactic' style, with related clauses juxtaposed rather than subordinated; he often uses parentheses, connectors meaning 'and' rather than subordinating conjunctions, and rhetorical questions or exclamations. He also has many short sentences. In part this produces greater clarity of comprehension, as small syntactical units make an immediate impression on the reader or audience, but on the other hand Virgil is less specific about the relationship between different clauses. Lucretius' hypotactic hexameters require more initial work to construe, but are ultimately more clear in their ability to make an argument: possibly we could suggest that this means that Lucretius wished to communicate a message on which he had a firm grasp, and Virgil did not (cf. in this volume Batstone's chapter 9 on *didaxis* and the *Georgics*). Even in English one should be able to see the paratactic style of, e.g. *Aen.* 4.1–6, 6.1–13, or 12.938–52 (the end of the poem), which offer little subordination, of only the simplest kind (a participle or two, a relative clause, a temporal clause). With sentence-structure too the question of variety and pleasure is important; in addition to those features just

---

[7] Cf. Norden (1981 [1916]) 376–90; Jackson Knight (1944) 180–9; Palmer (1961) 115–18; Quinn (1868) 414–40; Horsfall (1995) 231–2.

mentioned we should take note of Virgil's use of enjambment, which takes place when a thought is not complete at line-end but spills over into part of the next line. A poet's choice of end-stopped lines (favoured by Catullus in Poem 64) or enjambment allows for greater variety and for certain effects, as when a key word is not added until the second line; basically enjambment involves the interplay between the metrical unit (the line) and the syntactic unit (the sentence).

Perhaps more than any other Roman poet, Virgil makes use of what has been called 'theme and variation', or *interpretatio*, or *dicolon abundans*, the 'combination of two adjacent expressions apparently conveying the same idea, so that the second appears as a variation on the first'.[8] At the start of *Aeneid* Book 2, one finds 10–11 'to learn about our misfortune, and to hear the final struggle of Troy', 18–20 'they hid men in the horse, and filled the inside with armed soldiers', 56 'Troy would now stand, and Priam's tall citadel would remain', 92 'life in darkness and mourning', 108–9 'to flee and leave Troy behind, and to withdraw from the long war', 139–40 'punish for my escape, and make pay for my fault', 141 'the gods, and the divinities conscious of truth' (some of these are paraphrased rather than translated). At times the clauses look at the matter from differing perspectives; at times the second 'intensifies and explains the first' to increase pathos (Conte); at times the goal may seem simply to be verbal artistry and the reader's pleasure. The pervasiveness of the poet's interest in looking at matters from more than one perspective must not be overlooked; alternately, we might say that the reader or auditor is challenged to discover what is similar and different in the two formulations.

Hyperbaton, discussed above in the context of the separation of noun from adjective, is one of many ways Virgil violates the norms of prose, or even of Latin.[9] Translators, with their understandable desire to make sense, often 'fix' such constructions, producing a much tamer text than the original, and classroom translation and many commentaries often suggest that odd constructions are simply fancy equivalents of much blander ones. Virgil is particularly fond of hysteron-proteron (literally, 'later-sooner'), in which the logical sequence of actions is reversed, as in *Aen.* 2.353 *moriamur et in media arma ruamus*, 'let us die, and rush into the thick of battle'. Adjectives may modify not the word to which they logically apply, but another noun in the clause, in 'enallage' or 'transferred epithet'. In *Aen.* 5.139 *clara dedit sonitum tuba*, 'the clear horn gave a sound', it must be

---

[8] Conte (1993) 209; Henry (1873–92) called particular attention to the figure; cf. Williams (1968) 728; Quinn (1968) 423–8.

[9] Williams (1968) 726–30; Habinek (1985); Görler (1985) 265–75; Conte (1993) 208–9; Horsfall (1995) 225–31.

the sound that was clear, and *Aen.* 6.268 *ibant obscuri sola sub nocte,* literally seems to be saying 'they went, dark on a lone night', as both adjectives have switched position. Jackson Knight says that 'the point is the presence of some quality in the whole complex', but the poet and reader/audience must have taken pleasure in the inversion, which also determines how this 'quality' is to be perceived. Analogous syntactic inversion occurs also with the relationship between nouns and verbs: *Aen.* 10.269 *totumque adlabi classibus aequor,* suggests that 'the whole sea "slides forward" with ships', when it must be the ships that come forward on the sea, while in *Aen.* 2.487–8 *plangoribus aedes | femineis ululant,* 'the house wails with womanly cries', the personification of the house is produced by the transference of a statement like 'women filled the house with wailing'. As reviews of some recent commentaries have suggested, work needs to be done exploring and pinning down these features and their effects. This work must be wary of the danger of determining the ideology of the poet's time-period elsewhere, then substituting our knowledge of that ideology for full confrontation of the oddness of many of the things that Virgil says, and the way that he says them. But the work must be done.

Most obviously relevant to ideology is the claim that Virgilian sentences are often ambiguous. Virgil often offers words and sentences that can be interpreted in more than one way, and sometimes in diametrically opposed ways; he offers ambiguities or indeterminacies of syntax, some of which parallel larger problems of interpretation.[10] I have noted that Virgil's paratactic style involves sometimes being less specific about the relationship between clauses; Virgil's compact and concise hexameters also often omit the prepositions or other words or devices that might indicate more clearly the functions of modifiers.[11] In *Aen.* 6.466 *quem fugis? extremum fato quod te adloquor hoc est,* Aeneas' last words to Dido, Jackson Knight has suggested that *quem fugis* can mean not only 'From whom are you turning away?' but also 'What has the man become from whom you turn away?', that is 'Don't you see', or 'do you think', 'that I am a different man now?' In the rest of the line it is difficult to pin down the syntax or significance of *fato*; Jackson Knight suggests not only 'This is the last thing I speak to you by fate', but also 'It is fate's fault that I am talking to you, but it is the last time' or 'It is only by fate that this is the last time I talk to you', or even 'This talk to you is the last hope of joy that fate can ever let me

---

[10] On Virgilian ambiguity in general see Jackson Knight (1944) 191–229; Johnson (1976) (difficult but fundamental and underutilised); Williams (1983) 215–31; Lyne (1987); Batstone (1988); Fowler (1990); Thomas (1990); Martindale (1993b); Perkell (1994); Horsfall (1995) 229–30; O'Hara (1990), (1993), and (1994) may also seem relevant.

[11] Cf. Quinn (1968) 375–84, 394–414; Jackson Knight (1944) 214–16.

have.' These readings are mostly complementary; other ambiguities suggest more widely divergent possibilities. In *Aen.* 9.642–3 *iure omnia bella | gente sub Assaraci fato ventura resident*, clearly Virgil (through Apollo) says that all the wars to come will subside (*omnia bella ventura resident*) but there are also three adverbial modifiers, *iure*, 'rightly' (?), 'under the race of Assaracus (and Aeneas, Ascanius and Augustus)', and again *fato*, 'by fate'.[12] So is it 'rightly all the wars fated to come under the race of A. will subside' or 'all the wars to come are (rightly?) fated to subside under the race of A.'? The first seems more natural to me, but connects war and not peace with the race of Aeneas and Augustus, and the second better fits a confident Augustan interpretation of the poem, which predicts a new age of peace under Augustus. If the second is 'correct', does the reader (or must all readers) consider the first, and then completely reject it, or does the ambiguity remain, as reader-response and similar criticism seems to have established fairly firmly by now?[13] At *G.* 2.172 *imbellem avertis Romanis arcibus Indum*, as the Servian scholia note, Virgil appears to be saying that Augustus is 'repelling from Roman citadels the unwarlike Easterner', which seems a paltry feat; Servius suggests that *imbellem*, 'unwarlike', is proleptic: 'repel and so make unwarlike', but if the reader must consider both options, traces of the first must remain, as part of the reader's or auditor's experience of the line.[14]

At *Aen.* 4.165–6 *speluncam Dido dux et Troianus eandem | deveniunt*, 'Dido and the Trojan leader arrive at the same cave', translation cannot convey the way in which the *dux* seems only for a moment to be Dido, until *et Troianus* and the rhythm of the line specify that Aeneas is the *Troianus dux*.[15] At *Aen.* 4.19 *huic uni forsan potui succumbere culpae*, 'perhaps I might have yielded to this one – sin', *huic* seems to mean 'to him', 'to Aeneas', until Dido adds the word *culpae*; the effect is created by the slight hyperbaton. A different kind of temporary ambiguity occurs at *G.* 1.145, with the phrase *labor omnia vicit*. At first it is not quite clear, in this passage of considerable importance for the interpretation of the *Georgics*, whether this means the more optimistic 'toil overcame all

---

[12] On the frequent ambiguity of the word *fatum* in Virgil cf. Commager (1981).

[13] See Fish (1980) 47: the reader's 'temporary adoption of . . . inappropriate strategies is itself a response to the strategy of an author; and the resulting mistakes are part of the experience provided by that author's language, and therefore part of its meaning', and for Virgil see Batstone (1988); O'Hara (1993); Perkell (1989).

[14] Thomas (1988) *ad loc.*

[15] *Aen.* 4.165–6 almost = 4.124–5; Clausen (1987) 24 notes the ambiguity, and the recall of 1.364 *dux femina facti* ('a woman was in charge'); he suggests that 'ambiguity in Latin poetry is circumscribed and tends to be, as here, momentary and evanescent'. My next example is from Clausen (1987) 41–2; I also borrow his translation.

obstacles' or the more pessimistic 'toil occupied all areas of existence'. Then line 146 begins with the adjective *improbus*, characterising *labor* as 'insatiable', 'cruel', and then adds a second, clearly negative subject for *vicit* in *egestas*, 'poverty', 'need', which seems to remove the possibility of the optimistic interpretation, though some readers still cling to it; the effect is created by hyperbaton and enjambment.[16]

I close this section with three examples of ambiguous genitives, one each concerning Turnus, Aeneas, and Dido, and all involving the limitations of human knowledge; some may be sceptical of claims of ambiguity here. *Aen.* 10.501 *nescia mens hominum fati*, may suggest either the general 'Oh, how human minds are ignorant of fate!' or more specifically 'Oh, such ignorance (of Turnus, who has just killed Pallas) about the fate of human beings!' depending on which noun the genitive *hominum* modifies. What is at stake here is whether Turnus is to be thought of as making a mistake that any human being could make, or as being particularly foolish, in a way that you or I, fortunately, would not be. On *Aen.* 8.730 *miratur rerumque ignarus imagine gaudet*, the comment of Gransden (1976) spells out the possibilities: '*ignarus*: if taken absolutely . . . then "all unawares Aeneas takes pleasure in the pictures of things to come", if taken with *rerum* . . . "though ignorant of the events Aen[eas] takes pleasure in their representation".' At *Aen.* 4.65, when Dido consults omens to learn whether the gods approve of her love for Aeneas, Virgil says *heu vatum ignarae mentes*.[17] If *vatum* here is possessive genitive with *mentes*, this can mean 'alas, ignorant minds of prophets', which might suggest that prophets know nothing about the future, perhaps because, in this case, the gods will plot against Dido. Or, with *vatum* as objective genitive with *ignarae*, it can be 'minds ignorant of prophets and prophecy', which might suggest that the haruspices, or Dido and Anna themselves, had performed the rites incorrectly, or that Dido and Anna had misunderstood the haruspices. Here the reader's difficulty in handling the syntax of the genitive *vatum* is parallel or analogous to the difficulty both Dido and the reader have in interpreting the language of the entrails. For some reason, Dido does not learn from the sacrifices that her love for Aeneas is going to lead to a bad end. Because of Virgil's relentlessly ambiguous language, the reader does not learn exactly why this happens.

I have neglected so far to mention most of the sound-effects and rhetorical devices used by Virgil; analysis of a few short passages will illustrate a few of these. Many involve repetition of a word or sound, just as metre

---

[16] See Thomas (1988) *ad loc.*; Perkell (1989) 6, 97; Batstone (1988); and both Batstone and Braund in this volume.

[17] See O'Hara (1993).

involves repetition of rhythmic patterns; these devices work with metre to create and either fulfil or play with expectations (as do, on the larger level, thematic patterns of repetition[18] and responsion in the whole *Georgics*, *Aeneid*, and *Eclogues*). Alliteration is the repetition of initial consonant sounds, as in *Tityre tu* (the first words of *Ecl.* 1); both alliteration and assonance (closeness in sound among nearby words) appear in the g's, c's, v's, and m's in *Aen.* 4.1–4:

> at regina gravi iamdudum saucia cura
> vulnus alit venis et caeco carpitur igni.
> multa viri virtus animo multusque recursat
> gentis honos.

> But the queen, long pierced by deep desire,
> feeds the wound in her marrow, consumed by hidden fire.
> The man's manly courage[19] and his line's nobility come
> to her mind again and again.

Alliteration was important in Rome even before the influence of Greek models and so in high concentration will seem archaic, but gently responsive alliteration is sprinkled throughout Virgil. Attempts to describe the effect of alliteration on the reader, however, seem doomed to conjecture and subjectivity. Assonance often involves the repetition of vowel sounds; it and several other figures appear in lines on Orpheus' lament at *G.* 4.464–6:

> ipse cava solans aegrum testudine amorem
> te, dulcis coniunx, te solo in litore secum,
> te veniente die, te decedente canebat

> To soothe his pained love on the curved lyre,
> he sings of you, sweet wife, of you when alone on the shore,
> of you when day comes, of you when it departs.

The first line presents two and perhaps three interlocked noun–adjective pairs, if we count not only *cava testudine* and *aegrum amorem* but also *ipse solans*. Next comes an apostrophe, an address of the absent Eurydice, a figure often used to heighten emotional impact, and suggestive of the narrator's involvement with the character's suffering. These two lines present a kind of tricolon (on the shore, at dawn, at sunset), but the addition of the apostrophe makes it more like a tetracolon, with the two lines falling into four parts. They also feature anaphora, the repetition of a word (*te*)

---

[18] On repetition see Moskalew (1982) and Wills (1996).

[19] My slightly odd translation here is meant to bring out the etymological connection between *vir*, 'man', and *virtus*, 'manliness', 'courage', 'virtue'; on etymological word-play as an important aspect of Virgilian style see O'Hara (1996).

at the beginning of successive clauses, and alliteration and assonance in the t's and s's of 465 and finally the 'e' sounds of 466. Careful manipulation of vowel-sounds is not limited to assonance: elsewhere the patternings of a's, e's, and u's work with the apostrophe, anaphora and varied nominative constructions in the elegant and sad tricolon lamenting the death of Umbro at *Aen.* 7.759–60, *te nemus Angitiae, vitrea te Fucinus unda,* | *te liquidi flevere lacus* ('you the grove of Angitia, you Fucinus with its glassy waters, you the clear lakes lamented' – a bit more on this passage below).

Epanalepsis is the rhetorical, syntactically unnecessary repetition of a word or phrase from a previous line, to add emphasis, ornament, or pathos, producing the effect of lingering over a word or idea. It is common in the melancholy world of the *Eclogues*, as in 9.27–8 *superet modo Mantua nobis,* | *Mantua vae miserae nimium vicina Cremonae,* 'if only Mantua survives, Mantua alas too close to poor Cremona' (where the assonance is also noteworthy). It appears in less intense moments simply as ornament, as in *Ecl.* 6.20–1, *supervenit Aegle,* | *Aegle Naiadum pulcherrima,* 'Aegle came along too, Aegle most beautiful of nymphs', or *G.* 1.297–8 *at rubicunda Ceres medio succiditur aestu* | *et medio tostas aestu terit area fruges,* 'but reddening grain is cut in midday heat, in midday heat baked crops beaten on the threshing floor'. Used more sparingly in the *Georgics* and *Aeneid*, epanalepsis can suggest great pathos, as at *Aen.* 10.820–1 *vultum vidit morientis et ora,* | *ora modis . . . pallentia miris,* '[Aeneas] saw the face of the dying boy [Lausus], the face growing pale in a startling way.'

As with the elegant noun–adjective patterns and metrical effects discussed above, we may analyse the poet's deployment of these effects either in terms of aesthetics and their formal qualities, or in terms of their consequences for interpretation. Chief among the latter must be these stylistic features' potential for producing an emotional response, often one of pathos or sympathy: the link between style and emotion seems critical, but fraught with difficulty for any scholar attempting analysis. Here we can only briefly mention some possible approaches. One recent study (Farron (1993)) suggests that ancient readers sought and found nothing but emotion and pathos in a reading of the *Aeneid*; this extreme view is useful mainly as a warning against underestimating the role of pathos. In the passage from *Aeneid* Book 7 quoted just above, stylistic analysis of the pathos attached to the death of the Italian Umbro was the starting-point for Parry's celebrated 'Two voices of Vergil's *Aeneid*' (1966), in which attention to style and emotion produces considerable ideological consequences. Since Heinze we have also learned to speak of features of Virgil's style that encourage emotional and other types of identification with points of view other than those of the narrator: Otis popularised a rather different version of Heinze's idea that spoke of the poet's 'subjective' style.[20] In *Georgics* Book 4, to cite a classic example, Virgil's story of Orpheus seems more emotionally charged than the framing sections on Aristaeus (I have cited, two paragraphs above, three lines describing Orpheus' lament for Eurydice). This may tell us something about whether sympathy should lie with the doomed Orpheus or the successful Aristaeus, and the same technique colours the *Aeneid*'s presentation of the stories of Aeneas, Dido, Turnus, and countless minor characters. On this 'subjective style', Fowler's 1990 piece on 'deviant focalisation' offers an excellent discussion that briefly summarises recent studies, especially by Italian scholars, which reconceptualise it as part of Virgil's multiple 'voices' or 'points-of-view', or as 'deviant focalisation' or a 'dramatic' style. The problem of whether the 'subjective style' ultimately produces a carefully controlled work with a unified viewpoint to which dissenting voices are carefully subordinated, or instead offers as conflicting a plethora of voices and views as is found in any modern novel, will not be solved in this chapter, but Fowler and others have laid the groundwork for real progress (see also his chapter 17*a* in this volume). Valuable too for consideration of Virgil's emotional impact is Perkell's suggestion that in the *Eclogues*, *Georgics*, and *Aeneid* the poet aims to teach pity; for the *Georgics*, she says 'this lesson of pity, wherein the poet manipulates the reader's sympathy and elicits sorrow for loss, is the poet's mission in the poem'.[21] Not all would readily subscribe to this view, but it deserves serious consideration.

I began this chapter with Coleridge's comment on Virgil's 'language and metre', and turn at last to discuss Virgil's diction, a favourite topic of the modern commentator. Much of Virgil's vocabulary consists of ordinary Latin words, often in striking combinations (the *callida iunctura*, 'clever combination', of Horace, *Ars poetica* 47–8), but scholars talk profitably of features of Virgilian diction that are epic, archaic, poetic or unpoetic. The Greeks had what we may paradoxically call a natural artificial poetic language, developed over time from factors like the dialect spoken in the areas that produced epic or lyric or pastoral. Rome had to create an artificial poetic language rather in a hurry, and the first epicists Livius Andronicus and Ennius did so in part by the use of archaisms, or Homeric features like compounds, which are more rare in Latin than Greek. Thus 'epic' and 'archaic' are not easily distinguished, and features may seem at once Homeric and Ennian, or suggest an archaic quality, or even mimic the playful coinages of the Hellenistic or Neoteric poet. Pronounced alliteration, and the

---

[20] Cf. Heinze (1957 [1915]) 289–95 = (1993) 361–70; Otis (1964); concise summary in Boyle (1993) 88.

[21] Perkell (1989) 20–1; cf. too Perkell (1990).

paratactic style itself (both discussed above), also have an archaic flavour, but on the whole Virgil uses archaic forms sparingly, though more in the *Aeneid* than in the *Eclogues* and *Georgics*. It has been suggested that archaisms mark the speech of Virgil's gods, thus stressing the traditional aspects of Roman religion. In the *Aeneid* as a whole the use of archaisms suggests both tradition and the connotations or 'epic resonances' (Lyne) that accrue to words from their association with Rome's earliest epic: as noted above, the suggestion of Ennius (or Homer) can reinforce evocation of or dialogue with the earlier poet.

There is 'epic' or at least 'poetic' resonance also to many words more at home in poetry than prose, just a few of which are *ales* for *avis*, 'bird', *aequor* for *mare*, 'sea', *amnis* for *flumen*, 'river', *ensis* for *gladius*, 'sword', *arbusta* for the metrically intractable *arbores*, 'trees', *letum* for *mors*, 'death', *coniunx* for *uxor*, 'wife'. A number of these pairs are not quite synonyms, but there is more difference in tone than in denotation between them, and they add to the grandeur of especially the *Aeneid*, and to the sense that the poem belongs to 'a far-off imaginary world' (Williams) or '*another* time and order, distinct from the mundane present' (Lyne). Lyne comments further on the overall effect: 'poetry', he suggests, 'inclines to suggestive vocabulary, to words that are connotative rather than denotative'; he thus describes 'poetic diction' as 'words that are able to introduce into a poet's text resonances or connotations unavailable in the categories of ordinary language but available in another source'. Lyne cites three helpful examples:

> *Infit* in Virgil does not mean the same as *incipit*: its sense of 'begin (to speak)' has epic resonance; *olli*, *ollis* are dative forms of a pronoun that refers to epic characters, not to Everyman. You and I have never seen the *clipeus* of the archaizing poets: it is the defence of heroes from the epic tradition, of men who are not such as ourselves. Words such as these refer to objects and actions of a fabled world, a world *other* than our own. That is why they are chosen: to suggest such 'otherness'.

The term 'unpoetic' appears in the title of Axelson's short 1945 book *Unpoetische Wörter*, which, though controversial in some respects, has helped sensitise Latinists to the importance of thinking about a word's tone, which may have had a reasonably direct effect on the Romans, but which we must work harder to recover.[22] The most basic claim is that words rare in or absent from the 'higher' genres of poetry like epic help to define both epic and 'lower' genres like satire, and that the appearance

---

[22] Axelson (1945); Ross (1969); Williams (1968) 743–50 (sceptical); Jocelyn (1979); Watson (1985) (answers Williams); Knox (1986) on Ovid and Virgil; Harrison (1991) 287–8; Horsfall (1995) 219–22; and especially Lyne (1989).

of such words in, for example, Virgil, can be striking and significant. A tool for the recovery of such effects has been the *Thesaurus Linguae Latinae*, a survey of the usage of Latin words begun in 1900 and now in the p's, which scholars supplement by searches of particular poets with either traditional concordances (like Warwick's for Virgil), or, now, texts on CD-Rom like the Latin disk from the Packard Humanities Institute (work is under way to make the *TLL* computer-accessible). The most recent extended study of Virgilian diction, that of Lyne (1989), makes use of the Packard disk, but has won more praise for its theoretical Introduction than for the plausibility of many of Lyne's suggestions about individual words. Still, many suggestions convince. We must keep in mind how much Latin has been lost when we call words unpoetic or prosaic, but just as the use of poetic words generally adds a certain 'other-ness', the use of 'prosaic' or 'unpoetic' words may suggest more humble associations, in an eye-catching or striking way. At *Aen.* 4.266, Mercury in reminding Aeneas of his mission calls him *uxorius*, which suggests that he 'belongs' to a 'wife' like a possession, and is particularly striking because *uxor* and especially *uxorius* rarely appear in epic. The use of *scutum* at *Aen.* 10.505–6 when Pallas is brought home on his shield exploits its prosaic associations: 'in death, at this point, Pallas is an ordinary soldier' (Lyne; some reviewers have been sceptical here); the same claim has been made for the use of the prosaic *obitus* for Dido's death at 4.694–5 and the death of chieftains at 12.500–3. Throughout the battle-books 9–12, words of epic grandeur sometimes yield to words of prosaic ordinariness; this dovetails with the sense produced by other aspects of the *Aeneid* that the characters are both unlike us (whoever we are) in their heroic stature, and also more like us as ordinary beings than the heroic figures of Homer. The same type of research reminds us that diminutives, so common in the neoteric poetry of Catullus, appear a dozen times in the neoteric *Eclogues*, but rarely in the *Aeneid*, so that there is particular pathos to Dido's wish that 'some little (baby) Aeneas' (*parvulus Aeneas*, 4.328) would remain with her after he has departed.

Much must be omitted from an essay of this length.[23] I have tried to describe some of the more interesting and useful ways in which modern

---

[23] E.g. consideration of: abstract for concrete, anastrophe of prepositions, apposition (and enclosing apposition), brevity, bucolic diaeresis, caesura, chiasmus, colloquialisms, elision or synaloepha (one of the most significant omissions of this chapter), emphasis, epithets, four-word lines, four-syllable words at line-end, framing, geographical names, Graecisms, half-lines, hendiadys, hiatus, hyperbole, hypermetric lines, inverted *cum*, kakozelia, lists, lyricism, metaphor, metonymy, mythological names, neologisms, onomatopoea, parenthesis, periphrasis, personification, pleonasm, polyptoton, postponed connectives or particles, prepositions, punctuation, rhyme or homoioteleuton, simile, spondaic fifth feet, syllepsis, synecdoche, technical language, tenses, tmesis, and zeugma.

scholars have studied Virgil's style, and make some suggestions about the shape of future work. A modern full-length study of Virgilian style and poetic language is needed: the tools and talent to produce it now exist.

FURTHER READING

Although much important work on style in Latin poetry and in Virgil has been done in German, Italian, and French (see, e.g. the collection with updated bibliography edited by Aldo Lunelli, *La Lingua Poetica Latina* (third edition, Bologna, 1988), and the important appendices to E. Norden, *P. Vergilius Maro Aeneis Buch VI* (seventh edition, Stuttgart, 1981 [1916]), there is much accessible work in English. See the general discussions of Latin poetic style by L. R. Palmer, *The Latin Language* (London, 1961) 74–147 (111–18 on Virgil), L. P. Wilkinson, *Golden Latin Artistry* (Cambridge, 1963) and G. Williams, *Tradition and Originality in Roman Poetry* (Oxford, 1968) 682–782 (722–43 on Virgil). On Virgil see especially N. Horsfall, *A Companion to the Study of Virgil* (Leiden and New York, 1995) 217–48, who provides numerous further references; cf. too W. F. Jackson Knight, *Roman Vergil* (London, 1944) 180–281 (engaging, insightful, idiosyncratic); L. P. Wilkinson, 'The language of Virgil and Horace', *Classical Quarterly* n.s. 9 (1959) 181–92, reprinted in S. J. Harrison, ed., *Oxford Readings in Vergil's Aeneid* (Oxford, 1990) 413–28; W. A. Camps, *An Introduction to Virgil's Aeneid* (Oxford, 1960) 61–74 (concise and clear); K. Quinn, *Virgil's Aeneid: A Critical Description* (Ann Arbor, 1968) 350–440 (less impressive now than when New Criticism was new to Classical Studies); W. Moskalew, *Formular Language and Poetic Design in the Aeneid* (Leiden, 1982); R. O. A. M. Lyne, *Words and the Poet: Characteristic Techniques of Style in Vergil's Aeneid* (Oxford, 1989) (intelligent and bold, sometimes unconvincing); S. J. Harrison, *Vergil: Aeneid 10. With Introduction, Translation, and Commentary* (Oxford, 1991) 285–91; Richard F. Thomas, 'Callimachus back in Rome', pp. 197–225 in *Callimachus* (Hellenistica Groningana, vol. 1) eds. M. A. Harder, R. F. Regtuit, and G. C. Wakker (Groningen, 1993); and A. J. Boyle, ed., *Roman Epic* (London and New York, 1993) 86–94. Much can be expected from a forthcoming book-length study of the *Aeneid* by H. Gotoff, known for his studies of the style of Cicero and Caesar. On the *Eclogues* see R. G. M. Nisbet, 'The style of Virgil's *Eclogues*', *Proceedings of the Virgil Society* 20 (1991) 1–14, on the *Georgics*, L. P. Wilkinson, *The Georgics of Virgil: A Critical Survey* (Cambridge, 1969) 183–222 and R. F. Thomas, *Virgil, Georgics* (Cambridge, 1988) 1.24–32. Only moderate skills in Italian are needed to use the sections on 'lingua' and 'metrica' in the *Enciclopedia Virgiliana* articles on *Bucoliche*, *Georgiche*, and *Eneide* (Görler on the *Aeneid* is especially helpful), which give extensive bibliography up to and including 1982. Modern commentaries on Virgil tend to concentrate on matters of style; they have been extremely helpful to me in writing this chapter, and on most passages I discuss they provide references to further examples and discussions. See R. G. Austin, *P. Vergili Maronis Aeneidos Liber Quartus* (Oxford, 1955), *P. Vergili Maronis Aeneidos Liber Secundus* (Oxford, 1964), *P. Vergili Maronis Aeneidos Liber Primus* (Oxford, 1971), *P. Vergili Maronis Aeneidos Liber Sextus* (Oxford, 1977); R. D. Williams, *P. Vergili Maronis Aeneidos Liber Quintus* (Oxford, 1960), *P. Vergili Maronis Aeneidos Liber Tertius* (Oxford, 1961); C. J. Fordyce, *P. Vergili Maronis Aeneidos Libri VII–VIII with a*

Commentary (Oxford, 1977); K. W. Gransden, *Virgil, Aeneid Book VIII* (Cambridge, 1976), *Virgil, Aeneid Book XI* (Cambridge, 1991); P. R. Hardie, *Virgil, Aeneid Book IX* (Cambridge, 1994); S. J. Harrison, *Virgil, Aeneid 10. With Introduction, Translation, and Commentary* (Oxford, 1991); R. Coleman, *Vergil, Eclogues* (Cambridge, 1977); W. Clausen, *A Commentary on Virgil Eclogues* (Oxford, 1994); R. F. Thomas, *Virgil, Georgics*, 2 vols. (Cambridge, 1988); R. A. B. Mynors, *Virgil, Georgics. Edited with a Commentary* (Oxford, 1990).

17a

DON FOWLER

Virgilian narrative: story-telling

The *Aeneid* has a story to tell, of how Aeneas after the fall of Troy reaches Italy with a small group of followers (Books 1–6) and there fights a war with some of the native inhabitants which ends in his victory (Books 7–12). The plot of the *Aeneid* is quickly told, and not that long in the enactment, but its temporal outreach is enormous, from the prehistoric past to Virgil's own day and beyond (a time-scale Ovid will extend and parody in the *Metamorphoses*). Like all good stories, it also has much to say about story-telling itself, and the way we plot our ends in history: and at every point who speaks and who sees admits itself of more than one story.

Narrators

The narrator of the poem is a first-century BC Latin poet, whom it is easiest to call 'Virgil': he generally retains epic anonymity, but on occasions reveals his hand (e.g. 7.1, Caieta is buried *litoribus nostris*, 'on our shores', or 9.446–9, Nisus and Euryalus will be famous as long as the Roman father has power *si quid mea carmina possunt*, 'if my poems can (do) anything'). But from the beginning we meet other storytellers within the poem: the Muse who tells him the causes of events (1.8), the anonymous narrator who told Juno of the plot of the poem before it even began (1.20 *audierat*, 'she had heard . . .': compare Dido's desperate desire *Iliacos iterum demens audire labores*, 'to hear again in madness the Trojan labours', 4.78), the script of the Fates (1.260) based – or is it the other way round? – on a treatment by Jupiter himself, the Master Narrator of all. Scarcely (1.34 *vix*) has Virgil got going on the story when he is interrupted by Juno, complaining at the idea that she has to give up on *her* tale (1.37–9):

> mene incepto desistere victam
> nec posse Italiam Teucrorum avertere regem!
> quippe vetor fatis.

so I am to cease defeated from my beginning
and not be able to turn the Trojan king from Italy!
I suppose I am forbidden by the fates?

Her opening *mene incepto*, 'me from my beginning' echoes in sound[1] the opening word of the *Iliad, menin*, 'wrath', which Virgil himself could only translate (1.4, 11, 25): in turn she will be echoed by Aeneas (1.97–8 *mene Iliacis occumbere campis | non potuisse*, 'that I should not have been able to die on the plains of Troy'). *Inceptum*, 'beginning', is a common word for a literary enterprise (cf. *Georgics* 2.39): so Aeneas will begin his story in Book 2 with the word *incipiam*, 'I shall begin'. Juno's story will come to nothing: at the end of the poem, Jupiter will bid her *inceptum frustra summitte furorem*, 'submit your fury, begun in vain' (12.832). Or rather: it will amount to the *Aeneid* itself, the poem this vain fury constructs by its obstruction and delay.

Jupiter sets himself up as the god of ends in opposition to Juno as the demonic force which starts and restarts the action and will not let it be. He is first introduced with the mysterious words *et iam finis erat*, 'and already it was the end' (1.223: referring most obviously to the preceding scene where Aeneas and his men mourn their lost comrades): just before Aeneas had optimistically told his men *dabit deus his quoque finem*, 'god will give an end to these (troubles) too' (1.199), and just after Venus will despairingly ask her father *quem das finem, rex magne, laborum?*, 'What end are you giving, great king, to these labours?'(1.241). At the other end of the poem, Jupiter will himself echo her words to Juno at the beginning of the 'reconciliation' scene of Book 12, *quae iam finis erit, coniunx? quid denique restat?* 'What end will there ever now be, wife? What at last is left?' (12.793). Aeneas unknowingly echoes Jupiter's words when he addresses Turnus at 12.889: *quae nunc deinde mora est? aut quid iam, Turne, retractas?* 'What now at last is the delay? Or what now, Turnus, are you rehandling?' (parodying Turnus' misleading declaration at 12.11 *nulla mora in Turno*, 'there is no delay in Turnus': *retracto* can be a literary term, see Nisbet and Hubbard on Horace, *Odes* 2.1.38). Whenever Jupiter tries to bring things to an end, his wife frustrates him and creates *mora*, 'delay': whenever Juno and her allies introduce delay, in the end the story moves on. So Anchises in Book 2, having at first delayed, agrees to leave Troy when he sees the god's portent, with the words *iam iam nulla mora est*, 'now, now there is no delay' (2.701); and at another nodal point of departure Mercury tells Aeneas to leave Carthage with the words *heia age, rumpe moras*, 'come now, break all delays' (4.569). At the end of the

[1] See Levitan (1993) 14–15.

Aeneid, that is what Aeneas does (12.699 *praecipitat ... moras omnis, opera omnia rumpit*, 'he drives headlong all delays, breaks (off) all (other) works'). Right at the end there is a brief hesitation, as Aeneas delays the climactic killing of his enemy, but the poem finally ends with an act of composition, if not of composure: Aeneas *ferrum adverso sub pectore condit*, 'buries (founds, lays down) the iron in his adversary's chest' (12.950, recalling 1.5 *dum conderet urbem*, 'before he could found a city' and 1.33 *tantae molis erat Romanam condere gentem*, 'so weighty a task was it to found the Roman people'). The final killing is at once an end and a beginning, a foundational act for the new Rome like Romulus' killing of his brother (cf. 1.276–7 in Jupiter's prophecy, *Romulus excipiet gentem et Mavortia condet | moenia, Romanosque suo de nomine dicet*, 'Romulus will take over the race and found the Martial walls, and call (the people) Romans from his name'). There Jupiter's omission of the killing of Remus highlights its presence under his attempted erasure, reinforced by the echo of Ennius fr. 63 of the brothers' enmity, *certabant urbem Romam Remoramne vocarent*, 'they were contending as to whether they would call the city Remora or Roma'.

Oppositions

From beginning to end, the *Aeneid* similarly represents its own ends and beginnings in contention. The contest between Jupiter and Juno is fought on many levels. In the first half of the poem, Aeneas wanders around the Mediterranean trying to discover what the plot is: there are stories to help him, but they are easily misunderstood. Anchises, after consulting the history-books (3.102 *veterum volvens monimenta virorum*, 'pondering/ unrolling the records of ancient men', glossed later in 105 as *audita*, 'things heard') plausibly suggests Crete as their home, but is proved wrong by a plague. In Book 6, the dead Anchises gives him perhaps more reliable – but even less directly helpful – information about what will happen later in Roman history: we are also told that he instructed Aeneas in detail about what was to happen in Books 8–12 (6.890–2), but the narrator does not share this information with us, and Aeneas shows little sign of remembering it. Nevertheless, the second half of the poem has a stronger teleology, as despite Juno's efforts events move to their conclusion. Hence some[2] have seen a move in the poem from an Odyssean concern with repetition as return ('romance') to an Iliadic sense of repetition with variation ('epic'): instead of 'seeking his mother' (3.96), Aeneas becomes the new father of

[2] Quint (1993).

the Roman race, instead of going around in circles, the plot spirals on. The Trojan war is replayed in the second half, but this time the Trojans take on the role of the Greeks, and the Latins move from besieging the Trojan camp to themselves being besieged: Turnus becomes Hector, and Aeneas proves the *alius . . . Achilles*, 'Achilles II' prophesied by the Sibyl (6.89).

But while an opposition between the plots of the *Iliad* and the *Odyssey* is undoubtedly basic to the storytelling of the *Aeneid*, the terms of the opposition are less clear than this view suggests. Of the two Homeric epics, it is the *Odyssey* which has the strongest teleology: events move inexorably to their ordained conclusion, and the divine plot outlined at the beginning is finally justified (at *Od.* 24.351 Laertes exclaims 'Father Zeus, you gods still exist in Olympus . . .'). As many have noted, it is the *Odyssey* which provides the armature for the structure of the *Aeneid*, with a heterogeneous first half succeeded by a second half in which time and place get increasingly concentrated and claustrophobic as we move to the final act of vengeance. From the breadth of the Mediterranean we move to Ithaca, and then the palace, and finally the killing field of Book 22: similarly the *Aeneid* moves towards the pairing of Turnus and Aeneas, one-on-one outside the city gates. The final meeting in heaven between Athene and Zeus in *Odyssey* 24 is mirrored by the settlement reached by Juno and Jupiter in *Aeneid* 12: in both cases we are assured that there will now be peace and justice (cf. *Od.* 24.486, 483 with *Aen.* 12.821–2), that events have finally reached a resolution. Whereas Athene descends to earth to stop the conflict between Odysseus and the suitors' relatives, however, Juno mysteriously leaves her cloud (12.842) merely to disappear from the epic, and the resolution at the human level is messier and more disturbing. The *Iliad*, in contrast, while it looks to an end in the fall of Troy, within the compass of the poem ends only with a mutual recognition of shared pain, and has a much less strong sense of theodicy, for all that Zeus sends Hermes to guide Priam to Achilles. It is more easily assimilated to the paradigms of tragedy, to the eternal return of human suffering rather than any hope of an end. In so far, therefore, as the opposition between *Odyssean* and *Iliadic* plots works itself out in the *Aeneid*, it is arguably in the opposite sense to that suggested by Quint and others: the *Odyssey* represents closure, the *Iliad* the resistance to it formed by human pain. The question of the tendency of the plot of the *Aeneid*, whether it progresses linearly or goes round in circles, thus turns out to be another version of the debate over the ideological tendency of the poem; and the question of plot gets mirrored again at another level in the history of Virgilian criticism itself. Does criticism get anywhere, make progress, resolve issues, reach conclusions, or just eternally return to the same oppositions? Does it ask questions, or give answers?

Plot, story, book

The *Aeneid* displays the manipulations of order, duration, and frequency familiar from narratological theory, and raises the equally familiar problems that surround attempts to make precise what is at the level of plot or *fabula* or story ('what happened') and what at the level of the narration of the events of the plot, the way they are told (and the terms to use for each level . . .). The narrative of the *Aeneid* begins with Juno seeing Aeneas, making an angry speech, and stirring up a storm: it ends with Aeneas seeing the baldric of Pallas, making an angry speech, and killing Turnus. But as we have noted, the beginning and end of the *story* is much more problematic.

The most notable ruptures of narrative **order** are Aeneas' narration to Dido of the fall of Troy and Anchises' recital of the future history of Rome, itself not ordered by strict chronology, but there are many smaller *analepses* (flashbacks) and *prolepses* (anticipations). An opposition is conventionally made in relation to narrative **duration** between the balanced narration of epic, with a predominance of 'scenes' (where the time taken to narrate an event corresponds to its length and importance at the level of plot) over 'summaries' and 'slow-downs', and the more 'syncopated' narrative of elegy, in which major events of the story may be passed over briefly to concentrate on descriptive passages and emotional confrontations or monologues. This is as valid as any of the other markers of the generic opposition between epic and elegy: in fact, there is great variety in respect of the handling of narrative duration within the *Aeneid*. Devices such as ecphrasis (see ch. 17*b*) and simile which tend completely to suspend narration[3] are extensively used. The battle narratives of the second half might seem to be the place where one would most expect to find epic-style narrative regularity, but they are typically constructed around death-vignettes in which description and analepsis of the victim's past life tends to predominate over narration of the actual killing, and at the moment of death the focus may be on a bizarre detail rather than the expected narration of the killing. They also frequently contain direct speech. At 9.590–637, for instance, we have the famous death of Remulus Numanus at the hands of Iulus: three lines (590–2) introduce the killing in summary form, two (593–4) describe Remulus, three narrate his taunting of the Trojans (595–7), twenty-three (598–620) give his speech, four narrate Iulus' aiming (621–4), five give his prayer to Jupiter (625–9), five lines (630–4) narrate Jupiter's response and the shooting, two (634–5) give Iulus' vaunt, and two (636–7) describe the reaction of the Trojans. Although direct speech is sometimes

---

[3] Cf., however, Lyne (1989) 63–99.

classified as representing a 'scene' by narratologists, since it takes just as long to narrate as it did to be uttered, its effect is in fact to slow down a narrative, since its content can often be narrated more economically by indirect speech or narrator's report of speech-act: so in this example very little of the episode is devoted to narrative proper, and much more to comment, reflection, or reaction. Direct speech, one of the great markers of the epic style, is thus ambiguous in its effect on the progress of the narrative.

In talking of the Remulus Numanus 'episode' I am using the conventional Aristotelian language for narrative **segmentation**. The section arguably does not conclude at 637, as Virgil goes on to narrate the subsequent reaction of Apollo and Iulus' withdrawal from the conflict: a plausible incision for the end of the episode might be 663, though modern editors tend to mark a paragraph break later, at 671. The paragraphing of modern texts is a sometimes haphazard feature of the paratext (the features of a text which are not quite part of the text but affect interpretation[4]), but there are some obvious signals of division within the text such as *epiphonemata* (single-line summations, like 1.33 *tantae molis erat Romanam condere gentem*, 'such a task it was to found the Roman race') or other general comments, such as the pause for reflection with which Aeneas concludes his narrative of the death of Priam in Book 2 (554–8):

> haec finis Priami fatorum, hic exitus illum
> sorte tulit Troiam incensam et prolapsa videntem
> Pergama, tot quondam populis terrisque superbum
> regnatorem Asiae. iacet ingens litore truncus,
> avulsumque umeris caput et sine nomine corpus.

> This was the end of Priam's fates, this conclusion
> took hold of him by chance, viewing Troy in flames and
> Pergamum fallen: once the proud ruler over so many
> peoples and lands of Asia. He lies a huge trunk on the shore,
> a head torn from its shoulders, a body without a name.

Aeneas as internal narrator draws attention to the fact that the end of his telling of Priam's story coincides with the end of Priam, who has exited from story within story to become a corpse without a name (the modern reader may well think of the end of *The Name of the Rose*). The final detail on which Aeneas had concluded his narration before this reflection was the plunging of Pyrrhus' sword into Priam (2.552–3), the (sort of) action which will of course conclude the *Aeneid* itself (12.950: cf. also 10.536).

---

[4] Cf. Genette (1987).

At the end of the *Aeneid* narration will stop without any pause for reflection, but there is a clear element of *mise en abyme* (mirroring of the textual process within a text) within *mise en abyme* signalled by the segmentation: just as Aeneas' narrative is a story within a story which starts the poem off again (cf. 2.3 *infandum regina iubes* **renovare** *dolorem*, 'unspeakable, queen, is the pain you bid me **renew**'), so the Priam story within it ends the way the whole work will end. And then the story goes on.

It is this sort of internal segmentation which generates effects such as the mirroring of scenes between first and second halves: only when the textual continuum is allowed to be broken up into units can we seek correspondences between those units. The major segmentation of the *Aeneid* is the division into twelve 'books', which have a similar status to the chapters of a modern novel. The *Iliad* and the *Odyssey* were each divided into 24 books before or during the early Hellenistic period: although some of the divisions do not mark a strong break in the action, most produce a significant pause on some level. Some of the books have a strong sense of individual unity (e.g. *Iliad* 10 and *Odyssey* 11, both of which have been held for this reason to be additions to the original poems), and the numeration emphasises correspondences between the two Homeric poems: both the *Iliad* and the *Odyssey*, for instance, have climactic moments in their twenty-second books, with the killing of Hector and the suitors respectively. The book division of the *Aeneid* is much more strongly marked, however, and the book predominates as the main structural unit of the poem. The most obvious division is into two halves of six books, with a 'proem in the middle' in Book 7, ironically announcing not only a *maius opus*, 'greater work', but also a *maior ordo*, 'greater order or sequence': throughout the *Aeneid* more than the order of things enters into the usages of *ordo*, and this sequence begins immediately after the long order of Roman history outlined by Anchises (6.723, 754). But there is also a sense of three sets of four books (1–4 for instance deal with the 'digression' in Carthage, just as *Odyssey* 1–4 contains the details of Telemachus' journey), and other divisions are possible. The books in the first half tend to end on a death (2 Creusa, 3 Anchises, 4 Dido, 5 Palinurus, 6 Marcellus), while in the second half this is true only of 10 and 12: there is perhaps a particular parallel between 4 and 10 in this respect, suggesting a division within each half into 4 + 2. One particular aspect of the book structure is the way that some books may be seen as representing in a form of *mise en abyme* the entire work. This has been argued in particular for Books 3 and 5,[5] both of which begin with a sea voyage and end with a death, and in other ways

---

[5] Cf. Hershkowitz (1991) 69–76; Galinsky (1968) 157–85.

too may be seen as mirroring the larger work. This play with the segmentation and structure of the work is not just a matter of formalist games: the multiple and shifting structures connect different parts of the poem in different ways, and thus correspond to the multiplicity of ends and means at the ideological level.

Point of view

It is at the level of voice ('who speaks?') and especially mood ('who sees?', focalisation), however, that the storytelling of the *Aeneid* has seemed to impinge most directly on the wider questions of its interpretation. As already mentioned, while the narrator of the *Aeneid* on the whole avoids explicit intervention in the narrative, and pursues epic 'showing' rather than the 'telling' of discourse, the 'point of view' embodied in the poem is by no means always clear (a point which emerges already in comments on *persona* in the ancient commentary of Servius: see ch. 5). In 4.281–2, for instance, Aeneas' reactions to Mercury's reminder of his mission are described:

> ardet abire fuga dulcisque relinquere terras,
> attonitus tanto monitu imperioque deorum.

> he blazes to go away in flight and leave the sweet lands,
> astonished at so great a warning and command of the gods.

The epic narrator speaks, but as Servius notes it is more plausibly Aeneas who focalises *dulcis*: he is eager to depart, but also sees the land of Carthage as sweet because of his love for Dido (we may conjecture). Here the lexical choice of *dulcis* embeds the point of view of Aeneas: he sees, even though Virgil speaks. The following line too may be held to represent Aeneas' point of view rather than Virgil's, but in a less obvious way: while Virgil is not an obvious focaliser for *dulcis*, the description of the 'warning and order' of the gods as 'so great' (*tanto*) could be from the point of view of the primary narrator, but can also be read as a representation of how Aeneas feels in relation to what he has just heard. Similarly, there is nothing about the phrase *monitu imperioque deorum* 'by the warning and order of the gods' which cannot be from the primary narrator's point of view, but we may also read it as embodying Aeneas' move from seeing what Mercury said as a warning (which is in fact closest to the tenor of his speech, which contains only one imperative) to a view of it as an order. None of this is unambiguous, however. Although sometimes, therefore, we may be clear that we wish to see a character's point of view embedded in the text, at other times we may feel less sure about distributing the viewpoint between narrator and characters: it is a matter of interpretative choice. The position of the narrator towards the embedded focalisation is also dependent on the reader's choice: we may see Virgil as merely recording that a character felt in a particular way, or as sharing in that character's point of view with 'sympathy' or 'empathy'.

It is thus possible to draw very different conclusions about the tenor of the poem from Virgil's famous 'subjective style'.[6] We can see elements as focalised by the characters, or the narrator, or some mixture of the two: and we can use embedded focalisation either to 'solve problems' in the ideological tendency of the narrative or to introduce discordant notes. In 10.565–70, for instance, Aeneas is compared to the monstrous giant Aegaeon revolting against the gods: do we see this as a comment by the narrator on the monstrous nature of Aeneas at this point, or merely as the way he seems to his opponents? It is clear that questions like this cannot be solved by appeal to textual elements in themselves but depend on wider views of the poem's ideology. It has been argued that regardless of whether we see the narrator as sympathising with the embedded points of view or merely recording them, the coherency of the text is shattered and it becomes impossible to ascribe to it any dominant ideological tendency,[7] but this perhaps underestimates the ability of a sufficiently strong-willed critic to produce an overarching interpretation which keeps these other 'voices' suitably muted.

Singing and writing

In 9.774–7 Turnus in the fury of battle kills a poet:

> amicum Crethea Musis,
> Crethea Musarum comitem, cui carmina semper
> et citharae cordi numerosque intendere nervis,
> semper equos atque arma virum pugnasque canebat.

(Turnus killed) Cretheus the friend of the Muses,
Cretheus, companion of the Muses, who loved poems always
and lyres, and to stretch metres on strings,
who always used to sing of horses and arms of men, and battles.

The phrase *arma virum*, although here *virum* is genitive plural, 'of men' rather than the singular 'man' of the opening *arma virumque cano*, 'arms and the man I sing', links Cretheus to Virgil himself (variations on the opening two words continually return throughout the *Aeneid*). If Turnus

---

[6] Cf. e.g. Heinze (1915); Otis (1964); La Penna (1967) 220–44; Conte (1986) 141–84; Bonfanti (1985); Fowler (1990) 42–63.

[7] Cf. Conte (1986) 141–84.

had at this point opened the gates to his companions, he would have won the war and the poem would have been prematurely and wrongly concluded (9.757–9): instead he goes off and kills the poet. The final *canebat*, 'used to sing' (with a pathetic hint of 'but no more') links Cretheus to another singer, Iopas who sings an allegorical cosmic didactic poem at the end of Book 1 (742–3):

> hic canit errantem lunam solisque labores,
> unde hominum genus et pecudes, unde imber et ignes

> he sings of the wandering moon and the labours of the sun,
> the origin of the human race and animals, of rain and fire . . .

And we must not forget another singer who had a stunning effect on his audience, as Dido remarks to her sister after the end of Aeneas' story (4.13–14):

> heu, quibus ille
> iactatus fatis! quae bella exhausta canebat!

> ah, by what fates was he
> tossed! what wars drained dry he was singing!

Cano in Latin, however, means more than 'sing': it is also the word for 'prophesy' (Virgil in the opening prophesies a man as well as singing about one). This aspect of its usage brings in many more narratorial surrogates within the poem. Perhaps the most prominent is the Sibyl of Cumae, whose literary activity is described by Helenus in Book 3 (443–52):

> insanam vatem aspicies, quae rupe sub ima
> fata canit foliisque notas et nomina mandat.
> quaecumque in foliis descripsit carmina virgo
> digerit in numerum atque antro seclusa relinquit:
> illa manent immota locis neque ab ordine cedunt.
> verum eadem, verso tenuis cum cardine ventus
> impulit et teneras turbavit ianua frondes,
> numquam deinde cavo volitantia prendere saxo
> nec revocare situs aut iungere carmina curat:
> inconsulti abeunt sedemque odere Sibyllae.

> you will see a mad prophet/poet, who under the hollow crag
> sings fates and entrusts marks and names to leaves.
> Whatever the songs the virgin writes down on the leaves
> she places in order/metre and leaves them set apart in the cave:
> they stay unmoved in their places, nor depart from their order.
> But these same songs, when at the turning of the hinge a small wind

strikes them, and the door disturbs the tender leaves,
fly around the hollow cave, and she has no care to take them
or to call them back to their places or join together the songs:
without a message the people go away, and hate the site of the Sibyl.

So later in Book 6, when he finally meets the Sibyl, Aeneas begs her to sing herself, and not entrust her prophecies to writing (6.74–6):

> foliis tantum ne carmina manda,
> ne turbata volent rapidis ludibria ventis;
> ipsa canas oro.

> only do not entrust your songs to leaves,
> lest disturbed they fly a plaything for the swift winds;
> sing yourself I beg you.

Entrusted to writing, the prophecies of the Sibyl become unstable at the moment of reading: opening the door disturbs the order of the text beyond recall. Aeneas begs the Sibyl for full presence, in an attempt to avoid these instabilities, but the Sibyl's response is as ambiguous as all the prophecies of the *Aeneid*. As song, the *Aeneid* aspires to transcend the indeterminacies of its nature as text, as written text it embodies those indeterminacies. Even at the very moment that it embraces song at the opening of the poem, however, the narration is ambiguous. The 'man' of 'Arms and the man I sing ...' is obviously Aeneas, but equally obviously looks forward to another man, Augustus (6.791–4):

> hic vir, hic est, tibi quem promitti saepius audis,
> Augustus Caesar, divi genus, aurea condet
> saecula qui rursus Latio regnata per arva
> Saturno quondam

> this is the man, this is he whom you hear often promised to you,
> Augustus Caesar, the stock of god, who will found
> again the golden centuries in the fields ruled by Latin
> Saturn once

Virgil sings Aeneas and prophesies Augustus: the direct presence promised by song and prophecy is illusory from the start. Things as they are are always already changed on Virgil's guitar.

The stress on the indeterminacy of reception implied by the story of the Sibyl's *folia* – the implication that whatever fixity a text might possess, it disappears in the very act of reading which is necessary to give it meaning – is reflected in the other surrogates for the act of reception that we find in the poem. Whenever anyone hears someone else's tale (as the Trojans listen to Sinon, or Dido to Aeneas) or views a work of art (as Aeneas does in Books 1 and 8: see ch. 17*b*) or receives a prophecy, the *Aeneid* stresses the active role of the audience in the way that the message is taken, the way that their beliefs and emotions decide how they react to what is set before them. One may build on these internal surrogates to construct readers of the *Aeneid* who will similarly react in differing ways to its story: who may be reminded of past pain (2.3, 3.710) or stirred on to future glory (6.889), who may be taken in by the tale or maybe read with more suspicion. The story of the *Aeneid* necessarily does not end with the final flight of Turnus' soul (itself the result of Aeneas' 'reading' of the sword-belt of Pallas that Turnus was wearing), but begins at the point where the work's first readers pick up the book and start to unroll what Virgil has wrapped in darkness. That is when things really hot up, and start to happen: that is where the action really leads.

FURTHER READING

The best introductory works on narratology are by the two most celebrated practitioners, G. Genette, *Narrative Discourse* (Oxford, 1980) and M. Bal, *Narratology: Introduction to the Theory of Narrative* (London, 1985).

There is a bibliography of other introductory works, and of classical analyses influenced by narrative theory in I. J. F. De Jong and J. P. Sullivan, *Modern Critical Theory and Classical Literature* (*Mnemosyne* Suppl. 130) 282–4 (Leiden, 1994). De Jong's own *Narrators and Focalisers: The Presentation of the Story in the Iliad* (Amsterdam, 1987) is the most extensive treatment of a classical author.

For psychoanalytic narrative theory, see especially P. Brooks, *Reading for the Plot: Design and Intention in Narrative* (New York, 1985) and his more introductory *Psychoanalysis and Storytelling* (Oxford, 1994).

17b

ALESSANDRO BARCHIESI

Virgilian narrative: ecphrasis

In modern criticism the term 'ecphrasis' ('description') is used specific-ally to refer to a literary description of a work of art. In ancient criticism the term belongs to a much wider area of reference, covering both the visual force and the emotional impact of verbal art (not only poetry but historiography and rhetoric). Heroic epic, in particular, was held to be a narrative form oriented towards the production of visual effects and the re-creation of an eyewitness reaction to events. Virgil is particularly famous as a maker of impressive descriptions, including e.g. a dramatic study of a brook (*G.* 1.104ff.), a bold vision of monstrous snakes swimming in the Dardanelles (*Aen.* 2.203ff.), a miniature of a tame stag (7.483ff.). Didactic hexameter and heroic epic are alike very concerned with visual impact, although with divergent emphases: didactic poetry focuses on the typical and repeatable, while heroic poetry is a narrative of striking events, tradi-tionally geared towards the grandiose and the violent. Yet in both forms the challenge of representation is at stake: how adequate is the verbal med-ium to convey an impression of what is being described (whether the con-text requires that this be vivid and fresh, or realistic and typical, or unique and shocking)? More specifically, with regard to ecphrasis in the modern sense of a verbal re-creation of a visual work of art, verbal representation tests its own limits through a confrontation between literary description and representations in other media. In this case the verbal message will be measured both against direct perceptions of reality (or visual imagination) and against the model of the visual arts.

The present essay is concerned only with ecphrasis in the modern sense. The main texts are a series of substantial descriptions of artifacts, includ-ing engraved cups (*Ecl.* 3.36–47), a temple in northern Italy (*G.* 3.16–36), a temple in Carthage (*Aen.* 1.453–93), a temple in Cumae (*Aen.* 6.14–34), and a shield (*Aen.* 6.625–731). The interest of these passages does not lie in any documentary value: there is no reason to suspect that Vir-gil attempts to describe actual artifacts in any of these passages, and no

Roman reader would have imagined that they could actually go and see the objects. The cup is part of the bucolic world; the Italian temple is a symbolic project, not a real monument; the temples at Cumae and Carthage exist only in a narrative set eleven centuries before the Augustan age, and ten centuries before the total destruction of Carthage; the shield is manufactured by the god of metalwork. The reader can visit these monuments only with the aid of the poet's voice. The Palatine Temple of Apollo, the most magnificent of recent Roman monuments, is briefly glimpsed in miniature on the surface of an engraved shield (8.720).[1]

The inclusion in a general *Companion to Virgil* of a chapter devoted to these relatively brief texts may be justified by the relevance of the topic of ecphrasis to a number of concerns of recent criticism. In ecphrasis the narrative action is frozen: modern Virgilian criticism is very interested in the dynamics of narrative and plot (on narratology, see chapter 17a). In ecphrasis art, rather than action and character, becomes the focus; an interest in artistic self-reflexivity has been prominent in late twentieth-century study of classical literature. Finally, ecphrasis functions readily as the site of a confrontation between different ways of representing and imagining the world of reality. Our topic thus interacts with three major issues: the limits of narrative, the dimension of reflexivity, and the various approaches to realism and representation.

Competition

One important reason why ecphrasis matters is that Augustan culture places a strong emphasis on the visual. It has been shown that architecture and figurative art were focal areas for major cultural change in Rome; one cannot discuss issues like the Hellenisation of the Roman aristocracy, the formation of an Augustan political discourse, or the link between patronage and intellectuals, without realising that literature, and poetry in particular, could not pretend to the same degree of importance. As a leading verbal artist of this age, Virgil must have felt a pressure to define his art in competition with the claims of other artistic media. His project of a temple in *Georgics* 3 offers to Caesar a centrality and visibility superior even to the sophisticated strategies of public architecture. The reuse of Greek works of art of various styles and provenances, a highly visible feature of Augustan Rome, is paralleled through devices of intertextuality: in the proem to *Georgics* 3 Virgil takes on the challenge of imported Greek

---

[1] The Caesarian 'temple' at the beginning of *Georgics* 3 may also allude to the Palatine temple of Apollo (a monument already under construction in the late 30s).

statues (3.34 *Parii lapides, spirantia signa*, 'Parian marbles, statues that breathe'), and images of the gods (3.36 *Cynthius*) through his own appropriation of the praise poetry of Pindar and Callimachus; a marble temple of words requires the importation of Greek models, poetic instead of sculptural. The Carthaginian temple shows, in the reinvented world of twelfth-century Phoenician culture, the foundational role of art and myth in the process of colonisation and acculturation, and the iconography inevitably draws on Homeric epic. The shield of Aeneas mediates between the poetic tradition of the shield of Achilles and the contemporary world of real historical reliefs, honorary shields, and imperial cult.

Literary reflexivity

The visit to the Carthaginian temple illustrates the link between ecphrasis and artistic self-consciousness. The narrative function motivating the long description is provided in Aeneas' first reaction to the images: 'even here there is fame and pity for our suffering; this will bring salvation to us'; and the figurative programme of the temple does indeed show that the Trojan war is famous in Carthage. When Aeneas comments on the *bellaque iam fama totum vulgata per orbem* (1.457: 'warfare now famous through the whole world') he has some reason to be surprised – seven years after the fall of Troy, Phoenician wanderers have brought their repertory of images of the Trojan War to create a new monument in North Africa, but his readers have even more reason to pause. The Virgilian hero is meeting his own past, but this act of recollection through images is inscribed in a literary work where the past is also equivalent to the literary tradition. The temple at Carthage represents famous events narrated in the *Iliad* and the Epic Cycle; in fact the events are 'famous' through poetry and only secondarily – despite the riches of the Greek figurative tradition – through art. Thus the line could be tendentiously paraphrased 'wars made known through the whole Epic Cycle', *orbis* being the Roman equivalent of the Greek 'kyklos', and *vulgata* meaning 'trite', 'commonplace', a frequent judgement in ancient criticism on the quality of the Epic Cycle's predictable rehearsal of its subject-matter. So the description of the scenes of the Trojan War acts as a foil for Virgilian poetics: Virgil will invent a new 'Trojan' epic, an *Aeneid* which takes its point of departure from the Epic Cycle and particularly from the narrative tradition of post-war 'homecomings', but which then strays away, to assert a powerfully original project: a 'Trojan' epic which will be about the foundation of a new order and the recuperation of the Greek legacy within a different culture; a Roman epic poem which is also a charter myth for Roman epic. Aeneas, the spectator of the Trojan War in the Carthaginian temple, will become the narrator of its final chapter by the end of *Aeneid* 1. The new poem needs the Cyclic tradition, but it will not be simply a Roman continuation; it will confront the Cycle at an oblique angle.

The images in the temple are thus represented in the narrative, but also framed and miniaturised by the narrative. Their inclusion through ecphrasis invites the reader to consider the relevance of this secondary field of reference to the primary narrative; but the included description is compressed in such a way that a limit is established and a hierarchy of importance is reasserted. This is particularly significant given that epic ecphrases have a potential for becoming 'main stories', (for example the Shield of Herakles starts as heroic narrative but the narrative is then swallowed by a shield description) and that a particular tradition of modern epic (the so called epyllia, poems like Moschus' *Europa* and Catullus 64) had already exemplified the alternative: narratives that could be sidetracked and even engulfed by digressive descriptions.

There are similar implications in the case of the other major ecphrases of the *Aeneid*, the shield of Aeneas and the doors of the temple of Apollo at Cumae. In the second passage, the Sibyl interrupts the viewing of the mythological scenes with the wry comment 'this is not the right time for looking at such things' (6.37). This is, of course, a self-conscious nod towards the narrative problem of motivation and deferral (see below), but it may also be relevant that the ecphrasis contains allusions to Alexandrian and Neoteric models (Catullus 64, Callimachus), texts in which digression, excursus, and inset ecphrasis notoriously paralyse or thwart the progress of a 'natural' epic narrative.[2] The narrator has just paused to disclose what would have been Daedalus' choice of images – an untold story behind unseen representations. Virgil gestures towards the power of ecphrasis to branch out in the direction of alternative stories, before intervening to assert control over the progress of the narrative.

The shield of Aeneas looks back to the shield of Achilles and to the traditions of Homeric interpretation, but it is also relevant that the diction is often Ennian, and that the subject-matter has exactly the same temporal span as Ennius' *Annals* – from the birth of Romulus to the Roman triumphs of the present age (second quarter of the second century BC for Ennius, the 20s BC for Virgil) – and that the structure of the description is chronological, or in other words annalistic (cf. 8.629 *pugnataque in ordine bella*, 'the wars fought in chronological sequence'). This last feature

---

[2] The story of the Minotaur looks back to Catullus 64, and the description of the Labyrinth, a work of Daedalus replicated in the new artwork by the same master, recalls Callimachus' 'Hymn to Delos', 310–15.

is in contrast with the structure of the *Aeneid*, a new epic centred on a very short and dramatic sequence of events instead of a long, unbroken annalistic narrative. Significantly the temple in Carthage offers (1.456) *Iliacas ex ordine pugnas* ('battles at Troy in order'), but what the narrator in fact gives us looks like a non-chronological and emotional selection of the images, mediated through Aeneas as focaliser;[3] in other words, the reuse of Greek epic in the Carthaginian ecphrasis is in accordance with the poetics of the *Aeneid*, while the appropriation of Ennius and traditional Roman epic in the ecphrasis of the shield reflects a kind of antagonistic poetics, a road not taken. In all three cases, the issue of how to acknowledge influence is inseparable from the issue of how to resist influence.

Interpretation and the viewer

More than any other ancient poet Virgil stresses the importance of the viewing subject in the construction of visual meaning. The interpretation of the ornament of the cups in Eclogue 3 is the subject of a question in the text, and, like the riddles at the end of the poem, the correct reading of the images presupposes learning and interpretation, setting a challenge to the reader. The scenes of Iliadic themes in the temple at Carthage are related to Aeneas' experience of them; both a viewer and a part of the representation, Aeneas first marvels (1.456 *miratur*), then sees (1.456 *videt*; 1.466 *videbat*), and finally recognises (1.470 *agnoscit lacrimans*; 1.488 *se quoque ... agnovit*) – the use of *agnosco* shows that the reception of the images is inseparable from a set of previous experiences. This contrasts sharply with Aeneas' passive and superficial involvement in the visual disclosures of the shield: this ecphrasis in the future tense allows of no personal co-operation on the part of the viewer:

> oculos per singula volvit,
> miraturque ...
> ... et clipei non enarrabile textum ...
> Talia per clipeum Volcani. dona parentis,
> miratur rerumque ignarus imagine gaudet ...

he turns his eyes over each piece, in admiration ... and the shield's indescribable fabric ... he admires such things on the shield made by Vulcan, his mother's gift, rejoicing in their depiction of unknown events ...

> (8.618–19, 625, 729–30)

The centre of the shield is occupied by Caesar Augustus, a man who is a distant but recurring promise to Aeneas (6.791–2 *hic vir, hic est, tibi quem*

---

[3] Cf. ch. 17a, pp. 266–7.

promitti saepius audis, | *Augustus Caesar* ...). But we are not told whether Aeneas remembers seeing his image in the Underworld. It is therefore striking that the *princeps,* included in the very centre of the visual artifact, and displaced one millennium into the future, is represented as performing the act not only of viewing but of recognising:

> ipse sedens niveo candentis limine Phoebi
> dona *recognoscit* populorum aptatque superbis
> postibus; incedunt victae longo ordine gentes ...

> He himself, sitting at the snowy threshold of shining Phoebus, reviews the people's gifts, and hangs them at his proud door; the vanquished races move in long array ...   (8.720–2)

Thus Augustus is both the central figure on and the ideal spectator of the shield; as he watches the bringing of spoils and the triumphal procession, he trespasses over several layers of representation and becomes the privileged observer of the divine shield and of the Virgilian narrative itself. The 'gifts' to be affixed to the doorposts would be, typically, shields; the reader can imagine Aeneas watching a shield whose umbilical point is Augustus examining a shield ... (In a symmetrical *mise-en-abyme* the artist Vulcanus has 'fashioned shield[s]', *lapsa ancilia caelo* | *extuderat* 8.664–5, where the wording collapses the difference between the two levels of narration and description.) The visibility of the narrative (8.676 *cernere erat* ...) is of course a source of paradoxes. The *princeps,* represented atop a warship (8.680 *stans celsa in puppi*) and seated at the gleaming vantage-point of the Palatine temple (8.720 *sedens* ... *limine Phoebi*) has a panoramic view of Roman history, a concentric construct in which he is both centre and summit (cf. 8.675 *in medio* ... ; G. 3.16 *in medio mihi Caesar erit templumque tenebit*), both ultimate protagonist and observer, while the reader is rewarded with a teasing *videres* ('you could / might have seen', 8.676). The appearance of the Actian leader is also marked by the absence of ecphrastic markers: when he is introduced (*Augustus agens* ... *stans* ... *invectus* ... *sacrabat* ... *sedens*) he is the active subject in the representation, and the epic ecphrasis at this point eschews two devices that regularly mark images as the products of artifice: there is no mention of the artist as author of the image (no *fecerat* or *addit* or *extuderat*) and no reminder of the materiality of what is being described – amid a golden sea (8.672, 677), glittering silver dolphins (673) and bronze *rostra* (675) Augustus is just himself, a maker of history not an artist-made icon.

Ecphrasis and history

Yet this political function of ecphrasis is accompanied by a sense of reduction, of containment, of marginalisation. The shield of Aeneas is a substitute for an alternative epic poem, a poem which could have been Ennian, historical, written in tableaux, in sequential order, and focused on praise. We briefly encounter Catiline persecuted by infernal Furies, Agrippa leading his marines in martial alliteration (*arduus agmen agens*, 8.683); but Virgil offers this concentrated essence of a historical-epic poetics through the miniaturising device of ecphrasis. Only in the central blazon of the shield is Aeneas able to discover Rome, the future city which has been reshaped by Augustus into a counterpart of the prosperous town immortalised by Homer in the anonymous emblems of the cosmic shield of Achilles.[4]

Yet even when the internal viewer is a perfect model-reader of the images, Virgil suggests that viewing is a creative activity and that meaning is a matter for negotiation. Nobody can know more about the Trojan battles than Aeneas, but even he, the viewer of the temple of Juno in Carthage, can be seen to be a biased focaliser. His interpretation of the images as a sign of compassion and respect for the Trojan catastrophe is indeed reinforced by powerful contextual pointers – his solidarity with Dido, Dido's tragic view of the conflict and her source of information, the anti-war Greek/Trojan hero Teucer – but there are also counter-indications which set up a spiral of historical ironies: the ecphrasis is located in a temple of Juno, a goddess for whom the extinction of Troy is a triumph; the tale of Trojan empire and Trojan downfall is linked in turn to Greek triumph and Greek disaster (in the *Nostoi*, anticipated by the alarming image of Athena Ilias at 1.482[5]); to the rise of Carthage and the fall of the Carthaginian empire; after a span of a thousand years a war started by Juno's persecution of the Romans and Dido's curse on Aeneas will wipe out the citadel of Carthage, and a Roman general, a new and different Aeneas, will find tears of compassion for the mortality of empires (even Rome) at the very moment that his army methodically sacks and levels Carthage to the ground. Scipio will quote a Homeric passage on the destruction of Troy,[6] thus completing the cycle of destruction foreshadowed in the Virgilian ecphrasis; his compassion for the Punic city ironically complements Aeneas' compassionate reading of the figurative programme. Finally, perhaps (but Rome is still an empire,

---

[4] The panels on the shield of Achilles possess a generalising significance, and therefore prompted attempts at identification or allegorisation already in the classical period; when Virgil substitutes a contemporary Rome for the Homeric image of a prosperous and just town, he completes through imitation a process already initiated by the Homeric exegesis of his age.

[5] The goddess is represented as hostile to a Trojan supplication, in a precise counterpart to an Iliadic episode, but the description of the statue anticipates a prodigy which will announce, on the night of the sack of Troy, that Athena is now going to persecute *the Greeks* for their impious behaviour. The murder of Troilus, one of the most gruesome images in the temple, is both a precondition for the capture of Troy and the cause of divine retribution against Achilles.

[6] See Polybius' witness in Appian, *Punica* 132.

not a ruin . . .), a Roman poet will write the Carthaginian temple into his poem and re-create – with bitter self-consciousness? – an ur-Carthaginian culture whose central hearth is the charter-myth of Roman civilisation, Troy.

Motivation and deferral

The problems which ecphrasis imposes on a narrative poet are inseparable from its attractions; indeed, ecphrasis is practised by epic poets like Homer, Apollonius, Catullus and Virgil precisely because it poses a challenge for the poetics of narrative. The description of visual artifacts occupies a different level of complexity from description of natural objects within the world of the story. The poet manipulates words in response to images; two semiotic systems partially overlap, and in the process both images and words reveal their communicative potential as well as their limits. As a result of this dynamic, ecphrasis can incorporate its opposite, the retelling of events, sounds and movement. A rhetoric peculiar to ecphrasis suggests (often as a closural device) the paradox of cinematic silhouettes (1.493–7 *audetque viris concurrere virgo . . . regina . . . incessit*) and sonic tapestries (5.257 *saevitque canum latratus in auras*, 'the savage barking of dogs rises to the sky'). The textual medium explores the limits of visual communication as an indirect way of testing its own material limitations.

The economy of epic action is both unsettled and, more subtly, reinstated by ecphrasis. The description freezes the progress of the narrative: Achilles and Aeneas cannot go back to the battlefield – where their aid is urgently needed – before the text has exhausted its verbalisation of the figured shield. But epic poetics works precisely through the tension (meaningfully explored in the Goethe–Schiller discussion on 'epic deferral'[7]) between achieving closure and pursuing fullness of detail. The *Aeneid* is both strongly oriented towards an end, and constituted by the delays, interruptions and diversions that help to put off that desired end.

The immediate effect of the description of the shield is a sense of conspicuous consumption: the practical function of the episode, that of supplying the hero with a divine shield, is disproportionate to the effort expended by the narrator in visualising the work of art. Virgil wittily comments on this disparity when he shows his Cyclopes labouring at the forge, hammering the huge shield into shape and working to a rhythm (8.452–3 *illi inter sese multa vi bracchia tollunt | in numerum*, 'with great force they each raise their arms in measured rhythm') just as the epic poet is labouring at his rhythmic epic lines to shape the forthcoming verbal artwork. The

---

[7] See Heinze Hahn and Schmid (1981) 210–12.

first image on the shield reminds us of this labour of fashioning: the she-wolf is licking the twins into shape (8.634 *corpora fingere lingua*). In fact, when all is said and done, the shield will only briefly resurface as a talismanic, blazing sign (10.261–2, 271) and as a very efficient defensive weapon (10.884, 12.739–41) when the human sword of Turnus is shattered by the divine shield. The effort of Vulcan's team of blacksmiths, who have put off the making of a divine thunderbolt (8.426–32) for this more important task, leads to Aeneas' heroic achievement; of course the *vir* will need *arma* – the challenge has been gigantic, in that Virgil must mobilise Vulcan to create a worthy successor to the shield manufactured for Achilles in *Iliad* 18, the most impressive epic description ever.

There is an economic exchange between goal-oriented action and deferral: deferral, and description in particular, can slow down but also intensify the energy of the plot; on the other hand, the apparent inertia of descriptive inserts can be recuperated as a coded implementation of the main narrative. Turnus kills Pallas and we catch a glimpse of the booty, a swordbelt engraved with the slaughter of the Egyptian bridegrooms by their wives the fifty Danaids on their wedding night (10.497–99). The description interrupts a dramatic moment in which Turnus achieves a success that will ultimately determine his own death, as well as the end of the poem. The image functions as an interlude but it also triggers a search for motivation: a plurality of meaningful associations easily suggests itself. For example – and only by way of example – the image of the slaughter is a *nefas* (10.497) and Turnus is putting on responsibility for his action of slaying Pallas; finally he will be killed by Aeneas when Aeneas sees the swordbelt again. Moreover, the story is an Argive myth: Turnus himself is of Argive descent. It is a story of death disrupting a marriage, as befits the fate of both Pallas and Turnus. And some Roman readers could have seen a link between the first owner Pallas, eponymous hero of the Palatine hill, and the Portico of the Danaids recently inaugurated by Augustus in the precinct of the Palatine temple of Apollo; the figurative programme there was presumably associated with ideas of guilt and infernal expiation.

To draw out this last point, Virgil exploits to the full the potential for prefiguration offered by ecphrastic descriptions. The shield is of course a foreshadowing of Roman history, bridging the gap between Aeneas' family and the triumph of Augustus. The parallel vision of the future in Aeneid 6 itself has ecphrastic qualities, and one readily senses that the parade of Roman heroes, whose visible features are identified by Anchises (*aspice* . . .), has something to do with the growing taste for statues and heroic images of the past in Augustan Rome. The ecphrasis in Carthage appears to be merely retrospective, but the context of the poem acts like a powerful spotlight to create effects of foreshadowing. Almost all the images will, in one way or another, be reduplicated or inverted in the second half of the poem. The confrontation of Achilles and Priam (1.487) is a case in point: not only has Aeneas actually seen Priam die (Aeneas appears, precisely, in the role of a viewer at 2.499ff.), but the Homeric confrontation of Achilles and Priam will be replayed, with a difference, in the final scene of the *Aeneid*, when Aeneas, a different Achilles (6.89 *alius Achilles*),[8] kills Turnus as he re-enacts Priam's supplication ('in the name of your old father . . .').

In Virgil's dense epic narrative every descriptive pause opens itself to similar effects; a description like that of a chlamys embroidered with the abduction of Ganymede (5.250–7) might seem to withstand contextual motivation, but the resistance even of this image to narrative functionality yields to rereading: Trojan mythology is linked to the central preoccupation of book 5, continuity with the past, and the eroticism of the story of Jupiter and Ganymede prompts an association with the main love story of the poem, that of Nisus and Euryalus (5.294ff., a few lines after the ecphrasis). This whole range of effects is perfectly familiar to a reader who comes to it from the traditions of modern narrative and from contemporary studies of narrative poetics.

Finally, the problem of 'who views the images?' is intertwined with the problem of 'who tells the story?', and helps the reader to realise the importance of point of view and subjectivity. When the description has a focaliser, that is to say a character in the narrative who views the artifact, the reader needs to be aware that her perception of the images is mediated by the narrative voice, or voices, as well as by the perspective of the focaliser. This complexity cannot be isolated from the more general complexity of Virgilian narrative, and the problem of perceiving individual points of view against the background of a unified authorial vantage point is one familiar to readers and critics of Virgilian epic.

FURTHER READING

General

(Important for the critical approach and wide-ranging discussions and/or for the selection of Greek and Roman materials.) P. Friedlaender, *Johannes von Gaza, Paulus Silentiarius und Prokopios von Gaza* (Leipzig, 1912; repr. Hildesheim, 1962); (see

---

[8] The language of the Sibyl is, unsurprisingly, ambiguous and teasing. She offers to Aeneas a gloomy preview of the second half of the *Aeneid* as a replay of the Trojan war, and in that context the expected reference is to 'a new Achilles', i.e. Turnus as a powerful enemy of the Trojans, but since the normal Latin for this would be *alter Achilles*, while *alius* normally conveys an implication of difference, the prophecy also unfolds a reading of the story as a new but different *Iliad*.

also the new Kleine Pauly s.v. Ekphrasis, by Marco Fantuzzi and Christiane Reitz, forthcoming); W. Bühler, *Die Europa des Moschos*, Wiesbaden 1960; G. Ravenna, 'L'ekphrasis poetica di opere d'arte in latino', *Quaderni Istituto Filologia Latina Padova* 3 (1974) 1–51; A. Perutelli, *La narrazione commentata* (Pisa, 1979); M. Baxandall, *Patterns of Intention* (New Haven, 1985); E. W. Leach, *The Rhetoric of Space* (Princeton, 1988); J. Hollander, 'The Poetics of Ecphrasis', *Word and Image* 4 (1988) 209–18; S. Bartsch, *Decoding the Ancient Novel* (Princeton, 1989); D. Fowler, 'Narrate and describe: the problem of ecphrasis', *Journal of Roman Studies* 81 (1991) 25–35; M. Krieger, *Ekphrasis* (Baltimore and London, 1992); S. Goldhill and R. Osborne, *Art and Text in Ancient Greek Culture* (Cambridge, 1994); A. Laird, 'Sounding out ecphrasis: art and text in Catullus 64', *Journal of Roman Studies* 83 (1993) 18–30; W. Heffernan, *Museum of Words* (Chicago, 1993); J. Elsner, *Art and Text in Roman Culture* (Cambridge, 1996).

Specific papers on ecphrastic passages in the Aeneid

R. D. Williams, 'The pictures on Dido's temple', *Classical Quarterly* 10 (1960) 145–51; C. C. Breen, 'The shield of Turnus, the swordbelt of Pallas, and the wolf', *Vergilius* 32 (1986) 63–71; D. Clay, 'The archaeology of the temple to Juno in Carthage', *Classical Philology* 83 (1988) 195–205; R. F. Thomas, 'Virgil's ecphrastic centerpieces', *Harvard Studies in Classical Philology* 87 (1983) 175–84; A. Barchiesi, 'Rappresentazioni del dolore e interpretazione nell'Eneide', *Antike & Abendland* 40 (1994) 109–24; M. C. J. Putnam, 'Virgil's Danaid ecphrasis', *Illinois Classical Studies* 19 (1994) 171–89; *id.*, 'Dido's murals and Virgilian ekphrasis', *Harvard Studies in Classical Philology* (forthcoming).

18

ANDREW LAIRD

Approaching characterisation in Virgil[1]

Scrutiny of character has long been a concern of conventional literary criticism. As a result, the notion of character has come to be ignored or bypassed by critics and theorists who do not want to be conventional. They see the study of characterisation as the haven of connoisseurs. How-ever, characterisation involves a large set of questions which bear on fun-damental issues of textual interpretation. The way we attempt to answer common questions about Virgil's characters will determine – or be deter-mined by – the way we read Virgil's corpus in general.

For instance, a preoccupation with characters as 'types' (e.g. as epic or tragic figures) is often indicative of a generic reading of Virgil's poetry. Alternatively, to regard Virgilian characters as 'individuals' is to presup-pose that his poems function as forms of representation: simply postulat-ing the 'development' of a character like Aeneas involves an essentialised notion of a person which the *Aeneid* would then be supposed to portray. Again, appreciation of Virgil's construction of character could equally require a conception of his poems as forms of expression. In characterising Dido or anyone else, the poet is simultaneously characterising or express-ing himself. Such a view of character could entail a type of rhetorical cri-ticism of Virgil's poetry.

There are of course many other perspectives on character; this brief chapter cannot come anywhere near to providing an exhaustive account of their bearing on the *Eclogues, Georgics* and *Aeneid*. Instead, the first part of this discussion will outline the poetical features of style and narrative technique which contribute to Virgil's psychological characterisation. This

---

[1] I would like to thank an anonymous reader, Susanna Morton Braund, David West and especially the editor for helpful (and sometimes radical) criticisms. I was unable to follow all the advice I received and chose to avoid some issues altogether rather than to treat them inadequately. My purpose here is only to show the importance of two broader concerns (audience response to Virgil and the discursive nature of Virgil's texts) for discussions about characterisation – hence the genuinely apologetic title.

outline at least has the advantage of being pertinent to a variety of current conceptions of character and text. The second part of this chapter will consider the role audience response has – in terms of reception, intertextuality and ideology – in determining Virgil's characterisation.

I Characterisation as relation between poet and character

The fourth-century commentary on Virgil attributed to Servius offers a useful account of the various styles adopted in the *Eclogues*:[2]

> We have established then that there are these three styles of expression (*characteres dicendi*): one in which only the poet speaks, as is the case in three books of the *Georgics*; another dramatic one in which the poet nowhere speaks, as is the case in comedies and tragedies; the third is mixed, as is the case in the *Aeneid*: for there both the poet (*poeta*) and the personages he introduces (*introductae personae*) speak. All these styles (*characteres*) are suitable for bucolic verse as the book of *Eclogues* well shows. For it has one poem in which only the poet speaks, 'Muses of Sicily, let us sing of somewhat greater things' [Eclogue 4]. It has a mixed one, 'Arethusa, grant me this final endeavour' [Eclogue 10] – for in this poem he brings in Gallus as a speaker. The collection also employs the dramatic form as in the first eclogue and again in this third one . . .[3]

Servius gives us a model for understanding the relation between the poet and his characters (*introductae personae*) for each of Virgil's works. This actually provides a framework for understanding characterisation in formalist terms.[4] There are three types of characterisation to be drawn from Servius' model. Characters can be constituted (i) entirely by their thoughts or words in direct discourse (cf. *dramatis personae* in plays, or the speakers in Eclogue 3); (ii) by the poet's account of their attributes, thoughts or words in indirect discourse; and finally (iii) by a combination of their own words in direct discourse with the poet's account. This combination is obviously the way in which characterisation is most conspicuous in Virgil's narratival poetry: Eclogue 10, the Aristaeus epyllion in *Georgics* Book 4, and the *Aeneid*.

In addition to these three types of characterisation, it is worth noting that speakers portray *each other* in their words, as well as themselves. Consider the remarks of Evander to Aeneas about Mezentius in *Aeneid* 8.483–8, in which we are told he used to kill people by binding them to dead bodies.

---

[2] 'Servius' here refers to the Servian corpus as a whole. See Murgia (1975) for the tradition and Lazzarini (1989) for Servius' poetics.

[3] Servius on *Eclogues* 3.1 in Thilo and Hagen (1878–1902) 29.

[4] Compare (for example) Voloshinov (1926).

Such a testimony, though it comes from the mouth of Evander, says a great deal to the audience about what Mezentius is like, well before the tyrant has any sustained involvement in the action of the poem. Another lengthier example of one character constructing another who has yet to 'appear' is the account of Dido given by Venus to Aeneas in *Aeneid* 1.340–68.

In the rest of this section I shall concentrate on the second type of characterisation – that engineered by the poet's voice – rather than on the direct discourse of characters. Characters' own spoken words and thoughts have already received plenty of attention from critics[5] – yet most characters in Virgilian narrative are constituted by a combination of the poet's voice with the words of introduced speakers.

At the most basic level, Virgil can constitute or develop character simply by introducing a personage,[6] and explicitly mentioning personal attributes. He can directly state what a personage is like. In the *Aeneid*, epic epithets can accomplish this, e.g. *pius Aeneas* ('pious Aeneas'), *infelix Dido* ('unhappy Dido'). He can provide leading background information about a personage, e.g. the biographical sketch of Latinus in *Aeneid* 7.45–106 (cf. 1.340–68 and 8.483–8 discussed above).[7] The poet can also constitute character in a straightforward manner simply by reporting the speech of personages where the rendering is clearly in his own voice (e.g. *Georgics* 4.359–60, *alta iubet discedere late* | *flumina, qua iuvenis gressus inferret*, 'Cyrene ordered the waters to go wide apart along the route the young man would go'). An objection to the consideration of these 'techniques' in Virgil could be made on the grounds that such 'techniques' are employed by narrators all the time, and that proper characterisation should be regarded as a skill, and not as an inevitability. In response to this one could invoke Aristotle's conception of character (*ethos*) as both fact and value.[8]

However that may be, Virgil has other techniques of characterisation which are certainly more remarkable, because they are more psychological and because they are more particular to Virgil. The poet also constitutes or develops character by describing a personage's moods and emotions.

---

[5] E.g. Pöschl (1962); Heinze (1993); Highet (1972). Although Mackie (1988) does give attention to indirect discourse, he clearly privileges passages of direct discourse. Perutelli (1979a) and Fowler (1990) thoroughly examine narrative techniques which pertain to the second type of characterisation discussed here.

[6] The term 'personage' will designate *dramatis personae* (whether one or more) in the most basic sense. Cf. Bal (1985) 79: 'an actor is a structural position, while a character is a complex semantic unit'. My 'personage' corresponds (more or less) to Bal's 'actor'. I avoid 'person' because the word connotes more complex anthropological and philosophical categories.

[7] *Pace* Heinze (1993), 299.

[8] Aristotle, *Poetics* 1450a, 1454a and Halliwell (1987) *ad loc.*

He can tell us something about a personage which could not be gleaned from his or her actions or behaviour. For example, in Book 1 of the *Aeneid*, the narrator says of Aeneas' attempt to boost the morale of the Trojans (1.198–207):

> Talia voce refert curisque ingentibus aeger
> spem vultu simulat, premit altum corde dolorem.   (1.208–9)

> This was what he said out loud, but he was sickened by his huge troubles, as he put on a hopeful face and suppressed the grief that was deep in his heart.

These verses remind us that speeches in direct discourse do not necessarily convey all or any of a speaker's inner sentiments. This seems obvious enough, but it is often forgotten. Scholarly discussions of (e.g.) Aeneas' reply (4.333–61) to Dido after she has begged him not to leave Carthage frequently disregard the possibility that Aeneas is not giving full expression to his true feelings.[9]

Elaborate imagery can also be used to describe mental processes:

> At regina gravi iamdudum saucia cura
> vulnus alit venis et caeco carpitur igni.
> multa viri virtus animo multusque recursat
> gentis honos; haerent infixi pectore vultus
> verbaque nec placidam membris dat cura quietem.   (4.1–5)

> But the queen, afflicted for some time by a heavy care, nurtures the wound in her veins and is scorched by an unseen fire. The great courage of the man, the great nobility of his race coursed again and again through her mind; his face is fixed in her heart and his words cling to her, and the care deprives her limbs of peaceful sleep.

In these verses, Dido's psychological state is described in quasi-*physiological* terms: a sequence of metaphors evoking injury, disease and disturbed emotions interweaves incorporeal ideas with parts of Dido's body, so that material and conceptual notions begin to change places; Aeneas' features are almost abstracted, the *cura* in 4.5 becomes an almost concrete entity. The narrative is confusing in conveying Dido's confusion. Passages like these employ a kind of anatomic description to portray a character's psychology.

Virgil can also achieve psychological characterisation by constructing an outlook on the story which is not consistent with his own viewpoint, but which is consistent with the viewpoint of an agent in the story. This is a

---

[9] E.g. Mackie (1988) 86–8 following Page (1894) xviii. Cairns (1989) 52–4 is more balanced. Feeney (1983) 204–19 is an excellent treatment.

subtle and economic way of developing character by suggesting the attitudes or opinions of a particular individual or group.[10] An example of 'focalisation' can be found in *Aeneid* 4.281 – after Mercury has ordered Aeneas to leave Carthage:

> At vero Aeneas aspectu obmutuit amens,
> arrectaeque horrore comae et vox faucibus haesit.
> ardet abire fuga dulcisque relinquere terras,
> attonitus tanto monitu imperioque deorum.　　(4.279–82)

But Aeneas was dumbstruck and aghast at the apparition. His hair bristled with horror and his voice stuck in his throat. He burns to flee away and leave the sweet lands, overwhelmed both by so mighty a warning and the gods' power.

The lands of Carthage are 'sweet' (*dulcis*) in Aeneas' point of view: they would not be so to the poet, nor to an audience of patriotic Romans. *Abire fuga* ('to flee away') is not consistent with other narratorial references to the Trojans' grand journey to Italy. This too must be the way Aeneas sees it. Aeneas' state of mind is conveyed without explicit comment by the narrator or by the character himself.

There is a further order of psychological characterisation. Specific thoughts can be *rendered*, but still without actually allowing the personage being characterised to speak in place of the poet-narrator. An example of this device (free indirect discourse or 'FID') is to be found in *Aeneid* Book 4, directly after the verses previously quoted:

> heu quid agat? quo nunc reginam ambire furentem
> audeat adfatu? quae prima exordia sumat?　　(4.283–4)

Oh what should he do? With what words is he now to dare approach the queen in her rage? What should he choose as his opening words?

These rhetorical questions, though in the third person, none the less give the impression of a modification of the poet's voice. FID perhaps affords the most intimate technique of characterisation. In Virgilian narrative, FID is only slightly less common than soliloquies in direct discourse. However, identifying FID in Virgil is not always a straightforward matter. Consider these verses from *Georgics* 4 which present Orpheus' consternation once he realises he has lost Eurydice to the Underworld for ever:

> quid faceret? quo se rapta bis coniuge ferret?
> quo fletu Manis, quae numina voce moveret?
> illa quidem Stygia nabat iam frigida cumba.　　(G.4.504–6)

---

[10] See Genette (1980); de Jong (1987); Fowler (1990) and below p. 266.

What was he to do? Where could he go now his wife was snatched aw⌐
second time? With what lament could he move the Shades and what divin⌐
powers could he move with his voice? Indeed already cold she was drifting
away in a Stygian bark.

This final sentence could be a thought attributable to Orpheus: presented
in FID (like the rhetorical questions prior to it). Or it could be a perception focalised through Orpheus. Or again it could be the poet's discourse
entirely. These fine distinctions have varying implications for Virgil's characterisation. Verse 506 might continue to characterise Orpheus (by presenting his thoughts and perceptions). If not, it characterises the poet, however
trivially. Problems of interpretation like this indicate the constitutive role
readers and audiences have in determining characterisation. This will be
the concern of the remaining part of this chapter.

II Characterisation as relation between text and audience

When the distinction was first made in antiquity between texts in direct
speech, texts in the poet's own voice, and a mixture of the two (in Plato's
Republic 394b–c), it was applied to *all* kinds of narrative. Socrates' purpose in forming that distinction was to condemn mimetic poets, particularly
dramatists, who did not speak in their own voice and used direct discourse
to 'pretend' to be other people. Servius, however, applies the distinction to
Virgil's *œuvre* positively, to highlight the poet's dexterity. Servius' terminology constantly refers to the poet as a *speaker*. Virgil is not a colourless,
undetectable, neutral narrator but himself a character who is always present,
addressing his audience. Thus Virgil's constructed characters do not have
an independent *a priori* existence. They are *introductae personae* who are
conjured up by the poet.[11] Thus they also serve to characterise him. On at
least one occasion, a character's bearing on the poet is explicitly signalled.[12]

Our understanding of characters depends on our understanding of the
poet who presents them and vice versa. This is why the examination of
character and characterisation in literature has always been a matter of
opinion. We may be able to analyse the relation between poet and character in the ways I have already demonstrated, but a reader or audience
has to be involved for that relation to make sense. It is worth specifying
some areas in which interpretation has an inevitable though varying role
in the formation of character. An obvious one is characterisation achieved

[11] The issue of logical closure rears its head as soon as we think about character in any
depth. See Deutsch (1985), Fowler (1989).

[12] E.g. Hardie (1986) 59 on *Aen.* 9.774–9.

words, deeds and behaviour of personages. It is imposs-
comprehend these, let alone give an account of them,
some form of evaluation. The description of Aeneas'
a perfect paradigm:

icens ferrum adverso sub pectore condit
fervidus; ast illi solvuntur frigore membra
vitaque cum gemitu fugit indignata sub umbras.   (12.950–2)

Saying this he plunged the steel right into his opponent's breast, seething
with rage as he was. Turnus' limbs were dissolved in cold, and his life, with
a groan, fled indignantly down to the shades.

In these very final verses of the *Aeneid*, the poet-narrator neither explicitly praises nor explicitly blames Aeneas' action. Much has been made of
Virgil's use of the word *fervidus* ('seething with rage'). The word is used
in several contexts where intemperate behaviour is displayed, particularly
in the latter part of the poem. The word's deployment here has therefore
been seen as a slur on Aeneas: he lacks the self-control some readers expect
from him either as a Stoic role model or as a prototype of Augustan clemency (cf. Anchises' prescription to Aeneas in *Aeneid* 6.851–3). Yet the
qualities signified by *fervidus* would not be inappropriate for a Homeric
hero like Achilles or even Hector, whom Aeneas has himself presented to
his own son as an *exemplum* (*Aen.* 12.440). In the end, we can only make
of the word *fervidus* what we will. But what we make of it shapes not only
our opinion, but also our fundamental *perception* of Aeneas' character.

Responses to Virgil's uses of myth, literary sources, and even nomenclature fundamentally affect readers' constructions of his characters.[13] Recent
theories of intertextuality – which critics have not yet brought to bear on
the problem of character – provide the best framework for understanding
how these 'uses' work. Intertextuality highlights the reader's role in attributing qualities to a text – qualities (such as allusion) which were previously
thought to be objective and indisputable properties of the text-in-itself.
There are various means by which intertextuality can determine the formation of character in Virgil.

Personages in Virgil's poetry are bound to be fleshed out in different
ways by different readers in different times. Figures like Jupiter, Juno, Venus,
Hercules and Orpheus abound in ancient texts and later literary cultures.

---

[13] Names are not only suggestive because they are famous. Nomenclature can also be
intertextual by inviting allegorical or etymological interpretation, like Cacus (*kakos* in
Greek = 'bad'), Amata (= 'once loved' in Latin, cf. Lyne (1987) 14ff.). Early commentators
offer numerous glosses of characters' names. See Maltby (1991). Heinze (1993) 299 among
others has noted the 'late naming of names' as a narrative ploy in both Virgil and Homer.

They come to be perceived as self-standing, rather in the way that historical figures like Gallus (Eclogue 10) and Marcellus (*Aeneid* 6) are perceived. This is what makes us call these figures 'mythological': they transcend their portrayals in any one author. In fact none of these mythological or historical figures are self-standing: such personages will always be constructed by readers from any number of sources. One might consider the presentation of Polyphemus in *Aeneid* Book 3 as an example. Examining Virgil's particular characterisation of Polyphemus in the *Aeneid* in relation to Homer's Polyphemus in *Odyssey* Book 9 might at first appear to be a straightforward business. But the results of such an examination could never claim any kind of demonstrative status because they could never be decisive. For instance, constructions of Polyphemus derived from a response to Virgil's portrayal will influence an account of Virgil's transformation of Homer's portrayal. Thus, the degrees of communality between *Aeneid* 3 and *Odyssey* 9 can never be precisely assessed – any attempt to establish 'properly' or 'scientifically' their significance would be deeply misconceived.

Such complexities are most evident in the case of a major personage like Dido. Pease's erudite introduction to his commentary on *Aeneid* Book 4 assembles a remarkable number of 'sources' for Dido: Homer's Circe, Calypso and Nausicaa; Medea in Euripides, Apollonius and Varro Atacinus; Apollonius' Hypsipele; Catullus' Ariadne; Timaeus' account of Elissa preserved in Polyaenus; as well as historical accounts of Cleopatra and even Scribonia (the wife whom Augustus divorced).[14] Varying combinations and permutations of these figures provide filters and frames for all kinds of character construction. Readers, according to their ideological situation, will configure them in different ways.

As well as bearing on the identity of characters, consideration of Virgilian intertextuality also shows how the feelings and attributes of characters are affected by readers' determinations. Dido's expression of her loss of orientation followed by an attempt to recollect herself, after Aeneas has left Carthage, in *Aeneid* 4.596–7 is an example:

> infelix Dido, nunc te facta impia tangunt?
> tum decuit, cum sceptra dabas ...

> Unhappy Dido, are your impious deeds now affecting you? Once everything was fine when you used to hand out your sceptres ...

Dido is the only personage in the *Aeneid* to address herself by name. Homer's characters never address themselves in the second person, let alone by name.[15] But the device is found in a poem by Catullus:

---

[14] Pease (1935) 11–29. [15] Otter (1914).

> Miser Catulle, desinas ineptire,
> et quod vides perisse perditum ducas.
> fulsere quondam candidi tibi soles,
> cum ventitabas quo puella ducebat.　　　　(8.1–4)

Wretched Catullus, you should stop being silly, and consider as lost what you see has perished. Once suns shone brightly when you used to go about wherever the girl used to lead you.

The sense, structure and use of tenses in these two passages are clearly similar. Both speakers yielded authority to their former lovers. But as well as enhancing Dido's predicament, this intertext adds something else – it suggests that her association with Aeneas might have been a happy one (and not merely impious).

Descriptions of characters supplied by the poet himself can equally be determined by intertextuality. Some of Virgil's imagery conveniently demonstrates this. Lavinia is a personage to whom no spoken or thought discourse is ascribed at all. But this does not mean her feelings may not be discerned: Oliver Lyne has convincingly shown that the image of her blush and the simile used to develop it (*Aeneid* 12.64–9) evoke other literary portrayals of young virgins in love.[16] A 'further voice' is telling us Lavinia loves Turnus.[17]

Intertextuality also determines characterisation through the field of Virgil's reception in subsequent literary and cultural traditions. This field (i) mediates our responses to the formal techniques of characterisation treated earlier, and (ii) subsumes all the operations of intertextuality I have just discussed. I shall illustrate both principles in order. (These are illustrations, not proofs: characterisation is, again, a matter of opinion.)

(i)　In the English-speaking world the libretto of Purcell's opera *Dido and Aeneas* (1689) by Nahum Tate is certainly better known than the Latin text of Virgil's *Aeneid*. Aeneas' words at the end of Act II resemble *Aeneid* 4.283–4 quoted earlier:

> But ah what language can I try,
> My injured Queen to pacify?

However, this articulation is in direct discourse, where Virgil has FID: the rhetorical question is entirely attributable to Aeneas. Later on, Tate's libretto deviates radically from Virgil by showing Aeneas having a temporary change of heart (Act III, Scene 1). Notwithstanding the expression of Aeneas' sentiments given in the voice of Virgil's narrator, a reader going

---

[16] Lyne (1983a) and (1987) 114–22.　　[17] Lyne (1987) 121.

to *Aeneid* Book 4 from Purcell may well conclude that Virgil's Aeneas could either have or show more feeling.

(ii)   The notion of intertextuality may be opposed by those who seek to defend the unrealisable ideal of reading a text in the spirit in which it was written, and who will divide intertexts (on chronological grounds, and few others) into legitimate and illegitimate sources. None the less if the characters in Virgil have allegorical roles, they are bound to be intertextual with the texts which present the notions these characters are seen to symbolise. Hence Virgilian reception has considerable importance for appreciation of character as an intertextual feature. In his *Exposition of the Content of Virgil according to Moral Philosophy* (sixth century AD), Fulgentius offers this reading of *Aeneid* Book 4:

> Driven on by a storm and mist – symbolising a disturbed mind – Aeneas commits adultery. And when he has dallied for a long time, he gives up his immoral love at the urging of Mercury. Mercury is the god of reason. This symbolises that at the prompting of reason the more mature person breaks the bonds of lust.[18]

Such a characterisation of Mercury is unacceptable to commentators like Pease, who regard 'allegory as quite alien to Virgil's intention' and who see the Christian Fulgentius as the originator of 'excesses' of interpretation. Yet a contemporary scholar, Philip Hardie, is also able to characterise Mercury as 'Logos, Ratio, the unperverted word' by drawing only from *pre*-Virgilian traditions.[19]

At the beginning of this chapter I stated that responses to character in a text and responses to that text as a whole are interdependent. In conclusion it is worth considering the implications of my observations about characterisation for our reading of Virgil as a whole. The first part of this discussion put considerable emphasis on Virgil's more distinctive techniques of psychological characterisation. The *Eclogues*, *Georgics* and *Aeneid* are customarily regarded as three classic examples of three classical genres: bucolic, didactic and epic respectively. Yet some forms of psycho-narration Virgil employs – notably the use of suggestive imagery to convey emotional states, focalisation and FID – are *not* stereotypically 'classical'. They are generally regarded (however misguidedly) as hallmarks of modern, even modernist, writing. This prompts us to re-examine the grounds on which Virgil's works are considered *classical* in the sense of 'canonical' or 'standard'.[20]

---

[18] Translation from Hardison (1974) 74.   [19] Hardie (1986) 278.
[20] On this sense of 'classical', see Friederich (1974) 137 and Wellek (1965).

In showing the extent to which Virgil's readers in different times and climes are involved in shaping his characters and characterisation, the observations in the second part of this chapter are similarly disconcerting for our overall understanding of Virgil. Is any of *Virgil's* own character left by the time we have peeled away centuries of variously informed opinions? However, one inviolable principle ensures that our readings of Virgil's characters, and therefore of Virgil, will not be completely arbitrary. The characters are not self-standing. They cannot escape being understood as agents operating in the temporal sequence of the narratives in which we find them. Purcell's *Dido and Aeneas* illustrates this with a remarkable instance of closure. In her final aria Dido repeats the words:

> Remember me but – ah! – forget my fate!

She is of course asking for the impossible. Were it not for her fate Dido would not be remembered at all. The logic of narrative and the cultural tradition, which delimit Dido's character, have come to enhance her tragedy.

FURTHER READING

General studies (mostly on Aen.)

F. Cairns, *Virgil's Augustan Epic* (Cambridge, 1989), useful throughout; R. Heinze, tr. H. Harvey, D. Harvey and F. Robertson, *Virgil's Epic Technique* (Bristol, 1993); R. O. A. M. Lyne, *Further Voices in Vergil's Aeneid* (Oxford, 1987); C. J. Mackie, *The Characterisation of Aeneas* (Edinburgh, 1988); B. Otis, *Virgil: A Study of Civilised Poetry* (Oxford, 1964) (193ff. on G. 4).

Literary technique and characterisation in Virgil

G. B. Conte, *The Rhetoric of Imitation* (Ithaca, 1986), esp. 130–40 (on G. 4), 141–84 (on the *Aen.*); D. Feeney, 'The taciturnity of Aeneas', *Classical Quarterly* 33 (1983) 204–19; D. P. Fowler, 'Deviant focalization in Vergil's *Aeneid*', *Proceedings of the Cambridge Philological Society* n.s. 36 (1990) 42–63; A. Perutelli, 'Registri narrativi e il stilo indiretto libero in Virgilio', *Materiali e Discussioni* 3 (1979) 69–83 and 'L'episodio di Aristeo nelle *Georgiche*: structura e technica narrativa', *Materiali e Discussioni* 4 (1980) 59–76.

Virgil's characters and philosophy/ideology

Again Cairns, *Virgil's Augustan Epic, passim*; P. Hardie, *Virgil's Aeneid: Cosmos and Imperium* (Oxford, 1986) *passim*; A. S. Pease, ed., *P. Vergili Maronis Aeneidos Liber Quartus* (Harvard, 1935) 36–8, 42–3 (on Dido and Aeneas as *exempla* of Epicurean and Stoic values respectively – compare 'The intellectual physiognomy in characterisation', in G. Lucács, *Writer and Critic* (London, 1978) 149–88); C. Gill, ed., *The Person and the Human Mind: Essays in Ancient and Modern Philosophy* (Oxford, 1991).

Virgil's characters in later authors

Useful insights on Virgilian characterisation can be obtained from considering literary parody and elaboration: e.g. Ovid, *Metamorphoses* Books 13–14, *Fasti*, *Heroides*; the *Culex*; Fulgentius (translated in O. B. Hardison, ed., *Medieval Literary Criticism* (London, 1974) 69–80); Dante's presentation of Virgilian character in the *Commedia*; Scarron's seventeenth-century parody *Le Virgile Travesti*, ed. J. Serroy (Paris, 1988). A. La Penna, 'Fra Tersite e Drance: Note sulla Fortuna di un personaggio Virgiliano', in R. Chevallier, ed., *Présence de Virgile* (Paris, 1978) 347–66 investigates a specific character through reception.

General reading on characterisation

M. Bal, *Narratology: Introduction to the Theory of Narrative* (Toronto, 1985) 79–93 'From actors to characters' provides an important narratological 'anatomy' of character – the accounts of 'actors' 25–37, focalisation 100–14, and speech presentation 134–43, are also useful; B. Hochman, *Character in Literature* (Ithaca, 1985); D. Cohn, *Transparent Minds: Narrative Modes for Presenting Consciousness in Fiction* (Princeton, 1978); E. M. Forster, *Aspects of the Novel* (repr. Harmondsworth, 1976) 54–84 (on 'People'). A. Sinfield, *Faultlines: Cultural Materialism and the Politics of Dissident Reading* (Oxford, 1992) 52–79 challenges traditional humanist conceptions of character in Shakespeare and refers to a number of feminist and post-structuralist discussions.

Characterisation and the concept of 'person'

P. Heuzé, *L'image du corps dans l'œuvre de Virgile* (Collection de l'Ecole Française de Rome 36, 1985) deals thoroughly with the neglected role of the body and gesture in constituting Virgilian character; M. Carrithers, S. Collins and S. Lukes, eds., *The Category of the Person: Anthropology, Philosophy, History* (Cambridge, 1985) esp. Mauss on the Latin *persona* 13–19 and Momigliano's response 83–92.

19

ELLEN OLIENSIS

Sons and lovers: sexuality and gender in Virgil's poetry

One way or another, sexuality has always been a topic of interest to Virgil's readers. In his life of the poet, Suetonius reports that Virgil inclined toward the love of boys and that he addressed a favourite named Alexander under the name 'Alexis' in the Second Eclogue; Martial pretends to believe that it was this rosy-lipped young slave who excited the poet to compose his *Aeneid* (Mart. 8.5.11–20). It is only in the past two decades, however, that scholarly interest has begun to focus on the topic of 'sexuality and gender' in antiquity. The 'and' here covers a whole range of questions – for example, how is sexual difference represented in antiquity, how is it implicated with other kinds of socially constructed differences, is 'sexuality' a discrete concept or is it still awaiting its 'invention'? I will begin this essay by surveying Virgil's *Eclogues* (with side-glances at the *Aeneid*) to see what light they can shed on some of these issues. I will then turn to my central project, which is to sketch some of the ways sexual and gender differences help to articulate Virgil's poetry.

Symmetries and dissymmetries

Virgil's first full-length portrait of a lover privileges a homoerotic attachment. The Corydon of Eclogue 2 is modelled on the Cyclops of Theocritus' Eleventh Idyll; but whereas Theocritus' Cyclops is in love with the nymph Galatea, Virgil's country bumpkin dotes on the beautiful boy Alexis, a fellow slave who is his 'master's toy' (*delicias domini*, *Ecl.* 2.2). This portrait, as we have seen, was accorded special authority by ancient readers. Whatever its biographical resonance, it is true that the complaint of Virgil's passionate shepherd stands at the origin of a rich tradition of homoerotic pastoral.[1] Parallel to this tradition there develop readings that seek to circumscribe or erase the homoerotic content of the poem (the Fourth or

---

[1] E.g. Walt Whitman's aptly-entitled 'Calamus' poems (where *calamus* is at once the pastoral and the male sexual instrument).

'Messianic' Eclogue may have helped to assure the survival of Virgil's works, but the Second Eclogue posed significant problems to Virgil's Christian readers).[2] To this day, the presumption of heterosexuality is so strong that students of Latin regularly mistake 'Alexis' as a girl's name, even though the very first word of the eclogue, *formosum* (the masculine form of the erotically charged adjective 'lovely'), unambiguously signals that Alexis is a boy, a kind of male counterpart to the 'lovely Amaryllis' celebrated in the First Eclogue (*formosam ... Amaryllida, Ecl.* 1.5).

Still, it is worth noting that Virgil's Corydon (like Suetonius' Virgil, who was rumoured to have had an affair with a woman named Plotia) is not exclusively a lover of boys; one of Corydon's complaints identifies Alexis as the latest episode in an erotic history that includes a girl as well as a boy: 'wouldn't it have been better to endure Amaryllis' bitter temper and proud disdain, better [to love] Menalcas?' (*nonne fuit satius tristis Amaryllidis iras | atque superba pati fastidia? nonne Menalcan?, Ecl.* 2.14–15). A similar indifference to gender (this time with a heterosexual amour in the foreground – Gallus is in love with Lycoris) is manifest in Eclogue 10, where the obligatory love-interest of Gallus' Arcadian reverie may be supplied with equal facility by 'Phyllis or Amyntas' (*sive mihi Phyllis sive esset Amyntas*, 37). Again, in the singing contest of Eclogue 3, Damoetas celebrates Galatea, and Menalcas answers with praises of Amyntas; and while the gender of the beloved is not irrelevant here (for example, Amyntas' passion for hunting would be unseemly in Galatea), this difference is largely submerged in the symmetrical design of the contest, which invites us to compare not couples but couplets.

In this regard, Virgil's *Eclogues* conform to the conventions of Latin love poetry and also to the mores of significant segments of Roman society in the first century BC. Catullus sends kiss-laden poems to Juventius as well as Lesbia, Tibullus sighs for Marathus as well as Delia, and Horace accuses himself with perfect impartiality of loving 'a thousand boys, a thousand girls' (*mille puellarum, puerorum mille furores, Sat.* 2.3.325); Maecenas is reputed to have been infatuated with the actor Bathyllus, Cicero to have demanded kisses of his slave Tiro, and Catiline to have debauched (among numerous others) one Tongilius – and Maecenas, Cicero, and Catiline were all married men.[3] In the next century, Quintilian will lament that

---

[2] E.g. Erasmus' sanitised reading (designed to demonstrate how a clever teacher can make use even of potentially corrupting texts) of Eclogue 2 in *De Ratione Studii* and Spenser's heterosexual 'correction' of Virgil (with E. K.'s moralising commentary) in the January eclogue of *The Shepheardes Calendar*; see Goldberg (1992) 63–6.

[3] Cat. 48, 99; Tibull. 1.4.81–2; Tac. *Ann.* 1.54 (on Maecenas and Bathyllus); Pliny, *Ep.* 7.4 (on Cicero and Tiro); Cic. *Cat.* 2.4 (on Catiline and Tongilius). See further the material collected and discussed by Lilja (1983).

Roman children learn immorality at home, where they are exposed to 'our mistresses and our male concubines' (*nostras amicas, nostros concubinos, Inst.* 1.2.8); it is the father's sexual indulgence, not his sexual orientation, that Quintilian finds reprehensible. Our culture tends to divide the sexual universe according to the preferred gender of an individual's sexual partners – a scheme that yields heterosexuals, homosexuals, and bisexuals. In Virgil's Rome, however, what counted more was the role an individual took in sexual intercourse: 'penetrating' or 'penetrated', 'active' or 'passive', 'masculine' or 'feminine'. Sexual intercourse was articulated in terms of social hierarchies, and the 'senior' partner (older, higher-status, male) was expected to maintain and enact his seniority in bed. So long as Gallus played the man's part, that is, there would be nothing particularly scandalous about his enjoying an Amyntas as well as a Phyllis.[4]

Women, freedmen, and slaves were characterised by their penetrability; a freeborn Roman man who allowed himself to be penetrated was thereby degraded to their level. There was undoubtedly something that could be termed 'homophobia' in Rome, but it attached not to men who desired men but to men who acted like women, and in particular to men who chose 'passivity', 'enduring the woman's role' (*viri muliebria pati*), in Sallust's suggestive phrase (Sall. *Cat.* 13.3).[5] This unmanning 'passivity' could afflict either the spirit or the body or both; a man who succumbed to his passions – a man who devoted himself to satisfying the demands of his body – was 'soft', like the man who succumbed, in bed or on the battlefield, to another man. Hence the apparently paradoxical figure (to modern eyes) of the effeminate adulterer,[6] a figure epitomised in the classical tradition by Paris, the Trojan shepherd whose adulterous passions launched the Trojan war. Within the *Aeneid*, enraged rivals will often compare the epic's hero to his effeminate cousin, and with some warrant: both Paris and Aeneas come from the luxurious east, steal other men's brides, and enjoy the special favour of Venus. The dissonance between Aeneas' manly character and his suspiciously effeminate role contributes to the peculiar texture of his characterisation in the *Aeneid*.

The *Eclogues* dramatise every level of effeminate 'passivity'. The Second Eclogue ends when the passionate Corydon masters himself, turning from the absent beloved to a censorious self-apostrophe: 'Ah, Corydon, Corydon, what madness has taken hold of you! The half-pruned vine awaits you on

---

[4] This paragraph simplifies the ongoing debate surrounding Roman sexuality, on which see the items listed below under 'Further reading'.

[5] Cf. the Petronian phrase *muliebris patientia* (*Sat.* 9, 25); on this class of men, see Richlin (1993).

[6] See Edwards (1993) ch. 2.

the elm' (*Ecl.* 2.69–70). Corydon thus furnishes the answer to his purportedly rhetorical question, 'What limit can be set on love?' (*quis enim modus adsit amori*, 68), by himself setting a limit on his passion and on the poem. In the exchange of rustic insults that precedes the singing contest of Eclogue 3, Menalcas charges Damoetas with theft, and Damoetas replies by accusing Menalcas of being something less than a man (*Ecl.* 3.7–8): 'You ought to go easy on insulting *men* that way, remember! I know who [did] you while the goats looked on sideways' (*qui te transversa tuentibus hircis*). Grammatical and sexual categories mesh here perfectly. Although Damoetas leaves out the verb, the juxtaposition of subjective *qui* and objective *te* makes his jibe sufficiently clear: Menalcas is not a man but a boy, a *puer*, the passive and penetrated object of another man's desire. Let me underscore that what Damoetas' accusation targets is Menalcas' adoption of the object-position in sexual intercourse – not his 'homosexual' inclinations as manifested in his attachment to Amyntas. Indeed, far from confirming his 'homosexuality', Menalcas' subsequent allusions to Amyntas may be taken to refute Damoetas' accusation – as if to say 'ask Amyntas if I'm a boy or a man!' As the two shift from slinging insults to exchanging couplets, sexual parity is restored; *puella* and *puer* implicitly confirm the virile status of their respective lovers.[7]

On the other hand, while boys and girls may furnish equivalent erotic objects, they occupy different places in Roman culture. If we wanted to recast the Second Eclogue with a female beloved in place of Corydon's Alexis, for example, we would have to come up with something to replace the poem's central lines, where Corydon entices Alexis with the promise of music: 'Together with me in the forest you'll sing like Pan' (*mecum una in silvis imitabere Pana canendo*, 31). 'I have a pipe that Damoetas gave me', Corydon goes on to boast, 'saying with his dying breath "This now has you for its second [owner]"' (*et dixit moriens: 'te nunc habet ista secundum'*, 38). In this generational model, Corydon proposes to bestow on Alexis the musical and sexual instruction he himself received as a boy from Damoetas.[8] But the model is strictly pederastic. Girls are not presented with panpipes, for the good reason that this musical instrument is itself a girl – a transformation of Syrinx, Pan's elusive beloved. A *formosus puer* may grow up to be a pastoral singer who exchanges songs with his fellow shepherds; not so with a *formosa puella*.

In the world of Virgilian pastoral, girls are not singers; they do not perform; and while they are sometimes quoted, we never hear them speak.

---

[7] In Theoc. *Id.* 5 (Virgil's primary model here), parity is less readily restored, since the first singer puts himself in the position of Virgil's unspecified *qui*.

[8] Klein (1978) 9.

This pastoral (and thoroughly traditional) bias is encapsulated in Gallus' gender-specific fantasy of 'Phyllis weaving garlands, Amyntas singing' (*serta mihi Phyllis legeret, cantaret Amyntas, Ecl.* 10.41). When Silenus ransoms himself in the Sixth Eclogue, he offers his captors divergent gifts – for the boys, the knowledge of song; for the nymph Aegle, carnal knowledge (*carmina quae vultis cognoscite; carmina vobis,* | *huic aliud mercedis erit, Ecl.* 6.25–6). Aegle is not part of the poetic exchange; her 'payment' will take place offstage. The exclusion is further illustrated by Virgil's variation on Theocritus' Idyll 2 in Eclogue 8: whereas Theocritus brings the bewitching Simaetha directly before us, Virgil substitutes a masculine singer, the shepherd Alphesiboeus, who impersonates a love-stricken girl for the occasion.

In fact the exclusion of women from poetic intercourse might be termed the enabling exclusion of Virgilian pastoral. As the First Eclogue opens, Meliboeus discovers Tityrus 'reclining beneath the mantle of a spreading beech' (*patulae recubans sub tegmine fagi,* 1), 'teach[ing] the woods to re-echo "lovely Amaryllis"' (*formosam resonare doces Amaryllida silvas,* 5). The familiar scenario of the male singer celebrating his disembodied, disempowered female muse (should we imagine that Tityrus has authored a book of poems entitled 'Lovely Amaryllis'?)[9] is soon complicated, however. It turns out that Amaryllis is not only a poetic pretext but a good housekeeper – a marked improvement, according to Tityrus, over the profligate Galatea, under whose regime he never managed to make any money. It was only 'after Amaryllis took me, and Galatea let me go' (*postquam nos Amaryllis habet, Galatea reliquit,* 30), that he succeeded in saving enough to purchase his freedom. Tityrus thus owes his freedom not only to the godlike young man in the city but also to his frugal Amaryllis; it is because Amaryllis knows how to run a household that Tityrus can spend his time teaching the woods to echo her name. A similar distribution of roles underlies Meliboeus' dilemma in Eclogue 7:

> quid facerem? neque ego Alcippen nec Phyllida habebam
> depulsos a lacte domi quae clauderet agnos,
> et certamen erat, Corydon cum Thyrside, magnum. (*Ecl.* 7.14–16)

> What was I to do? I had no Alcippe or Phyllis
> at home to pen the new-weaned lambs,
> and here there was a great contest on, Corydon against Thyrsis.

Meliboeus decides to neglect his duties and attend the contest. But what should interest us here is the role played by women in the shepherd's domestic economy. Men can enjoy poetry with a clear conscience so long as there are women available to take care of the home. Let us note that

---

[9] On this paradigm see Wyke (1987).

the distinction between male and female here has partially displaced the (structurally homologous) distinction between free and slave. The shepherd-slaves whose labour supports their masters' leisure turn themselves into local masters by identifying slave-women with the subordinate instrumentality that is their common lot.

The paradigm is confirmed by its remarkable inversion in Book 8 of the *Aeneid*, where Venus seduces her husband Vulcan into supplying armour for her son (her son by her lover Anchises, not by Vulcan!). 'Chained fast by eternal love' (*aeterno . . . devinctus amore*, *Aen.* 8.394), Vulcan accedes to her request and then falls into her embrace. He rises betimes to do her bidding – at the hour, Virgil tells us, when a weaving woman stirs up the fire and rouses her servants to their spinning, all for the purpose of 'keeping her husband's bed chaste and rearing her little sons' (*castum ut servare cubile | coniugis et possit parvos educere natos*, 412–13). The ironies multiply. The scene most obviously recalls Thetis' embassy to Hephaestus in *Iliad* 18, but it also bears traces of another Homeric episode featuring the god of fire – the story of how the lovers Aphrodite and Ares were trapped in the 'unbreakable chains' forged by Hephaestus (Hom. *Od.* 8.266–99). But in the Virgilian scene it is the faithful husband, not the adulterous wife, who is 'chained'. And it is conscientious Vulcan, not inconstant Venus, who plays the part of the dutiful housewife.

The opposition between masterful leisure and servile labour complicates the opposition between masculine and feminine in the *Eclogues* and also in Virgil's Rome. Activity is central to the traditional conception of Roman *virtus* ('manly excellence'). Leisure can be construed both as a masculine privilege and as a form of slack and effeminate self-indulgence; the self-discipline of a Vulcan is, accordingly, at once servile and manly.[10] This complication is illustrated by a parallel grammatical oddity in the First and Second Eclogues. In the First Eclogue, we might expect Tityrus to say 'after I took Amaryllis, and abandoned Galatea'; instead, he identifies himself as the passive object of which the women dispose (*postquam nos Amaryllis habet, Galatea reliquit*, 30). Again, in the Second Eclogue, we might expect the dying Damoetas to say not 'this pipe has you' (*te nunc habet ista*, 38) but 'this pipe is yours' (i.e. *tu nunc habes istam*). In each case, the feminine instrument in some sense 'possesses' its masculine master.

The *Eclogues* and *Georgics*

The First Eclogue presents two versions of Amaryllis. The beloved who is celebrated by Tityrus as he 'teach[es] the woods to re-echo "lovely

[10] On active *virtus*, see e.g. Sall. *Cat.* 6.5, 7.5; on the paradoxes of *mollitia*, see Kennedy (1993) 38–9.

Amaryllis"' (*formosam resonare doces Amaryllida silvas*, 5) is a figure of plenitude; in this foreshortened exchange, the name is no sooner sounded than it is resonantly returned. Amaryllis the prudent housekeeper, by contrast, is bound up with delayed but more tangible returns – a hand weighed down with coins, the belated achievement of freedom (27–35). These two Amaryllises are emblematic of two strains within Virgilian pastoral, strains which might be termed, somewhat loosely, the pleasurable and the useful, or the pastoral and the georgic. Within the *Eclogues*, the housekeeper's world of labour, economy, and temporality is never far from view. The farmer's fruitful labour provides a contrastive backdrop to Corydon's flower-laden song in the Second Eclogue; it is the sight of cattle dragging the plough home (*aratra iugo referunt suspensa iuvenci*, 66) that recalls the forlorn singer to his senses at the eclogue's end. In the foreground of the *Eclogues*, however, cattle are not yoked to the plough, drawing the straight lines of georgic verse, but free to wander as they graze. Accordingly, when Tityrus celebrates his benefactor, it is for enabling 'my cows to wander, as you see, and me to play what I wish on my rustic pipe' (*meas errare boves, ut cernis, et ipsum | ludere quae vellem calamo . . . agresti*, 9–10). To the undirected activity denoted by verbs such as *errare* and *ludere* there seems to correspond a kind of pastoral sexuality – aberrant, unproductive, non-purposive, playful, pre- or extra-marital. Within this world, the perverse passion that makes Pasiphae wander (both in her mind and over the mountains – see *Ecl.* 6.47, 52), becomes matter for a song that makes 'Fauns and wild animals dance' (*ludere*, 28).

There is little space for this kind of playful errancy within the *Georgics*. Although pastoral matters take up much of *Georgics* 3, which deals with animal husbandry (horses and cattle, sheep and goats), the emphasis is now squarely on production, both of offspring and of marketable goods such as cheese and wool. The roles uneasily conjoined in Tityrus' Amaryllis, of housekeeper and beloved, are now rigorously separated. With her ugly head, enormous neck, shin-length dewlaps, big feet, and shaggy ears (G. 3.52–5), the cow Virgil recommends for breeding purposes is the very inverse of an erotic object – designed exclusively for use, not pleasure. Love is no longer fuel for communal song-making but a dangerous force threatening communal order. Whereas Tityrus could hymn 'lovely Amaryllis' without provoking the competitive rage of Meliboeus, in the *Georgics* two bulls lock horns in fierce battle over a 'lovely heifer' (*formosa iuvenca*, G. 3.219 – a passage that will be recalled in a simile that decorates the duel of Aeneas and Turnus, rivals for the hand of Lavinia, near the end of the *Aeneid*). The excessive heat of sexual passion may produce pastoral poetry, but it is inimical to georgic productivity. The best way to make your animals strong is to keep them chaste (*non ulla magis viris industria firmat | quam Venerem et caeci stimulos avertere amoris*, G. 3.209–10). Bulls should be isolated, since 'the sight of a female wears away their strength bit by bit, and burns them' (*carpit enim viris paulatim uritque videndo | femina*, 215–16). This devouring passion finds its external equivalent in the fiery plague (*aestu*, 479; *ignea*, 482) that supplies Book 3's grim finale.[11] Virgil's closing image is of the contaminated hides and rotting fleeces of the plague-ridden animals, a deadly 'clothing' (*invisos . . . amictus*, 563) that, like the legendary poison-soaked garments wielded by Medea and Deianeira, consumes in fire all those it touches (*contactos artus sacer ignis edebat*, 566).

This nightmare image of intercourse, contact breeding death, is balanced by the daydream of georgic productivity that concludes Book 2. The scene is notable for the disappearance of women and indeed of sexuality as such, which is displaced by the labour of agriculture. 'The farmer parts the earth with the curved plough' (*agricola incurvo terram dimovit aratro*, G. 2.513), an emblematic gesture that suffices to sustain 'fatherland, small grandchildren, herds of cattle, and deserving bullocks' (*hinc patriam parvosque nepotes | sustinet, hinc armenta boum meritosque iuvencos*, 514–15). It is as if this single seminal gesture completed the farmer's labour; after this, it is not the farmer but 'the year' that is busy 'without rest', yielding its various fruits, both vegetable and animal (*nec requies, quin aut pomis exuberet annus | aut fetu pecorum*, 516–17, etc.). 'Meanwhile', the farmer enjoys the pleasures of a well-ordered home:[12]

> interea dulces pendent circum oscula nati,
> casta pudicitiam servat domus, ubera vaccae
> lactea demittunt, pinguesque in gramine laeto
> inter se adversis luctantur cornibus haedi.   (G. 2.523–6)

> Meanwhile his sweet children cling to his kisses, the chaste home
> guards its purity, cows let down milky udders, fat kids
> on plush grass wrestle in pairs with opposed horns.

No desire complicates these harmonies. Effectively absorbed by the 'chaste house' and the milk-rich cows, emblems of obedient sexuality and maternal abundance, the wife who produced the farmer's 'sweet children' is nowhere to be seen. Even the animal life is carefully contained. Playful kids displace

---

[11] On the various 'fires' of G. 3, see Ross (1987) 185–6.

[12] Here *interea* can be taken to mean 'in the interstices of his labours'; but the grammar of the passage, which displaces the farmer from the laborious subject position in lines 516–22, suggests a fantasy of leisure.

the vying bulls that will disrupt Book 3, and the multiple cows, diffusing the problem posed by the individual female (whether 'lovely heifer' or breed cow), image fecundity without sexuality.

The culmination of this imagery comes in the fourth and final book of the *Georgics*, where Virgil turns his attention to bees. These marvellous creatures propagate their kind without 'indulging in intercourse' (*neque concubitu indulgent*, G. 4.198); instead the females 'themselves from leaves and sweet-scented grasses collect their children' (*ipsae e foliis natos, e suavibus herbis | ore legunt*, 200–1), in a golden-age fantasy of propagation as pre-agricultural 'gathering'. The long mythological excursus on the adventures of Aristaeus (primordial bee-keeper) that concludes the book operates according to a kind of poetic and sexual justice. Aristaeus loses his swarm of chaste bees because he fails to control his own sexuality – he pursues Orpheus' bride Eurydice and causes her death; and he gets his bees back when he initiates the bizarre variation on asexual reproduction known as *bougonia*, wherein a bullock, its orifices chastely sealed, is pounded to death, producing a new swarm from its devastated but intact body.[13]

Although it is Aristaeus' wayward desire for Eurydice that launches his troubles, the focus of mistrust here is not masculine but feminine sexuality. When Aristaeus descends into the waters, he returns in two senses to the source: to the home of his mother and to the source of all waters and hence of all life. This source is rewritten, however, as a masculine origin, derived from 'father Oceanus' (G. 4.382), to whom Cyrene bids her son pour a libation. Although it is Cyrene who ultimately tells her son what he actually needs to do to get his bees back, the labour of restoration centres on a consultation of the male deity Proteus, who recounts another descent, Orpheus' descent into the Underworld in quest of his lost Eurydice. The fate of Orpheus suggests, moreover, that the displacement of Cyrene is essential to Aristaeus' success. The first shades Orpheus encounters in the Underworld are the shades of mothers (*matres*, G. 4.475), and in the end he will be torn to pieces by enraged mothers (*matres*, 520; compare the love-maddened mares who rend Glaucus at G. 3.266–8). Orpheus is punished for 'looking back' – both for his inability to endure delay and for his orientation toward the maternal source. In this georgic version of pastoral, repetition emerges as a reproductive failure: Orpheus is a tragic Tityrus, forever sounding the name of his lost beloved. It is Aristaeus, the master of seasonal time, who succeeds in making not words but bees.

---

[13] G. 4.295–314. In the event Aristaeus is instructed to perform a more conventional sacrifice (see G. 4.538–58); agricultural production cannot be divorced, ideologically speaking, from sexual reproduction.

The *Aeneid*

In certain respects, the articulation of gender in the *Aeneid* proceeds along familiar lines: Virgil associates the feminine with unruly passion, the masculine with reasoned (self-) mastery. In narrative terms, this tends to mean that women make trouble and men restore order. The *Aeneid* tells repeated versions of this story, most often with the goddess Juno in the role of instigator. In Book 1, Juno incites Aeolus to unleash the winds in a storm that serves as a figurative as well as strategic expression of her rage; this storm is soon quelled by her brother Neptune, who famously checks both his own emotions and the winds' motions – breaking off in mid-reproach and recalling himself to the business at hand: 'whom I – but it is more important to compose the riled waves' (*quos ego – sed motos praestat componere fluctus*, *Aen.* 1.135). In Book 5, Juno stirs the Trojan matrons to set fire to their ships; Jupiter responds, answering Aeneas' prayers, with a dousing rain. And in Book 7 Juno sends the fury Allecto to stir up a storm of war – a storm that will finally be stilled by Jupiter, with Juno's consent, at the epic's conclusion.

Women are 'primitive' in the *Aeneid* in that they are linked to (maternal, material, narrative) origins. Juno's first words in the epic bespeak this linkage: 'am I to give up what I've begun?' (*men[e] incepto desistere*, *Aen.* 1.37). Indeed, Juno not only speaks of beginnings here, she actually voices the angry first word of Homer's *Iliad*: *menin*, 'wrath'.[14] Women tend to be repeaters, 'mindful' (*memor*) of the past and blind or violently resistant to the future (Dido is only a partial exception to this rule, as we will see). The most painful such repeater is Hector's widow Andromache, whom Aeneas encounters in Book 3 'pouring a libation to the ashes and calling upon the Shades' (the verse surrounds her name with 'ashes' and 'Shades': *cineri Andromache manisque*, *Aen.* 3.303).[15] By contrast, the uncomplicatedly virtuous women of the epic, Aeneas' first Trojan wife and his destined Italian bride, prove their virtue precisely by submitting to the masculine plot of history – Creusa by accepting her relegation to the past, Lavinia by not resisting her exploitation for the future.

Where women tend to cling to origins, men are oriented toward ends. Jupiter makes his first appearance surrounded by the language of 'ultimacy': 'and now it was the end, when Jupiter from the summit of aether . . .' (*et iam finis erat, cum Iuppiter aethere summo*, *Aen.* 1.223).[16] It is father Anchises who shows Aeneas the grand parade of future Romans in the Underworld of Book 6, and it is the forward-thinking Latinus (and not

---

[14] On Juno and beginnings, see Feeney (1991) 138; on Juno's Iliadic word, Levitan (1993) 14.
[15] See Quint (1993) 58–9.   [16] Feeney (1991) 137–8.

Amata – the angry queen forms a marked contrast to the gracious Arete of Homer's *Odyssey*) who welcomes his prospective son-in-law to the shores of Italy. This gendering of origins and ends is underscored by a curious episode of paternal misinterpretation in *Aeneid* 3, where the Trojans receive an oracle from 'father' Apollo (*pater*, 89). Aeneas' descendants are destined to rule in their ancestral land:

> Dardanidae duri, quae vos a stirpe parentum
> prima tulit tellus, eadem vos ubere laeto
> accipiet reduces. Antiquam exquirite matrem.   (*Aen.* 3.94–6)

> Sturdy sons of Dardanus, the land that first bore you
> from the stock of your ancestors will welcome you returning
> at her abundant teat. Seek out your ancient mother.

Aeneas' father takes the 'ancient mother' to be Crete, the original home of the Trojan Magna Mater or Great Mother (*hinc mater cultrix Cybeli*, 111). But upon their arrival in Crete, the Trojans are afflicted with plague. A dream-visitation from the household gods corrects the father's error – Apollo meant not Crete but Italy, the land which begot 'Dardanus and father Iasius, the origin of our race' (*hinc Dardanus ortus | Iasiusque pater, genus a quo principe nostrum*, 167–8). Anchises took the maternal figuration of the oracle too literally. Troy's 'ancient mother' is, it turns out, the province not of mothers but of fathers who father sons; the 'abundant teat' is not a woman's breast but the land's fertility.

The disjunction between metonymic origins and metaphoric ends is essential to Virgil's epic. The new, abstract fatherland cannot accommodate Aeneas' flesh-and-blood father; Anchises will not live into the epic's second, Italian half.[17] But it is above all mothers who must be left behind. At the end of *Aeneid* 2, Aeneas describes how he fled the fires of Troy, taking his father on his shoulders and his son by the hand and instructing his wife to 'follow at a distance' (*longe servet vestigia coniunx*, 711). This troubling arrangement produces a beautiful emblem of paternal hierarchy – Anchises above Aeneas above Ascanius – and also enables Aeneas (or Virgil) to fulfil the promise of the emblem by losing Creusa. In this reworking of the Orpheus story, Aeneas loses his wife because he looks back too late (*nec prius amissam respexi*, 741).[18] When he discovers his loss, he retraces his steps and redescends into the city, where he is met by the shade of his wife, who explains that her death was willed by 'the gods' great mother' (788) and admonishes him to look after their son Ascanius (789). Aeneas

---

[17] Quint (1993) 60–1.   [18] Putnam (1988) 41–5.

responds by imitating Odysseus' triple attempt to embrace the ghost of his mother Anticleia (*Od.* 11.206–8, cf. *Aen.* 2.792–4). Troy has become an underworld, a place of dead mothers.

But the woman most memorably abandoned as the epic traverses the distance between Troy and Rome is of course Dido. Like Creusa, Dido blends the features of mother and bride. Homerically speaking, she resembles both Arete and Nausicaa (the dominant model for *Aeneid* 1–4 is Odysseus' sojourn among the Phaeacians): she joins the power, influence, and regal presence of the mother to the impressionable heart and Diana-like beauty of the daughter. The blend yields an oddly maternal passion. It is Cupid, disguised as Aeneas' son, who makes Dido fall for his 'pretend' father (*falsi*, *Aen.* 1.716). Near the start of Book 4, the love-sick queen, 'captivated by his father's image, keeps Ascanius in her lap, hoping to cheat her unspeakable love' (*gremio Ascanium genitoris imagine capta | detinet, infandum si fallere possit amorem*, 84–5). And to the departing father she laments that she has no 'little Aeneas playing in the palace, whose face at least would bring you back' (*si quis mihi parvulus aula | luderet Aeneas, qui te tamen ore referret*, 328–9). Dido's preoccupation with Aeneas' son may be an effect of, or indeed one reason for, her kinship with Euripides' Phaedra – the queen who killed herself for love of her stepson Hippolytus.[19] But the language of delusion that runs through these passages (*falsi*, *imagine*, *fallere*, *luderet*) also aligns Dido's cross-generational desire with Andromache's desire to conflate the future with the past. Unlike Creusa, Dido seeks to detain both son and father by her maternal side.

As Book 4 progresses, Dido comes to imagine venting not her love but her rage upon both father and son:

> non potui abreptum divellere corpus et undis
> spargere? non socios, non ipsum absumere ferro
> Ascanium patriisque epulandum ponere mensis?
>
> (*Aen.* 4.600–2)

Couldn't I have caught his body, torn it apart, scattered it
over the waves – put his companions to the sword – Ascanius too –
and set him as a dish for his father's table?

This fantasy of revenge evokes both Medea's treatment of her brother's body (scattered over the waves behind her fugitive ship) and Procne's of her son's (served to her adulterous husband for dinner); somewhere in the background, perhaps, is Medea's murder of her children. The theme of the murderous mother certainly colours Dido's dreams, albeit in a curiously

---

[19] See Hardie in this volume, p. 322.

inverted form. In these dreams, Dido is not the pursuer but the pursued; in flight from a savage Aeneas, she wanders dazed and alone – like the crazed Pentheus and fury-ridden Orestes of Greek tragedy, Virgil tells us, in one of his most extraordinary similes (*Aen.* 4.465–73). Let us recall that Pentheus was torn to pieces by his Bacchant-mother, and that Orestes risked the same fate at the jaws of his mother's Furies. Although Dido is identified with the victimised sons here, she is also akin to their maddened mothers. In the event Dido will play both roles – she dreams these dreams the night before she commits suicide.

What of Aeneas' actual mother? Like Dido, the goddess Venus appears before Aeneas at once as a mother and as a potential erotic partner. After her son's arrival in Libya, she comes to meet him in the guise of a virgin huntress – one so lovely that Aeneas mistakes her for Diana (Virgil thus conflates the antithetical goddesses of sexuality and chastity). This virginal Venus is functionally akin to the Phaeacian princess who is the first person Odysseus encounters after being washed ashore on Scheria. The link between Venus and Nausicaa is mediated by Diana/Artemis, to whom both are compared by their epic's respective heroes. In an elaborate simile in Book 4, Virgil will also compare Dido to Diana; the Homeric role of Nausicaa is shared out between Venus and Dido. The point is that Venus presents herself to her son in the guise of a marriageable girl, offering him a kind of preview of Dido. The incestuous undertones are amplified by the echoes of another famous encounter involving the disguised goddess of love and an awestruck mortal: the meeting of Aphrodite with her future lover Anchises – Aeneas' father! – in the Homeric Hymn to Aphrodite. It is as if all heterosexual desire were incestuous, a recursive movement in time and space.

Women sometimes threaten to arrest not only the plot-line but the life-line of their child-lovers. When Aeneas recognises the departing goddess, she instantly regains her maternal status. Aeneas' complaint – 'why do you so often mock your son with false images? why are you cruel too?' (*quid natum totiens, crudelis tu quoque, falsis | ludis imaginibus?, Aen.* 1.407–8) – is loosely modelled on Odysseus' speech to his mother when her shade eludes his embrace. But Aeneas' bitter 'you cruel too' has a more ominous ring. The phrase derives from Eclogue 8 (47–8): 'savage Love taught the mother to stain her hands with her children's blood; you too are cruel, mother' (*crudelis tu quoque, mater*). The cruel mother of the eclogue may be Medea, the child-killing mother, or Venus, the mother of 'savage Love'. But the very fact that the referent is unclear draws the two mothers together. Whatever we make of this tangle of lovers and mothers – Venus, Medea, Creusa, Nausicaa, Dido – we can at least remark that the knot in which they are twined in the first half of the *Aeneid* is disturbingly tight.

One burden of the *Aeneid* is to disentangle this knot. In so far as incestuous unions come to figure narrative regress, the plot of the epic depends on the separation of maternal origins from marital ends; otherwise, Aeneas will reproduce only the past, not the future. In the epic's second half, accordingly, Dido splits into the two simpler and more easily contained figures of Amata and Lavinia: the mad mother, doomed to kill herself for love of her quasi-son Turnus, and the chaste daughter who is destined to be the hero's bride. In this economy, the mother absorbs all of Dido's passion, preserving the daughter as an almost perfectly cold blank.[20] If Virgil takes care not to realise Lavinia as a character, one reason is that she is and must remain – for Aeneas if not for Turnus – little more than the hypostasis of the 'Lavinian shores' (*Lavinia . . . | litora, Aen.* 1.2–3) through which Troy must pass en route to becoming Rome. A plausible and more interesting alternative to Lavinia is furnished by the heroic Italian warrior Camilla, another virginal avatar of Dido. Like Dido, Camilla is associated with Penthesileia (compare *Aen.* 1.491 and 11.662), the Amazon warrior with whom Achilles was fabled to have fallen in love the moment he killed her. But whereas Dido does indeed die on her lover's sword, as Penthesileia on Achilles', Camilla is killed not by Aeneas in hand-to-hand combat (as we might perhaps have expected) but by a minor warrior who strikes with a spear, from a distance, as if to avoid falling a victim to her charms. Virgil does not grant Aeneas an interview with Camilla any more than with Lavinia. Aeneas cannot be allowed the kind of like-minded union Odysseus praises to Nausicaa in *Odyssey* 6 (182–4) because Virgil's epic regularly construes heterosexual desire as the enemy, never the support, of social order. The only woman Aeneas embraces in the epic's second half is Venus, who comes to him bearing gifts, rather as Cupid bore gifts to Dido in Book 1. But these gifts are the weapons fashioned by Vulcan; the ardour instilled in her son by this seductive mother[21] is for war and for the future.

So far I have been writing as if passion distorted only Virgil's women – as if men uniformly displayed the Olympian calm of Virgil's Jupiter. That is, of course, very far from the truth. Passion may be gendered female, but it afflicts men as readily as women. We have already seen the ease with which Dido's erotic passion converts to (ultimately suicidal) violence; the two fires burn with a single heat. Throughout the *Aeneid*, men too 'burn'

---

[20] The snake Allecto hurls at Amata at *Aen.* 7.346–55 is a lurid realisation of the snaky embrace of Cupid in *Aen.* 1 (compare, e.g. the language of *Aen.* 1.688 and 7.350–1). Numerous details also link Cupid with the fiery, snaky figures of *Aen.* 2 discussed by Knox (1966); Cupid is in effect a miniature Trojan Horse who comes bearing gifts for Dido, and the fall of Dido reworks the fall of Troy, this time with Aeneas in the role of aggressor.

[21] See Putnam (1995) 43.

with various passions – for love, for blood, for glory, for death. We can see the process of translation at work when Turnus departs for battle at the start of Book 12. In this strangely triangulated scene, Turnus and Amata converse in the presence of Lavinia. When Amata tries to dissuade her 'fiery son-in-law' (*ardentem generum*, 55) from battle, declaring that she will not 'be taken prisoner and see Aeneas my son-in-law' (*nec generum Aenean captiva videbo*, 63), a red blush spreads across Lavinia's 'flaming cheeks' (*flagrantis . . . genas*, 65), creating an effect, Virgil tells us, of Indian ivory stained with blood-red purple, or lilies mixed with roses. The meaning of this corporeal, rubricated text remains controversial. Does it bespeak Lavinia's modesty, or her love of Turnus, or her love of Aeneas? The staining of white by red certainly suggests a symbolic deflowering, a suggestion underscored by the echoes of Catullus 64, where the marriage bed of Peleus and Thetis is agleam with 'Indian ivory' and draped in 'purple' (Cat. 64.48–9), and *Iliad* 4 (141–7), where Menelaus' bloodstained thighs are compared to ivory stained with purple. But Lavinia's blush may be less the external expression of her hidden emotions than a lateral mani-festation of the contagion of desire. There is a kind of textual intercourse at work here, a metonymic spread of fire, from Turnus to Amata to Lavinia and back to Turnus, in whom Lavinia's blush kindles both sexual desire and battle lust: 'love riots in him and fastens his face on the virgin; he burns all the more for arms' (*illum turbat amor figitque in virgine vultus; | ardet in arma magis*, 70–1). Turnus sallies forth to a battle in which he will be wounded in the thigh, like Homer's Menelaus, and then killed by Aeneas, in a death which enacts the displaced and inverted consummation of his desire for Lavinia.

Martial and marital wounds are consanguineous throughout the epic. This convergence is most fully realised in the ghastly 'penetration' of the only female fighter of the epic; the spear that pierces Camilla's nipple and drinks her blood (*sub exsertam donec perlata papillam | haesit virgineumque alte bibit acta cruorem*, Aen. 11.803–4) figures a grotesquely accelerated sexual maturation, from virgin to bride to nursing mother.[22] But warriors such as Euryalus, Lausus, Pallas, and Turnus also die in language that assimilates death to defloration.[23] It is not by chance that Pallas' baldric is decorated with depictions of the ill-fated husbands of the Danaids, slaugh-tered on the eve of their wedding night. Although it is the reluctant brides who commit the murder, Virgil's description sees only the young men, 'a band of youths foully murdered, and bloody bedchambers' (*caesa manus iuvenum foede thalamique cruenti*, Aen. 10.498), as if to suggest that the

---

[22] Fowler (1987) 195.   [23] Fowler (1987); Mitchell (1991).

battlefield were itself the bloody bedchamber. But there are figurative as well as literalised 'wounds' in the epic's second half. It is after his arrival in Italy that Aeneas himself comes to experience the kind of pain he earlier inflicted on the queen of Carthage. The person who thus 'wounds' Aeneas, moreover, is not Lavinia or Camilla but the young warrior Pallas, Evander's son, who accompanies Aeneas into battle in Latium.[24] Like its Homeric counterpart, the relationship between Achilles and Patroclus (itself often interpreted as homoerotic by post-Homeric readers), this relationship is doomed to end tragically. It is altogether fitting that Aeneas veils Pallas' flowerlike corpse with a robe woven by the hands of Dido.[25]

It may be worth asking why this erotic relation remains subtextual – why, if Pallas is the true successor of Dido, Virgil does not depict Aeneas and Pallas as lovers. One reason is cultural: unlike Greece, Rome never sanctioned sexual love between free men. Another reason is generic: like the Homeric epics, and like his own *Georgics*, Virgil's foundational epic focuses on familial reproduction. Heterosexual unions figure alternative futures; Dido and Lavinia embody lands where Aeneas may plant the seed of his new city. Homoeroticism is not rooted in this way in Rome's master narrative; it contours the plot but remains ultimately extraneous to it. And yet it often seems as if homoeroticism, both here and in the *Eclogues*, were the more fulfilling choice. In Eclogue 3, Galatea may flirt with her lover (64–5), but Amyntas goes hunting with his (66–7); in Eclogue 10, the pain Lycoris inflicts on Gallus is answered by the devotion Virgil lavishes on his beloved friend (73–4). Within the *Aeneid*, Virgil comes closest to representing a homoerotic couple with Nisus and Euryalus, the Trojans who volunteer for a doomed night mission in *Aeneid* 9. We have already met these two in Book 5 (295–6), where Virgil casts Euryalus as a fair beloved and Nisus as his lover, famous for 'his honourable love for the boy' (*amore pio pueri*; the qualifying adjective is crucial). In Book 9, all goes well until they are spotted by the enemy; they flee through the forest – Nisus emerging safely, Euryalus lost and left behind. The scene that follows recalls Aeneas' search for Creusa at the end of Book 2: like Aeneas, Nisus belatedly looks back, retraces his steps, calls out the name of his beloved, and finally finds him. But unlike Creusa, Euryalus is still alive. In a horrifying scene of displaced, triangulated intercourse, Euryalus' body is broken open (*candida pectora rumpit*, 432) before his friend's eyes; Nisus rushes to take vengeance on the killer and then falls dead in his turn, speared through, over Euryalus' corpse. Their deaths elicit from Virgil a famously enigmatic epitaph,

---

[24] See Putnam (1995) 27–49 (40–1 on Aeneas' 'wound').

[25] The verb is *obnubit* (*Aen.* 11.77), which carries suggestions of bridal veiling; see Putnam (1995) 39–40.

'fortunate pair!' (*fortunati ambo*, 446) – an apostrophe tinged with irony, perhaps, but also laden with pathos. This dying-together is in effect the epic's most fully consummated marriage.

If masculinity means the ability to harness passions, no character in the *Aeneid* is fully masculine – not even Jupiter. Near the very end of the epic, Jupiter and Juno come to terms, and Juno finally cedes her rage and accedes to Rome's destiny. The goddess has hardly nodded her consent when Jupiter initiates the fated destruction of Turnus by dispatching two snaky Furies, daughters of night (*Aen.* 12.845–8); 'these are found', Virgil tells us, in a truly astonishing line, 'by the throne of Jupiter and at the threshold of the savage king' (*hae Iovis ad solium saevique in limine regis | apparent*, 849–50). Virgil is remembering the incorporation of the Eumenides within Athens at the close of the *Oresteia*. But the allusion does not account for Virgil's terrifying hendiadys, 'the throne of Jupiter and the threshold of the savage king'. Jupiter does not merely deploy Juno's Furies from a distance; the 'savage king' has appropriated his wife's characteristic epithet. Rome is forged in a furious fire, like the shield of Aeneas. And Jupiter, like Vulcan, not only wields but internalises the instrumental flames.

As this chapter attempts to show, gender roles are complicated and crossed throughout Virgil's poetry, which gives us passionate men, rational women, backward-looking sons, and forward-thinking mothers, as well as their more predictable counterparts. Virgil's representations of gender and sexuality are shaped, moreover, by generic considerations; poetic, agricultural, and national 'production' entail corresponding sexual arrangements. Yet each genre places men in the foreground. In the *Eclogues*, women enable but do not perform pastoral song; in the *Georgics*, their ideal place is the deep background of the fruitful landscape and household. This relegation is dramatised by the *Aeneid*, which kills off its most visible and powerful women (Dido, Amata, Camilla) while preserving Lavinia as an instrument of dynastic reproduction. This asymmetry may reflect overarching cultural prejudices. And yet we might imagine other configurations. The poetic exchanges of the *Eclogues* might have featured women as well as men; this heterosexual model will be fully explored by later pastoral poets.[26] The *Georgics* might have featured an encomium of the resourceful mother and household-manager – something like the praise of old-fashioned womanhood delivered by Horace's Second Epode and sixth 'Roman' ode (Hor. *Epod.* 2.39–48, *Carm.* 3.6.39–41). And the *Aeneid* might have celebrated

---

[26] E.g. in dialogue-poems such as Andrew Marvell's 'Clorinda and Damon'. There is in principle no reason Virgil had to respect the Theocritean precedent of men-only contests; he might have found inspiration in Catullus' dialogue of Acme and Septimius (Cat. 45).

its marriage plot along familiar romantic lines. While generic differences allow some varieties to emerge, sexual hierarchies are carefully preserved in a productive dialectic that passes from song to home to nation.[27]

FURTHER READING

Sexuality and gender in ancient Rome

A. Richlin, *The Garden of Priapus*, (2nd edn, Oxford, 1991); A. Richlin, 'Not before homosexuality: the materiality of the *cinaedus* and the Roman law against love between men', *Journal of the History of Sexuality* 3 (1993) 523–73; C. Edwards, *The Politics of Immorality in Ancient Rome* (Cambridge, 1993, esp. chs. 1 and 2); C. A. Williams 'Greek love at Rome', *Classical Quarterly* 45 (1995) 517–39; T. N. Habinek, 'The invention of sexuality in the world-city of Rome', in T. N. Habinek and A. Schiesaro, eds., *The Roman Cultural Revolution* (Cambridge, 1997); J. P. Hallett and M. B. Skinner, eds., *Roman Sexualities* (Princeton, forthcoming).

Sexuality and gender in Virgil's poetry

(Most recent work on Virgil encompasses this topic; below are listed a few more specialised studies.)

T. M. Klein, 'The Greek shepherd in Vergil, Gide, Genet and Barthes', *Helios* 6 (1978) 1–32; D. Gillis, *Eros and Death in the Aeneid* (Rome, 1983); D. Fowler, 'Vergil on killing virgins', in M. Whitby *et al.*, eds., *Homo Viator: Classical Essays for John Bramble* (Bristol, 1987) 185–98; R. N. Mitchell, 'The violence of virginity in the *Aeneid*', *Arethusa* 24 (1991) 219–38; M. C. J. Putnam, 'Possessiveness, sexuality, and heroism in the *Aeneid*', in *Virgil's Aeneid: Interpretation and Influence* (Chapel Hill, 1995) 27–49.

---

[27] This chapter has benefited from the comments of Alessandro Barchiesi, Charles Martindale, John Shoptaw, and my research assistant Lesley Lundeen, and from the unpublished Virgilian ruminations of my Yale colleague Howard Stern. All translations are my own.

20

PHILIP HARDIE

Virgil and tragedy

Since antiquity Virgil the epicist has also been viewed as Virgil the tragedian; Martial describes him simply as *Maro cothurnatus*, 'Virgil in buskins'
(5.5.8, 7.63.5). The task of collecting the numerous parallels between the
Aeneid and tragedies both Attic and Roman was well under way by the
time of the late-antique commentators Servius and Macrobius. But why
should the poet who set out to write the definitive Roman epic include so
many elements from the distinct (if historically related) genre of tragedy?

A recent study shows the inseparability of formal study of tragic sources
for the *Aeneid* from wider questions of interpretation. Oliver Lyne exploits
an allusion to the Sophoclean Ajax in the characterisation of Aeneas to
reinforce a prevalent modern reading of the *Aeneid* as a 'tragic' (with a
small 't') poem: 'a further [non-epic] voice naggingly insinuates a quite
different message',[1] a message that makes of the poem a pessimistic, even
subversive and anti-Augustan epic. Here the opposition of 'epic' and 'tragic'
implies a conflict between the *Aeneid*'s function as a public panegyric of
Roman history and the valuation to be given to the private experience of
loss and grief. Implicit also is a reading of Attic tragedy that emphasizes
the psychological experience and moral dilemmas of its characters. But this
individualistic approach to tragedy is itself but one of a range of possible
responses to that genre. An examination of the tragic elements in the
Aeneid within conceptual frameworks developed over the last few decades
for the analysis of Attic tragedy leads to two general conclusions: first, that
the *Aeneid* is 'tragic' at deeper levels of structure than has perhaps yet been
realised; and secondly, that the evaluative use of the term 'tragic' (or
'pessimistic', 'anti-Augustan') leads to an over-simplified opposition of two
points of view holding out the possibility of a final arbitration. By contrast
recent studies of Attic tragedy have argued that the agonistic forms of the
genre yield not simple and final judgements, but a dialectic of proliferating

[1] Lyne (1987) 12.

complexity. My claim, in short, is that the *Aeneid* is a problematic text, in the sense that has been given to the term 'problematic' since Vernant in his classic 1969 paper on 'Tensions and ambiguities in Greek tragedy'[2] asserted that 'tragedy turns reality into a problem'.

First, a sketch of attempts earlier in this century to define the tragic in the *Aeneid*. Richard Heinze used Aristotelian terms in placing the tragic qualities of the *Aeneid* at the centre of critical attention: for Heinze Dido, in the 'tragic epyllion'[3] of *Aeneid* 4, is a tragic protagonist who undergoes a sudden *peripeteia* ('reversal'), as she falls from the summit of her dream of bliss to meet her unhappy death. Heinze makes the sudden *peripeteia* a central structural feature in Virgil's dramatisation of the more even tenor supposed natural to epic narrative; with this is associated the emotional goal of *ekplexis* ('amazement'), traced directly to Aristotle's definition of the function of tragedy as the arousal of the emotions of pity and fear.[4] The emotionality of the *Aeneid* is undeniable; Heinze looks only to the Greek tragic tradition, but it is important for the *Aeneid* that Roman adaptations of Greek tragic models accentuated even further the genre's striving after pathos.[5] Heinze inaugurates a line of critics who use the *Poetics* as a scaffolding for their reading of the *Aeneid* or of episodes within it.[6] Repeated attempts have been made to use Aristotle's slippery term *hamartia* to gain a foothold on the problem of attributing guilt or innocence to the major figures of Dido and Turnus;[7] this is particularly important for the debate as to whether Turnus is an 'enemy of the state' or a tragic hero.

Anglo-Saxon criticism in the earlier part of this century, influenced by Hegelian concepts of the tragic as popularised by A. C. Bradley,[8] tended to a more abstract formulation of the conflicts in the *Aeneid*: thus E. E. Sikes: 'The Fourth Book is a tragedy, and the essence of tragedy is a conflict, not only of wills but of rights. Both Aeneas and Dido have their points of view, which demand our sympathy, though of course we are not required to sympathize equally.'[9] More recently R. B. Egan has discussed the problem of *pietas* in the *Aeneid*, referring to the episode of the mother of Euryalus in Book 9, but with implications for our reaction to

---

[2] Vernant and Vidal-Naquet (1981) ch. 2.   [3] Heinze (1993) 96.

[4] Heinze (1993) 251–8, 370–3.

[5] Argenio (1961) 198–212; Traina (1974) 113–65, 202. For the possible wider influence of the passionate heroines of Roman tragedy on Augustan poetry see Griffin (1985) 203, 208–10.

[6] Dido: Wlosok (1976). Turnus: von Albrecht (1970).

[7] E.g. Moles (1984); Schenk (1984).   [8] Bradley (1909).

[9] Sikes (1923) 190; for another example of this kind of reading see Glover (1912) 175.

the last scene of the poem:[10] 'The simple tragic truth of the matter is that a heroic act of *pietas* in the *Aeneid* may also be an act of the greatest moral repugnance, that one and the same act embodies two antagonistic principles.' Egan thinks of the competing family duties in the *Oresteia* and the *Antigone*. The *Antigone* is the classic example of an Attic tragedy that is standardly read in this way; Simon Goldhill comments that 'Since Hegel's reading of the play, it has been difficult not to consider the text of the *Antigone* in terms of dialectic and opposition . . . It is difficult . . . to read the *Antigone* without making not only moral judgements but the sort of one-sided moral judgements that the play itself seems to want to mark as leading to tragedy.'[11] This observation on the way that critics fall into the trap of mirroring movements made *within* a tragic text is one that Virgilian critics might ponder.

Both Aristotelian and Hegelian versions of 'tragic' criticism of the *Aeneid* tend to place great weight on the experience of the individual actors in the epic: the former through an emphasis on Aristotle's discussions of the tragic protagonist, the tragic flaw, and the arousal of the tragic emotions; the latter through a sympathy with the experience of the individual subject crushed between the clashing rocks of incompatible abstractions. In a generalised usage the word 'tragic' is often used by Virgilians as virtually synonymous with 'private', in the standard opposition of 'private' and 'public' voices, where for 'public' may be read 'epic'. The recent privileging of the 'private' over the 'public' is a symptom of liberal humanism's interest in the individual subject and his or her responsibility for exercising personal choice in the face of vast supra-personal forces or institutions. The consequence for readings of the *Aeneid* is to locate true value in the interior experiences of an Aeneas, a Dido, a Turnus, of suffering parents and children, exposed to the impersonal and inhuman structures of militarism and absolutism.

The paradigm shift in much recent criticism of Attic tragedy has been away from a focus on individual psychology and morality to a concern with political, social, and cultural relationships. The tragic self is understood not so much as the heroic individual struggling for self-determination, but as the *locus* of contesting roles within the structures of gender, household, and city. The search for solutions to the moral dilemmas thrown up by tragic plots has given way to an analysis of the tensions and problematics that emerge when the structures of the *polis* are tested to breaking-point.[12] Tragedy's fascination with liminality and transgression is given historical

---

[10] Egan (1980).   [11] Goldhill (1986) 88–9.   [12] A good survey in Segal (1986).

context as a discursive engagement with the tensions of the rapidly developing society of fifth-century Athens, as the democracy struggles to come to terms with the shifting relationship between the collective and the individual, between mass and elite, and with changing roles in household and city.

How might we use this kind of criticism in reassessing the presence of the 'tragic' in Virgil's epic? To see how the narrow focus on the moral and psychological may be widened, with the help of a tragic model, to include the historical and political, we can turn to the end of the *Aeneid*.[13] Aeneas' killing of Turnus is one of the most 'personal' moments in the epic, and readers are under pressure to pass judgement according to their sense of the individual moral worth and humanity of Aeneas and his victim. But although the hero's vengeful violence appears to result from an intensely private passion, the omniscient narrator has inserted it within a more extensive closural structure that determines both human and divine action. In the final scene Aeneas first throws a spear that exceeds even the force of the thunderbolt (12.921–3); at the end the *coup de grâce* is delivered by a man 'ablaze with fury (*furiis*) and terrible in his anger' (946–7). Allusion to Jupiter's weapon, the thunderbolt, is associated with the eruption of a hellish fury (texts of Virgil's day did not distinguish between *furiis* 'fury' and *Furiis* 'the Furies'); this combination unfolds along the temporal axis the contradiction of a single moment a hundred lines before when, in the last divine action of the poem, Jupiter sends down to earth a Fury (here referred to as a *Dira*, the embodiment of god's wrath, *dei ira*). The Fury rushes down with the stormy force later attributed to Aeneas' spear: with 12.855 'she flies and is carried to earth on a swift whirlwind', compare 923 '[the spear] flies like a black whirlwind'. Juturna, Turnus' sister, recognises that this apparition seals her brother's fate. Aeneas' apparently private impulse to kill Turnus is in fact pre-scripted on the divine level. The unsettling use by the supreme Olympian of an agent normally associated with the Underworld, with its re-enactment in the Fury-like vengeance of Jupiter's vicar Aeneas, has a tragic model in Aeschylus' *Oresteia*, whose plot is finally resolved by an alliance between the Olympian gods and the Erinyes when the latter are naturalised as honorary citizens of Athens in their cave below the Acropolis. The specifically Roman implication of the finale to the legendary story of Aeneas and Turnus is suggested by the awesome description of the Capitol, the hill of Jupiter at the centre of what will be Rome, at 8.349–50 'already in those days the dread (*dira*)

---

[13] For further details see Hardie (1991); see also the discussions by Tarrant and Braund above.

religious awe of the place terrified the fearful countryfolk'. Jupiter's capacity for furious violence has been previously revealed to us when we saw 'the father himself' among the 'dread (*dirae*) shapes' of the Olympian gods busy with the destruction of Troy at 2.617–23. An etymological pun in the Jupiter and Dira scene in Book 12 imports another Roman overtone (849–50): the Dirae 'appear' (*apparent*) at the throne of Jupiter, like the *apparitores*, the attendants of Roman magistrates. As agent of official violence the Dira may be compared to the lictors, with their rods and axes (and at this point we may well remember the 'cruel axes' of that other father, the first consul Brutus, who put love of country and freedom before mercy to his son, 6.817–23). This all adds up to a socio-political issue that concerns the structures of state-control, rather than (simply) a problem of the behaviour of the individual hero. Virgil raises the question of the relationship between legitimate power, let us call it the *pax Augusta*, and arbitrary violence. Put like that, this is hardly a new reading; the point to stress is that this problematisation of the end of the poem reflects the structures of Attic tragedy. One may also compare the interminable debate over the meaning of the death of Turnus with the discussion by recent Aeschylean critics of the way in which the apparently decisive conclusion of the *Oresteia* works against its own status as a *telos* (how can the Erinyes *both* be socialised as the 'Kindly Ones' *and* retain their deterrent efficacy as a principle of fear at the heart of the Athenian democracy?).[14] While in formal terms the ending of the *Aeneid* is very *un*tragic, because of its unforeseen abruptness, it is highly tragic both in the sense of personal tragedy, and also in the sense of the problematisation of social and political structures.

Vernant, in an essay entitled 'The historical moment of tragedy in Greece' (1968), develops the thesis that fifth-century Attic tragedy is the product of the particular conditions of fifth-century Athenian society, struggling to come to terms with the vast changes involved in the full realisation of the city-state, as older values collide with the new legal and political systems. While the changes in Roman society involved in the transition from the Republic to the principate were not on the scale of the changes experienced in the fifth-century BC city-state, nevertheless if there is a 'tragic moment' (to use Vernant's phrase) in the history of Rome, it is the years around the Battle of Actium (31 BC) when Octavian and the Roman people had to negotiate the institutional and ideological gap between the

---

[14] See also Vernant in Vernant and Vidal-Naquet (1981) 23 n. 3 on the ambivalent balance between Peitho and the Erinyes in the *Eumenides*. The Zeus of Aeschylus' *Supplices* presides over both an Olympian sky and the infernal shadows.

discredited structures of the Republic and the unproven and potentially repugnant alternative. This is in many ways a more critical moment in the history of Rome than what Biliński, arguing for an analogy between the conditions of fifth-century Athens and those prevailing in Rome at the time of the introduction and flourishing of tragedy in the latter city, refers to as the 'heroic age' of the third and second centuries BC.[15] The French school of Vernant and his associates has focused on the problem of the relationship between the collective of the city-state and the individual, above all the heroic and pre-eminent individual of pre-democratic social organisations. Homer already explores the problem of heroes who are expected to serve the interests of their group altruistically, but are encouraged at the same time (and indeed in the pursuit of the communal good) to strive for a competitive, individualistic superiority. In tragedy this instability *within* the Homeric system intensifies when it becomes the instability of two different systems, one old and one new, rubbing up against each other.

If tragedy examines the problems raised by the survival of an obsolescent heroic individualism, Augustan epic has to confront the inverse problem, the emergence of a new autocratic individualism out of the collectivity of the *res publica*. This is already clear from the example of the killing of Turnus: the manifestation of state-sanctioned terror and violence (Jupiter's Fury–lictor) in the unpredictable behaviour of the single hero Aeneas anticipates the problem, ever-present in the Empire, of containing and averting the anger of one man, the emperor; while the course of action notoriously rejected by Aeneas, the sparing of his enemy, images the flip-side of that coin in Julius Caesar's advertisement of the virtue of clemency (the autocrat's gracious forbearance from venting his anger). Another passage where a reading of the specifically Roman problems of the relationship between individual and collective yields a 'tragic' interpretation of the kind here proposed is the Marcellus episode at the end of *Aeneid* 6, the premature death of a young man at the end of the first half of the poem that corresponds to the premature death of Turnus at the end of the second half. The 'tragedy' of Marcellus is frequently read in terms of personal loss and grief, often with the further appeal to the familiar opposition of public and private voices, as if the death of Marcellus were somehow the cost of the glorious fulfilment of empire. But the death of the emperor's nephew also highlights a structural problem within the principate; the terms of the problem are set up when Anchises presents the last figure in the main parade of Roman heroes, Fabius Cunctator, 6.845–6 *tu Maximus ille es, | unus qui nobis cunctando restituis rem*, 'You are that Maximus, the one

---

[15] Biliński (1958) 11.

man who by delaying restores our state.' An individual hero, one man, the 'greatest man' (*maximus*), who single-handedly restores the collective, the *res* (*publica*), to itself. This is obviously a powerful precedent in a line of heroes that will culminate in the one *princeps*, Augustus, who claimed to have restored the *res publica*. Anchises in fact quotes almost verbatim a famous line from Ennius' second-century BC epic on Roman history.

The Marcellus coda reveals one of the dangers in a system where the community is dependent on the presence of the one great man. Anchises first points to an earlier great Marcellus, another version of the Republican 'one man', a pre-eminent individual (856 'in victory he towers over all men') who preserves the republic (857–8 *rem Romanam . . . sistet*, 'he will hold fast the Roman state'). The line of Marcellus was to have excelled even itself in the person of the younger Marcellus, snatched prematurely from Rome by the jealous gods; his unrealised potential to be the greatest of all Romans is expressed through a comparison with all others of the Trojan–Romulean race (857–9). The funeral enacted verbally at the end of Book 6 replaces the triumph that would surely have followed from his irresistible military might (879–81), the triumph whose absence is the more strongly felt through the structural homology between this last scene in the Parade of Heroes and the last scene on the Shield of Aeneas at the end of Book 8, the triple triumph of Augustus. The general reference in 870 to 'the Roman stock' lightly veils the real point at issue, that Marcellus was being groomed for the succession; the continuity not so much of the 'Roman race', but of the Julian *gens* (789–90 *omnis Iuli | progenies*) was threatened by his death, starkly revealing the fragility of a system in which the security of the state depends on the physical survival of one man and his heir. The succession was indeed to prove one of the most intractable problems of the principate. Augustus himself delivered the funeral speech at the public funeral of Marcellus before burying his nephew in his own Mausoleum, that colossal architectural statement of the presence in the city of Rome of the one man and his family.

The endings of Books 6 and 12 are equally problematic in their own ways, but grief, private and public, at the death of a potential successor is easier to talk about openly than is the dark necessity of the anger of the autocrat. In dealing with the first Virgil speaks directly of contemporary events, but in approaching the latter he works through the events of a remote legendary past. At the beginning of *Georgics* 3 the poet offers us the fantasy of his own sideshow to Octavian's triple triumph of 29 BC. The imaginary temple to Caesar Octavian contains the sculptural equivalent of a historical epic on the achievements of the contemporary hero (26–33); in the lines that immediately precede (24–5) we hear of theatrical performances.

Virgil offers us no hint of what as poetic *triumphator* he will produce on this stage, but we might think of the famous stage-work that was actually produced at games in Rome in 29 BC to celebrate the victory at Actium, the tragedy *Thyestes* by Virgil's close friend Lucius Varius Rufus, a work that may have used events from the Greek legendary past to comment on the stirring events of the immediate past. The contrast between Varius' legendary tragedy and the historical 'epic' embodied in the poetic temple draws our attention to Virgil's strategic decision to write a *legendary* rather than a *historical* epic. There is a metonymical relation of cause and effect between the story of Aeneas and the history of Augustus, a relation that serves the panegyrical and epic function of 'praising Augustus through his ancestors' (as Servius describes the 'intention' of the poem). But more important is the metaphorical relation between the events of the legendary past and those of more recent history, and this is the relation between past and present in Attic tragedy. Virgil's decision to write an *Aeneid* rather than an *Augusteid* is the crucial point of liberation from the panegyrical straitjacket of historical epic into the freedom to problematise the issues of Roman history and of the principate.

Aeneid 8 offers in microcosm the whole structure of the past–present relationship in the poem, and provides a measure of the difference between legendary problematisation and contemporary panegyric. The Roman part of the book begins and ends with narratives of heroic victory and celebration, first the story of Hercules and Cacus with the ensuing hymn of the Salii, and secondly the scenes on the Shield of Aeneas of the Battle of Actium and the triple triumph. It is not easy to deconstruct the panegyrical content of the Shield: the scene of Actium presents an easy contrast between, on the one side, the orderly formation of Augustus attended by Italians and Romans, citizens and gods, and backed up by his admiral Agrippa, and on the other side the disorderly and heterogeneous barbarian rabble of the forces of Antony, accompanied not by an Agrippa, but by the unspeakable 'Egyptian wife', whose presence confuses categories of gender (a woman in the front line) and of nationality (an Egyptian allied with a Roman). The turning-point of the battle itself is narrated through the defeat of the monstrous and hybrid Egyptian gods by the Graeco-Roman Olympians. The distant type of the victory at Actium is the victory of Hercules over Cacus on the site of Rome, but, as many have noted, Virgil goes out of his way to blur – to problematise – the simple dichotomy between Olympian hero and chthonic monster: the hero of reason falls prey to a fiery fury that seems the more proper quality of the fire-breathing monster Cacus. The hero of civilisation and future god falls below the level of humanity into a semi-bestial passion. Attic tragic treatments of Heracles provide parallels for this destructuring of the categories of beast, man, and god, for example the first stasimon of Sophocles' *Trachiniae* describing the fight between Heracles and the river-god Achelous in such a way that the son of Zeus almost merges into the bull-form of his adversary. The qualitative difference in *Aeneid* Book 8 between the Actium scene and the Hercules and Cacus narrative reflects the 'tragic distancing' operative in the latter episode.

Hercules is the extreme example of the transgressive hero, the hero who confuses boundaries, and through whom the tragedians explore liminal situations; but liminality is a constant feature of all tragedy, as the French school with its anthropological and structuralist roots has made abundantly clear.[16] The *Aeneid* lends itself pre-eminently to an analysis in terms of liminality, and tragic models are never far away. The whole plot of the *Aeneid* is one of transition, of the geographical passage from the sacked Troy to new cities in Italy, during which Aeneas and his people must pass from their old identity to the possibility of a new identity as ancestors of the Roman race. Large-scale narratives of passage are ultimately of epic rather than tragic derivation, and there is much to be gained for an understanding of the *Aeneid* from recent structuralist-type analyses of the passage of Odysseus in the *Odyssey* from the masculine world of war at Troy to resocialisation in his Ithacan household. In Aeneas the Odyssean liminal roles of outcast and suppliant are yet more completely realised in a hero who is an exile rather than a homecomer. The *Aeneid* is also full of smaller narratives of passage and liminality that correspond at the level of the history of the individual to the epic's wider narrative of the passage of a nation over the centuries; the closest models for these individual histories are tragic, particularly in cases of a liminality that ends in catastrophe rather than in successful passage from one status to another.

One of the most obviously 'tragic' features of the *Aeneid* is the series of promising young people who die before their time (including Marcellus). The strong emotional impact of these stories cannot be downplayed, but beyond the *pathos* lie the abstract structures familiar above all from the Greek institution of the *ephebeia*, the practices and roles associated with the passage from childhood to adulthood, whose patterns, classically analysed in Vidal-Naquet's essay on 'The Black Hunter',[17] are now seen to pervade such tragedies as Aeschylus' *Oresteia*, Sophocles' *Philoctetes*, and Euripides' *Bacchae*. *Aeneid* Book 9 is full of ephebic characters, most of whom fail to make it to adulthood; the one exception is Ascanius, whose killing of Numanus is applauded by Apollo as the act by which the boy

---

[16] See Segal (1986) 38–41. [17] Vidal-Naquet (1981).

realises *uirtus* (manliness/courage). Ascanius thus fulfils the epic model of the successful ephebe as represented by Odysseus' son Telemachus. The immediate foil to this success story is the tale of Nisus and Euryalus in which may be recognised many ephebic motifs. The two youths are 'black hunters', operating at night, not killing in open fight but trickily slaughtering the enemy as they sleep. Once discovered they take refuge in what has become their natural environment during their 'continual hunting' (9.245) since they arrived in Italy, the dark woods, in which the hunters now become the hunted. When Euryalus is captured Nisus continues to operate from cover, his spearthrows as unseen as any non-hoplite arrow, until the death of his beloved Euryalus forces him into the open to fight fair with his flashing sword; but this final burst of light, far from leading to the dawn of adulthood, seals his return to the darkness, this time of death. The cut-flower simile of Euryalus' death (435–7), with its allusion to the Catullan inversion of the epithalamial motif in poem 11 (the flower 'touched' by the plough), weaves into the ephebic pattern the corresponding female passage from virginity to womanhood,[18] reminding us that the dominant image of marriage in the *Aeneid* is the tragic one of wedding-as-funeral, the *thalamus* as tomb.[19]

Similar patterns structure the story of that most liminal of Virgilian characters, the Amazon Camilla, who confuses the boundaries between hunting and war, the pastoral wilderness and the warfare of an urban civilisation, feminine and masculine roles,[20] as she tries to reverse her passage into the realm of Diana when as a baby she crossed over the raging river Amasenus bound to the spear of her father. Unlike Nisus and Euryalus, she succeeds for a time in entering the adult male world of war, enjoying one of the most spectacular *aristeiai* in the epic, before she makes the fatal mistake of confusing the battlefield with a hunting-ground; the pointed placing of the words *uenatrix* 'huntress' and *bellatrix* 'warrior-woman' (7.805, 11.780) highlights the source of her tragedy in this confusion of roles.

Camilla is in many respects a mirror-image of Dido, and an investigation of liminality will usefully supplement the established tragic readings of the Dido episode, and also shift the emphasis somewhat away from the psychologistic towards the social and cultural aspects of Dido's 'tragedy'. Like Aeneas, Dido has a history of exile; when we first meet her she appears successfully to have made the transition from one role (dependent wife) to another (supreme monarch). But the intersection of her story with

[18] See Fowler (1987).   [19] Seaford (1987).
[20] Catullus 63 would be an easy object for this kind of analysis in pre-Virgilian Latin poetry: see Griffin (1985) on tragic influence in Cat. 64 and 68.

that of the Trojan exile casts her back into a state of confusion – of liminality – that is resolved only by her death. The emblem of this confusion is the figure who in Book 1 first informs Aeneas (and the reader) about Dido, Venus. The goddess of love is disguised as a virgin, and Aeneas initially takes her for one of Diana's nymphs, or for the virgin goddess of hunting herself. There is an element of the metatheatrical about Venus' entrance: in preparation for the drama to unfold, she has put on costume, and, as E. L. Harrison has shown,[21] her account of the earlier history of Dido takes the shape of a Euripidean prologue, and she is appropriately shod in the buskin (*cothurnus*, 337). A combination of Venus and Diana in a tragic context evokes the goddesses whose power struggle mirrors on the divine level the impossible contradictions in which Euripides' Phaedra is involved; it is as if Virgil has rolled into one the opening and closing epiphanies in the *Hippolytus*, Aphrodite in the prologue and Artemis as *dea ex machina*. Dido herself combines features both of Hippolytus – she has vowed herself to perpetual chastity after her first husband's death – and of Phaedra – as a woman whose established status is disrupted by an illicit passion that gets the better of her sense of shame and modesty (*pudor, aidos*). As in the *Hippolytus* the human drama is played out through a polarity of civilisation and the wild: it is when Dido goes out into the wilderness in which Aeneas met Venus that she succumbs to her passion, as Venus once again demonstrates her power in what should be the domain of Diana (perhaps partly because Dido fulfils Phaedra's fantasy of racing over the mountains in the hunt). On her return Dido figuratively brings back wild nature into the city when she rages through Carthage like a Bacchant on Mount Cithaeron (300–3); later in her dreams she once more experiences the sensation of an exile far from civilisation, lines followed immediately by the famous simile at 469–73 comparing Dido to Pentheus and Orestes on the tragic stage, a jarring pointer to the theatricality of the story. In her desperate musings on the night before Aeneas' departure she fantasises about a complete escape from a civilisation in which social roles and sexuality are irreconcilably opposed, 550–1. Dido is the victim of transgressions of a kind thoroughly at home in Attic tragedy.

Reflection on recent criticism of Attic tragedy reveals the pervasiveness of tragic patterns in the *Aeneid*. This may be another answer to Brooks Otis' question of how Virgil managed to reinvigorate the flagging tradition of Graeco-Roman epic and thus produce *the* Roman classic text;[22] furthermore the 'tragic' quality of the *Aeneid* was an important condition for the

---

[21] Harrison (1972–3).   [22] Otis (1964) ch. 2 'The obsolescence of epic'.

successful production of further imperial epics: an 'epic of problematics' might be a fair label for the continuing line of Ovid's *Metamorphoses*, Lucan's *Bellum ciuile*, and Statius' *Thebaid* (the influence of specific tragic models is particularly important in the epics of Ovid and Statius). There remains the literary-historical question of the degree of Virgil's originality in writing a 'tragic epic'. Heinze[23] saw close parallels to *his* list of dramatic features in the *Aeneid* (concentration of dramatic interest, striking reversals, careful psychological motivation) in what we know of the so-called peripatetic school of historiography; Heinze speculates on the possible presence of such features in the lost Hellenistic epic, but thinks it unlikely that the Roman epic poet Ennius was a predecessor of Virgil in this respect. One might on the other hand press Servius' comment on *Aeneid* 2.486ff. that 'this passage has been taken from the fall of Alba', probably referring to the account of the sack of Alba Longa in Book 2 of Ennius' *Annals*, and ask whether Ennius' narrative was already characterised by the tragic qualities found in Virgil's narrative of the destruction of Priam's palace. Ennius, in fact, was a tragedian as well as an epicist (a combination also seen in Livius Andronicus, Naevius, Varius Rufus, and Ovid – a Roman tradition, perhaps).

The surviving Hellenistic epic of Apollonius is a more certain precedent; the use of tragic models particularly in Book 3 of the *Argonautica* is well known, and Virgil will have received an impulse to his dramatic presentation of Dido from the Apollonian Medea. Richard Hunter has shown the presence in the characterisation of Jason of the ephebic patterns of Attic tragedy and other earlier Greek literature,[24] and Apollonius may here too be a mediator between tragedy and the *Aeneid*.

There is also the question of Roman tragedy itself. The fragmentary evidence at least allows us to see that Virgil drew extensively on the Roman tragedians, and it is often difficult in particular instances to judge whether a Roman tragedy or its Greek original is the primary model.[25] The storm that opens the *Aeneid* corresponds to the storm in *Odyssey* Book 5, but is heavily indebted in detail to *nostos*-storms in Roman tragedy (Pacuvius' *Teucer* and Accius' *Clytaemestra*); Wigodsky suggests as the reason 'the rarity of other storm scenes in early Latin literature' (85).[26] Alternatively it may be that through this opening salvo of tragic imitations Virgil stakes his claim to be the continuator of the Roman tragic tradition. Note also how Virgil (through Juno) remotivates the *second* half of the epic through heavy tragic allusion: Allecto is closely related to the personification

---

[23] Heinze (1993) 371–3.   [24] Hunter (1988).
[25] Wigodsky (1972) 90ff.; Stabryla (1970); Zorzetti (1990).   [26] Wigodsky (1972) 85.

of frenzy, *Lyssa*, in Euripides' *Heracles*, and Virgil's descriptions of the effects of the Fury may draw on Latin tragedies on Dionysiac themes (the centrality of Furies in the plot and of Maenads in the imagery of the *Aeneid* is itself a mark of the poem's tragic quality; neither are at all prominent in Homeric epic). In both Books 1 and 7 Juno, like an attentive theatre-goer, mentally rehearses old plays as examples to imitate in her own behaviour. At 1.39–45 she remembers the death of Oilean Ajax in the version of Accius,[27] while at 7.319–22 she tries to use Ennius' *Alexander* as the script for the future history of the Trojans in Italy. In *Aeneid* Book 1 there is something of an overdetermination of tragic introductions, first through Juno and then through Venus' Euripidean 'prologue' to the history of Dido. It may be no accident that in the great Hellenistic city which Aeneas sees rising in the wastes of Africa theatres seem to be the most eye-catching feature (1.427–9).

Although Accius (d. after 86 BC) had been the last major Roman writer of new tragedies, there had been regular productions of tragedies through the first century BC. Late Republican writers of tragedies, whether for stage performance or recitation, include C. Asinius Pollio, a close literary associate of Virgil and probably the author of the tragedies 'worthy of Sophocles' praised at the beginning of Eclogue 8,[28] as well as Varius, author of the *Thyestes* performed in 29 BC. The slender evidence surviving suggests that in their plays Pollio and Varius may have aspired to create a new, 'classic', stage in the development of Roman tragedy, challenging directly the great tragedians of fifth-century Athens;[29] Virgil perhaps subscribed to this ideal in his own epic rewritings of tragedy. But in the event the number of tragic productions in Augustan Rome rapidly dwindles, for whatever reasons.[30]

Virgil's use of tragedy needs also to be assessed against the background of the cultural and ideological functions of Roman Republican tragedy. A line of Italian scholars has sought to find in their reconstructions of third- and second-century BC tragedies direct reflections of the contemporary class struggle;[31] but criticism of this political criticism has not been lacking.[32] Eckhard Lefèvre argues that a major difference between Attic

---

[27] Degl' Innocenti Pierini (1980) 41 n. 50 suggests that Accius' picture of the blasted Ajax may be indebted to a Hellenistic gigantomachy; this would yield a ring-composition with Aeneas' final Gigantomachic blasting of Turnus.

[28] See Nisbet and Hubbard on Horace, *Odes* 2.1.9–12.   [29] Tarrant (1978) 258–61.

[30] Bibliography at Biliński (1958) 51 n. 99.

[31] Pastorino (1957); Biliński (1958); Lana (1958–9); Argenio (1961).

[32] For a balanced overview of the issues see La Penna (1979). The ancient sources make it plain that in the later Republic and under the Empire the theatre was a place for direct political expression on the part of the *plebs*: Abbott (1907); Tengström (1977); Nicolet (1976) 483–94.

tragedy and the Roman adaptations lay in the panegyrical character of the latter, the result of the overpowering pressure of the ideology of a Roman historical destiny that drains the truly tragic from Roman tragedies.[33] Another way of putting it would be to say that Roman tragedy tends to the epic, understood as the genre of praise poetry. If so, Virgil's adaptations of tragic models represent a movement in the opposite direction, producing a 'tragic epic', where 'tragic' is to be understood in terms of the categories both of Aristotle and of Vernant and his school. The closest approximation to an Accian stage tyrant in the *Aeneid* is Mezentius, but the reader's response to the Etruscan king is problematised by the paradoxical combination in his person of tyrannical bestiality with heroic virtue and parental piety.[34] But whatever our assessment of the nature of Republican tragedy, it may be dangerous to underestimate the part played by Virgil himself in forging an amalgam of the commemorative, panegyrical tradition of historical epic with the problematics of Attic legendary tragedy.

FURTHER READING

General on the tragic qualities of the Aeneid

R. Heinze, *Virgil's Epic Technique* (tr. of 3rd edn (1915) by H. and D. Harvey and F. Robertson) (Bristol, 1993) esp. 251–8, 370–3; N. W. De Witt, 'The second *Aeneid* as a drama', *Classical Journal* 20 (1925) 479–85; W. Jackson Knight, *Roman Vergil* (3rd edn Harmondsworth, 1966); K. Quinn, *Virgil's Aeneid: A Critical Description* (Michigan, 1968) 323–49; J. Foster, 'Some devices of drama used in *Aeneid* 1–4', *Proceedings of the Virgil Society* 13 (1973) 28–41; J. W. Hunt, *Forms of Glory. Structure and Sense in Virgil's Aeneid* (Carbondale and Edwardsville, 1973).

Virgil and Greek tragedy

B. C. Fenik, 'The influence of Euripides on Vergil's *Aeneid*', diss. Princeton (1960); A. König, *Die Aeneis und die griechische Tragödie: Studien zur imitatio Technik Vergils* (Berlin, 1970); P. R. Hardie, 'The *Aeneid* and the *Oresteia*', *Proceedings of the Virgil Society* 20 (1991) 29–45.

Individual characters and episodes

Dido: K. Quinn, 'Virgil's tragic queen', *Latin Explorations: Critical Studies in Roman Literature* (London, 1963) 29–58; J. L. Moles, 'Aristotle and Dido's *hamartia*', *Greece & Rome* 31 (1984) 48–63; C. Collard, 'Medea and Dido', *Prometheus* 1 (1975) 131–51.

Aeneas and Ajax: R. O. A. M. Lyne, *Further Voices in Vergil's Aeneid* (Oxford, 1987) 8–12.

Mezentius: A. La Penna, 'Mezenzio: una tragedia della tirannia e del titanismo antico', *Maia* 32 (1980) 3–30.

---

[33] Lefèvre (1976) 43.   [34] La Penna (1980).

Virgil and Roman tragedy

N. Zorzetti, s.v. *Tragici Latini, Enciclopedia Virgiliana*, vol. 5 (Rome, 1990) 245–7 (convenient summary of known allusions); M. Wigodsky, *Vergil and Early Latin Poetry* (Wiesbaden, 1972); J. Griffin, 'The influence of drama', *Latin Poets and Roman Life* (London, 1985) ch. 10. Approaches to the political function of Republican tragedy: B. Biliński, *Accio ed i Gracchi. Contributo all storia della plebe e della tragedia romana*, Accad. Polacca di Scienze e Lettere, Biblioteca di Roma, Conferenze, fascicolo 3 (Rome, 1958); F. F. Abbott, 'The theatre as a factor in Roman politics under the Republic', *Transactions of the American Philological Association* 38 (1907) 49–56. On Augustan tragedy: R. J. Tarrant, 'Senecan drama and its antecedents', *Harvard Studies in Classical Philology* 82 (1978) 213–63, at 258–61.

21

FIONA COX

Envoi: the death of Virgil

In 1930 Europe celebrated the bimillennium of Virgil's birth. The celebrations fell in the middle of Mussolini's dictatorship (1922–43), strengthening the links that Mussolini sought to establish between his Italian regime and ancient Rome. The *Aeneid*, singing of the birth of a new city and a new empire, helped to validate Mussolini's imperialist policies, and in 1936 a new Italian empire was born. In the same year the Austrian writer Hermann Broch began to meditate upon Virgil's position in the modern world and by 1937 he had conceived his novel *The Death of Virgil*.[1] This envoi will focus in particular on Broch's novel, since it probes and anticipates many of the anxieties attached to twentieth-century responses to Virgil.

The opposed political approaches to Virgil offered by Mussolini and the anti-Fascist Broch typify the variety of Virgilian studies proliferating at this time. A renaissance of interest in Virgil was due not solely to the bimillennium, but more suggestively to the sense of crisis pervading Europe in the *entre-deux-guerres* period. George Steiner has observed that after the First World War the European ear became more attuned to the Virgilian voice of exile than to the Homeric cry of triumph.[2] Such a claim seems validated by the wealth of Virgilian biographies published in the 1920s and 1930s. Amongst the most significant was André Bellessort's *Virgile, son œuvre et son temps* (1920), a celebration of a 'Fascist' Virgil whom Bellessort wished to portray at the head of a new cultural tradition rooted in France. This partisan approach was maintained by Bellessort's pupil Robert Brasillach, who was eventually executed for Nazi collaboration and whose book *Présence de Virgile* (1931) strives to portray a modern-day Fascist Virgil: *On a voulu que le lecteur pût commencer ce livre comme s'il s'agissait de l'histoire d'un jeune Italien de 1930*.[3] But the most influential

---

[1] I refer throughout to Jean Starr Untermeyer's translation of *The Death of Virgil* in the OUP Twentieth-Century Classics collection.

[2] Steiner (1990) 10. See also Ziolkowski (1993) 6.   [3] Brasillach (1931) 250.

of these biographies was Theodore Haecker's *Vergil, Vater des Abendlandes* (1933, translated into English in 1934 by A. W. Wheen as *Virgil, Father of the West*), which was also written in response to the current situation in Europe, but was politically opposed to the vision of Brasillach and Bellessort. It may seem somewhat paradoxical that the German Haecker also claims Virgil as the father of Western civilisation, but his Virgil is no nationalist poet. Rather he is the *'anima naturaliter christiana* of antiquity' who transcends the idea of nation and to whom the Western world owes so great a debt.[4]

Haecker exerted an enormous influence upon Broch, not only bestowing a Christianised Virgil upon him but also evoking in similar terms the atmosphere of the age.[5] The theme of the masses fascinated Broch to the point where he wrote a treatise on mass hysteria: he will surely have recognised a kindred spirit when reading Haecker's depiction of the character of their times:

> The strong and real sense – it is not knowledge – that every man has today, of a break, a break through, a new dawn, is suddenly converted by the spirit of the time to hysteria, so that he sees not merely a new period but a new era approaching. (p. 17)

Broch's description evokes an atmosphere which is ripe for the arrival of an imperial leader to guide the masses into this new era:

> they screamed out of themselves and to themselves that somewhere in the thicket there must exist an excellent one, an extraordinary voice, the voice of a leader to whom they need only attach themselves so that in his reflected glory, in the reflection of the jubilation, the intoxication, the power of the imperial divinity they might with a gasping, wild, bullish thundering assault still be able to clear an earthly path out of this entanglement of existence. (p. 73)

The Death of Virgil pivots around Virgil's eventual realisation that he has contributed to this infernal confusion by presenting through the *Aeneid* a lie which he asks his readers to accept as reality, namely the glorious beauty of empire. Broch has projected into the legend of Virgil's demand that the *Aeneid* should be burnt his own modernist awareness of the inadequacy and dishonesty of art. Lawrence Lipking observes pertinently that Broch was writing under the same circumstances that drove Curtius to

---

[4] Haecker (1934) 17.

[5] T. S. Eliot also stressed the importance of a Christian Virgil to Western civilisation, although his Virgil is one with a noble idea of empire, glorying in civilisation despite the cost, and so differs radically from Haecker's (and Broch's) vision. See 'What is a Classic?' (pp. 53–71) and 'Virgil and the Christian world' (pp. 121–31) in Eliot (1957).

wonder if any more classics would be born, and Eliot to think that all his work might end in fire. Moreover the destruction of the *Aeneid* would sound the death-knell of Western civilisation, as it would also annihilate all that the *Aeneid* had inspired.

On one level Broch's novel may be seen as a somewhat idiosyncratic account of Virgil's last hours, written at a time which fostered biographical accounts of Virgil. But far from being no more than a biographical study *The Death of Virgil* displays anxieties which later surfaced as subjects of critical theory. The title itself suggests an affinity with Roland Barthes' essay *The Death of the Author* (1968) which argues against the conception of the author as a source of texts. This argument depends upon loss of authorial control, and it is interesting that Broch also depicts a Virgil unable to control his work, swept away in autonomous verbal currents. Barthes' call for recognition of the author's diminished role helped to develop the concept of intertextuality, the relationships that texts forge independently with other texts. An intertextual approach to Broch, liberating us from the chronological constraints of influence, enables us to see not only how Virgil enhances Broch, but also how Broch modifies our readings of Virgil.

The novel's very title announces its intertextual nature. This is furthered by the use of prefatory quotations, two of which come from the *Aeneid* and one from Dante's *Inferno*. The first, *fato profugus* (*Aen.* 1.2), suggests that Virgil is driven by fate as much as his creation Aeneas. This loss of authority is a leitmotif throughout the work, and exacerbates Virgil's insecurity and sense of exile:

> Only at the edge of his fields had he walked, only at the edge of his life had
> he lived. He had become a rover, fleeing death, seeking death, seeking work,
> fleeing work ... a lodger in his own life.   (p. 5)

This life has gone round in circles, has consisted of flight after flight. The balancing phrases of the chiasmus contribute to the feeling of suspension as Virgil's life has been spent in the interstices of 'fleeing death, seeking death, seeking work, fleeing work'. But it is in just such an ephemeral place that poetic inspiration came: 'Flight, oh flight! oh dusk, the hour of poetry ... oh poetry was anticipation but not quite departure, yet it was an enduring farewell' (p. 50). The passage expands on 'no longer, but not yet', a phrase which recurs constantly throughout the book. The suspension mirrors that which underpins the *Aeneid*, situated as it is between the past of lost Troy and the glorious future of Rome which stands outside the text. Only at the point of death does Virgil realise that this twilight hour is the prelude to the final homecoming: 'never was the earth nearer the heart of light nor light closer to the earth than in the approaching dusk at the two boundaries of night' (p. 8). Broch's vision casts new shades of meaning upon *umbra*, a word which closes not only the *Aeneid* but also Eclogues 1 and 10. The ambivalence of Virgil's shade, at times restful, at times harmful to flocks and poets, reinforces the ambivalent power of poetry. Furthermore, Broch's inheritance of Dante's Christian Virgil endows *umbra* with a metaphysical quality: he follows the pattern set by Dante, who imprisoned his Virgil within a twilight from which, because of his pagan status, he was unable to emerge into the light of Paradise.

The nearer Virgil comes to death, the further he enters into this twilight where the greatest of earthly perceptions are born. Here, all of his past has spilled over into his present. It is a rich past: like Tennyson's *Ulysses* he has become a part of all that he has met. Significantly in the following extract the word used of Virgil's life is 'einverwoben', 'interwoven'. Since texts are literally 'woven structures' it is the smallest of etymological jumps to move from 'interwoven' to *intertextum* and to hear Virgil's voice in all the texts he has ever encountered:

> interwoven with them all, ... interwoven and losing himself in happenings and objects, interwoven and losing himself in countries and their cities, how buried all this and yet how immediate ... he knew simultaneously his own life, knew it to be carried by the stream and counter-stream of night in which past and future cross each other ... he himself in the center of the plaza as if someone had wanted to bring him to the center of his own being, to the cross-roads of his worlds, to the center of his world, compliant to fate.
>
> (p. 21)

The passage again stresses Virgil's loss of control and his failure to reach a centre, the stability of a present tense despite all his wanderings. To see his life as intertextual opens up the interpretation of *fato profugus* still further, so that it signifies 'driven by past literary voices, by what has been said'. Literary theorists such as Genette and Blanchot have used the image of the labyrinth to denote the intertextual infinity of voices linking text to text. It is interesting that Broch also speaks of a 'maze of voices' in which Virgil is imprisoned, assailed by the 'anarchic voices and their grasping arms ... voices of the second, voices of the year, voices of the aeon' (p. 71). Virgil's fate, embodying the notion of past voices and of destiny, is unable to restore a centre that has failed to hold. The whole book is devoted to his attempts to recover a mythical circle of completion like that depicted at the end of Dante's *Paradiso*, where human beings are united with their final selves and all the texts of the world are bound in absolute harmony. Virgil's distance from such perfection is evidenced by his imprisonment in 'the enormous cavern of night from which there was no release' (p. 70), where he cries out '... oh, he must again behold the stars' (p. 76). The plea echoes the prefatory quotations where Broch has placed the closing lines of the *Inferno*:

> The leader and I entered upon that hidden road to return into the bright world, and without caring to have any rest we climbed up, he first and me second, so far I saw through a round opening some of the fair things that Heaven bears; and thence we came forth to see again the stars.

Virgil's prefiguring of Dante's words establishes his suffering in a similar hell from which he has not yet emerged to see the stars. Although he hopes for the voice of a leader to guide him from his entangled existence, he senses that such a voice would have to stand outside the earthly sphere. He himself is condemned to repeat himself and other people, to turn words over so often that they lose all human meaning. He may have attempted to shore up fragments against his ruin, but he has succeeded only in entering the inhuman circularity of art:

> constrained to return constantly into its own beginning which was
>   its end and hence pitiless
> pitiless towards human sorrow which meant no more to art
> than passing existence, no more than a word, a stone, a sound or a color
> to be used for exploring and revealing beauty
> in unending repetition.   (p. 101)

The realisation that art cannot express the reality of humanity results in the bitterest of cries as Virgil reaches the horrible, but necessary, conclusion that all he had sought to achieve through the *Aeneid* was a failure, a mere simulacrum of achievement. He perceives the *Aeneid* as a piece of writing as futile as the prophecies which flit around the Sibyl's cave, disappointing all who come to consult them (*Aen* 3. 443–52):

> the translucent and glittering pictures of his life's landscape, once so dazzling, had grown dim, had withered and dried away, his verses which he had twined about them had dried up and fallen away, all this had blown away like faded leaves.   (p. 75)

As if to recognise the failure of his life's work were not enough, a still more horrifying realisation dawns upon Virgil, that the words which he has written will play their part in the barbaric wars that human beings wage against each other – the scope of interpretation is an uncontrollable infinity, allowing for all the possibilities of evil:

they read the unspeakable prose behind the poem of words, and what they read consisted no longer of lines, but of an endless immense space stretching out on all sides to infinity, a space in which the sentences did not follow one another in order, but covered each other in infinite crossings and were no longer sentences ... At every spot where the sentence waves and sentence cycles crossed one another, there war, lifeless and callous, conducted by human beings essentially dead, came into view, there the feud of the gods could be seen in all its godlessness, there too was revealed the nameless murder in a nameless sphere. (p. 160)

The disorder and autonomy of the sentences depicted here foreshadow the attempts of much modernist literature to depict this very disorder. In the context of this volume it is perhaps more significant that it also anticipates recent classical criticism such as John Henderson's 'Lucan/The word at war', which helps to unfold the terrible prose behind the clashing narrative currents of Lucan's *Pharsalia*, itself a parody of the *Aeneid*. Furthermore it is interesting that Virgil, Lucan and Broch are all intertextual presences in Claude Simon's novel *La Bataille de Pharsale* (1969), where the narrative rapidly degenerates into *La Bataille de la phrase*.

The terror of witnessing the horror that he has furthered creeps over Virgil in an absolute stillness and evidences still further his lack of control. He becomes the Aeneas who gazed mutely over the devastation of his fatherland as a shepherd watching the destruction of the land (*Aen.* 2.302–17), but the landscape in Broch is as putrefied as Hades – no bird will fly across it (*Aen.* 6.239–41) – and in desperation he echoes the words of Jupiter (*Aen.* 12.793) by asking where the end to all this was to be found:

and he too was waiting: with uplifted arms he waited with dream and landscape, he gazed over the still pastures on which the cattle were grazing without motion, he perceived the muteness of the motionlessly burning brands, and no bird flight moved across the pavilion of the air ... oh, when was the end to be? Where was the end to be found? When would the desecration be quaffed to the last drop? Was there a nethermost stage to this deepening silence? And then it seemed to him that just such an ultimate stage had been achieved. For he saw the mouths of men gaping at one another full of terror, no sound wrenched itself from the dry clefts and no-one understood the other. (p. 185)

This breakdown of communication is the ultimate realisation of the many instances in Virgil's poetry where humans are unable to relate to one another. In Broch's depiction, however, the collapse into silence is unsoftened by melancholy: memories of his former luxury of expression now contribute to Virgil's realisation that he must burn the *Aeneid*. This realisation dawns upon him in the second of the book's four sections. Although this is the bleakest section of the book, its closing chords are sweetened by a 'voice of such great loneliness that it glowed like a single star in the darkness' (p. 168). Virgil is at last emerging from his hell to behold a star. Its solitary status links it to the star over Bethlehem, and like this star it leads the way to Christianity: 'it revealed itself as the tone-picture of the annunciating deed: "Open your eyes to Love!"' (p. 187).

The journey towards the innocence of the final Christian arrival is a journey back to the innocence of childhood, and so it is unsurprising that figures from Virgil's distant past should assert their presences. The two most important are Plotia, beloved by Virgil, and the boy Lysanias, Virgil's other love, who sometimes appears under the name of Alexis in allusion to the Second Eclogue. They are figures sent to guide Virgil as once Virgil and Beatrice guided Dante. Virgil tells Plotia of his hitherto fruitless search and of the relief he is at last beginning to glimpse;

> Retained, retained ... yes, I thought to hold fast to everything, everything that had happened and that was why nothing could succeed.   (p. 274)

> '... then came the voice, then I heard it, and now there is light ...'
> '... and now it is you who are leader.'
> 'Driven by self and by fate, there was no question of leading, scarcely a guide for myself, and still less a guide for the others.'   (p. 224)

The passages explain in part the last of the prefatory quotations:

> '... da iungere dextram
> da genitor, teque amplexu ne subtrahe nostro.'
> sic memorans, largo fletu simul ora rigabat.
> ter conatus ibi collo dare bracchia circum
> ter frustra comprensa manus effugit imago
> par levibus ventis volucrique simillima somno.
>
> (*Aen*. 6. 697–702)

'O Father, give me your hand to hold, give it to me. Do not withdraw from my embrace.' As he spoke thus his face was wet from his flowing tears. Three times there he tried to throw his arms about his father's neck, but three times the image, seized in vain, slipped away like thin air and very like winged sleep.

Virgil's poetry is used to point to the futility of the images which he had tried to posit as firm reality. In his eventual realisation that Aeneas also had returned as 'an empty symbol' from the Underworld, Virgil acknowledges that only death will clear all the vain metaphors from the path of true perception.

The nearer Virgil comes to death, the more insistent becomes the Christian imagery, especially in the form of allusions to Dante. Broch echoes Dante's Statius, who likened the earthly Virgil to a traveller holding behind his back a lantern to illumine for others the path that had been dark for him, as now the child Lysanias held 'the very ring . . . which sent out this radiance, a mantle of light over his shoulders . . . the way-showing smile of a star held aloft in the hands of the boy' (p. 387). This smile gains in importance towards the end of the journey. Virgil himself had foreseen it in his Fourth Eclogue, where he closes with an injunction to the child to smile at its mother. This smile becomes the smile binding Madonna and child, but also 'a faceless smile at rest in itself' (p. 398). Even here the journey is uncompleted – 'the great human sense of wandering beat on in him' (p. 403) – but eventually Virgil comes to a final point and realises that it is the word which he is still unable to clasp, because its very nature eludes expression: 'he could not hold fast to it, he might not hold fast to it; incomprehensible and unutterable to him; it was the word beyond speech' (p. 416). Virgil alone is able to come home to himself. Unlike Dante he cannot return to earth and describe the final perfection; the text and the reader are left still in an exile of imperfection and metaphor.

The loss of control and sense of exile that pervade Broch's novel have become dominant elements of recent critical theory, and it is interesting to observe the parallels between The Death of Virgil and recent Virgilian readings informed by this theory. We have already seen how the conflicts tormenting the dying hours of Virgil opened his eyes to the warring narrative currents within the Aeneid itself. This perception is validated not only by the contending Virgilian receptions of Broch's own time but also W. R. Johnson's observation that twentieth-century interpreters of Virgil could be classified as belonging to either the 'European school' or the 'Harvard school', the former presenting Aeneas' achievements in a positive light despite the cost (as does Eliot), the latter highlighting the darker and more disquieting aspects of the poem (Johnson himself, Adam Parry, Wendell Clausen, Michael Putnam). The anxiety of Broch's Virgil anticipates much of the criticism of the Harvard school, in particular Parry's highly influential essay 'The two voices of Virgil's Aeneid' (1963), which examines Virgil's public voice of triumph and private voice of regret, as well as Johnson's remarkable analysis of the Aeneid's sinister forces, Darkness Visible: A Study of Virgil's Aeneid (1976). More recently Denis Feeney has demonstrated the difficulty of gaining control over Fama or the narrative currents of the Aeneid in The Gods in Epic (1991), while Philip Hardie has focused attention on the suspended quality of the Aeneid in The Epic Successors of Virgil (1993). I have already observed Broch's echoes in John Henderson's article on Lucan's *Pharsalia*, which is itself a parody of the *Aeneid* ('Lucan/The word at war') and Henderson's acute analysis is developed still further in Jamie Masters' equally penetrating book *Poetry and Civil War in Lucan's Bellum Civile* (1992).

Through its vigorous yet lyrical depiction of art's futility *The Death of Virgil* has become one of Europe's most significant modernist novels. Paradoxically Broch's condemnation of art has itself served as an inspiration for new art. In France Jean Barraqué planned a musical meditation longer than Wagner's *Parsifal* and Bach's *St Matthew Passion* combined, although he completed only a few sections of *La Mort de Virgile* before his death. In Britain the writer and academic Gabriel Josipovici has written movingly of his Jewishness and indicated the importance of Broch's account to his own play *Vergil Dying*. Extracts from this play and an essay describing its genesis were published in Charles Martindale's *Virgil and his Influence* (1984), which itself commemorates the bimillennium of Virgil's death. Despite these artistic tributes and despite George Steiner's persistent and passionate advocacy of the novel, the indifference with which it has been received among British classicists remains largely unaltered. Such obduracy is highlighted still further by the warm reception that *The Death of Virgil* has received on the continent as an important piece of Virgilian criticism, especially in France.

To say that *The Death of Virgil* is the twentieth century's most important response to Virgil seems no exaggeration. It is an astonishing piece of literature, but far more than this it is a critique of Virgil's *œuvre* that anticipates the main trends of subsequent Virgilian criticism. It is a novel which shows in the most chilling terms how a work of art can extend far beyond the author's control and imaginings, how it can be used to validate the destruction of thousands of lives. There is, however, another more optimistic side to this phenomenon which testifies to Broch's inability also to control his work. *The Death of Virgil* was written in a period which seemed to have seen the death of culture, when all that was most artistically exquisite seemed to be infested by ghastly possibilities. From these apparent wastelands, however, a host of new responses to Virgil have been born. Far from quelling the Virgilian tradition *The Death of Virgil* stands at the head of a new line of Virgilian studies which are underpinned by a recognition of the *Aeneid*'s guilty past, but which ultimately testify to Virgil's ability to help to articulate and survive the twentieth century.

FURTHER READING

Barthes, Roland (1968) 'La mort de l'auteur', tr. Stephen Heath in Barthes (1977) *Image–Music–Text*. New York

Blanchot, Maurice (1971) *Le Livre à venir*. Paris

Broch, Hermann (1945) *Der Tod des Vergil*, tr. Jean Starr Untermeyer (1983) *The Death of Virgil*. Oxford

Eliot, T. S. (1957) *On Poetry and Poets*. London

Feeney, D. C. (1991) *The Gods in Epic*. Oxford

Genette, Gérard (1981) *Palimpsestes: la littérature au second degré*. Paris

Haecker, Theodore (1934) *Virgil. Father of the West*, tr. A. W. Wheen. London

Hardie, Philip (1993) *The Epic Successors of Virgil*. Cambridge

Henderson, John (1987) 'Lucan/The Word at War', *Ramus* 16: 122–65

Johnson, W. R. (1976) *Darkness Visible: A Study of Virgil's Aeneid*. Berkeley

Josipovici, Gabriel (1980) *Vergil Dying*. Windsor

Lipking, Lawrence (1981) *The Life of the Poet*. Chicago and London

Martindale, Charles, ed. (1984) *Virgil and his Influence*. Bristol

Parry, Adam (1966) 'The two voices of Virgil's *Aeneid*', in Steele Commager, ed., *Virgil: A Collection of Critical Essays*. Englewood Cliffs, NJ

Steiner, George (1975) *After Babel*. London

   (1990) 'Homer and Virgil and Broch', in *London Review of Books*, 12 July, 10–11

Ziolkowski, Theodore (1993) *Virgil and the Moderns*. Princeton

DATELINE

Some of these dates are necessarily approximate or speculative.

BC

1200	Traditional date of Trojan War
753	Legendary foundation of Rome
750	Cumae colonised by Greeks
700	Composition of *Iliad* and *Odyssey*; Hesiod, *Works and Days*
510	Traditional date of expulsion of kings of Rome and foundation of the Republic
270	Apollonius of Rhodes, *Argonautica*; Theocritus active
264–241	First Punic War with Carthage
218–202	Second Punic War
172	Ennius, *Annales*
152	Cato the Elder, *Origines*
149–146	Third Punic War; destruction of Carthage
106	Births of Pompey and Cicero
100	Birth of Julius Caesar
98	Birth of Lucretius
87	Birth of Catullus
76	Birth of Pollio
70	Birth of Virgil, 15 October; first consulate of Pompey and Crassus
69	Births of Gallus and Maecenas
65	Birth of Horace
63	Births of Octavian and Agrippa; consulate of Cicero
62	Death of Catiline
60	First triumvirate of Pompey, Crassus and Caesar
59	Catullus active

55	Virgil in Mediolanum; traditional date of his assumption of the *toga virilis*. Second consulate of Pompey and Crassus; death of Lucretius
54	Death of Catullus
53	Crassus killed at Carrhae
51	Cicero, *De republica*
49	Civil War begins
48	Battle of Pharsalus (Thessaly); Pompey killed in Egypt; Caesar in Alexandria
46	Suicide of Cato the Younger at Utica; dictatorship of Caesar
45	Caesar adopts Octavius as heir
44	Assassination of Caesar by Cassius and Brutus, 15 March; Octavian in Rome
43	Birth of Ovid; second triumvirate formed by Antony, Lepidus and Octavian; proscriptions; death of Cicero
42	Battle of Philippi; defeat and deaths of Cassius and Brutus; Virgil begins composition of *Eclogues*
41	Octavian distributes confiscated land to veterans
40	Consulate of Pollio; reconciliation of Octavian and Antony
38	Virgil and Varius introduce Horace to Maecenas
37	Virgil begins composition of *Georgics*; Virgil and Horace accompany Maecenas on a diplomatic mission to Brundisium
35	Horace, *Satires* 1
31	Battle of Actium; defeat of Antony and Cleopatra
30	Octavian in Egypt; deaths of Antony and Cleopatra; Horace, *Satires* 2 and *Epodes*
29	Virgil completes *Georgics* and begins composition of *Aeneid*; Octavian celebrates triple triumph; Propertius and Tibullus active
27	Octavian receives title 'Augustus'
26	Propertius extols Virgil's work on *Aeneid*
23	Virgil reads extracts from *Aeneid* to Augustus and Octavia at Nola; effective end of Maecenas' literary patronage; Horace, *Odes* 1–3
20	Horace, *Epistles* 1; Ovid, *Amores*, first edition
19	Virgil leaves for Greece to finish the *Aeneid*, becomes ill and dies on return to Italy at Brundisium, 21 September; buried in Naples; *Aeneid* published posthumously by Varius and Plotius; death of Tibullus
15	Birth of Germanicus; Ovid, *Heroides*, first collection
13	Horace, *Odes* 4 and *Epistles* 2 completed
8	Deaths of Maecenas and Horace

AD

1	Ovid, *Amores*, second edition, *Ars amatoria* and *Remedia amoris* completed
2	Ovid begins composition of *Metamorphoses* and *Fasti*
4	Death of Pollio; Augustus adopts Tiberius
8	Ovid's exile
14	Augustus dies; succeeded by Tiberius
17	Ovid dies in exile

SELECTED DATES IN THE RECEPTION OF VIRGIL

Some of these dates are necessarily approximate or speculative.

AD

62	Calpurnius Siculus, *Eclogues*
95	Quintilian, *Institutio oratoria*
384	Servius, commentator on Virgil, active
397	St Augustine, *Confessions*
400	Macrobius, commentator on Virgil, active
500	Fulgentius, commentator on Virgil, active
800	Charlemagne crowned Holy Roman Emperor
1321	Dante, *Divina Commedia*
1380	Chaucer, *House of Fame*
1513	Gavin Douglas, translation of *Aeneid*
1517	Earl of Surrey, translation of *Aeneid* 2 and 4
1579	Spenser, *The Shepheardes Calender*
1581	Torquato Tasso, *Gerusalemme Liberata*
1590	Spenser, *The Faerie Queene*, Books 1–3
1596	Spenser, *The Faerie Queene*, Books 4–6
1637	Milton, *Lycidas*
1674	Milton, *Paradise Lost*
1689	Purcell, *Dido and Aeneas*
1697	Dryden, *Aeneid*
1930	Bimillennium celebrations of Virgil's birth
1944	T. S. Eliot, 'What is a Classic?'
1945	Herman Broch, *The Death of Virgil*
1951	T. S. Eliot, 'Virgil and the Christian world'

WORKS CITED

Abbott, F. F. (1907) 'The theatre as a factor in Roman politics under the Republic', *Transactions of the American Philological Association* 38: 49–56

von Albrecht, M. (1970) 'Zur Tragik von Vergils Turnusgestalt: Aristotelisches in der Schlusszene der Aeneis', *Festschrift E. Zinn*, 1–5. Tübingen

Alexander, J. J. G. (1969) 'A Virgil illuminated by Marco Zoppo', *Burlington Magazine* III: 514–17

(1994) *The Painted Page*. London

Allen, D. C. (1970) *Mysteriously Meant. The Rediscovery of Pagan Symbolism and Allegorical Interpretation in the Renaissance*. Baltimore

Alpers, P. (1979) *The Singer of the Eclogues*. Berkeley

Anderson, R. D., Parsons, P. J., and Nisbet, R. G. M. (1979) 'Elegiacs by Gallus from Qaṣr Ibrîm', *Journal of Roman Studies* 69: 125–55

Anderson, W. S. (1957) 'Virgil's second *Iliad*', reprinted in Harrison (1990) 239–52

Arendt, H. (1961) *Between Past and Future*. New York

Argenio, R. (1961) 'Retorica e politica nelle tragedie de Accio', *Rivista di Studi Classici* 9: 198–212

Arnold, M. (1964) *Essays in Criticism: First and Second Series*. London and New York

Augustine, St (1912) *Confessions*, tr. William Watts. Loeb Classical Library, 2 vols. Cambridge, MA

Austin, R. G. (1927) 'Virgil and the Sibyl', *Classical Quarterly* 21: 100–5

(1955) *P. Vergili Maronis Aeneidos Liber Quartus*. Oxford

(1964) *P. Vergili Maronis Aeneidos Liber Secundus*. Oxford

(1968) '*Ille ego qui quondam*', *Classical Quarterly* 18: 107–15

(1971) *P. Vergili Maronis Aeneidos Liber Primus*. Oxford

(1977) *P. Vergili Maronis Aeneidos Liber Sextus*. Oxford

Axelson, B. (1945) *Unpoetische Wörter: Ein Beitrag zur Kenntnis der lateinischen Dichtersprache*. Lund

Bakhtin, M. (1981) *The Dialogic Imagination. Four Essays*, tr. C. Emerson and M. Holquist. Austin

(1984) *Problems of Dostoevsky's Poetics*, tr. C. Emerson. Minneapolis

Bal, M. (1985) *Narratology: Introduction to the Theory of Narrative*. Toronto and London

Ball, R. (1991) 'Theological semantics: Virgil's *Pietas* and Dante's *Pietà*', in Jacoff and Schnapp (1991) 19–36

Barchiesi, A. (1984) *La traccia del modello: effetti omerici nella narrazione Virgiliana.* Pisa

(1994) 'Rappresentazioni del dolore e interpretazione nell'Eneide', *Antike und Abendland* 40: 109–24

Bardon, H. (1950) 'L'Enéide et l'art des XVIe–XVIIIe siècles', *Gazette des Beaux Arts* 37: 77–90

Barnes, T. D. (1981) *Constantine and Eusebius.* Cambridge, MA

Barnes, W. R. (1995) 'Virgil: the literary impact', in Horsfall (1995)

Barolini, T. (1984) *Dante's Poets: Textuality and Truth in the Comedy.* Princeton

Barrell, J. and Bull, J., eds. (1974) *The Penguin Book of English Pastoral Verse.* London

Barthes, R. (1968) 'La mort de l'auteur', tr. S. Heath in Barthes (1977)

(1977) *Image–Music–Text.* New York

(1989) *The Rustle of Language*, tr. R. Howard. Berkeley

Bartsch, S. (1989) *Decoding the Ancient Novel.* Princeton

Basnett, S. (1991) *Translation Studies*, rev. edn. London and New York

Baswell, C. (1995) *Virgil in Medieval England.* Cambridge

Batstone, W. W. (1984) *Georgics I: Studies in Meaning and Criticism*, diss. University of California, Berkeley

(1988) 'On the surface of the *Georgics*', *Arethusa* 21: 227–45

Baxandall, M. (1985) *Patterns of Intention.* New Haven

Baxter, R. T. S. (1972) 'Virgil's influence on Tacitus in Books 1 and 2 of the *Annals*', *Classical Philology* 67: 246–69

Bellessort, A. (1920) *Virgile, son œuvre et son temps.* Paris

Benjamin, W. (1970) *Illuminations*, tr. Harry Zohn. London

Bernard, J. D., ed. (1986) *Vergil at 2000: commemorative Essays on the Poet and his Influence.* New York

Bews, J. (1972) 'Virgil, Tacitus, Tiberius and Germanicus', *Proceedings of the Virgil Society* 12: 35–48

Biliński, B. (1958) *Accio ed i Gracchi. Contributo alla storia della plebe e della tragedia romana* (Accad. Polacca di Scienze e Lettere, Biblioteca di Roma, Conferenze, fasc. 3). Rome

Binder, G. (1971) *Aeneas und Augustus: Interpretationen zum 8. Buch der Aeneis.* Meisenheim

Bing, P. (1993) 'Aratus and his audiences', in Schiesaro *et al.* (1993) 99–129

Blanchot, M. (1971) *Le Livre à venir.* Paris

Bloom, H. (1973) *The Anxiety of Influence: A Theory of Poetry.* London

(1995) *The Western Canon: The Books and School of the Ages.* London

Blunt, A. (1967) *Nicolas Poussin.* London

Bonfanti, M. (1985) *Punto di vista e modi della narrazione nell'Eneide.* Pisa

Bosci, U. *et al.*, eds. (1976) *Enciclopedia Dantesca*, 6 vols. Rome

Bowersock, G. W. (1971) 'A date in the *Eighth Eclogue*', *Harvard Studies in Classical Philology* 75: 73–80

Bowra, C. M. (1933–4) 'Aeneas and the Stoic ideal', *Greece & Rome* 3: 8–21

Boyle, A. J. (1975) *Ancient Pastoral.* Victoria

ed. (1979) *Virgil's Ascraean Song: Ramus Essays on the Georgics.* Berwick, Victoria

(1986) *The Chaonian Dove: Studies in the Eclogues, Georgics, and Aeneid of Virgil.* Leiden

(1993) 'The canonic text: Virgil's *Aeneid*', in Boyle, ed. *Roman Epic*. London and New York

Bradley, A. C. (1909) 'Hegel's Theory of Tragedy', *Oxford Lectures on Poetry*, 69–95. Oxford

Brasillach, R. (1931) *Présence de Virgile*. Paris

Braund, S. M., and Gill, C., eds. (forthcoming) *The Passions in Roman Thought and Literature*. Cambridge

Breen, C. C. (1986) 'The shield of Turnus, the swordbelt of Pallas, and the wolf', *Vergilius* 32: 63–71

Broch, H. (1945) *Der Tod des Vergil*, tr. J. S. Untermeyer (1983) *The Death of Virgil*. Oxford

Brooks, P. (1984) *Reading for the Plot: Design and Intention in Narrative*. New York and London

(1994) *Psychoanalysis and Storytelling*. Oxford

Büchner, K. (1955) 'P. Vergilius Maro', *Real-Encyclopädie der Classischen Alter-tumswissenschaft* 8a.1021–486

Bühler, W. (1960) *Die Europa des Moschos*. Wiesbaden

Burck, E. (1929) 'Die Komposition von Vergils Georgika', *Hermes* 64: 279–321

Burrow, C. (1993) *Epic Romance: Homer to Milton*. Oxford

Cafritz, R. C., Gowing, L., and Rosand, D. (1988) *Places of Delight: The Pastoral Landscape*. London and Washington

Cairns, F. (1989) *Virgil's Augustan Epic*. Cambridge

Callman, E. (1974) *Apollonio di Giovanni*. Oxford

Cameron, A. (1995) *Callimachus and His Critics*. Princeton

Campbell, M. (1977) *Pietro da Cortona at the Pitti Palace. A Study of the Plan-etary Rooms and Related Projects*. Princeton

Camps, W. (1969) *An Introduction to Virgil's Aeneid*. Oxford

(1971) *Literary Style: A Symposium*. Oxford

Carcopino, J. (1930) *Virgile et le Mystère de la IV Eglogue*. Paris

Carrithers, M., Collins, S. and Lukes, S., eds. (1985) *The Category of the Person: Anthropology, Philosophy, History*. Cambridge

Chalker, J. (1969) *The English Georgic*. London

Chambers, D. D. C. (1993) *The Planters of the English Landscape Garden: Botany, Trees and the Georgics*. London and New Haven

Champlin, E. J. (1978) 'The life and times of Calpurnius Siculus', *Journal of Roman Studies* 68: 95–110

Chaucer, G. (1987) *The Riverside Chaucer*, eds. L. D. Benson *et al.*, 3rd edn. Boston

Chevallier, R., ed. (1978) *Présence de Virgile*. Paris

Clausen, W. (1964a) 'An interpretation of the *Aeneid*', *Harvard Studies in Classical Philology* 68: 139–47

(1964b) 'Callimachus and Latin poetry', *Greek, Roman and Byzantine Studies* 5: 181–96

(1972) 'On the date of the *First Eclogue*', *Harvard Studies in Classical Philology* 76: 201–6

(1986) 'Cicero and the New Poetry', *Harvard Studies in Classical Philology* 90: 159–70

(1987) *Virgil's Aeneid and the Tradition of Hellenistic Poetry*. Berkeley

(1994) *A Commentary on Virgil Eclogues*. Oxford

(1995) 'Appendix', in Horsfall, ed. *A Companion to the Study of Virgil*. Leiden

Clay, D. (1988) 'The archaeology of the Temple to Juno in Carthage', *Classical Philology* 83: 195–205

Clay, J. S. (1993) 'The education of Perses', in Schiesaro *et al.* (1993) 23–34

Cohn, D. (1978) *Transparent Minds: Narrative Modes for Presenting Consciousness in Fiction*. Princeton

Coleman, R. (1977) *Vergil, Eclogues*. Cambridge

(1982) 'The Gods in the *Aeneid*', *Greece & Rome* 29: 143–68

Collard, C. (1975) 'Medea and Dido', *Prometheus* 1: 131–51

Commager, S., ed. (1966) *Virgil: A Collection of Critical Essays*. Englewood Cliffs, NJ

(1981) 'Fateful words: some conversations in *Aeneid* 4', *Arethusa* 14: 101–14

Comparetti, D. (1966) *Virgil in the Middle Ages*, tr. E. F. M. Benecke, 2nd edn. London

Conrad, C. (1965) 'Traditional patterns of word-order in Latin epic from Ennius to Virgil', *Harvard Studies in Classical Philology* 69: 195–258

Consoli, D. and Ronconi, A. (1976) 'Virgilio' and 'Echi Virgiliani', in Bosci *et al.* (1976)

Conte, G. B. (1966) 'Il Proemio della *Pharsalia*', *Maia* 18: 42–53

(1986) *The Rhetoric of Imitation: Genre and Poetic Memory in Virgil and Other Latin Poets*. Ithaca, NY and London

(1992) 'Proems in the middle', *Yale Classical Studies* 29: 147–59

(1993) Review of Harrison (1991), *Journal of Roman Studies* 83: 208–12

(1994a) *Latin Literature. A History*. Baltimore and London

(1994b) *Genres and Readers: Lucretius, Love Elegy, Pliny's Encyclopedia*, tr. G. W. Most. Baltimore and London

Cooper, H. (1977) *Pastoral: Mediaeval into Renaissance*. Ipswich

Courcelle, J. (1984) *Lecteurs paiens et lecteurs chrétiens de l'Enéide*. Mémoires de l'Académie des inscriptions et belles-lettres, n.s. 4, 2 vols. Rome

(1985) 'Les illustrations de L'Enéide dans les manuscrits du Xe au XVe siècle', *Collection de l'Ecole Française de Rome* 80: 395–409

Courtney, E. (1993) *The Fragmentary Latin Poets*. Oxford

Crusius, O. (1899) 'Cento', *Real-Encyclopädie Der Classischen Altertumswissenschaft* 3.1929–32

Curtius, E. R. (1953) *European Literature and the Latin Middle Ages*, tr. W. R. Trask. London, Henley and New York

Dahlmann, H. (1954) *Der Bienenstaat in Vergils Georgica*, Akad. der Wissen. Und der Lit. Mainz 10: 547–62. Wiesbaden

Daintree, D. (1990) 'The Virgil commentary of Aelius Donatus – black hole or "éminence grise"?', *Greece & Rome* 37: 65–79

Davis, C. T. (1993) 'Dante and the Empire', in R. Jacoff, ed. *The Cambridge Companion to Dante*, 67–79. Cambridge

Deroux, C., ed. (1980) *Studies in Latin Literature and Roman History*. Brussels

Derrida, J. (1981) 'The Law of Genre', *Glyph* 7: 176–229

Deutsch, H. (1985) 'Fiction and fabrication', *Philosophical Studies* 47: 201–11

Dietz, D. B. (1989) 'Elementi di una poetica Serviana', *Studi Italiani di Filologia Classica* 82: 56–109, 240–60

(1995) 'Historia in the commentary of Servius', Transactions of the American Philological Association 125: 61–97

Douglas, G. (1957–64) Virgil's Aeneid Translated into Scottish Verse, ed. D. F. C. Coldwell, 4 vols. Edinburgh and London

Dover, K. J. (1978) Greek Homosexuality. Cambridge, MA

Dryden, J. (1987) The Works of Virgil in English: Volumes V and VI, eds. W. Frost and V. A. Dearing. Berkeley, Los Angeles and London

Duckworth, G. (1969) Virgil and Classical Hexameter Poetry: A Study in Metrical Variety. Ann Arbor

DuQuesnay, I. M. Le M. (1979) 'From Polyphemus to Corydon', in West and Woodman (1979)

(1981) 'Vergil's First Eclogue', in F. Cairns, ed. Papers of the Liverpool Latin Seminar Third Volume, 29–182. Liverpool

Eden, P. T. (1975) A Commentary on Virgil: Aeneid VIII. Leiden

Edwards, C. (1993) The Politics of Immorality in Ancient Rome. Cambridge

Egan, R. B. (1980) 'Euryalus' mother and Aeneid 9–12', in Deroux (1980) vol. 2, 157–76

Eliot, T. S. (1951) Selected Essays. London

(1957) On Poetry and Poets. London

Elsner, J. and Masters, J., eds. (1994) Reflections of Nero. London

Empson, W. (1935) Some Versions of Pastoral. London

Fantuzzi, M. and Reitz, C., eds. (forthcoming) Ekphrasis

Faral, E. (1924) Les Arts Poétiques du XIIe et du XIIIe Siècle. Paris

Farrell, J. (1991) Vergil's Georgics and the Traditions of Ancient Epic: The Art of Allusion in Literary History. New York and Oxford

(1992) 'Literary allusion and cultural poetics in Vergil's Third Eclogue', Vergilius 38: 64–71

Farron, S. (1993) Vergil's Aeneid: A Poem of Grief and Love. Leiden and New York

Feeney, D. C. (1983) 'The taciturnity of Aeneas', Classical Quarterly 33: 204–19

(1984) 'The reconciliations of Juno', reprinted in Harrison (1990) 339–62

(1986) 'History and revelation in Vergil's Underworld', Proceedings of the Cambridge Philological Society 32: 1–24

(1991) The Gods in Epic. Oxford

(1997) Literature and Religion at Rome: Cultures, Contexts, and Beliefs. Cambridge

Fenik, B. C. (1960) 'The influence of Euripides on Vergil's Aeneid', diss. Princeton

Fish, S. E. (1980) Is There a Text in This Class? The Authority of Interpretative Communities. Cambridge, MA, and London

Fordyce, C. J. (1977) P. Vergili Maronis Aeneidos Libri VII–VIII with a Commentary. Oxford

Forster, E. M. (1976) Aspects of the Novel. Harmondsworth

Foster, J. (1973) 'Some devices of drama used in Aeneid 1–4', Proceedings of the Virgil Society 13: 28–41

Foster, K. (1977) The Two Dantes and Other Studies. London

Foucault, M. (1977) Language, Counter-Memory, Practice: Selected Essays and Interviews, tr. P. Kamuf. New York and London

Fowler, D. P. (1987) 'Vergil on killing virgins', in Whitby et al. (1987) 185–98

(1989) 'First thoughts on closure: problems and prospects', Materiali e Discussioni 22: 75–122

(1990) 'Deviant focalisation in Virgil's *Aeneid*', *Proceedings of the Cambridge Philological Society* 36: 42–63

(1991) 'Narrate and describe: the problem of ekphrasis', *Journal of Roman Studies* 81: 25–35

(1994) 'Arts and the Mantuan', review of Ziolkowski (1993), *Times Literary Supplement* 11 February, p. 25

(1995) 'From epos to cosmos: Lucretius, Ovid, and the poetics of segmentation', in Innes, *et al.* (1995) 1–18

Fraenkel, E. (1964) *Kleine Beiträge zur klassischen Philologie*. Rome

    (1990) 'Aspects of the structure of *Aeneid* 7', reprinted in Harrison (1990) 253–76

Friederich, F. (1974) 'Classicism', in A. Preminger, ed. *The Princeton Encyclopedia of Poetry and Poetics*. Princeton

Friedlaender, P. (1962) *Johannes von Gaza, Paulus Silentiarius und Prokopios von Gaza*, 2nd edn (1st edn 1912, Leipzig). Hildesheim

Frost, R. (1962) 'For John F. Kennedy. His inauguration', *In the Clearing*, 28–30. New York

Frost, W. (1982) 'Translating Virgil, Douglas to Dryden: some general considerations', in Mack and deForest Lord (1982) 271–86

Gadamer, H.-G. (1975) *Truth and Method*, tr. W. Glen-Doepel. London

Gagarin, M. (1990) 'Ambiguity of *Eris* in the *Works and Days*', in Griffith and Mastronarde (1990)

Gale, M. (1991) 'Man and beast in Lucretius and the *Georgics*', *Classical Quarterly* 41: 414–26

Galinsky, G. K. (1968) '*Aeneid* V and the *Aeneid*', *American Journal of Philology* 89: 157–85

    (1988) 'The anger of Aeneas', *American Journal of Philology* 109: 321–48

    (1994) 'How to be philosophical about the end of the *Aeneid*', *Illinois Classical Studies* 19: 191–201

    (1996) *Augustan Culture: An Interpretive Introduction*. Princeton

Genette, G. (1980) *Narrative Discourse*, tr. C. Lewin. Cornell

    (1981) *Palimpsestes: la littérature au second degré*. Paris

    (1987) *Seuils*. Paris

Georgii, H. (1912) 'Zur Bestimmung der Zeit des Servius', *Philologus* 71: 518–26

Geymonat, M. (1995) 'The transmission of Virgil's works in antiquity and the Middle Ages', in Horsfall (1995)

Gibson, W. S. (1977) *Bruegel*. London

Gill, C., ed. (1991) *The Person and the Human Mind: Essays in Ancient and Modern Philosophy*. Oxford

Gillis, D. (1983) *Eros and Death in the Aeneid*. Rome

Glover, T. R. (1912) *Virgil*. London

Goldberg, J. (1992) *Sodometries: Renaissance Texts/Modern Sexualities*. Stanford

Goldberg, S. M. (1995) *Epic in Republican Rome*. Oxford

Goldhill, S. D. (1986) *Reading Greek Tragedy*. Cambridge

Goldhill, S. D. and Osborne, R. (1994) *Art and Text in Ancient Greek Culture*. Cambridge

Goodyear, F. R. D. (1981) *The Annals of Tacitus*, vol 2. Cambridge

Goold, G. P. (1970) 'Servius and the Helen episode', *Harvard Studies in Classical Philology* 74: 101–68

(1992) 'The voice of Virgil: the pageant of Rome in *Aeneid 6*', in T. Woodman and J. Powell, eds. *Author and Audience in Latin Literature*, 110–23. Cambridge

Gorgemanns, H. and Schmidt, E. A., eds. (1976) *Studien zum antiken Epos*. Meisenheim

Görler, W. (1985) 'Eneide: la lingua', *Enciclopedia Virgiliana* 2: 262–78. Rome

Gransden, K. W. (1976) *Virgil, Aeneid Book VIII*. Cambridge

  (1984) *Virgil's Iliad: An Essay on Epic Narrative*. Cambridge

  (1991) *Virgil, Aeneid Book XI*. Cambridge

  (1996) *Virgil in English*. Harmondsworth

Graves, R. (1962) 'The Virgil cult', *The Virginia Quarterly Review* 38: 13–47

Griffin, J. (1979) 'The Fourth *Georgic*, Virgil and Rome', *Greece & Rome* 26: 61–80

  (1984) 'Augustus and the poets: "Caesar qui cogere posset"', in Miller and Segal (1984) 189–218

  (1985) *Latin Poets and Roman Life*. London

  (1986) *Virgil* (Past Masters series). Oxford and New York

  (1992) 'Virgil', in Jenkyns (1992) 125–50

Griffin, M. (1989) 'Philosophy, politics, and politicians at Rome', in M. Griffin and W. R. Barnes, eds. *Philosophia Togata. Essays on Philosophy and Roman Society*, 1–37. Oxford

Griffith, M. (1983) 'Personality in Hesiod', *Classical Anthology* 2: 37–65

Griffith, M. and Mastronarde, D. J., eds. (1990) *Cabinet of the Muses: Essays on Classical and Comparative Literature in Honor of Thomas G. Rosenmeyer*. Atalanta

Gurval, R. A. (1995) *Actium and Augustus: The Politics and Emotions of Civil War*. Ann Arbor

Haber, J. (1994) *Pastoral and the Poetics of Self-Contradiction: Theocritus to Marvell*. Cambridge

Habinek, T. N. (1985) 'Prose cola and poetic word-order: observations on adjectives and nouns in the *Aeneid*', *Helios* 12: 51–66

  (1997) 'The invention of sexuality in the world-city of Rome', in T. N. Habinek and A. Schiesaro, eds. *The Roman Cultural Revolution*. Cambridge

Haecker, T. (1934) *Virgil, Father of the West*, tr. A. W. Wheen. London and New York

Hagendahl, H. (1958) *The Latin Fathers and the Classics*. Göteborg

Hallett, J. P. and Skinner, M. B., eds. (forthcoming) *Roman Sexualities*. Princeton

Halliburton, D. (1981) *Poetic Thinking: An Approach to Heidegger*. Chicago

Halliwell, S. (1987) *The Poetics of Aristotle*. London

Halperin, D. M. (1983) *Before Pastoral: Theocritus and The Ancient Tradition of Bucolic Poetry*. New Haven and London

Hamon, P. (1975) 'Clausules', *Poétique* 6: 496–526

Harder, M. A., Regtuit, R. F., and Walker, G. C., eds. (1993) *Callimachus*. Gronigen

Hardie, P. R. (1986) *Virgil's Aeneid: Cosmos and Imperium*. Oxford

  (1991) 'The *Aeneid* and the *Oresteia*', *Proceedings of the Virgil Society* 20: 29–45

  (1993) *The Epic Successors of Virgil: A Study in the Dynamics of a Tradition*. Cambridge

  (1994) *Virgil, Aeneid Book IX*. Cambridge

(1995) Review article, 'Virgil's epic techniques: Heinze ninety years on', *Classical Philology* 90: 267–76

Hardison, O. B. ed. (1974) *Medieval Literary Criticism*. London

Harrison, E. L. (1972–3) 'Why did Venus wear boots? Some reflections on *Aeneid* 1.314f.', *Proceedings of the Virgil Society* 12: 10–25

Harrison, S. J. (1989) 'Augustus, the poets, and the *spolia opima*', *Classical Quarterly* 39: 408–14

  ed. (1990) *Oxford Readings in Vergil's Aeneid*. Oxford and New York

  (1991) *Vergil, Aeneid 10. With Introduction, Translation, and Commentary*. Oxford

  ed. (1995) *R. G. M. Nisbet: Collected Papers on Latin Literature*. Oxford

Harrison, T. W. (1967) 'English Virgil: the *Aeneid* in the XVIII century', *Philologica Pragensia* 10: 1–11, 80–91

Hawkins, P. S. (1991) 'Dido, Beatrice and the signs of ancient love', in Jacoff and Schnapp (1991) 113–30

Heaney, S. (1991) *Seeing Things*. London

  (1995) *The Redress of Poetry: Oxford Lectures*. London and Boston

Heffernan, W. (1993) *Museum of Words*. Chicago

Heidegger, M. (1968) *What is Called Thinking*, tr. J. Glenn. New York

  (1971) *Poetry, Language, Thought*, tr. A. Hofstadter. New York

Heinze, R. (1915) *Vergils epische Technik*, 3rd edn (4th edn 1957, Stuttgart). Leipzig and Berlin

  (1993) *Vergil's Epic Technique*, tr. H. and D. Harvey and F. Robertson. Bristol

Heinze Hahn, K. and Schmid, I. eds. (1981) *Briefe an Göethe*, vol. 2, 1796–8. Weimar

Helgerson, R. (1992) *Forms of Nationhood*. Chicago and London

Henderson, J. (1987) 'Lucan/The word at war', *Ramus* 16: 122–65

Henry, J. (1873–92) *Aeneidea, or Critical, Exegetical, and Aesthetical Remarks on the Aeneid*, 5 vols. London, Dublin and Edinburgh

Hershkowitz, D. (1991) 'The *Aeneid* in *Aeneid* 3', *Vergilius* 37: 69–76

Heuzé, P. (1985) *L'Image du corps dans l'œuvre de Virgile* (Collection de l'Ecole Française de Rome). Rome

Highet, G. (1972) *The Speeches in Virgil's Aeneid*. Princeton

Hirsch, E. D. (1967) *Validity in Interpretation*. New Haven and London

Hochman, B. (1985) *Character in Literature*. Cornell

Holland, L. A. (1935) 'Place names and heroes in the *Aeneid*', *American Journal of Philology* 56: 202–15

Hollander, J. (1988) 'The poetics of ecphrasis', *Word and Image* 4: 209–18

Hope, C. (1971) 'The "Camerini d'Alabastro" of Alfonso d'Este', *Burlington Magazine* 113: 641–50

Hopkinson, N. (1988) *A Hellenistic Anthology*. Cambridge

Horsfall, N. M. (1971) 'Numanus Remulus: ethnography and propaganda in *Aeneid* 9: 598ff', reprinted in Harrison (1990) 305–15

  (1974) 'Virgil's Roman chronography: a reconsideration', *Classical Quarterly* 68: 111–15

  (1981) 'Virgil and the conquest of chaos', reprinted in Harrison (1990) 466–77

  (1987) 'Myth and mythography at Rome', in Bremmer and Horsfall, *Roman Myth and Mythography, Bulletin of the Institute of Classical Studies* Suppl. 52. London

(1988) 'Camilla o i limiti dell'invenzione', *Athenaeum* 66: 31–51

(1991) Review of P. Brugisser, *Romulus–Servianus, Classical Review* 41: 242–3

(1995) *A Companion to the Study of Virgil, Mnemosyne* Suppl. 151. Leiden and New York

Hunt, J. W. (1973) *Forms of Glory. Structure and Sense in Virgil's Aeneid.* Carbondale and Edwardsville

Hunter, R. L. (1988) '"Short on heroics": Jason in the *Argonautica*', *Classical Quarterly* 38: 436–53

Innes, D. C., Hine, H. and Pelling, C., eds. (1995) *Ethics and Rhetoric: Essays for Donald Russell on his 75th Birthday.* Oxford

degl' Innocenti Pierini, R. (1980) *Studi su Accio.* Florence

Iser, W. (1993) *The Fictive and the Imaginary: Charting Literary Anthropology.* Baltimore and London

Jackson Knight, W. F. (1944) *Roman Vergil* (3rd edn 1966). London

Jacoff, R., ed. (1993) *The Cambridge Companion to Dante.* Cambridge

Jacoff, R. and Schnapp, J. T., eds. (1991) *The Poetry of Allusion: Virgil and Ovid in Dante's Commedia.* Stanford

Janko, R. (1995) 'Reconstructing Philodemus' *On Poems*', in Obbink (1995) 69–96

Jenkyns, R., ed. (1992) *The Legacy of Rome: A New Appraisal.* Oxford

Jocelyn, H. D. (1964–5) 'Ancient scholarship and Virgil's use of republican Latin poetry', *Classical Quarterly* 14: 280–95 and 15: 126–44

(1979) 'Vergilius Cacozelus (Donatus *Vita Vergilii* 44)', in F. Cairns, ed. *Papers of the Liverpool Latin Seminar Second Volume*, 67–141. Liverpool

Johnson, W. R. (1976) *Darkness Visible: A Study of Virgil's Aeneid.* Berkeley and Los Angeles

Johnston, P. (1980) *Vergil's Agricultural Golden Age. A Study of the Georgics, Mnemosyne* Suppl. 60. Leiden

Jones, C. P. (1978) *The Roman World of Dio Chrysostom.* Cambridge, MA

Jones, J. W. J. (1960–1) 'Allegorical interpretation in Servius', *Classical Journal* 56: 217–26

de Jong, I. F. (1987) *Narrators and Focalizers: The Presentation of the Story in the Iliad.* Amsterdam

de Jong, I. F. and Sullivan, J. P. (1994) *Modern Critical Theory and Classical Literature, Mnemosyne* Suppl. 130. Leiden

Josipovici, G. (1980) *Vergil Dying.* Windsor

Kallendorf, C. ed. (1993) *Vergil (The Classical Heritage*, vol. II). New York and London

Kaster, R. A. (1980) 'Macrobius and Servius: *Verecundia* and the grammarian's function', *Harvard Studies in Classical Philology* 84: 219–62

(1988) *Guardians of Language: The Grammarian and Society in Late Antiquity.* Berkeley

(1995) *Suetonius: De grammaticis et rhetoribus.* Oxford

Kennedy, D. F. (1983) 'Shades of meaning. Virgil, *Ecl.* 10.75–77', *Liverpool Classical Monthly* 8: 124

(1987) 'Arcades ambo: Virgil, Gallus and Arcadia', *Hermathena* 143: 47–59

(1993) *The Arts of Love: Five Studies in the Discourse of Roman Love Elegy.* Cambridge

Kenney, E. J. (1973) 'The style of the *Metamorphoses*', in J. W. Binns, ed. *Ovid*, 116–53. London

Kenney, E. J. and Clausen, W. V., eds. (1982) *The Cambridge History of Classical Literature*, vol. II: *Latin Literature*. Cambridge

Kermode, F. (1966) *The Sense of an Ending*. Oxford and New York

(1968) 'A Babylonish dialect', in C. B. Cox and A. P. Hinchcliffe, eds., *T. S. Eliot: The Waste Land. A Casebook*, 224–35. London

(1975/1983) *The Classic: Literary Images of Permanence and Change*. London

(1988) *History and Value*. Oxford

(1990) *Poetry, Narrative, History*. Oxford

Kitson, M. (1960) 'The "Altieri Claudes" and Virgil', *Burlington Magazine* 102: 312–18

Klein, T. M. (1978) 'The Greek shepherd in Vergil, Gide, Genet and Barthes', *Helios* 6: 1–32

Klingner, F. (1967) *Virgil: Bucolica, Georgica, Aeneis*. Zurich and Stuttgart

Knauer, G. N. (1964a) *Die Aeneis und Homer*. Göttingen

(1964b) 'Vergil's *Aeneid* and Homer', *Greek, Roman and Byzantine Studies* 5: 61–84

Knox, B. M. W. (1966) 'The Serpent and the Flame: the imagery of the second book of the *Aeneid*', in Commager (1966) 124–42

Knox, P. E. (1986) *Ovid's Metamorphoses and the Traditions of Augustan Poetry*, Camb. Philol. Soc. Suppl. vol. 11. Cambridge

König, A. (1970) *Die Aeneis und die Griechische Tragödie: Studien zur imitatio Technik Vergils*. Berlin

Krieger, M. (1992) *Ekphrasis*. Baltimore and London

Kromer, G. (1979) 'Didactic tradition in Vergil's *Georgics*', in Boyle (1979) 7–21

Laird, A. (1993) 'Sounding out ecphrasis: art and text in Catullus 64', *Journal of Roman Studies* 83: 18–30

Lamacchia, R. (1984) 'Cento', *Enciclopedia Virgiliana* 1. 734–7

Lamberton, R. and Keaney, J., eds. (1992) *Homer's Ancient Readers*. Princeton

Lana, I. (1958–9) 'L' "Atreo" di Accio e la leggenda di Atreo e Tieste nel teatro tragico romano', *Atti Accad. Scienze Torino* 93: 291–385

Langmuir, E. (1976) '*Arma virumque*: Niccolo dell' Abate's *Aeneid Gabinetto* for Scandiano', *Journal of the Warburg and Courtauld Institutes* 39: 151–70

La Penna, A. (1967) 'Sul cosidetto stile soggetivo e sul cosidetto simbolismo di Virgilio', *Dialoghi di Archeologia* 1: 220–44

(1978) 'Fra Tersite e Drance: Note sulla Fortuna di un personaggio Virgiliano', in Chevallier (1978) 347–61

(1979) 'Funzione e interpretazioni del mito nella tragedia arcaica latina', in *Fra teatro, poesia e politica romana*, 49–104. Turin

(1980) 'Mezenzio: una tragedia della tirannia e del titanismo antico', *Maia* 32: 3–30

Laugesen, A. T. (1962) 'La Roue de Virgile. Une page de la théorie littéraire du Moyen Age', *Classicalia & Medievalia* 23: 248–73

Lazzarini, C. (1984) 'Historia/Fabula: forme della costruzione poetica Virgiliana nel commento di Servio all'Eneide', *Materiali e Discussioni* 12: 117–44

(1989) 'Elementi di una poetica serviana. Osservazione sulla costruzione del racconto all'Eneide', *Studi Italiani di Filologia Classica* 7: 56–109, 241–60

Leach, E. W. (1974) *Vergil's Eclogues: Landscapes of Experience*. Ithaca
  (1981) 'Georgics 2 and the Poem', *Arethusa* 14: 35–48
  (1988) *The Rhetoric of Space*. Princeton.
Lee, G. (1984) *Virgil: The Eclogues*, Harmondsworth
Lee, R. W. (1967) *Ut pictura poesis. The Humanistic Theory of Painting*. New York
Leech, G. N., and Short, M. H. (1981) *Style in Fiction: A Linguistic Introduction to English Fictional Prose*. London and New York
Lefèvre, E. (1976) *Der Thyestes des Lucius Varius Rufus. Zehn Überlegungen zu seiner Rekonstruktion*. Wiesbaden
Lefkowitz, M. (1981) *The Lives of the Greek Poets*. London
Levey, M. (1957) 'Tiepolo's treatment of a classical story at Villa Valmarana. A study in eighteenth-century iconography and aesthetics', *Journal of the Warburg and Courtauld Institutes* 20: 298–317
Levitan, W. (1993) 'Give up the beginning? Juno's mindful wrath (*Aeneid* 1.37)', *Liverpool Classical Monthly* 18: 1–15
Lewis, C. S. (1955) *Surprised by Joy: The Shape of my Early Life*. London
Lilja, S. (1983) 'Homosexuality in Republican and Augustan Rome', *Commentationes Humanarum Litterarum* 74. Helsinki
Lipking, L. (1981) *The Life of the Poet: Beginning and Ending Poetic Careers*. Chicago and London
Llewellyn, N. (1984) 'Virgil and the visual arts', in C. Martindale, ed. *Virgil and his Influence*, 117–40. Bristol
Long, A. A. and Sedley, D. N. (1987) *The Hellenistic Philosophers*, 2 vols. Cambridge
Loughrey, B. ed. (1984) *The Pastoral Mode: A Casebook*. London and Basingstoke
Low, A. (1985) *The Georgic Revolution*. Princeton
Lucács, G. (1978) *Writer and Critic*. London
Lunelli, A. ed. (1988) *La Lingua Poetica Latina*, 3rd edn. Bologna
Lyas, C. (1992) 'Intention', in D. Cooper, ed. *A Companion to Aesthetics*. Oxford
Lyne, R. O. A. M. (1978) *Ciris: A Poem Attributed to Virgil*. Cambridge
  (1983a) 'Lavinia's blush', *Greece & Rome* 30: 55–64
  (1983b) 'Virgil and the politics of war', *Classical Quarterly* 33: 188–203
  (1987) *Further Voices in Vergil's Aeneid*. Oxford
  (1989) *Words and the Poet: Characteristic Techniques of Style in Vergil's 'Aeneid'*. Oxford
  (1995) *Horace: Behind the Public Poetry*. New Haven
Mack, M. and deForest Lord, G., eds. (1982) *Poetic Traditions of the English Renaissance*. New Haven and London
Mackail, J. W. (1930) *Virgil's Aeneid*. Oxford
Mackie, C. J. (1988) *The Characterisation of Aeneas*. Edinburgh
Maltby, R. (1991) *A Lexicon of Ancient Latin Etymologies*. Leeds
Marouzeau, J. (1940) 'Virgile linguiste', *Mélanges de philologie et de littérature anciennes offerts à Alfred Ernout*, 259–65. Paris
  (1949) *Quelques aspects de la formation du Latin littéraire*. Paris
  (1962) *Traité de Stylistique Latine*, 4th edn. Paris
Martindale, C. A., ed. (1984) *Virgil and his Influence*. Bristol
  (1993a) *Redeeming the Text: Latin Poetry and the Hermeneutics of Reception*. Cambridge

(1993b) 'Descent into Hell: reading ambiguity, or Virgil and the critics', *Proceedings of the Virgil Society* 21: 111–50

(1996) 'Ruins of Rome: T. S. Eliot and the presence of the past', *Arion* 3rd series 3: 102–40

Masters, J. (1992) *Poetry and Civil War in Lucan's Bellum Civile*. Cambridge

(1994) 'Deceiving the reader: the political mission of Lucan *Bellum Civile* 7', in Elsner and Masters (1994) 151–77

Mayor, J. B., Warde Fowler, W. and Conway, R. S., eds. (1907) *Virgil's Messianic Eclogue, its Meaning, Occasion and Sources*. London

Miles, G. B. (1975) '*Georgics* 3.209–294: *Amor* and civilisation', *California Studies in Classical Antiquity* 8: 177–97

(1980) *Virgil's Georgics: A New Interpretation*. Berkeley

Miller, F. and Segal, E., eds. (1984) *Caesar Augustus: Seven Aspects*. Oxford

Mitchell, R. N. (1991) 'The violence of virginity in the *Aeneid*', *Arethusa* 24: 219–38

Mitsis, P. (1993) 'Committing philosophy on the reader: didactic coercion and reader autonomy in *De Rerum Natura*', in Schiesaro *et al.* (1993) 111–28

Moles, J. L. (1984) 'Aristotle and Dido's *hamartia*', *Greece & Rome* 31: 48–63

Momigliano, A. (1960) *Secondo contributo alla storia degli studi classici*. Rome

Montrose, L. A. (1983) 'Of gentlemen and shepherds: the politics of Elizabethan pastoral form', *English Literary History* 50: 415–59

Moskalew, W. (1982) *Formular Language and Poetic Design in the 'Aeneid'*, *Mnemosyne* Suppl. 73. Leiden

Most, G. (1987) 'The "Virgilian" *Culex*', in Whitby *et al.* (1987)

Mühmelt, M. (1965) *Griechische Grammatik in der Vergilerklärung*. Munich

Murgia, C. (1975) *Prolegomena to Servius 5: The Manuscripts*. Berkeley

Mynors, R. A. B. (1990) *Virgil, Georgics. Edited with a Commentary*. Oxford

Nagle, B. R. (1983) 'Open-ended closure in *Aeneid*', *Classical World* 76: 257–63

Nagy, G. (1996) *Poetry as Performance*. Cambridge

Nicolet, C. (1976) *Le métier de citoyen dans la Rome républicaine*. Paris

Nisbet, R. G. M. (1991) 'The style of Virgil's *Eclogues*', *Proceedings of the Virgil Society* 20: 1–14

(1995) 'Virgil's Fourth *Eclogue*: Easterners and Westerners', in Harrison (1995) (= *Bulletin of the Institute of Classical Studies* (1978) 59–78)

Norden, E. (1916) *P. Vergilius Maro Aeneis Buch VI*, 2nd edn (3rd edn 1926, Liepzig; 5th edn 1970, Stuttgart; 7th edn 1981, Stuttgart). Leipzig

Nugent, S. G. (1992) 'Vergil's "voice of the women" in *Aeneid* v', *Arethusa* 25: 255–92

Nuttall, A. D. (1992) *Openings: Narrative Beginnings from the Epic to the Novel*. Oxford

Obbink, D., ed. (1995) *Philodemus and Poetry: Theory and Practice in Lucretius, Philodemus, and Horace*. Oxford

O'Hara, J. J. (1990) *Death and the Optimistic Prophecy in Vergil's Aeneid*. Princeton

(1993) 'Dido as "interpreting character" in *Aeneid* 4.56–66', *Arethusa* 26: 99–114

(1994) 'They might be giants: inconsistency and indeterminacy in Vergil's war in Italy', *Colby Quarterly* 30: 206–26

(1996) *True Names: Vergil and the Alexandrian Tradition of Etymological Wordplay*. Ann Arbor

Oksala, T. (1978) *Studien zum Verständnis der Einheit und der Bedeutung von Vergils Georgica, Commentationes Humanarum Litterarum* 60. Helsinki

O'Loughlin, M. J. K. (1978) *The Garlands of Repose: Studies in the Literary Representations of Civic and Retired Leisure*. Chicago

Orlin, L., ed. (1975) *Janus: Essays in Ancient and Modern Studies*. Ann Arbor

Otis, B. (1964) *Virgil: A Study in Civilized Poetry*. Oxford

(1972) 'A new study of the *Georgics*', *Phoenix* 26: 40–62

Ott, U. (1969) *Die Kunst des Gegensatzes in Theokrits Hirtengedichten*, Spudasmata 22. Hildesheim

Otter, H. (1914) *De Soliloquiis Quae in Litteris Graecorum et Romanorum Occurrunt Observationes*. Marburg

Page, T. E., ed. (1894) *The Aeneid of Virgil I–VI*. London

(1898) *P. Vergilii Maronis Bucolica et Georgica*. London

Palmer, L. R. (1961) *The Latin Language*. London

Panofsky, E. (1939) 'Iconography and iconology: an introduction to the study of Renaissance art', in *Studies in Iconology: Humanistic Themes in the Art of the Renaissance*. New York

Parry, A. (1966) 'The two voices of Virgil's *Aeneid*', in Commager (1966) 107–23 (reprinted from *Arion* 2 (1963) 66–80)

(1972) 'The idea of art in Virgil's *Georgics*', *Arethusa* 5: 35–52

Pastorino, A. (1957) *Tropaeum Liberi. Saggio sul Lucurgus di Nevio e sui motivi dionisiaci nella tragedia latina arcaica*. Arona Paideia

Patterson, A. M., ed. (1984) *Roman Images*. Baltimore and London

(1988) *Pastoral and Ideology: Virgil to Valéry*. Oxford

Pearce, T. E. V. (1966) 'The enclosing word-order in the Latin hexameter I, II', *Classical Quarterly* 16: 140–71, 298–320

Pease, A. S., ed. (1935) *P. Vergili Maronis Aeneidos Liber Quartus*. Cambridge, MA

Perkell, C. (1981) 'On the Corycian gardener of Vergil's Fourth *Georgic*', *Transactions of the American Philological Association* 111: 167–77

(1986) 'Vergil's theodicy reconsidered', in Bernard (1986) 67–83

(1989) *The Poet's Truth: A Study of the Poet in Virgil's Georgics*. Berkeley

(1990) 'On *Eclogue* 1.79–83', *Transactions of the American Philological Association* 120: 171–81

(1994) 'Ambiguity and irony: the last resort?', *Helios* 21: 63–74

Perutelli, A. (1979a) 'Registri narrativi e stile indiretto libero in Virgilio', *Materiali e Discussioni* 3: 69–83

(1979b) *La Narrazione Commentata*. Pisa

(1980) 'L'episodio di Aristeo nelle Georgiche: struttura e technica narrativa', *Materiali e Discussioni* 4: 59–76

Pfeiffer, R. (1968) *A History of Classical Scholarship from the Beginnings to the End of the Hellenistic Age*. Oxford

Phaer, T. (1596) *The Thirteene Bookes of Aeneidos*. London

Poggioli, R. (1975) *The Oaten Flute: Essays on Pastoral Poetry and the Pastoral Ideal*. Cambridge, MA

Poliakoff, M. B. (1985) 'Entellus and Amycus: Virgil, *Aen.* 5.362–484', *Illinois Classical Studies* 10: 227–31

Poole, A. and Maule, J., eds. (1995) *The Oxford Book of Classical Verse in Translation*. Oxford

Porter, D. H. (1987) *Horace's Poetic Journey*. Princeton

Porter, J. I. (1992) 'Hermeneutic lines and circles: Aristarchus and Crates on the exegesis of Homer', in Lamberton and Keaney (1992) 67–114

Posch, S. (1969) *Beobachtungen zur Theokritnachwirkung bei Vergil*, Commentationes Aenipontanae 19

Pöschl, V. (1962) *Virgil's Poetic Art*, tr. M. Seligson. Michigan

Powell, A., ed. (1992) *Roman Poetry and Propaganda in the Age of Augustus*. London

Powell, J. G. F. (1990) *Cicero: Laelius, On Friendship and the Dream of Scipio*. Warminster

Preimesberger, R. (1976) 'Pontifex romanus per Aeneam praedesignatus. Die Galleria Pamphily und ihre Fresken', *Römisches Jahrbuch für Kunstgeschichte* 16: 221–87

Preminger, A. and Brogan, T. V. F., eds. (1993) *The New Encyclopedia of Poetry and Poetics*. Princeton

Putnam, M. C. J. (1970) *Virgil's Pastoral Art: Studies in the Eclogues*. Princeton

(1975) 'Italian Virgil and the idea of Rome', in Orlin (1975) 171–200

(1979) *Virgil's Poem of the Earth: Studies in the Georgics*. Princeton

(1988) *The Poetry of the Aeneid: Four Studies in Imaginative Unity and Design*, 2nd edn (1st edn 1965). Ithaca

(1990) 'Anger, blindness and insight in Virgil's *Aeneid*', *Apeiron* 23: 7–40

(1994) 'Virgil's Danaid Ekphrasis', *Illinois Classical Studies* 19: 171–89

(1995) *Virgil's Aeneid: Interpretation and Influence*. Chapel Hill and London

(forthcoming) 'Dido's murals and Virgilian ecphrasis', to appear in *Harvard Studies in Classical Philology*

Quinn, K. (1963) 'Virgil's tragic queen', *Latin Explorations: Critical Studies in Roman Literature*, 29–58. London

(1968) *Virgil's Aeneid: A Critical Description*. London and Ann Arbor

Quint, D. (1989) 'Repetition and ideology in the *Aeneid*', *Materiali e Discussioni* 23: 9–54

(1993) *Epic and Empire: Politics and Generic Form from Virgil to Milton*. Princeton

Raaflaub, K. and Toher, M. (1990) *Between Republic and Empire: Interpretations of Augustus and his Principate*. Berkeley

Ravenna, G. (1974) 'L'ekphrasis poetica di opere d'arte in Latino', *Quaderni Istituto Filologia Latina Padova* 3: 1–51

Rawson, E. (1985) *Intellectual Life in the Late Roman Republic*. Baltimore and London

Reeve, M. D. (1983) '*Appendix Vergiliana*', in Reynolds (1983) 437–40

Reeves, G. (1989) *T. S. Eliot: A Virgilian Poet*. Basingstoke

Rehm, B. (1932) *Das geographische Bild des alten Italien in Vergils Aeneis*, *Philologus* Suppl. 24.2. Liepzig

Reynolds, L. D., ed. (1983) *Texts and Transmission*. Oxford

Richlin, A. (1991) *The Garden of Priapus*, 2nd edn. Oxford

(1993) 'Not before homosexuality: the materiality of the *cinaedus* and the Roman law against love between men', *Journal of the History of Sexuality* 3: 523–73

Ricoeur, P. (1991) *A Ricoeur Reader: Reflection and Imagination*, ed. M. J. Valdes. New York and London

Rosati, G. (1979) 'Punto di vista narrativo e antichi esegeti di Virgilio', *Ann. Scuol. Norm. di Pisa*, Class. di Lett. e Fil. Pisa

Rosenmeyer, T. G. (1969) *The Green Cabinet: Theocritus and the European Pastoral Lyric.* Berkeley

Ross, D. O., Jr (1969) *Style and Tradition in Catullus.* Cambridge, MA
  (1975) *Backgrounds to Augustan Poetry: Gallus, Elegy, and Rome.* Cambridge
  (1987) *Virgil's Elements: Physics and Poetry in the Georgics.* Princeton

Schama, S. (1995) *Landscape and Memory.* London

Schenk, P. (1984) *Die Gestalt des Turnus in Vergils Aeneis.* Königstein

Schiesaro, A. (1994) 'Seneca's *Thyestes* and the morality of tragic *furor*', in Elsner and Masters (1994) 196–210

Schiesaro, A., Mitsis, P. and Clay, J. S., eds. (1993) *Mega nepios Il distinatario nell'epos didascalico*, vol. 31 of *Materiali e discussioni per l'analisi dei testi classici.* Pisa

Seaford, R. (1987) 'The tragic wedding', *Journal of Hellenic Studies* 107: 106–30

Sedley, D. N. (1989) 'Philosophical allegiance in the Greco-Roman world', in M. Griffin and W. R. Barnes, eds. *Philosophia Togata. Essays on Philosophy and Roman Society*, 97–119. Oxford

Segal, C. (1966) 'Orpheus and the Fourth *Georgic*: Vergil on nature and civilization', *American Journal of Philology* 87: 307–25
  (1986) 'Greek tragedy and society: a structuralist perspective', *Interpreting Greek Tragedy*, 21–47. Ithaca and London

Sellar, W. Y. (1877) *The Roman Poets of the Augustan Age. Virgil.* Oxford

Serroy, J., ed. (1988) *Le Virgile Travesti.* Paris

Sforza, F. (1935) 'The problem of Virgil', *Classical Review* 49: 97–108

Sharrock, A. R. (1994) *Seduction and Repetition in Ovid's Ars Amatoria II.* Oxford

Sidney, P. (1973) *An Apology for Poetry*, ed. G. Shepherd. Manchester

Sikes, E. E. (1923) *Roman Poetry.* London

Simon, C. (1969) *La Bataille de Pharsale.* Paris

Sinfield, A. (1992) *Faultlines: Cultural Materialism and the Politics of Dissident Reading.* Oxford

Singleton, C. S., tr. (1970–5) *Dante: The Divine Comedy*, 3 vols. Princeton

Skutsch, O. (1985) *The Annals of Q. Ennius.* Oxford

Smith, B. H. (1968) *Poetic Closure. A Study of How Poems End.* Chicago

Smith, S. (1993) *Subjectivity, Identity, and the Body: Women's Autobiographical Practices in the Twentieth Century.* Bloomington and Indianapolis

Snell, B. (1953) *The Discovery of the Mind: The Greek Origins of European Thought*, tr. T. G. Rosenmeyer. Cambridge, MA

Soubiran, J. (1966) *L'Elision dans la poésie Latine.* Paris

Spenser, E. (1976) *The Faerie Queene*, ed. A. C. Hamilton. London

Spofford, E. W. (1981) *The Social Poetry of the Georgics.* Salem

Spurr, M. S. (1986) 'Agriculture and the *Georgics*', *Greece & Rome* 33: 164–87

Stabryla, S. (1970) *Latin Tragedy in Virgil's Poetry.* Wrocław

Stehle, E. M. (1974) 'Virgil's *Georgics*: the threat of sloth', *Transactions of the American Philological Association* 104: 347–69

Steiner, G. (1975) *After Babel: Aspects of Language and Translation* (2nd edn 1992). London and New York

(1990) 'Homer and Virgil and Broch', review of Harrison (1990), in *London Review of Books*, 12 July, pp. 10–11

Steiner, T. R. (1975) *English Translation Theory 1650–1800*. Amsterdam and Assen

Stevenson, T. B. (1983) *Miniature Decoration in the Vatican Virgil. A Study in Late Antique Iconography.* Tübingen

Stocker, A. F. (1963) '*Servius servus magistrorum*', *Vergilius* 9: 9–15

Stuart, D. R. (1922) 'Biographical criticism of Vergil since the Renaissance', *Studies in Philology* 19: 1–30

Suerbaum, W. (1981) 'Von der Vita Vergiliana über die Accessus Vergiliani zum Zauberer Virgilius. Probleme – Perspektiven – Analysen', in Temporini and Haase (1981) Welt II, 31.2: 1156–1262. Berlin

Surrey, H. H. Earl of (1964) *Poems*, ed. E. Jones. Oxford

Syme, R. (1939) *The Roman Revolution.* Oxford

(1957) *Tacitus.* Oxford

(1959) 'Livy and Augustus', *Harvard Studies in Classical Philology* 64: 27–87

Tanner, M. (1993) *The Last Descendant of Aeneas. The Hapsburgs and the Mythic Image of the Emperor.* New Haven and London

Tarrant, R. J. (1978) 'Senecan drama and its antecedents', *Harvard Studies in Classical Philology* 82: 213–63

(1985) *Seneca: Thyestes.* Atlanta

Taylor, L. R. (1934) 'Varro's "De gente populi Romani"', *Classical Philology* 29: 221–9

Temporini, H. and Haase, W., eds. (1981) *Austief und Niedergang der Romischen Welt.* Berlin

Tengström, E. (1977) 'Theater und Politik im kaiserlichen Rom', *Eranos* 75: 43–56

Terravent, G. de (1967) 'Présence de Virgile dans l'art', *Mémoires de l'Académie Royale Belgique. Classe des Beaux Arts* 12 (2e série): fasc. 2

Thilo, G. and Hagen, H., eds. (1878–1902) *Servii Grammatici Qui Feruntur in Vergilii Carmina Commentarii.* Leipzig

Thomas, E. (1880) *Essai sur Servius et son commentaire sur Virgile.* Paris

Thomas, R. F. (1982) *Lands and Peoples in Roman Poetry*, Cambridge Philological Society Suppl. vol. 7. Cambridge

(1983a) 'Virgil's ecphrastic centrepieces', *Harvard Studies in Classical Philology* 87: 175–84

(1983b) 'Callimachus, the Victoria Berenices and Roman poetry', *Classical Quarterly* 33: 92–113

(1986a) 'From *recusatio* to commitment', in F. Cairns, ed. *Papers of the Liverpool Latin Seminar*, vol. 5, 61–73. Liverpool

(1986b) 'Virgil's *Georgics* and the art of reference', *Harvard Studies in Classical Philology* 90: 171–98

(1987) 'Prose into poetry: tradition and meaning in Virgil's *Georgics*', *Harvard Studies in Classical Philology* 91: 229–60

(1988) *Virgil, Georgics*, 2 vols. Cambridge

(1990) 'Ideology, influence, and future studies in the *Georgics*', *Vergilius* 36: 64–73

(1993) 'Callimachus back in Rome', in Harder *et al.* (1993) vol. I.

Thompson, L. and Winnick, R. H. (1976) *Robert Frost: The Later Years 1938–63*. New York

Thornton, A. (1976) *The Living Universe. Gods and Men in Virgil's Aeneid.* Leiden

Thrale, H. (1942) *Thraliana*, ed. K. C. Balderston, 2 vols. Oxford

Timpanaro, S. (1986) *Per la storia della filologia Virgiliana antica, Quaderni di 'Filologia e critica'* 6. Rome

Traina, A. (1974) *Vortit Barbare. Le traduzioni poetiche da Livio Andronico a Cicerone.* Rome

Vernant, J.-P. and Vidal-Naquet, P. (1981) *Tragedy and Myth in Ancient Greece.* Brighton

Veyne, P. (1988) *Roman Erotic Elegy: Love, Poetry, and the West*, tr. D. Pellauer. Chicago and London

Vidal-Naquet, P. (1981) 'The Black Hunter and the origins of the Athenian *ephebeia*', in Gordon, ed. *Myth, Religion and Society*, 147–62. Cambridge

Virgilio nell'arte e nella cultura europea (1981) exhibition catalogue, ed. M. Fagiolo, Biblioteca Nazionale Centrale. Rome

Voloshinov, V. N. (1926) 'Slovo v zhizni i slovo v poezii', *Zvesda* 6; forthcoming translation 'Discourse in life and discourse in poetry', in W. Godzich, ed. *Writings of the Bakhtin Circle.* New Haven

Waddell, H. (1976) *More Latin Lyrics from Virgil to Milton.* London

Warde-Fowler, W. (1918a) *Virgil's Gathering of the Clans.* Oxford

(1918b) *Aeneas at the Site of Rome.* Oxford

Warwick, H. H. (1975) *A Vergil Concordance.* Minneapolis

Watkins, J. (1995) *The Specter of Dido: Spenser and Virgilian Epic.* New Haven and London

Watson, P. (1985) 'Axelson revisited: the selection of vocabulary in Latin poetry', *Classical Quarterly* 35: 430–48

Weinstock, S. (1971) *Divus Iulius.* Oxford

Wellek, R. (1965) 'The concept of classicism and classic in literary scholarship', *International Comparative Literature Association, Proceedings of the 4th Congress*

Wells, F. H. (1970) *Poems on Affairs of State Volume 6: 1697–1704.* New Haven and London

West, D. A. (1969) 'Multiple-correspondence similes in the *Aeneid*', *Journal of Roman Studies* 59: 40–9

(1975–6) '*Cernere erat*: the shield of Aeneas', reprinted in Harrison (1990) 295–304

(1995) '"Cast out theory": Horace Odes 1.4 and 4.7', Classical Association Presidential Address

West, D. A. and Woodman, T., eds. (1979) *Creative Imitation and Latin Literature.* Cambridge

Whitby, M., Hardie, P., and Whitby, M., eds. (1987) *Homo Viator: Classical Essays for John Bramble.* Bristol

White, P. (1993) *Promised Verse: Poets in the Society of Augustan Rome.* Cambridge, MA, and London

Wigodsky, M. (1972) *Vergil and Early Latin Poetry*. Wiesbaden

Wilkinson, L. P. (1950) 'The intention of Virgil's *Georgics*', *Greece and Rome* 19: 19–28

(1959) 'The language of Virgil and Horace', *Classical Quarterly* 9: 181–92

(1963) *Golden Latin Artistry*. Cambridge. Reprinted Bristol and Norman, OK, 1985

(1969) *The Georgics of Virgil: A Critical Survey*. Cambridge

(1970) 'Pindar and the Proem to the Third Georgic', *Festschrift K. Büchner*, 286–90. Wiesbaden

Williams, C. A. (1995) 'Greek love at Rome', *Classical Quarterly* 45: 517–39

Williams, G. (1968) *Tradition and Originality in Roman Poetry*. Oxford

(1983) *Technique and Ideas in the Aeneid*. New Haven and London

Williams, R. (1973) *The Country and the City*. London

Williams, R. D. (1960a) *P. Vergili Maronis Aeneidos Liber Quintus* Oxford. Reprinted Bristol, 1981

(1960b) 'The pictures on Dido's Temple', *Classical Quarterly* 10: 145–51

(1961) *P. Vergili Maronis Aeneidos Liber Tertius*. Oxford. Reprinted Bristol, 1981

(1964) 'The Sixth Book of the *Aeneid*', *Greece and Rome* 11: 48–63

(1966–7) 'Servius, commentator and guide', *Proceedings of the Virgil Society* 6: 50–6

Wills, J. (1987) 'Scyphus – a Homeric hapax in Virgil', *American Journal of Philology* 108: 455–7

(1996) *Repetition in Latin Poetry: Figures of Allusion*. Oxford

Wimmel, W. (1973) *'Hirtenkrieg' und arkadisches Rom: Reduktionsmedien in Virgils Aeneis*, Abh. d. Marburger Gelehrten Gesellschaft, Jahrg. 1972: 1. Munich

Wine, H. (1994) *Claude: The Poetic Landscape*. London

Wiseman, T. P. (1971) *New Men in the Roman Senate 139 B.C. – 14 A.D.* Oxford

(1979) *Clio's Cosmetics*. Leicester

de Witt, N. W. (1925) 'The Second *Aeneid* as a drama', *Classical Journal* 20: 479–85

Wlosok, A. (1976) 'Virgils Didotragödie. Ein Beitrag zum Problem des Tragischen in der *Aeneis*', in Görgemanns and Schmidt (1976) 228–50

Wofford, S. L. (1992) *The Choice of Achilles: The Ideology of Figure in the Epic*. Stanford

Woodbridge, K. (1970) *Landscape and Antiquity: Aspects of English Culture at Stourhead 1718–1838*. Oxford

Wordsworth, W. (1947) *The Poetical Works*, eds. E. de Selincourt and H. Darbyshire. Oxford

Wright, D. H. (1993) *The Vatican Vergil. A Masterpiece of Late Antique Art*. Princeton

Wyke, M. (1987) 'Written women: Propertius' *Scripta Puella*', *Journal of Roman Studies* 77: 47–61

Zanker, P. (1988) *The Power of Images in the Age of Augustus*. Ann Arbor

Zetzel, J. E. G. (1973) '*Emendavi ad Tironem*: some notes on scholarship in the second century A.D.', *Harvard Studies in Classical Philology* 77: 225–43

(1981) *Latin Textual Criticism in Antiquity*. Salem

(1983a) 'Catullus, Ennius, and the poetics of allusion', *Illinois Classical Studies* 8: 251–66

(1983b) 'Recreating the canon: Augustan poetry and the Alexandrian past', *Critical Inquiry* 10: 83–105

(1989) '*Romane Memento:* justice and judgement in *Aeneid 6*', *Transactions of the American Philological Association* 119: 263–84

(1996) 'Natural law and poetic justice: a Carneadean debate in Cicero and Virgil', *Classical Philology* 91: 297–319

Ziolkowski, T. (1993) *Virgil and the Moderns.* Princeton

Zorzetti, N. (1990) s.v. *Tragici Latini, Enciclopedia Virgiliana*, vol. 5, 245–7. Rome

INDEX

Note: references in **bold** refer to illustrations.

academic and non-academic reception,
  distinction between 39
accent, stress 245
Accius 324
Actium, Battle of 169, 191, 199, 316
addressees, in *Georgics* 132–5
*Aeneas, Anchises and Ascanius fleeing
  Troy* (Bernini) **8**, 98
Aeneas
  anger of 214–16, 288
  characterisation of 285–6, 288
  as internal narrator 263–5
  killing of Turnus 83–4, 89, 179, 181,
    188, 206; interpretations 214–16;
    tragedy 315–16
  link with Augustus 178–9, 318–19
  and Milton 88–9
  and models/types 225–6, 228
  and Ovid 62–3
  point of view 266–7
  sexuality 296
  and T. S. Eliot 45–7, 48–9
  and *umbra* 163–4
  and visual arts 96–7, 100–1
  see also Anchises; shield of Aeneas
Aeneas sacrificing **1b**
Aeneid
  archaic lore 194–5
  audience's role in 270
  book division of 264–6
  and Broch's *Death of Virgil* 328, 331,
    332–5
  Chaucer's summary of 22
  complicity with power 53
  cosmology 209–10
  direct speech in 263–4, 285
  ecphrasis 271–80

gender and sexuality in 303–10
and history 51–2, 183, 191–5
and Homer 151–2, 229–30, 262
  inversion of images 280; female role
    299
Italy described in 189–96
kingship debate 216
and landscape art 99–100
liminality in 320–2
and Lucan 65–7, 183, 332
marriage image in 321
men and sexuality 307–10
metapoiesis 236–7
in Middle Scots 22
and Milton 87–90
multiple perspective 179
narrative structure 189
narrators 259–61, 285
opening 160
Ovid's response to 62–3, 183
passion in 307–8
past–present relationship in 318–20
plot 23, 151–2, 263–6, 320
premature deaths of ephebic characters
  320–1
prophetic element 85, 196–200
repetition 146–7, 153
rhetorical structure 236
Rome depicted in 24–5, 188–9,
  200
ruptures of order 263–4
'singing' (*cano*) 160–1
time in 236, 259, 263
tragedy in 312–25
translatio imperii 53, 153
viewpoints 266–7, 280, 286
women in 303–7